Ludovico Ariosto
An Annotated Bibliography of Criticism
1956–1980

LUDOVICO ARIOSTO
An Annotated Bibliography of Criticism
1956–1980

Robert J. Rodini
Salvatore Di Maria

University of Missouri Press

Columbia
1984

Library of Congress Cataloging in Publication Data

Rodini, Robert J.
    Ludovico Ariosto: an annotated
bibliography of criticism, 1956–1980

    Continues: Bibliografia della critica ariostea, 1510–
1956 / Giuseppe Fatini.
    1. Ariosto, Lodovico, 1474–1533—Criticism and inter-
pretation—Bibliography. I. Di Maria, Salvatore.
II. Fatini, Giuseppe. Bibliografia della critica
ariostea, 1510–1956. III. Title.
Z8043.R62 1984 [PQ4599]   851'.3   84–2196
ISBN 0–8262–0445–7

To Our Parents

Contents

Preface

This annotated bibliography for the years 1956–1980 is intended as a guide to critical scholarship on the writings of Ludovico Ariosto. With some variations, it is a continuation of the only comprehensive bibliography for the period preceding 1956, the indispensable volume of Giuseppe Fatini, which annotates chronologically 3,624 items: *Bibliografia della critica ariostea, 1510–1956* (Florence: Le Monnier, 1958). In carrying on Fatini's task, we have also included the year 1956, listing, however, only those items that do not appear in his volume. On the other hand, no attempt has been made to include items published before 1956 and not included in Fatini; to have done so would have entailed Herculean efforts to track down the obscure. We are convinced from our own necessary and frequent references to Fatini's bibliography that few items of any great significance escaped the compiler's attention; not surprisingly, those few that did were, for the most part, published abroad.

During the nearly quarter century embraced by this bibliography—years that saw the celebration of the six-hundredth anniversary of Ariosto's birth (1974) and, consequently, the organization of congresses and the publication of numerous commemorative volumes—several bibliographies of Ariosto criticism have appeared, some with brief annotations. None is an exhaustive compilation of articles, essays, monographs, and notes; however, they were all helpful in our efforts to be as thorough as possible and often provided important leads in a search for information not otherwise readily available. Of interest for articles appearing in regional publications of Emilia-Romagna and often dealing with matters tangential to a critical evaluation of Ariosto the writer is Domenico Medici's "La Bibliografia della critica ariostesca dal 'Fatini' ad oggi (1957–1974)," *Bollettino storico reggiano* 7, no. 27 (1974): 63–150. Unfortunately, Medici's compilation appeared in one of the Ariosto anniversary issues of a publication with very limited circulation and almost unobtainable outside Italy. A supplement to Medici's interesting but incomplete and often inaccurate list was compiled by Renzo Cremante and published together with his review of the anniversary issues in *Studi e problemi di critica testuale* 18 (1979): 229–44. Also of use in the preparation of this volume were the following bibliographies or bibliographical essays: Tiziano Ascari, "Rassegna di studi ariosteschi (1954–1960)," in *Atti e memorie dell'Accademia di Scienze Lettere e Arti di Modena*, 6th ser., vol. 3 (1961): 161–77; Guido Baldassarri, "Tendenze e prospettive della critica ariostesca nell'ultimo trentennio (1946–1973)," *La Rassegna della letteratura italiana*, 7th ser., vol. 79, nos. 1–2 (1975): 183–201; Aldo Borlenghi,

Ariosto, 2d ed. (Palermo: Palumbo, 1974); Renzo Frattarolo, "Ariosto 1974," *Accademie e biblioteche d'Italia* 42, no. 6 (1974): 426–66; Joseph Gibaldi, "Bibliography of Ariosto in England and America," in *Ariosto 1974 in America*, edited by Aldo Scaglione (Ravenna: Longo, 1976), pp. 159–77; Paolo Paolini, "Situazione della critica ariostesca," in *Per l'Ariosto*, special issue of *Italianistica* 3, no. 3 (1974): 3–22, published in 1976 by Marzorati in Milan; and Alessandro Tortoreto, "Ariosto e Tasso: saggio bibliografico (1957–1974)," *Studi tassiani* 24, nos. 1–2 (1974): 71–78. The foregoing list is, of necessity, selective; it does not include often substantial bibliographies appended to monographic studies on Ariosto (and noted in the appropriate entry) or bibliographies devoted to writers upon whom Ariosto had significant influence, especially Torquato Tasso, Edmund Spenser, and Miguel de Cervantes. Finally, any bibliographer in the humanities is indebted to the annual compilations of the Modern Language Association, the bibliographic narratives in *Year's Work in Modern Language Studies*, and the numerous standard reference works that, by now, are the starting places for any bibliographical undertaking.

This bibliography is devoted essentially to critical scholarship on the entire corpus of Ariosto's works or on his influences in Italy and abroad. With few exceptions, it does not list items that are of peripheral interest and that, not infrequently, appear in regional journals published in Emilia-Romagna. Exception has been made in the case of entries that have been judged of interest to Ariosto studies even if not literary in nature. No bibliography is complete; we have tried, however, to include all the critical literature devoted to the Ferrarese poet and to the literature that comments on Ariosto in an important way, though concerned primarily with another figure or with a topos. As all bibliographers know, the latter items are the most elusive; often they come to one's attention by chance. We hope, nevertheless, that what we have included attests to Ariosto's growing importance to students of narrative and romance in Western culture. In addition to monographs, critical essays, and significant prefaces to editions of Ariosto's works, we have included doctoral dissertations written in the United States and, to the degree possible, abroad. However, few countries systematically publish lists and abstracts of dissertations written for advanced degrees and, consequently, we can make no claim to thoroughness for European dissertations, for example. The decision to include North American dissertations was based on several factors. From 1956 through 1980, over twenty-five doctoral dissertations on Ariosto or concerned with Ariosto in a significant way are listed in *Disssertation Abstracts, Dissertation Abstracts International,* and *American Doctoral Dissertations.* In a relative way, this means that a substantial amount of Ariosto scholarship, in North America especially, is in dissertation form and available only by special order. By annotating the dissertation abstracts available and by providing relevant bibliographical information, we intended to inform scholars who do not reside in North America of much significant work that often goes unnoticed. For dissertations that were revised and published as monographs before 1980, we have entered the monograph title and relevant bibliographical information; for dissertations published in monograph form after that date, we have listed the abstract and relevant information from *Dissertation Abstracts* or, after July 1969, *Dissertation Abstracts International*, as well as the publication information. Furthermore, encyclopedia and biographical dictionary entries have been included only if analytical. Finally, it should be noted that the decision not to include book reviews was made after extensive deliberation. The conclusion was that completeness becomes even more problematic for reviews than for primary entries; that many reviews are brief notices of no critical importance; and that selecting reviews for inclusion becomes arbitrary.

A few words on the mechanics of the listing. For all entries first published before 1956 and then reprinted, with or without revisions, between 1957 and 1980, reference is made to the Fatini entry and, except in cases of substantial revision, no annotation is provided. Recent editions of "classic" studies on Ariosto, such as the commentaries of Galilei, the several essays of the nineteenth-century scholar Francesco De Sanctis, or the views of Hegel, to name a few, have not been included because there would be little chance (and perhaps necessity) of a complete listing of such publications; in any case, such items are included by Fatini. In the case of modern studies with several editions, every attempt has been made to note the latest edition. When it seemed of possible importance to the reader, we have indicated the first edition. Collections of essays entirely or largely devoted to Ariosto are entered under the title of the volume if a general editor is not named, and the relevant contents are listed; the annotation, however, appears under the entry for the specific item, listed by author. For articles published in more than one journal, published in a journal as well as in a volume of essays, or republished in a collection, the primary entry lists the most recent printing, with information on earlier publications provided in the annotation. If the same text was published on more than one occasion and has significant variations in title, the variant is given; if not, only the journal or volume is noted, with relevant bibliographical information. The entries are arranged alphabetically for ease of access.

Incorporated into the annotations are frequent quotations from the text with page references, which are also given when a point seemed especially relevant and it was felt that the exact location would aid the reader. Quotations in major foreign languages, including Italian, French, German, and Spanish, have not been translated, on the assumption that the individual consulting the bibliography would have a working knowledge of these languages. With languages less frequently known by American and Western European scholars, we have translated or paraphrased in English. Names of authors and editors in languages that must be transliterated have been cited as shown in the annotated work.

Finally, the bête noire of any bibliographer is the item that cannot be located, even by the most diligent and enterprising reference librarian. In such instances and if it seemed of critical interest, we cited the item and its source, providing whatever useful information possible. Bibliographers are inclined to feel that if their efforts were of no avail, the scholar researching a subject with a limited amount of time will certainly not be able to turn up the obscure; on the other hand, the possibility of chance encounters or of finding oneself in an out-of-the-way library always exists and if our citation gives a lead, so much the better. The finder can have the satisfaction of a discovery that defied our efforts.

In compiling and editing this bibliography, we have received assistance at all stages of preparation from many colleagues and friends almost too numerous to mention. However, we would like to express our appreciation to those who have been most involved in the project or who have shown interest by keeping an eye out for a title that might have escaped our attention. For help with library legwork, editing, translating, and proofreading: Keala Jewell, Ilona Klein, and especially Amy Scarr, the bibliographer's dream assistant. For providing assistance with the frustrations of Italian libraries: Signorina Fiorella Ginanneschi of the Istituto Nazionale di Studi sul Rinascimento (Palazzo Strozzi, Florence); the several patient (and, alas, nameless) young assistants in the Sala Periodici and Sala di Consultazione of Florence's Biblioteca Nazionale Centrale; the staff of the Biblioteca Comunale Ariostea (Ferrara) and, in particular, Dott. Luciano Capra, its director and a leading Ariosto scholar; Dott. Maurizio Festanti, director of the Biblioteca Municipale "A. Panizzi" in Reggio Emilia. For a variety of things, including helpful advice, our colleagues James O. Bailey, Gino Casagrande, Gail Geiger, Christopher Kleinhenz, Arnold Miller, Bonner Mitchell, Nicholas Rand, Marian Rothstein, J. Thomas Shaw, James Steakley, Lawrence L. Thomas, Andrew D. Weiner, and particularly John R. Roberts, a model bibliographer. For financial assistance in the final stages of compilation and manuscript preparation, the Research Committee of the Graduate School of the University of Wisconsin. Our greatest debt is to the several units of the Memorial Library of the University of Wisconsin and of the O. Meredith Wilson Library of the University of Minnesota: at Interlibrary Loan at the University of Wisconsin, Priscilla Neill and Judy Tuohy, and at the University of Minnesota, Erica Linke; in Reference at the University of Wisconsin: Elizabeth Breed, Marguerite Christensen, Louise Henning, Bonnie Kalmbach, Lynn Magdol, Ann Pollock, Eleanor Morgan Rodini, Ruth Sanderson, Willa Schmidt, Charles Spetland, Jean Thompson, and Jeanine Thubauville.

R. J. R.
S. Di M.
Madison
May 1984

Abbreviations and Terms
Used in the Annotations

ADD	*American Doctoral Dissertations*
CC	*Cinque Canti* (Ariosto)
DAI	*Dissertation Abstracts International*
DC	*La Divina Commedia* (Dante)
DQ	*Don Quixote* (Cervantes)
FQ	*The Faerie Queene* (Spenser)
GL	*La Gerusalemme Liberata* (Tasso)
OF	*Orlando Furioso* (Ariosto)
OI	*Orlando Innamorato* (Boiardo)
Dispense	Text of published university lectures
Fatini	Giuseppe Fatini, *Bibliografia della critica ariostea*, 1510–1956 (Florence, 1958).
Medici	Domenico Medici, "La Bibliografia della critica ariostesca dal 'Fatini' ad oggi (1957–1974)," *Bollettino storico reggiano* 7, no. 27 (1974): 63–150.

Except in the case of commonly used abbreviations (e.g., *MLN*, *PMLA*), all journals are listed by full name.

Bibliography

᪥ 1. AGNELLO, NINO. "Spunti favolistici e aneddotici nelle *Satire* di Ludovico Ariosto." *Aspetti letterari* (Naples), nos. 5–6 (1966): 42–53.
Modeled after Horace's *Sermones*, the satires are essentially literary in character, as made evident by Ariosto's use of fable, apology, and anecdote. Analyzes the structure of these elements in the satires, compares specific instances to classical and popular sources, and concludes that they serve to maintain, through variety and good humor, the median tone of Horace, to lend a note of authority to the moral stance, and, in some instances, to act as a means of closing the composition.

᪥ 2. ———. "Tecnica dell'Ariosto nel *Furioso* (tecnica del congedo)." *Ausonia* 29, nos. 3–4 (1974): 11–25.
Discusses Ariosto's technique in the *congedo* and in the prologue to the cantos of the *OF*. Shows that the *congedo*, or leave taking—normally directed to the audience—is free of the popular, moralizing, medieval elements present in Pulci and Boiardo. Suggests that the prologue, though often characterized by a courtly tone, follows the chivalric tradition of commenting on the characters' deeds and on the poet's own achievements. Notes that at times Ariosto uses it to comment on the nature of man, as well as on the role of God as ultimate judge of man and human history.

᪥ 3. ———. "Il viaggio di Rinaldo in Italia nell'*Orlando Furioso*." *Ausonia* 32, nos. 1–2 (1977): 25–29.
Notes that the unusually lengthy description of Rinaldo's journey between Mantua and Urbino (*OF* 42–43) not only reveals the poet's familiarity with the region but also provides him the opportunity to praise the deeds of the Este family and to invoke God's protection of Ferrara and its leaders. Suggests that the episode also serves as an idyllic pause before the dramatic and epic finale of the battle between Ruggiero and Rodomonte.

᪥ 4. ———. "Ariosto e Virgilio: da Eurialo e Niso a Cloridano e Medoro," *Ausonia* 34, nos. 1–2 (1979): 28–38.
Discusses Ariosto's use of his source (book 9 of the *Aeneid*) for the Cloridano and Medoro episode (*OF* 18–19), noting that he structures his episode closely after Virgil but with several modifications and innovations that adapt the epic-tragic tone of Virgil to the chivalric-romance tone of the *OF*.

5. AGUILERA, EMILIANO M. Preface. In *Orlando Furioso*, by Ludovico Ariosto, translated into prose by Manuel Aranda Sanjuan, 1:vii–xv. 2 vols. Barcelona: Editorial Iberia, 1958.
Summary preface on the life and career of Ariosto. No critical evaluation.

6. ALBINI, UMBERTO. "Ariosto scrittore latino." *Terzoprogramma*, nos. 2–3 (1974): 14–23.
Discusses the tonal qualities of some of Ariosto's Latin love lyrics and epigrams, noting his early use, among other things, of ironic contemplation, parody, and the variety of reactions to the vicissitudes of life evidenced in his more mature work. Occasional references to echoes of his Latin verse in the *OF*.

7. ALHAIQUE, ROSANNA PETTINELLI. "Tra il Boiardo e l'Ariosto: il Cieco da Ferrara e Niccolò degli Agostini." *La Rassegna della letteratura italiana*, 7th ser., vol. 79, nos. 1–2 (1975): 232–78.
Studies the stylistic, thematic, and lexical borrowings in the *OF* from Agostini's continuation of the *OI* and from Cieco da Ferrara's *Il Mambriano*, noting that a study of Ariosto's cultural formation for the composition of a romance epic should be based on poems contemporary to him rather than on the French romance tradition. Cites a similar conclusion reached by Carlo Dionisotti, "Appunti sui *Cinque canti* e sugli studi ariosteschi," in *Studi e problemi di critica testuale* (entry 265), 369–92, especially pp. 377–79. Considers a variety of themes (e.g., flight, pp. 242–48), structural techniques (pp. 240–42), and variants on Boiardo's episodes and shows how Agostini, Cieco, and Ariosto employ them in ways that reveal the latter to be a superior poet in his ability to incorporate traditional materials into an organic poetic conception.

8. ALLEN, DON CAMERON. *Mysteriously Meant: The Rediscovery of Pagan Symbolism and Allegorical Interpretation in the Renaissance.* Baltimore and London: Johns Hopkins University Press, 1970.
Notes Ariosto's use of allegory in the *OF* as one of the elements used to assure "variety and keep the reader's interest" (p. 283). States that the Renaissance commentators on the text gave allegorical interpretations that exaggerated the author's probable intentions. See especially pp. 283–86.

9. ALLEN, FRANK. "Ariosto and Browning: A Reexamination of 'Count Gismond.'" *Victorian Poetry* 11, no. 1 (1973): 15–25.
On Browning's use of the Ginevra-Ariodante episode (*OF* 4–6) in his poem "Count Gismond" and his modification of the source "to reinterpret stereotyped and conventional behavior to create a more psychologically realistic dramatic conflict" (p. 15).

⊷§ 10. ALMANSI, GUIDO. "Tattica del meraviglioso ariostesco." In *Ludovico Ariosto: lingua, stile e tradizione*, edited by Cesare Segre (entry 789), pp. 175–93. Milan: Feltrinelli, 1976.

Suggests three principal divisions of the fantastic elements ("meraviglioso") in the *OF*: "practical" fantasy, which is introduced matter-of-factly and which, through a mediated or low-keyed tone, tends to make of the unusual something banal and unexceptional; "incredulous" fantasy, wherein doubt about the reality of the moment is structured into the narrative; and "onyric," or true fantasy. In all instances, the reader is unprepared for the change from the verisimilar to the fantastic due to Ariosto's tightly controlled narrative tone that, the author suggests, is intended to insure the fluidity of the reading process, always hampered by an emotionally charged style.

⊷§ 11. ALONGE, ROBERTO. See Getto, Giovanni, Roberto Alonge, Guido Baldi, and Giorgio De Rienzo, *Storia della letturatura italiana*, entry 351.

⊷§ 12. ALONSO, DÁMASO. Prologo. In *Romance de Angélica y Medoro*, by Luis de Góngora y Argote, pp. 9–38. Madrid: Ediciones Acies, 1962.

Summary account of the fortune of Ariosto's Angelica and Medoro episode in Spanish literature, as well as a brief comparative analysis of Ariosto's narrative and Góngora's version, noting in particular the stylistic differences between the original and the mannered adaptation of the Spanish poet.

⊷§ 13. ALPERS, PAUL J. *The Poetry of "The Faerie Queene."* Princeton, N.J.: Princeton University Press, 1967. Reprint. Columbia and London: University of Missouri Press, 1982. 415p.

Examines Spenser's major borrowings from the *OF*, concluding that his interest lay with characters "in a poetically interesting situation, as opposed to an individual with a unique moral nature" (p. 194) and, therefore, that his major inspiration came from the Italian text itself and not, as has often been claimed, from a reading of the sixteenth-century allegorists of the *OF*. See especially chapter 6, "Spenser's Use of Ariosto," pp. 160–99.

⊷§ 14. ANCESCHI, GIUSEPPE. "Panizzi e Boiardo." In *Il Boiardo e la critica contemporanea*, edited by Giuseppe Anceschi, pp. 11–27. Atti del Convegno di Studi su Matteo Maria Boiardo. Scandiano-Reggio Emilia, 25–27 aprile 1969. Biblioteca dell'*Archivum Romanicum*, 1st ser., vol. 107. Florence: Leo S. Olschki, 1970.

Discusses the genesis of Antonio Panizzi's edition of Boiardo and Ariosto (*Orlando Innamorato of Matteo Maria Boiardo and Orlando Furioso of Ludovico Ariosto, with an Essay on the Romantic Narrative Poetry of the Italians. Memoirs and Notes by Antonio Panizzi*. London: William Pickering,

1830–1834, 9 vols.) prepared while the editor was in political exile in England and held the chair of Italian studies at University College, London. Gives particular attention to the historical significance of the edition of the *OI* and to the one-volume essay on the Italian epic romance—one of the first to note in Boiardo the confluence of the Carolingian and Arthurian traditions (p. 22).

15. ANCESCHI BOLOGNESI, SELENE. "Era nata a Reggio Emilia la figlia del re del Catai?" In *Ludovico Ariosto*, pp. 563–74. Convegno internazionale (entry 475). Rome: Accademia Nazionale dei Lincei, 1975.
Observations on the character of Angelica in both the *OI* and the *OF*; identifies Antonia Caprara as Boiardo's inspiration for the character.

16. ANONYMOUS. *L'Arioste en France*. Paris: Istituto Italiano di Cultura; Ferrara: Sciaca Arti Grafiche, 1974. Pages unnumbered.
Catalog of exhibition of works by Ariosto published in France. Descriptive entry for each item. Divided into five sections: French editions of the *OF* in Italian; editions of French translations of the *OF*; French translations or imitations of parts of the *OF*; translations of the *OF* in languages other than French and published in France; other works of Ariosto, either in the original or in translation, published in France. First part of catalog contains reproductions of selected title pages (e.g., of the 1544 Lyon translation, one of the oldest), woodcuts, and samples of designs for editions (e.g., by Léonard Gaultier and Gustave Moreau).

17. ANONYMOUS. *Mostra bibliografica ariostea nel V centenario della nascita di Ludovico Ariosto*. Catalogo. Rome: Biblioteca Statale Angelica, 1974. 63p.
Catalog of 1974 exhibition of *Ariosteana* in the Biblioteca Angelica, Rome, including editions of the poet's work and both biographical and critical studies. Includes 272 entries: 106 editions, plus critical studies. Five plates.

18. ANONYMOUS. "Prince of Poets / Anniversary. Ariosto, a Leading Light of the Renaissance." *MD (Medical Newsmagazine)* 18, no. 6 (1974): 129–36.
Brief commemorative essay on Ariosto's life and his importance to Renaissance culture, with summary commentary on his most important work.

19. *Antologia della letteratura italiana*. See Vitale, Maurizio, entry 893.

≈§ 20. APOLLONIO, MARIO. "Arioto." In *Opere di Ludovico Ariosto*, edited by Mario Apollonio, 1:1–58. 2 vols. Milan: Rizzoli, 1956.
First edition 1944; Fatini, 3340.

≈§ 21. ——. Introduzione. In *Orlando Furioso*, by Ludovico Ariosto, edited by Mario Apollonio and Pio Fontana, pp. 7–37. 2d ed. Brescia: La Scuola, 1968.
Discussion of the evolution of Ariosto's poetics against the backdrop and as a product of the complexities of early sixteenth-century European culture, under the weight of political disturbances and in constant flux with the broadening horizons of new geographical and scientific discoveries. Sees Ariosto's work as based in reality, as a constant dialogue with reality, and as a celebration and preservation of man's essence and individualism against the nullifying forces of the world. Observes that the structure of the *OF* is a metaphor of the new mathematical geography of the world: "Tutto il mondo è uguale, tutto ritorna al suo principio, ogni punto della superficie di una sfera è equidistante dal centro" (p. 17).

≈§ 22. A[QUILECCHIA], G[IOVANNI]. "Ariosto, Ludovico." In *The New Encyclopaedia Britannica: Macropaedia*, 1:1151–52. 30 vols. 15th ed. Chicago: Encyclopaedia Britannica, Inc., 1979.
Brief account of Ariosto's life and literary activities, as well as a traditional evaluation of the poet's character.

≈§ 23. ARENS, J. C. "Olimpia aan Birenus: een Heroide van G. Brandt naar Stof van Ariosto." *Spiegel der Letteren* 7 (1963–1964): 129–31.
Notes that Geeraardt Brandt's alexandrine "Heroide" (1646) of Ovidian inspiration is probably indebted to Ariosto's Olimpia episode (*OF* 9, 10, and 11), which he knew through the 1615 French translation of de Rosset.

≈§ 24. ARGENTI, RAIMONDO. "Il Poeta Lodovico Ariosto fu titolare del beneficio di Santa Maria dell'Oliveto." *La Libertá* 8, no. 35 (1959): 12.
Brief history of the church of Montericcio, constructed by Benedictines and for which Ariosto held a benefice from 1507 to 1515.

≈§ 25. ARIOSTO, LUDOVICO. *Orlando furioso*. Secondo l'edizione del 1532 con le varianti delle edizioni del 1516 e del 1521, edited by Santorre Debenedetti and Cesare Segre. Bologna: Commissione per i testi di lingua, 1960. 1697p.
Critical edition of the text based on the 1516 (A), 1521 (B) and 1532 (C) manuscripts. Edition begun by Santorre Debenedetti (Bari: Laterza, 1928). In a note to the text (pp. 1649–97), Segre credits Debenedetti with the editing of cantos 1–8 and 12–32, and describes his criteria for the collation of

available manuscripts for this edition, as well as his task of reconstructing Debenedetti's methodology. Proceeds to discuss and group six tables of variants among the A, B, and C manuscripts, distinguishing between printing errors and discrepancies attributed to the printers' interpretation of the "lezioni," or graphic and phonetic representation of the textual elements.

◄§ 26. ———. *The Comedies of Ariosto*. Translated, edited, and with an introduction by Edmond M. Beame and Leonard C. Sbrocchi. Chicago and London: University of Chicago Press, 1975. 322p.

Introduction (pp. vii–xlv) traces the evolution of Italian theater before Ariosto, especially Ferrarese theater under Este patronage. Discussion of all of Ariosto's comedies, noting the playwright's debt to Roman comedy and to the Italian novella tradition. Consideration of Ariosto's contribution to the development of erudite comedy in the sixteenth century. Views Ariosto as a "noteworthy critic of his society, censuring its artificiality, its folly, and its corruption" (p. xxxviii).

◄§ 27. ARRÓNIZ, OTHÓN. *La influencia italiana en el nacimiento de la comedia española*. Madrid: Editorial Gredos, S.A. (Biblioteca Románica Hispánica), 1969. 339p.

Discusses the probable influence of Ariosto's *Il Negromante* on Juan de Timoneda's *Comedia llamada Cornelia* (1559), noting, however, the superiority of Ariosto's comedy and Timoneda's failure to imitate the most successful aspects of his model. See especially pp. 134–42.

◄§ 28. ARTHOS, JOHN. *On the Poetry of Spenser and the Form of Romances*. London: George Allen & Unwin, Ltd., 1956. 207p.

Notes that for a reader of English literature, the OF appears to be a Catholic poem, having as its central theme the marriage of Ruggiero and Bradamante. Considers the poem as a romance without epic figures and identifies as its greatest point of interest "the intricate movement of life" (p. 118). Points to the poem's contemporaneity. Concludes that the questing figures in the OF "are not like the figures of Spenser's poem, or many another romance, wanderers in a forest following some holy light, but in the forests of Ariosto . . . they are individuals in a slaughter-house about to be abandoned, half the time mad with jealousy or love" (p. 129). See especially pp. 115–31.

◄§ 29. ASCARI, TIZIANO. "Rassegna di studi ariosteschi (1954–1960)." In *Atti e memorie dell'Accademia di Scienze Lettere e Arti di Modena*, 6th ser., vol. 3 (1961): 161–77.

Review essay with a critical evaluation of the following: Antonio Piromalli, *Motivi e forme della poesia di Ludovico Ariosto* (1954); Riccardo Bacchelli, "Arte e genio dell'Ariosto poeta della poesia" and "Codicillo ariostesco," in

Ludovico Ariosto, *Tutte le opere* (1958); Mario Marti, "Il tono medio dell'*Orlando furioso*," *Convivium*, n.s. 23 (1955); Enzo Turolla, "Dittologia e *enjambement* nell'elaborazione dell'*Orlando furioso*," *Lettere italiane* 10 (1958); Antonio Baldini, *Ariosto e dintorni* (1958); Emilio Zanette, *Conversazioni sull'"Orlando Furioso"* (1958); Anna Carlini, "Progetto di edizione critica delle liriche di Ludovico Ariosto," *Giornale storico della letteratura italiana* 135 (1958); Cesare Segre, "Studi sui *Cinque Canti*," *Studi di filologia italiana* 12 (1954); Carlo Dionisotti, "Per la data dei *Cinque Canti*," *Giornale storico della letteratura italiana* 137 (1960).

►§ 30. ATCHITY, KENNETH JOHN. "Renaissance Epics in English," *Italica* 50, no. 3 (1973): 435–39.
Comments briefly on four editions of translations of the OF printed in the preceding two decades: Allan Gilbert's prose rendition (1954), "accurate but often awkward" (p. 435); Rudolf Gottfried's edited selections from Harington's 1591 translation (1963); the complete Harington translation with an introduction by Robert McNulty (1972); and Stewart A. Baker and A. Bartlett Giamatti's edition of the 1831 William Stewart Rose translation (1968). Concludes that the Rose translation is the most serviceable to date.

►§ 31. AUREAS, HENRI. *Un Général de Napoléon: Miollis*. Paris: Les Belles Lettres, 1961. 210p.
Includes the text of Sextius de Miollis's (1759–1828) letter to the citizens of Reggio Emilia exhorting them to honor Ariosto with a monument (pp. 85–86); also contains a brief account of Miollis's sponsorship of the transference of Ariosto's tomb to its present site in the library of the university (6–7 June 1801).

►§ 32. BACCHELLI, RICCARDO. "Codicillo ariostesco." *Nuova antologia* 469, fasc. 1873 (1957): 9–20.
Fatini, 3599.

►§ 33. ———. *La Congiura di Don Giulio d'Este, e altri scritti ariosteschi.* 2d ed. Milan: Mondadori, 1966. 688p.
First edition 1931; Fatini, 2533.

►§ 34. ———. "Nel Mare dell'*Orlando Furioso*." *Approdo letterario*, n.s. 14, no. 44 (1968): 3–26.
Originally published as preface to *Orlando Furioso*, by Ludovico Ariosto, pp. ix–xvii. 3 vols; illustrated by Fabrizio Clerici. Milan: Electa Editrice, 1967.
Essay on the nature of Ariosto's irony and satirical bent, on his moral perspective and political involvement, and on the structural patterns in the

narrative of the *OF*, concluding with a discussion of Fabrizio Clerici's illustrations, which are considered inspired for having captured the spirit of the poem. Notes that Ariosto's satire and irony manifest "il senno popolare italiano, di temperata, appunto sennata ironia, critica, non negativa, moderante, non distruttiva, ironica e magari sardonica, non sarcastica e irridente" (p. 6). Draws a parallel with Francesco Guicciardini's attitude in the face of a pessimistic world view, noting that Guicciardini was "virile in quanto prescrive d'operare malgrado e contro ogni scettica conclusione" and that his was a "pessimismo stoico" (p. 12). Discusses the *OF* as a political apologia for the Este dynasty and a strong defense of its policies. Notes several lines of thematic and tonal development in considering how the work should be read, including a progression from the intensely fantastic ("favolistica"), toward "la sobrietà d'una poesia umana anche nello straordinario e stupefacente" (p. 21), and toward the sublime, i.e., "la scoperta involontaria, la legge segreta, la fatalità finale insita e celata nel soggetto, anzi nell'impresa per sé stessa avventurosa e d'inattendibili sviluppi" (p. 9).

⊷§ 35. ――――. "Ariosto 'solstiziale.'" In *Per l'Ariosto* (entry 623). Special 1976 issue of *Italianistica* 3, no. 3 (1974): 165–66.
Notes Ariosto's presence in his writings and that in the *CC* there is "un accenno della varia e complessa melanconia ariostesca" (p. 166).

⊷§ 36. ――――. "Esperienza ariostesca." *La Rassegna della letteratura italiana*, 7th ser., vol. 79, nos. 1–2 (1975): 5–6.
Brief observations on tonal and stylistic qualities of Ariosto's eclogue describing the attempted conspiracy of Don Giulio d'Este in 1505 and their reflections in Ariosto's more mature compositions.

⊷§ 37. BACCINI, DANILO, ed. *Orlando furioso: sunti-commento-analisi dei personaggi-curiosità ariostesche.* 2 vols. Rome: Le Muse, 1970. 714p.
Volume 1 contains a popularized introduction to a reading of the *OF*, touching upon commonplaces and stating traditional evaluations of the poet's attitudes and vision of the world (pp. 5–155). Summary and brief discussion of each canto. Selected letters of Ariosto, a short review of criticism before De Sanctis, and a summary of the *CC* (2:619–706). Includes bibliography, 1:155, and index of characters, 2:707–10.

⊷§ 38. BADINI, GINO. "Reggio al tempo dell'Ariosto dalle relazioni del Guicciardini e da documenti d'archivio." In *Lodovico Ariosto: il suo tempo la sua terra la sua gente* (entry 468). Estratto dal *Bollettino storico reggiano* 7, no. 25 (1974): 35–41.
Notes the importance of Francesco Guicciardini's correspondence (sixteen volumes published by Roberto Palmarocchi, 1938–1951, and Pier Giorgio

Ricci, 1954–1970) while governor of Reggio (1517–1523) to a study of the political events of the period (e.g., papal domination) and to greater knowledge of important citizens of the region.

◄§ 39. BAEHR, RUDOLF. "Das Porträt der Alcina in Ariosts *Orlando Furioso* (VII, 10–15)." *Italienische Studien* (Vienna: Italienisches Kulturinstitut 1 (1978): 5–17.

Analysis of Ariosto's description of Alcina (*OF* 7.10–16). Suggests that the details evolved from the Neoplatonic interest in the nature of beauty. Argues that the description is fundamentally of two types: "descriptio personarum extrinseca" (p. 7), and a portrait employing the rhetorical norms of classical Latin descriptions. Concludes that Ariosto's portrait of ideal beauty serves as a basis for many similar descriptions among his contemporaries.

◄§ 40. BAILLET, ROGER. *Le monde poétique de l'Arioste: essai d'interprétation du "Roland Furieux."* Lyon: Editions l'Hermès, 1977. 544p., plus appendixes.

Notes the failure of both traditional and more recent criticism to identify a coherent structure in the *OF* and proceeds to demonstrate that the poem is in fact characterized by a well-defined poetic message. Through a discussion of formal and thematic elements of the poem, such as imagery, narrative sequences, major characters, types of adventures, and their diversity of tones, argues that Ariosto subscribes to the humanist ideal of the Golden Age as well as to a monarchic ideology, the latter reflected in his eulogy of the Este dynasty. Considers the *OF* a new *Aeneid*, or an "Estéide" (passim) that celebrates the coming of a Golden Age in Ferrara and specifies that contrary to a traditional Utopian vision, Ariosto's moves from the real world of his city to the platonic Ideal. Discusses this view of the poem by pointing out that the world of the *OF*, in directing the chaotic toward a structured universe or toward a harmonious whole, has as its dynamics the opposition of Good and Evil and represents the victory of perfection. On a different level, such a victory is represented by Bradamante and Ruggiero, whose path is that of all beings in search of perfection. After observing that the narrative of the *OF* is primarily important as the medium for the communication of the dynastic and Utopian message, suggests that the content of the work is to be found in the conscious complicity between the style of the discourse and its message, or "dans la forme même du poème dont la structure est *concordia discors*" (p. 535). Extensive bibliography for the years 1956–1976, pp. 538–41.

◄§ 41. BALACI, ALEXANDRU. *Ludovico Ariosto, contemporanul nostru.* (In Rumanian.) Bucharest: Albatros, 1974. 233p.

Parts of this monograph are revisions of "În cetatea lui Ariosto," *România literară* (Bucharest) 32 (1972): 32; "Structuri armonice în *Orlando Furioso*,"

Steaua (Cluj) 9 (1974): 42–44; "Spiritul armoniei," Secolul XX (Bucharest) 163 (1974): 79–83; "La 500 de ani: Ariosto si comediile lui," Teatrul (Bucharest), no. 10 (1974): 63–65.

Introduction to Ariosto and his works, focusing on the reflection in his writings of the Renaissance ethos and on the modernity of his perspective on life. States that Ariosto can be defined as the poet of harmony (p. 17), which in his work manifests itself as the ordering of a polymorphous, complex reality. Discussion of Ariosto's life as courtier in the service of the Este and brief analysis of the minor works. Considers the sources of the OF, the main narrative threads of the poem, and, in particular, the important role of women in the poem. Concludes that the OF exalts the individual and that Ariosto is our contemporary in his perception of the situation of the individual in a multidimensional reality.

*§ 42. BALDACCI, LUIGI, ed. Lirici del Cinquecento. With revisions of the second edition by Giuseppe Nicoletti. Milan: Longanesi, 1975.

Brief biographical note and comment on Ariosto's lyric poetry, in pp. 189–90. Notes a spiritual affinity between Ariosto and Horace in the lyrics while "la forma dell'imitare resta sì vagamente in un ambito petrarchistico [and] la sostanza sentimentale è espressa in una luce pagana e immediata che niente ha che fare con i prefabbricati itinerari spirituali dei bembiani. Di Orazio la lirica dell'Ariosto risente il sapore realistico" (pp. 189–90). Bibliography of selected editions of the lyric poetry. Annotated selections of his verse contained in pp. 191–206.

*§ 43. BALDASSARRI, GUIDO. "Tendenze e prospettive della critica ariostesca nell'ultimo trentennio (1946–1973)." La Rassegna della letteratura italiana, 7th ser., 79, nos. 1–2 (1975): 183–201.

Brief survey of the major trends in Ariosto criticism from the late 1940s to the early 1970s, noting the particular contributions in the early postwar period of Carlo Grabher and Walter Binni, whose Metodo e poesia di Ludovico Ariosto (1947) is seen as an important beginning in the revision of Crocean methodology regarding Ariosto (p. 186). Discusses the polemical stance in the 1950s against certain idealistic criticism and the significant philological and stylistic studies of Dionisotti, Segre, and Caretti. Indicates several important studies on Ariosto's use of sources and, for the later period, the contributions of Eduardo Saccone and Mario Santoro, significant for the application of new critical methods to a reading of the OF, especially, and for new light shed on the irrational components of Ariosto's Weltanschauung (p. 194). Extensive bibliography for the period 1946–1973 (pp. 195–201).

*§ 44. BALDI, GUIDO. See Getto, Giovanni, Roberto Alonge, Guido Baldi, and Giorgio De Rienzo, Storia della letteratura italiana, entry 351.

◆§ 45. BALDINI, ANTONIO. *Ariosto e dintorni.* Caltanissetta-Rome: Salvatore Sciascia, 1958. 223p.
Collection of short pieces that originally appeared in newspapers and journals, including the brief essays contained in his *Ludovico della tranquillità. Divagazioni ariostesche* (Bologna: Zanichelli, 1933); Fatini, 2706. See also Fatini, Index, p. 695.

◆§ 46. ———. "Sette capitoli sul *Furioso.*" In *Orlando Furioso,* by Ludovico Ariosto, edited by Gabriele Baldini, 1:vii–lxi. 2 vols. Bologna: Zanichelli, 1964.
Introduction to this edition is composed of several articles that were published earlier as indicated and, with one exception, annotated in Fatini: "Nota a un giudizio sull'*Orlando Furioso,*" *La Cultura* 31 (1912): 531–37; 563–71; 594–605; 628–35 (Fatini, 2032); selected pages from *Ludovico della tranquillità. Divagazioni ariostesche.* Bologna: Zanichelli, 1933, pp. 63–70; 91–98; 107–11 (Fatini, 2706); from "Stazioni dell'ottava rima." In *Cattedra d'occasione* (1941), pp. 61–69; preface to *Le Più belle pagine di Ludovico Ariosto.* Milan: Treves, 1928 (Fatini, 2373).

◆§ 47. BALESTRINI, NANNI. "Ariosto realista: le satire." *Terzoprogramma,* nos. 2–3 (1974): 24–33.
Considers the process and rhetorical devices by which autobiographical fact—"realismo"—in the satires becomes literature, written in a style described as "basso, colloquiale e comico," and representing the poetic resolution of a conflict between art and social reality (p. 28). In the last satire, "il cerchio si chiude. L'umiliazione patita dall'intellettuale che deve necessariamente dipendere dalla classe dominante, e insieme il fallimento delle sue aspirazioni d'innalzamento sociale, si risolvono nel pacato equilibrio dei versi delle *Satire* che suggellano l'accettazione della condizione prima tanto vituperata e combattuta" (p. 32).

◆§ 48. BALL, ROBERT. "Poetic Imitation in Góngora's 'Romance de Angélica y Medoro.'" *Bulletin of Hispanic Studies* 57 (1980): 33–54.
Góngora's imitation and mutation of the Angelica and Medoro episode in both the *OF* and Lope de Vega's *La hermosura de Angélica* as a commentary on the process of poetic creation.

◆§ 49. BALMAS, ENEA. "Note sulla fortuna dell'Ariosto in Francia nel Cinquecento." In *Premio Città Monselice per una traduzione letteraria. Atti del Quinto Convegno sui problemi della traduzione letteraria: Le Prime traduzioni dell'Ariosto,* no. 6, pp. 3–32. Monselice: A Cura dell'Amministrazione Comunale, 1977.
Considers the nature of Ariosto's great popularity in sixteenth-century

France (two prose translations of the *OF* in eighteen editions, two partial verse translations, several imitations of the *OF*, and an equal interest in the minor works) and discusses the interest of the Pléiade in Ariosto and, in particular, the imitations of Ariosto in Du Bellay's lyric poetry. Notes that, given a different historical and sociological context, in France the reading of Ariosto was distorted, to the point of misunderstanding (p. 29), and that Ariosto was done a great disservice by prose translations that treated the *OF* as a reworking of traditional epic material and failed to capture its ironic and ambiguous nuances. States that the Pléiade read Ariosto as a love poet and used him as an anti-Petrarchan model, to be imitated to go beyond the rigid schemes of the Italian lyric tradition. In analyzing several of Du Bellay's lyric imitations, concludes that the French poet attempts to capture the sensuality of Ariosto's lyrics, but completely overlooks their ambiguity and irony.

≈§ 50. BALSAMO, LUIGI. "L'Industria tipografico-editoriale nel ducato estense all'epoca dell'Ariosto." In *Il Rinascimento nelle corti padane: società e cultura*, ed. Paolo Rossi et al., pp. 277–98. Bari: De Donato, 1977.
Development of printing, editing, and marketing of books during Ariosto's lifetime; notes that the 1516 *OF*, subsidized in part by Cardinal Ippolito, was one of the few works of Este court poets published in Ferrara, both because of poor commercial prospects and of inferior work (p. 293).

≈§ 51. BÁN, IMRE. "Le *Roland Furieux* de l'Arioste, modèle du style littéraire de la Renaissance." In *Littérature de la Renaissance: à la lumière des recherches soviétiques et hongroises*, edited by N. I. Balachov, T. Klaniczay, and A. D. Mikhaïlov, pp. 251–66. Budapest: Akadémiai Kiadó, 1978.
Identifies the poetic style in the *OF* as exemplary of the aesthetic taste of the High Renaissance in Italy, the expression of its "esprit hédoniste et utopique" (p. 266) and briefly analyzes the stylistic elements characteristic of the *OF*, including spectacle and compositional harmony and grandeur in the multiplicity of thematic variations. Notes that stylistic elements are dictated by Ariosto's humanism—"la présentation totale de l'homme dans ses valeurs corporelles et psychiques" (p. 254)—and by a utopian conception of his poetic world.

≈§ 52. BARATTO, MARIO. *La commedia del Cinquecento (aspetti e problemi)*. 2d ed. Vicenza: Neri Pozza, 1977. 157p.
Focuses on the innovative aspects of Ariosto's theater, noting in particular in the evolution of his plays from 1508 to 1528 the constant maturation of dramatic technique and the increasing concern for the scenic representation of a contemporary, civic reality. Discusses the function of the servant Corbolo

in *La Lena* (1528), who exemplifies the birth of a "modern" character, here one who is conscious of his classical origins and at the same time of his contemporary dimensions. Briefly discusses *La Lena* as contradicting the "serena prospettiva della città comica ideale" (p. 111) in its satirical analysis of an increasingly corrupt society. Also notes the significance of Ariosto's theater to the attempts in the early sixteenth century to rival classical authors (pp. 44–45) and to the establishment of a typology of comic theater: "L'Ariosto cerca . . . di elaborare un primo abbozzo tipologico (personaggi e azione) della commedia, di costruire lo schema di quello che può essere il sistema comico" (p. 67).

◆§ 53. ———. "La Fondazione di un genere (per un'analisi drammaturgica della commedia del Cinquecento)." In *Il Teatro italiano del Rinascimento*, edited by Maristella de Panizza Lorch, pp. 3–24. Milan: Edizioni di Comunità, 1980.

Specifies the nature of Ariosto's importance as the founder of vernacular comedy and, in particular, of a modern theatrical language. Defines his use of "nova comedia" in reference to the 1508 production of *La Cassaria*, noting that it was intended both in the Terentian sense (i.e., "non ancora rappresentata perché non ancora imitata da un autore precedente") and to identify the play as one not modelled on a specific classical text (p. 6). Considers as fundamental to Ariosto's "new" dramaturgy a theatrical language or discourse between the playwright and his public, exemplified in the 1508 *La Cassaria* by the referential nature of the stage set representing Ferrara and a new comic language, intended to be recognized as both contemporary and grounded in classical tradition. Argues that *La Cassaria* establishes "un nesso tra spazio scenico e ritmo verbale," thus opening the possibility of multiple rapports between play and audience (p. 9). In the 1509 *I Suppositi*, the poetics of Ariosto's theater becomes more complex in the assimilation of the classical tradition into the reflection of a contemporary world. Concludes: "Elaborando, da vero uomo di teatro, una *commedia cittadina* per un *pubblico di corte*, accettando dunque gli elementi essenziali della sua *situazione di autore*, l'Ariosto imprime al 'genere' in formazione il sigillo della sua indiscussa autorità, e ne dimostra insieme il possibile funzionamento: l'agibilità, sul piano teatrale, del nesso antichi-contemporaneo" (p. 19).

◆§ 54. BARBARISI, GENNARO. "Foscolo, Ariosto, Omero: (a proposito di una recente edizione foscoliana)." *Giornale storico della letteratura italiana* 134, fasc. 405 (1957): 86–94.

Points out that Ugo Foscolo's criticism of Ariosto stems from his aversion to the *ottava rima*, which he saw as not only constraining poetic expression but also tending to prolong the narration through a dispersion into the non-essential, a tendency irreconcilable with his own "gusto della parola poetica"

(p. 92). Notes, however, that when Foscolo abandoned his own prejudices and sought out Ariosto's poetic voice, he was capable of extraordinary critical perceptions.

✍§ 55. BÀRBERI SQUAROTTI, GIORGIO. "Le figure dell'Eden." In his *Fine dell'idillio, da Dante a Marino,* pp. 263–342. Genoa: Il Melangolo, 1978.

Considers the function of the Edenic garden from the Earthly Paradise of Dante's *Purgatorio* to the Garden of Pleasure in Marino's *Adone,* discussing, in particular, the topos in several works of Boccaccio, in Poliziano's *Stanze per la giostra,* in the *Hypnerotomachia Poliphili,* and as the basis for the garden of Armida in Tasso's *GL.* Discusses the function of the topos in the *OF* in relation to its traditional significance in Italian literature of the medieval and early Renaissance periods, noting that in Ariosto's poem the garden of perfection and pleasure is no longer symbolic of a state of innocence, nor does it serve as a refuge, but it is rather "lo spazio dove si è esercitato il culmine dell'inganno e del tradimento": by entering Alcina's garden, Ruggiero arrives "non nello spazio d'amore e di piacere . . . ma piuttosto in quello della menzogna, dell'amore mentito" (p. 305). Views Alcina's garden as essentially ambiguous in nature, a realm of continuously changing moral perspectives (p. 310), concluding that it is essentially the opposite of the idyllic earthly paradise, leading those who fall into the snares of its attractions— fraudulent love—to a vegetal rather than spiritually elevated condition. See especially pp. 303–11.

✍§ 56. ———. "Nei dintorni del *Furioso.*" In his *Fine dell'idillio, da Dante a Marino,* pp. 105–16. Genoa: Il Melangolo, 1978.

Also in *Terzoprogramma,* nos. 2–3 (1974): 42–51.

Situates the composition of the *OF* in the cultural and historical background of Renaissance Italy and, in particular, Ferrara, during a period of major political and social change, highlighted by the invasion of Charles VIII. Compares the *OF* and *OI* as reflecting two different cultural moments, symbolized by central motifs of madness and love-chivalry, respectively. Notes that the *OF* is a poem of disharmonies, reflecting a world of traditions and rational behavior intruded upon by madness and corruption, and that Orlando is emblematic of an ambiguous nature, at once possessing courage and insanity, and characterized by nobility and irrational violence (pp. 109– 10). States that the increasing use of the idyll and pastoral motif in the *OF* and afterward is symptomatic of a need to seek refuge from grim realities. Sees in the *OF* a resolution, a celebration of human capacities in the face of a world gone mad, but notes that as a poem representing the multiple possibilities for the human spirit, it gives way to the rigid structure and close-ended epics of the late sixteenth century.

❧ 57. BARILLI, RENATO. "Il Boiardo e l'Ariosto nel giudizio del Rajna." In *Il Boiardo e la critica contemporanea*, edited by Giuseppe Anceschi, pp. 61–72. Atti del Convegno di Studi su Matteo Maria Boiardo. Scandiano–Reggio Emilia, 25–27 aprile 1969. Biblioteca dell'*Archivum Romanicum*, 1st ser., vol. 107. Florence: Leo S. Olschki, 1970.

Evaluates the critical importance of Pio Rajna's *Le Fonti dell'"Orlando furioso"* (1876). Argues that the positivistic basis of the study, dismissed by much subsequent criticism, has, in fact, provided some essential groundwork for the most valid understanding of the *OF*'s historical importance in the evolution of the romance genre. Notes, particularly, Rajna's recognition of the profound difference between the *OI* and the *OF*, the former conforming to traditional structural patterns (e.g., success or complete failure in obtaining the object of desire) and revealing a poet who marks a culminating point in the history of the Italian romance epic; the latter, rather than a continuation of a tradition, a radical breaking away toward modern romance forms and anticipatory of the *DQ*—"una tendenza . . . allo spostamento e alla deviazione rispetti ai fini ufficialmente perseguiti" (p. 71).

❧ 58. BARLUSCONI, GIOVANNA. "*L'Orlando furioso* poema dello spazio." In *Studi sull'Ariosto*, presentazione di Enzo Noè Girardi, pp. 39–130. Milan: Vita e Pensiero (Pubblicazioni dell'Università Cattolica del Sacro Cuore), 1977.

Extensive analysis of how space is organized and manipulated in the *OF*, concluding that it functions essentially as a reflection of the interior world of Ariosto's protagonists. Argues that the loci of the narrative serve as vortices of energy, each with a semantic charge that radiates into a multiplicity of, characteristically, simultaneous or vertically structured actions. Examines the semantic value or nucleus of several place-situations ("luoghi-situazioni," p. 53), for example, the fountain, characterizing the movement back to the locus as an "assorbimento a spirale" (p. 101). Notes the plurality of perspectives on a spatial context by several characters or the same character on several occasions as fundamental to the deep structure of the poem, in which the protean nature of the spatial dimension reveals the constantly shifting mental world of a protagonist.

❧ 59. BAROCCHI, PAOLA. "Fortuna dell'Ariosto nella trattatistica figurativa." In *Critica e storia letteraria. Studi offerti a Mario Fubini*, 1: 388–405. 2 vols. Padua: Liviana, 1970.

Surveys the fortunes of the *OF* in sixteenth– and seventeenth–century treatises on art, noting that *OF* 33.2 (1532 edition only), with its references to several Renaissance artists, was repeatedly cited as evidence of Ariosto's superior judgment and authority, especially apparent in his inclusion of Michelangelo. Discusses the authority of the *OF* among treatise writers as a source of the symbolic-emblematic significance of certain colors and of the most effective artistic representation of human emotions (especially in Giovanni Paolo Lomazzo, *Trattato dell'arte della pittura, scoltura et architettura*, 1584); notes the several parallels drawn between the structural elements of the OF and architectural design. Concludes that painters were frequently recommended to study Ariosto—an example of Renaissance *ut pictor poeta*.

◆§ 60. BARROSO FILHO, JOSÉ ACÚRCIO. "Ariosto e Tasso: História e Fantasia." *Revista de Letras* (Ceará, Brazil) 1, no. 2 (1978): 5–16.
Contrasts the OF and the GL in the context of the historical periods in which their authors lived. Considers the OF a major expression of Renaissance culture, reflecting a serene acceptance of life, moral sobriety, the individual's passions and sentiments, and a sense of equilibrium, all elements that confer on the poem's narrative "um andamento pacato, largo e uniforme" (p. 15). Contrasts the subjectivism and gloom of Tasso's GL with Ariosto's harmonious view of life.

◆§ 61. BASILE, JOSÉ. "Premessa a uno studio della poetica ariostesca." In his *Forma simbolica ed allegorica nei 'Rerum vulgarium fragmenta' ed altre cose*, pp. 27–47. Assisi-Rome: B. Carucci, 1971.
Also in *Paragone* 21, no. 248 (1970): 111–26.
Observations on the ethical principles (e.g., *aurea mediocritas*) that inform Ariosto's aesthetic in the OF; on the poem as a function of an essentially skeptical outlook on one's ability to dominate life forces; on the nature of the aesthetic classicism of the poem and in particular the structure of the *ottava*.

◆§ 62. BASILONE, GIUSEPPE. *Guida allo studio dell'"Orlando Furioso" per gli alunni delle scuole medie*. 14th ed. Naples: Federico e Ardia, 1961. 135p.
First edition 1932; Fatini, 2591.

◆§ 63. BASSANI-NARDI, ISABELLA. "La Fortuna dell'Ariosto in Francia nell'Ottocento e nel Novecento." *Bollettino storico reggiano* 8, no. 30 (1975): 1–18.
Brief discussion of the critical fortune of Ariosto in France during the sixteenth century and his diminishing influence in the seventeenth century with the triumph of classicism. Notes a short-lived revival of interest in Ariosto during the second half of the eighteenth century, especially in the critical evaluations of Voltaire. Interest in Ariosto during the nineteenth century was almost exclusively among literary specialists: concludes that with French romanticism Ariosto's influence was minimal, whereas there began an era of critical interpretations of the OF. Reviews the major critical perspectives on Ariosto in nineteenth-century France and their importance to the under-

standing of critical writing on Ariosto in nineteenth-century Italy. Synthesizes and identifies the critical importance of the views of Pierre-Louis Ginguené, who, with Ugo Foscolo, reflects "una nuova concezione della poesia che ormai era nell'aria: la poesia si identifica con lo stile, e 'lo stile non è veste esteriore ma forma interna del mondo del poeta'" (quotes Raffaello Ramat, *La critica ariostesca* [1954], p. 102, on p. 9); of Jean-Charles-Léonard Simonde de Sismondi, who initiates romantic criticism on Ariosto by acknowledging in the poet "il diritto di creare un'opera priva di unità, e riconosce a sé stesso, in quanto critico, il diritto di amare e di apprezzare una poesia che non ubbidisce ad alcuna regola" (pp. 9–10); of the uniquely romantic criticism of Edgar Quinet, who viewed the *OF* as the very image of the human spirit in Renaissance culture. Summary discussion of selected twentieth-century critical views, including those of Henri Hauvette, (*L'Arioste et la poésie chevaleresque à Ferrare au début du XVIème siècle*, 1927) and the unpublished thesis of Nicole Oprandi, "L'expression artistique du mouvement dans le *Roland Furieux*," University of Nice, 1973, 2 vols. Concludes that interest in Ariosto among current French critics is relatively limited.

◆§ 64. BASTIAENSEN, MICHEL. "La ripetizione contrastata nel *Furioso*." *La Rassegna della letteratura italiana*, 7th ser., vol. 74, no. 1 (1970): 112–33.
Defines as "contrastata" the technique of repetition of two or more thematically related narrative elements in varying order. Using graphs, discusses several types of devices for repetition in the *OF*: the anaphoric, which allows the poet to return to a narrative line after an *excursus*; "commutazione," used to initiate a new action or episode (p. 117); and those that take their names from projections on a graph: M, "vetta," (p. 120), "a ghimel," (p. 124), and "a denti di sega" (p. 128). Terms the latter extended repetitions since often they involve repetition through synonyms and semantic equivalents. Notes that extended repetition has a psychological importance for it reflects the movement of the thought process that does not proceed in a linear fashion, having "nulla di continuo" (p. 131). Concludes that contrastive repetition reveals the melodic and pictorial qualities of Ariosto's poetry as well as his complete control over his material.

◆§ 65. ⸺. "La cité des femmes." *La pensée et les hommes* (Revue mensuelle de philosophie et de morale laïques, Brussels) 20, no. 5 (1976): 133–42.
Notes the important role accorded women in the *OF*, from the poem's opening words to the episode of the city of homicidal women. Considers mythological and primitive female societies, such as the Amazons and the

Lemnians, from which Ariosto could draw for his episode. Observes that in the OF, the all-female society is counter-balanced by the misogynous group led by Marganorre (OF 37). Suggests that within the context of the sixteenth-century *querelle des femmes*, Ariosto seems to propose his own poetic resolution: in a world of harmony, a battle of the sexes has no place and, accordingly, both contingents are destroyed, the homicidal women by Astolfo's thunderous horn and the women-haters by the tragic end of Marganorre himself.

◄§ 66. ———. "Varianti e colori nel *Furioso*." *Giornale storico della letteratura italiana* 155, fasc. 489 (1978): 526–50.

Detailed account and analysis of Ariosto's emendations in the use of chromatic terms and expressions in the three editions of the OF. Views the poet's definitive changes as linguistic, lexical, and rhythmic improvements and suggests that the use of color is one of Ariosto's aesthetic choices. Notes that the variants reflect the poet's supreme effort to conceal all traces of strain in the creative process.

◄§ 67. ———. "La Nave magica di Gloricia." *Italianistica* 9, no. 2 (1980): 234–50.

Discusses various possible sources of the metamorphosis of a drawing of a ship into an actual flying vessel in the episode of Gloricia (CC 86). Focuses on the similarities between this particular Ariostean animation of an inorganic object and episodes in the *Life of San Leone Taumaturgo, Archbishop of Catania* and in Folengo's *Baldus*, but concludes by arguing that contextual specificity and individuality confer greater originality on Ariosto's invention.

◄§ 68. BATKIN L[EONID MIKHAILOVICH]. "Renessansnyi mif o cheloveke" (The Renaissance myth of man). *Voprosy literatury* 9 (1971): 112–33.

Consideration of the Renaissance ethos in Italy, noting that one of the most important aspects of the Renaissance myth of being was its plastic, unfinished, and limitless nature. Discusses the importance of the fantastic adventure romance, particularly the OF, in the representation of the Renaissance myth of the individual. Discussion of Ariosto's use of magic as a device for underscoring the multiplicity of nature and for representing the potentially infinite possibilities in phenomena. Argues that the entire narrative of the poem in its constant transitions from one uncompleted event to another represents a picture of the Renaissance in its dynamic nature and of a world in which man is free and godlike.

◄§ 69. ———. *La Concezione rinascimentale del mondo nel poema dell'Ariosto*, 1978.

Unavailable; cited in Iginio De Luca, "Rassegna della letteratura italiana in URSS." *Lettere italiane* 32, no. 1 (1980): 99–100. Source identifies item as a monograph ("volume") without additional information; title is presumably a translation of the original Russian.

🔖 70. BATTAGLIA, ROBERTO. "Il Realismo dell'Ariosto." In *I Metodi attuali della critica in Italia*, edited by Maria Corti and Cesare Segre, pp. 47–52. Turin: ERI, 1970.
Excerpted from "L'Ariosto e la critica idealistica," *Rinascita* 7 (1950): 141–50; Fatini, 3446.

🔖 71. BATTAGLIA, SALVATORE. *Mitografia del personaggio*. 3d ed. Milan: Rizzoli, 1970. 547p.
Briefly notes the significance of the *OF* in the context of the period of historical crisis during which it was conceived and relates it to perspectives on the individual and his world in the *DC* and in Boccaccio's *Decameron*: "in quell'immensa arena dell'esistenza che è l'*Orlando Furioso*, il senso della vita e soprattutto la coscienza dei destini umani si è fatta ambigua, o per lo meno è avviata verso soluzioni a doppia faccia. Si avverte distintamente che la prospettiva morale allenta il controllo di cui l'avevano dotata Dante e Boccaccio. Nella *Divina Commedia* e nel *Decameron* i protagonisti, qualunque sia la loro sorte e la loro rispettiva condotta, si comportano con impegno totale. Per loro la vita e la realtà sono una cosa seria, anche se la personale esperienza possa palesarsi angusta o meschina o futile e perfino comica. Nell'*Orlando Furioso*, viceversa s'insinua un atteggiamento che tende a sospingere le passioni verso un'aria di malizioso incanto. E la vita, pur conservando la propria ricchezza e fertilità, rimane come sospesa ed elusa in un clima di favola, d'ironia, di esorbitanza. . . . E gli uomini si dissolvono nei loro stessi desideri e illusioni, e i loro sentimenti svaniscono nel ritmo precipitoso del caso, e la ruota della fortuna si tramuta nella gara del tempo, e ogni cosa si logora nell'eterna vicenda del mondo" (p. 133).

🔖 72. ———. "Ludovico Ariosto." In *La Letteratura italiana*, edited by Salvatore Battaglia and Giancarlo Mazzacurati, vol. 2, *Rinascimento e barocco* (1974), pp. 55–70. 4 vols. Florence: Sansoni, 1971–1974.
Also in Salvatore Battaglia, *Le Epoche della letteratura italiana: medioevo; umanesimo; rinascimento* (Naples: Liguori, 1965–), pp. 677–97.
Brief introduction to Ariosto, characterized as an author whose creations all contain some aspects of his own nature but as one who refuses to reveal himself completely. Notes that his comedies represent the flux of life and show little interest in character; that the satires, a self-portrait, represent the "umano quotidiano" as opposed to the *OF*'s representation of the "umano immaginoso" (p. 63). Suggests that both Boccaccio's *Decameron* and the *OF*

portray a total society in which "si esplica una trama inesauribile di relazioni, contrasti, incontri" (p. 67). Concludes that the *OF* is essentially concerned with the illusory aspects of life, noting that the episode of Astolfo on the moon and the image of the Castle of Atlante are most emblematic of this theme.

➣ 73. BEAME, EDMOND M. See Ariosto, Ludovico, *The Comedies of Ariosto*, entry 26.

➣ 74. BECCALUVA, LINO. "L'*Orlando Furioso* tradotto in vernacolo bolognese." *Il pescatore reggiano* (Reggio Emilia) 120 (1966): 131–33.
Mention of the rare translation of the *OF* by Eraclito Manfredi into Bolognese dialect and published in 1865. Unavailable; cited in Medici, 173.

➣ 75. ———. *Ariosto*. Modena: STIG, 1974. 297p.
Summary account of Ariosto's life and times; brief account of works; no critical analysis. Contents: "Vita," pp. 25–76; "Genesi fondamentale dell'*Orlando Furioso*," pp. 77–90; "*Orlando Furioso*: analisi estetica," pp. 91–160 (summary of the narrative despite chapter heading); "Opere minori," pp. 163–84; "Le Commedie," pp. 185–94. Text of *La Lena*, pp. 197–275. Includes appendixes with documents pertaining to Ariosto's life, as well as fifty-three illustrations.

➣ 76. BELLINI, GIUSEPPE. "L'Ariosto nell'America ispanica." In *Per l'Ariosto* (entry 623). Special 1976 issue of *Italianistica* 3, no. 3 (1974): 189–201.
Discusses Ariosto's influence on Alonso de Ercilla y Zúñiga, and through him on Juan de Castellanos, Pedro de Oña, Inca Garcilaso de la Vega, and Bernardo de Balbuena, whose *Bernardo* has been judged a baroque variation on an Ariostean theme (p. 194). Observes that while Italian literature exerted a continuing influence on Spanish America, it is only in the nineteenth century that one finds significant evidence of Ariosto's presence, especially in Rubén Darío's *Prosas profanas* (1896) and *El canto errante* (1907). Concludes by noting that in the twentieth century, Latin American interest in Ariosto has been kept alive by Borges, a self-proclaimed "lector y relector de Dante y Ariosto" (quoted on p. 198).

➣ 77. BELLOCCHI, UGO. *Il Mauriziano. Gli affreschi di Nicolò dell'Abate nel "nido" di Lodovico Ariosto*. Reggio Emilia: Poligrafici, 1967. 244p.
Republished in the series "Monumenti" of the *Deputazione di Storia Patria delle Antiche Province Modenesi*. Modena: Aedes Muratoriana, 1974.
Extensively documented commentary on Ariosto's associations with the Mauriziano of the Malaguzzi family. Detailed history of the property, inven-

tories of rooms, and an analysis of the frescoes of Nicolò dell'Abate. Color and black-and-white reproductions.

◄§ 78. ———. "Il fenomeno giornalistico al tempo dell'Ariosto." In *Lodovico Ariosto: il suo tempo la sua terra la sua gente* (entry 468). Estratto dal *Bollettino storico reggiano* 7, no. 25 (1974): 43–54.

Noting the means by which news was circulated before the invention of printing and before the widespread use of type—letters, *avvisi*, manuscript circulars—indicates important holdings in Italian archives of such "journalistic" materials and lists with complete manuscript information the most important such documents, from 1497 to 1533, that Ariosto might have consulted and that are in the Archivio di Stato of Modena.

◄§ 79. BELLOCCHI, UGO, AND BRUNO FAVA. *L'Interpretazione grafica dell'"Orlando Furioso."* Reggio Emilia: Banca di Credito Popolare e Cooperativo, 1961. 58p, with 108 reproductions.

Traces the history of illustrations of the *OF* from the sixteenth century, noting the technical excellence of many graphic representations but the general failure to duplicate the artistic genius of the poem, whose structural complexities make pictorial representation exceedingly difficult.

◄§ 80. BELVEDERI, RAFFAELE. "Ludovico Ariosto nel V Centenario della nascita." In *Ferrara e l'Ariosto*, by Raffaele Belvederi, Virgilio Ferrari, and Arturo Malagù, pp. 81–99. (La *Ferrariae Decus* nel V Centenario della nascita del poeta.) Ferrara: S.A.T.E., 1974.

Summary review of critical perspectives on Ariosto, stating the need for extensive research on the historico-cultural period in which the poet had his formation and created his literary works. Considers as neglected by critics the poetry-history nexus in the case of Ariosto, an area of research that would reveal "quale ampiezza di orizzonti avesse il poeta ferrarese e quanto profonda fosse la sua conoscenza della storia, della geografia a delle condizioni politiche, come pure degli uomini passati e contemporanei" (p. 88). Describing the *OF* as a "riflessione poetica su una realtà operante e viva" (p. 91), briefly considers the historical moment—geography, personalities, culture—as reflected in the poem.

◄§ 81. BENDER, JOHN B. *Spenser and Literary Pictorialism.* Princeton: Princeton University Press, 1972. 218p.

States that its "general purpose is to theorize and illustrate some formal and rhetorical solutions to the problem of embodying visual experience in poetic language" and, through an analysis focused on Spenser, "to provide prolegomena to a critical history of pictorial rhetoric which would classify the diverse uses of visual materials in poetry" (p. 3). Cites as an example of descriptive poetry Ariosto's detailed description of Alcina (*OF* 7.11–15), noting that "Ariosto excels at such exhaustively systematic and structured description. . . . Ariosto's descriptions are conceived not only analytically, but antithetically. Alcina's hair is blond but 'no gold' is brighter; her eyes are black but dazzlingly bright. . . . Logic, wit, parody, and even cynicism are the sinews of Ariosto's descriptions, just as his rendering of action and gesture in narrative. He seems unwilling to force us to confine our view to surfaces without anatomizing and polarizing their components and substructures. . . . Ariosto's images have visual components, but their structure is essentially analytical and discursive, not reiterative and parallel; their shape is open, not formally closed" (pp. 39–40). Argues, in contrasting Ariosto's pictorial style with Spenser's, "Ariosto's wit, his ironic objectivity, his skeptical poise, all are incompatible with the visual concentration so notable in Focused imagery. [See "A Mode of Pictorialism: Focusing," pp. 40–67.] He writes perfectly conceptualized and formally controlled poetry in which description is used illustratively; the effect is a continuous but abstracted and diffused awareness of an imagined visual world. Ariosto tends to move directly from surface to ideas about them. Spenser lingers over the surfaces themselves and makes them seem to contain ever more significance without necessarily making the significance wholly intelligible" (pp. 55–56). Ariosto cited frequently, but see especially pp. 35–40, 44–45, and 53–59.

82. BENSON, PAMELA JOSEPH. "Independence and Fidelity: The Contributions of the *Querelle des Femmes* to the *Orlando Furioso*." *DAI* 39, no. 8 (1979): 4969A. (Columbia University, 1978. 157p.)

Argues that the early Renaissance *querelle des femmes*, beginning in an important way with Boccaccio's *De claris mulieribus*, had a profound influence both on Ariosto's presentation of women in the *OF* and on the entire conception of the poem. Identifies and discusses the major debates in the poem on the topic of women's infidelity, concluding that Ariosto is testing contemporary ideas about women against each other and against the action of the stories. Concludes that Ariosto is at once attacking a traditional misogynistic double standard and upholding fidelity as an ideal. Examination of the central role of Bradamante, the "model of an accomplished woman," and the significance of her search for and marriage with Ruggiero, noting that this important narrative thread "infuses the whole poem with a domestic spirit absent from classical epic."

83. ———. "An Unrecognized Defender of Women in the *Orlando Furioso*." *Italica* 57, no. 4 (1980): 268–70.

Suggests that Ariosto's mention of "Capel" (*OF* 37.1) is a reference to Galeazzo Flavio Capra (1487–1537), known as Capella, author of an influential tract, *Della eccellenza et dignità delle donne* (1525), that demonstrates the "moral, intellectual, and physical superiority of women to men" (p. 269), a view consistent with Ariosto's own encomium in canto 37.

◈§ 84. BENVENUTI, ANTONIA. "'Timoteo, l'onor de' Bendedei' (*Orl. Fur.*, XLII, 92)." *Giornale storico della letteratura italiana* 140, fasc. 431 (1963): 482–88.
Catalog of poems attributed to Timoteo Bendedei, the Ferrarese poet who, according to Ariosto, *OF* 42.92, praised Beatrice d'Este.

◈§ 85. BERTINETTO, PIER MARCO. "Il Ritmo della prosa e del verso nelle commedie dell'Ariosto." In *Ludovico Ariosto: lingua, stile e tradizione*, edited by Cesare Segre (entry 789), pp. 347–77. Milan: Feltrinelli, 1976.
Close analysis of structure and use of the *endecasillabo sdrucciolo* in the comedies in verse. Suggests that Ariosto, in experimenting with a relatively new form (the erudite comedy), was attempting to find a means of expression less rigidly structured than the verse of lyric and epic tradition, but one that would suggest, within the framework of a measured metrical system, the spontaneity of the spoken vernacular. Details the characteristics of Ariosto's *endecasillabo sdrucciolo*, especially the variety of accentual patterns, concluding that the rhythmical structure is entirely free and unpredictable and that the tension of prose speech is maintained within the verse form.

◈§ 86. BERTINI, GIOVANNI MARIA. "Ludovico Ariosto e il mondo ispanico." *Estudis Romanics* (Barcelona) 9 (1961, but 1966): 269–82.
Considers the impact of the Italian Renaissance on Spain and, in particular, the significance of both the extent of Ariosto's popularity and the way in which the OF was adapted by Spanish writers and read by the public, which regarded it in the context of medieval Spanish chivalric heroism rather than as a poem with an essentially antiheroic spirit. Notes the debt of Garcilaso de la Vega and other lyric poets to Ariosto, whose poem provided the grace and lyrical sensitivity that were instrumental in shaping the course of Spanish Renaissance poetry.

◈§ 87. BESOMI, OTTAVIO. "Una censura secentesca all'*Orlando Furioso*." In his *Esplorazioni secentesche*, pp. 209–55. Padua: Antenore, 1975.
Discusses Tommaso Stigliani's "Censura," a free-verse critique of the OF, listing the merits and shortcomings of the poem identified by Stigliani. Notes that in the context of the sixteenth-century polemic over Ariosto and Tasso, Stigliani is to be considered a *tassista*. Text of the "Censura" on pp. 247–53.

◈§ 88. BETTI, FRANCO. "Annotazioni sul paesaggio nell'*Orlando Furioso*." *Italica* 45, no. 3 (1968): 329–44.

Observes that the descriptive realism characterizing the landscape in the *OF* is not a mere end in itself but serves to give life to the "immagine evocata" (p. 332). Finds that the landscape is charged with thematic significance, in that it is often transformed or deformed to reflect that state of mind of a character.

≈§ 89. BEZZOLA, RETO R. "L'Oriente nel poema cavalleresco del primo Rinascimento." In *Venezia e l'oriente fra tardo medioevo e Rinascimento*, edited by Agostino Pertusi, pp. 495–510. Florence: Sansoni, 1966.
Also in *Lettere italiane* 15, no. 4 (1963): 385–98.
Traces the treatment and function of the Far East in Italian chivalric poetry of the early Renaissance and concludes that with Pulci, Boiardo, and Ariosto, the Orient loses its realistic representation and becomes an exotic place of fable, magic, and illusion.

≈§ 90. BIGI, EMILIO. "Appunti sulla lingua e sulla metrica del *Furioso*." In his *La Cultura del Poliziano e altri studi umanistici*, pp. 164–86. Pisa: Nistri-Lischi, 1967.
Also in *Giornale storico della letteratura italiana* 138, fasc. 422 (1961): 239–53.
Uses the Debenedetti-Segre listing of variants in the three editions of the *OF* (1516; 1521; 1532) to comment on various stylistic aspects of the poem. Discusses Ariosto's use of the *enjambement* and defends him against Parodi's charge that in the *OF* the rhyme is often weak and prosaic (p. 177; see Ernesto G. Parodi, "La rima e i vocaboli in rima nella *Divina Commedia*" [1896], in his *Lingua e letteratura; studi di teoria linguistica e di storia dell'italiano antico*, edited by Gianfranco Folena, 2:215–16. 2 vols. Venice: Neri Pozza, 1957). Gives selected examples of rhyme endings, noting the poet's preference for the dactylic and the *equivoca*, or ambiguous (p. 185).

≈§ 91. ———. "Vita e letteratura nella poesia giovanile dell'Ariosto." *Giornale storico della letteratura italiana* 145, fasc. 449 (1968): 1–37.
Discusses Ariosto's youthful literary activity, namely the composition of the Latin *capitoli*, noting in particular references to real experiences: early loves, family problems, court life, and the influences of the poet's teachers. Finds that in these youthful poems the poet already condemns the irrational aspects of life and especially human passions, war, and political intrigues. Characterizes the Latin poetry as "un tentativo di esprimere . . . un senso acuto dell'imperfezione della vita pratica, che cerca un polemico rifugio nell'aristocratico e difficile impegno letterario" (p. 36) and concludes by suggesting its relationship to Ariosto's more mature compositions: the polemical tone of the opposition of life and literature in his early works "tende a transformarsi

in un rapporto dinamicamente equilibrato" (p. 36). In the 1516 *OF* particularly, a sense of the irrational in life is pervasive yet is at one with a lucid recognition of the limits imposed upon our existence and does not result in an embittered denial of life; and the poetic transfiguration of the poet's perspective on life "perde il suo antico carattere di scontrosa evasione e acquista essa stessa ['la trasfigurazione letteraria'] la consapevoleza sottilmente ironica del proprio limite, della propria natura di stilizzazione appunto tutta letteraria di quella irriducible realtà" (p. 37).

◀§ 92. ———. "Ariosto, Ludovico." In *Dizionario critico della letteratura italiana*, 1:113–33. 3 vols. Directed by Vittore Branca; edited by Armando Balduino, Manlio Pastore Stocchi, and Marco Pecoraro. Turin: UTET, 1973.
Summary view of Ariosto's life and works. Notes originality of his comedies; discusses the chivalric romance tradition before the *OF* and the sociopolitical reality of the satires. States that the 1532 *OF* perfects the earlier editions. Surveys major critical contributions to the study of the poet and his writings. Bibliography, pp. 131–33.

◀§ 93. ———. "Aspetti stilistici e metrici delle *Rime* dell'Ariosto." *La Rassegna della letteratura italiana*, 7th ser., vol. 79, nos. 1–2 (1975): 46–52.
Also in *Notiziario culturale italiano* (entry 573) 15, no. 3 (1974): 69–75.
Documents evolving styles, or "maniere" of Ariosto's Italian lyrics, from the earliest period in the courtly tradition of late humanism, to the application of Petrarchesque-Bembesque formalism, to Ariosto's own stylistic exigencies. "Egli crede nella letteratura, e in particolare in quella di orientamento petrarchesco-bembiano, come strumento di controllo e di dominio della realtà varia e incomposta delle passioni e della Fortuna; ma della letteratura, di quella letteratura, egli conosce anche il limite, la natura, appunto, tutta letteraria, e conosce quanto della realtà sfugge a quel controllo e a quel dominio. Donde l'impiego senza dubbio costante e convinto, ma con un notevole margine di elasticità e con un certo distacco che può arrivare . . . al sorriso e all'ironia" (p. 50).

◀§ 94. ———. "Le Liriche volgari dell'Ariosto." In *Ludovico Ariosto*, pp. 49–71. Convegno internazionale (entry 475). Rome: Accademia Nazionale dei Lincei, 1975.
Partially summarizes his "Vita e letteratura nella poesia giovanile dell'Ariosto." *Giornale storico della letteratura italiana* 145, fasc. 449 (1968): 1–37.
Summary view of the current hypotheses regarding the chronology of Ariosto's vernacular lyrics and the poet's own intentions in their regard; con-

cludes by stating that the poet selected and revised only a group of poems
and that this was done prior to 1525 and the period of his most mature
compositions. Noting that the lyrics selected for revision remain haphazardly
arranged and in no way constitute an organic whole in the tradition of Petrarch's *Canzoniere*, proceeds to study the lyrics that were unretouched and
those that underwent revision, categorizing the groupings according to characteristic lyrical style, or "maniere" (p. 53). Identifies in the former group a
homogeneous set of ten *capitoli*, characterized in theme and style by the
courtly manner ("cortigiana," pp. 53–54) or by the courtly Petrarchism of
fifteenth-century Ferrarese lyrics. In the lyrics of the second group, i.e.,
those that underwent revision, notes the significant influence of Petrarchistic
Bembism and an attempt, with mixed success, to bring a personal and inven-
tive note to his poetry while remaining within the constraints of traditional
lyric compositions. Identifies as of particular importance experimentation
with rhythm and meter, repetition, and the use of inversion for emphasis.
Concludes that Ariosto subscribed to the literary modes of Petrarch and
Bembo as a means of "controllo e dominio" (p. 67), but realized the difficulties of forcing reality to conform to such models.

☙ 95. ———. "Ideali umanisitici e realtà storica nell'*Orlando furioso*." *Libri e documenti* 2, no. 1 (1976): 1–7.
   Noting that Ariosto was vitally interested in the problems of his age and in
the "problemi della vita pratica" (p. 1), argues that the *OF* (1516), rather
than a form of literary escapism, reflects the poet's personal situation and the
sociopolitical and cultural crises of the peninsula at the end of the fifteenth
century. States that Ariosto, fully aware of the new realities of his age, creates
in his works a controlled balance between these harsh realities and the humanistic ideals of an earlier period. This equilibrium, evident in the poet's
personal life, is important to the *OF*, where life is represented both in its
harsh realities and in its ideals: human reason, honor, love, and loyalty are
juxtaposed with the destructive forces of fortune, the irrational, and human
passions. The poet's irony signals his awareness of polarities. Considers the
aesthetic equilibrium maintained in the poem in the context of Ariosto's view
of art as a means to "creare un mondo più bello, più nobile, più rispondente
agli ideali di quello in cui viviamo, o almeno trasfigurare e stilizzare il vero
in forme armoniose e rasserenatrici" (p. 5). Concludes that the structural and
historical dimensions of the 1516 edition must be taken into account when
evaluating the later editions: believes that whereas the 1521 edition was
simply an attempt to perfect the poem, in the final edition, by means of the
additions, there is a new thematic balance that reflects "non solo la più tran-
quilla situazione privata del poeta nei suoi ultimi anni di vita, ma anche il
rasserenamento dell'orizzonte politico ferrarese ed europeo dopo la pace di
Cambrai e gli accordi di Bologna" (p. 7).

✧ 96. ———. "Il Leopardi e l'Ariosto." In *Leopardi e la letteratura italiana dal Duecento al Seicento*, pp. 215–28. Atti del IV Convegno internazionale di studi leopardiani. Recanati, 13–16 settembre 1976. Florence: Leo S. Olschki, 1978.

Discusses Leopardi's changing attitude toward Ariosto during the evolution of his concept of the poetic, noting the early interest in Ariosto as a "natural" and spontaneous poet (p. 217) and his later reservations regarding Ariosto, whose work he classified as the last example of "irrecuperabile poesia antica e naturale" (p. 218), preferring Tasso as the first modern poet with a sense of the nothingness of life (p. 218). Notes the relative scarcity of borrowings from Ariosto and concludes, after an analysis of several lexical and verse borrowings, that Leopardi's principal interest was in elements that conformed to his poetics of the vague, indefinite, pathetic, and pessimistic.

✧ 97. BILINSKI, BRONISLAW. "Le risonanze ariostee nella poesia romantica polacca." In *Ludovico Ariosto*, pp. 253–95. Convegno internazionale (entry 475). Rome: Accademia Nazionale dei Lincei, 1975.

Discusses the interest in Italian literature among writers of the Polish romantic period and the particular attention given to the epic tradition and poets such as Tasso and Ariosto. Considers in particular the influence of Ariosto on Adam Mickiewicz and Juliusz Słowaki. Selected bibliography of Polish editions and translations of the *OF* and of critical studies (pp. 291–95).

✧ 98. BINNI, WALTER. *Ludovico Ariosto*. Turin: ERI, 1968. 317p.

Critical commentary on the poet's life and works. In two parts, with selections of the works under consideration. First part provides a biographical sketch followed by a series of biographical data; highlights aspects of the poet's personality through a discussion of his letters; notes the sensual and hedonistic tone of the lyric poetry; argues that the comedies, rather than imitations of classical models, reveal the poet's taste for plot, intrigue, dialogue, structure of scenes, etc., foreshadowing the presence of comic and theatrical dimensions in the *OF* (p. 121); notes that in the satires the poet reveals his ability to pass from the realistic to the fantastic. Second part, "Il capolavoro," proposes an integral reading of the *OF* in the context of Ariosto's poetics or conception of life, identified as a cosmic harmony between the real and the fantastic. Considers various aspects of the poem, noting that the narrative rhythm, in its changes from one episode to another, reflects the flux of life (p. 232), that the passage from the real to the fantastic is achieved through the deformation of the real (p. 246), and that the fantastic is brought to the dimension of reality by means of irony, which is aimed at empty myths and unfounded beliefs (p. 270). Compares the styles of the three editions and discusses the problems of dating the *CC*.

☙ 99. ———. Introduzione. In *"Orlando furioso" e opere minori scelte*, edited by Walter Binni, pp. iii–xx. Florence: Sansoni, 1969. First edition 1942; Fatini, 3305.

☙ 100. ———. *Metodo e poesia di Ludovico Ariosto*. Messina-Florence: D'Anna, 1970. 182p. First edition 1947; Fatini, 3379.

☙ 101. ———. "*Le Lettere* e le *Satire* dell'Ariosto nello sviluppo e nella crisi del Rinascimento." In his *Due Studi critici: Ariosto e Foscolo*, pp. 11–59. Rome: Bulzoni, 1978.

Revision of "Le *Lettere* e le *Satire* dell'Ariosto," in *Ludovico Ariosto*, Convegno internazionale (entry 475) (Rome: Accademia Nazionale dei Lincei, 1975), pp. 133–69. Also in *La Rassegna della letteratura italiana* 79, nos. 1–2 (1975): 53–84.

Maintains that both the letters and satires reveal important aspects of Ariosto's complex personality as well as ideological, cultural, and artistic experiences, which surface in the 1532 *OF*. Argues that the letters constitute significant historical documentation of the political turmoil of the day, provided the poet with invaluable writing experience and reflect his sense of humanity, compassion, and understanding of human nature, which often distinguishes the narrative tone of the *OF*. Insists that the satires, in attacking prevailing false values among both the humanists and the clergy, attest to Ariosto's awareness of the cultural and moral crises of his epoch. Concludes that, although minor works, they reveal important insights into Ariosto the poet and the man.

☙ 102. BINNI, WALTER, AND RICCARDO SCRIVANO. "Ludovico Ariosto." In their *Introduzione ai problemi critici della letteratura italiana*, pp. 132–37. Messina-Florence: G. D'Anna, 1967.

Summary historical perspective on Ariosto criticism.

☙ 103. BIONDI, ALBANO. "Streghe ed eretici nei domini estensi all'epoca dell'Ariosto." In *Il Rinascimento nelle corti padane: società e cultura*, edited by Paolo Rossi et al., pp. 165–99. Bari: De Donato, 1977.

Representation of magic in the *OI* and in the *OF* is an aesthetic transposition of popular beliefs and in the epic allows for passage from the real to the imaginary. Notes, however, the complexity of the social, philosophical, and scientific dimensions of belief in the supernatural in Ferrarese society and discusses its historical context.

☙ 104. BLACKBURN, WILLIAM. "Spenser's Merlin." *Renaissance and Reformation* 4, no. 2 (1980): 179–98.

Argues that Spenser's Merlin—the magician, prophet, and artificer portrayed in the *OF*, one of the English poet's sources—is also a poet figure and consequently of major importance to the treatment of art throughout the *FQ*.

⋙ 105. BLASUCCI, LUIGI. "La *Commedia* come fonte linguistica e stilistica del *Furioso*." In his *Studi su Dante e Ariosto*, pp. 121–62. Milan-Naples: Ricciardi, 1969.
Also with title "Ancora sulla *Commedia* come fonte linguistica e stilistica del *Furioso*." In *Giornale storico della letteratura italiana* 145, fasc. 450–51 (1968): 188–231.
Mentions critical studies that have established Ariosto's debt to the *DC*, particularly Cesare Segre's "Un repertorio linguistico e stilistico dell'Ariosto: la *Commedia*" (in his *Esperienze ariostesche* [1966], pp. 51–83). Examines linguistic expressions, stylistic devices, and themes and episodes of Dantesque origin, pointing out that Ariosto often mediates his source by enriching it with classical (Horace, Virgil) and chivalric tradition. Suggests that Dante's influence on Ariosto is more textual than contextual (pp. 132, 162) and underscores this point by showing that both Pulci and Tasso used the *DC* in a more literal and contextual sense (pp. 153, 155).

⋙ 106. ———. "Un Esempio del 'metodo' ariostesco: la sosta a Cipro (*Furioso*, XVIII, 136–140)." In his *Studi su Dante e Ariosto*, pp. 163–74. Milan-Naples: Ricciardi, 1969.
Discusses the unexpected stop of the five knights on Cyprus on their way to France from Damascus. Suggests that the unusually lengthy description of the island's beauty and tranquillity, although apparently unrelated to preceding and following events, has an important unifying function: it serves to create a pause between the "vicenda contrastata di Damasco" (p. 167) and the storm encountered by the knights soon after they leave the island. Points out that the pause reflects Ariosto's view that from Fortune's "ordine scompigliato può nascere, imprevisto, un altro ordine" (p. 174).

⋙ 107. ———. "Nota sull'enumerazione nel *Furioso*." In his *Studi su Dante e Ariosto*, pp. 113–20. Milan-Naples: Ricciardi, 1969.
Originally published as second part of "Osservazioni sulla struttura metrica del *Furioso* (con una nota sull'enumerazione)." In *Giornale storico della letteratura italiana* 139, fasc. 426 (1962): 169–218.
Views enumeration in the *OF* as the poetic transcription of reality in motion. Suggests that the technique, found in Petrarch as analysis or as the representation of stasis, in Ariosto is a Pythagorean abstraction or a transfiguration of action and movement into number.

⋙ 108. ———. "Osservazioni sulla struttura metrica del *Furioso*." In his *Studi su Dante e Ariosto*, pp. 73–112. Milan-Naples: Ricciardi, 1969.
Originally published as first part of "Osservazioni sulla struttura metrica del *Furioso* (con una nota sull'enumerazione)." In *Giornale storico della letteratura italiana* 139, fasc. 426 (1962): 169–218.
Discusses in detail the rhythmic, semantic, and syntactic structure of Ariosto's *ottava*. Notes that the originality of the Ariostean octave, defined as a harmonious microcosm characterized by rhythmic and syntactic unity, consists in the fusion of Boccaccio's narrative syntax and Petrarch's lyricism. Suggests that the octave is divisible into symmetric units (4–4; 4–2–2; 6–2; 2–2–2–2) and examines the melodic, rhythmic, and semantic importance of the final verse of a unit ("versi di clausola," p. 96).

⋙ 109. ———. *Studi su Dante e Ariosto.* Milan-Naples: Ricciardi, 1969. 203p.
Includes "Osservazioni sulla struttura metrica del *Furioso*"(entry 108); "Nota sull'enumerazione nel *Furioso*" (entry 107); "La *Commedia* come fonte linguistica e stilistica del *Furioso*" (entry 105); "Un esempio del 'metodo' ariostesco: la sosta a Cipro (*Furioso*, XVIII, 136–140)" (entry 106).

⋙ 110. ———. "Riprese linguistico-stilistiche del *Morgante* nell'*Orlando Furioso*." In *Ludovico Ariosto: lingua, stile e tradizione*, edited by Cesare Segre (entry 789), pp. 137–55. Milan: Feltrinelli, 1976.
Also in *Giornale storico della letteratura italiana* 152 (1975): 199–221.
Considers several lexical and stylistic borrowings from the *Morgante* in the *OF* and concludes that, especially in Ariosto's use of enumeration (a technique he had in common with Pulci and for which he was clearly indebted to the author of the *Morgante*), we can discern how different the stylistic systems of the two poets were: in the tradition of the burlesque poets, Pulci used the technique to enhance the richness of the verse and to create a lexical spectacle ("spettacolo," p. 155); for Ariosto, enumeration was integral to the structure of the octave, with a precise metrical function, often relating in a contrapuntal or symmetrical way to other enumerative elements within the strophe or in a preceding or subsequent one and thus lending to the dynamic quality of the narrative plane.

⋙ 111. BONADEO, ALFREDO. "Il lamento di Sacripante." *Italica* 41, no. 4 (1964): 355–83.
Considers Sacripante's lament (*OF* 1.41–44) and his encounter with Angelica, noting that the inconsistencies in the character's behavior and the calculating astuteness of Angelica point to a departure from the prevailing Petrarchan and Neoplatonic concepts of love. Explains that Ariosto's attitudes informing the episode date back to his own youthful experiences, in

particular with a woman named Maria, when he began to realize that love often hinges on calculation and vulgarities.

113. ———. "Amore e cavalleria nell'*Orlando Furioso.*" *DAI* 26, no. 10 (1966): 6029. (University of California, Berkeley, 1965. 260p.)
Uses a "historical approach" to analyze several episodes of the *OF*, concluding that the poem is imbued with the spirit of a culture "whose values develop from an effort to assess and to understand man and his world according to more objective, and at the same time, more human criteria." Notes that the patina of tradition (e.g., the Neoplatonic elements in the love motif of canto 1) frequently serves to heighten the irony of a poetic vision anchored in reality.

113. ———. "L'Avventura di Rinaldo." *PMLA* 81, no. 3 (1966): 199–206.
Consideration of *OF* 4 and 5 and Rinaldo's defense of Ginevra in the context of Ariosto's perspective on the institution of chivalry. Argues that while Rinaldo's failure to follow Charlemagne's orders ("non segue una via predeterminata che lo porti ad una precisa meta, ma 'or una et or un'altra via,'" p. 199) and his undertaking of Ginevra's cause is in keeping with the chivalric pursuit of "self-realization" (p. 201) through adventures, Rinaldo also reveals a "maniera tutto ideale [of perceiving and judging reality], sia esso pure spontaneo e generoso, questo persistere nel corso d'azione intrapresa anche quando esso si rivela erroneo e in bisogno di modificazione ed adattamento alla cangiante situazione del reale, questa ferma volontà di tenere alta la bandiera di una causa ideale e non abbassarla nemmeno di fronte all'evidenza che quella causa smente" (p. 203). Notes that in a culture such as Ariosto's, dominated by political calculation and oppression, the chivalric spirit is of necessity alien to reality and can only express itself in the most fantastic, amusing, and futile manner.

114. ———. "Olimpia." *Italica* 45, no. 1 (1968): 47–58.
Considers the nature of Olimpia's love for Bireno (*OF* 9–11), noting that it is born of her need to love and stimulated by his youth and beauty. Argues that Bireno is merely the "catalizzatore" (p. 52) and object of her passions and that the one-sided relationship recalls in several respects Ariosto's own love for Alessandra Benucci, which was based on externals unable to satisfy the poet's more mature needs, "le esigenze più mature, profonde ed umane del poeta" (p. 56). Suggests that Ariosto was aware of Leone Ebreo's *Dialoghi* (1501–1502) on the two types of love, one appetitive and the other deriving from the appreciation of enduring qualities such as virtue, intellect, and grace.

🖙 115. ———. "Note sulla pazzia di Orlando." *Forum Italicum* 4, no. 1 (1970): 39–57.

Analysis of Orlando's frustrated passion and eventual madness in the context of medieval concepts of the origins and ends of human love. Argues that the drama of *OF* 23 results from the inability of the protagonist to reconcile his preconceptions of the lover / love-object relationship of courtly tradition and the realities of a situation that do not correspond to a rigidly "systematic idealism" (Johan Huizinga, *The Waning of the Middle Ages*). Concludes that "La grandezza di Ariosto e la sua particolare originalità consistono nel fatto che dell'amore egli ha rappresentato il dolore, l'illusione e la delusione non come esperienza nobilitante, esultante e mistica, ma eminentemente come esperienza umana, concreta, di disperazione" (p. 49).

🖙 116. BONDANELLA, PETER E., AND J. E. RIVERS. "Sacripant and Sacripante: A Note on Proust and Ariosto." *Romance Notes* 11, no. 1 (1969): 4–7.

Authors note that *Miss Sacripant*, Elstir's portrait of Odette de Crécy in *A la recherche du temps perdu*, brings to mind the episode of Sacripante and Angelica, *OF* 1. Considers thematic similarities between the two literary instances, especially the rose-virginity topos and its sexual-amatory implications in both Proust and Ariosto.

🖙 117. BONFANTINI, MARIO. "Ariosto e il *Furioso*." In his *Le Opere e le persone*, pp. 53–84. Padua: Liviana, 1976.

First published in his *Ariosto* (Lanciano: R. Carabba, 1934); Fatini, 3089.

🖙 118. BONIFAZI, NEURO. "Ariosto, il paladino e le lettere infedeli." In his *Le lettere infedeli. Ariosto, Leopardi, Manzoni*, pp. 1–120 and introduction, pp. xxiv–xxxiv. Rome: Officina, 1975.

Extensive analysis of Ariosto's letters, satires, and the *OF* based on the critical premise that writing is an act of deception that leaves to the reader the decodification of the text. Argues that in the letters, writing is unfaithful ("infedele") in that it tends to conceal from the receiver the sender's true feelings. Maintains that the relationship between sender and receiver is paradigmatic of that between son and father or servant and master, noting that Ariosto's letters are meant to satisfy his debt toward his employers. The sender's stated concern that the content of his letters—especially those of the Garfagnana period—might bore the receiver tends to reveal Ariosto's own dissatisfaction and boredom ("fastidio") with his assignment. Observes that his proclaimed pleasure over events that do honor to his patron (the receiver) is often colored by the fact that it is expressed in a relatively irrelevant place in the "scrittura," usually at the end of the text. Proceeds to discuss at length the opposition fidelity-infidelity in the *OF* through an analysis of selected characters such as Alcina, Olimpia, and Bradamante.

◆§ 119. BORGESE, G[IUSEPPE] A[NTONIO]. "L'Ariosto nel mondo degli invisibili." In his *Da Dante a Thomas Mann*, edited by Giulio Vallese, pp. 152–90. Milan: Mondadori, 1958.
Fatini, 2487.

◆§ 120. BORLENGHI, ALDO. "Regolarità e originalità della commedia del Cinquecento." In his *Studi di letteratura italiana dal '300 al '500*, pp. 122–230. Varese-Milan: Istituto Editoriale Cisalpino, 1959.
Discusses all of Ariosto's plays, focusing on the circumstances of their composition and production. Finds that Ariosto's novelty lies especially in his awareness of the comic language and his use of proverbs, in his realism—namely in the detailed description of games such as "zara"—and in his attempt to represent contemporary taste and ideals. Considers Ariosto's theater one of the most eloquent examples of the ambitions, experimentations, and originality that characterize Renaissance comedy in Italy. See especially pp. 174–206.

◆§ 121. ———. Nota. In *Commedie*, by Ludovico Ariosto, edited by Aldo Borlenghi, 1:5–13. 2 vols. Milan: Rizzoli, 1962.
Brief discussion of the social, theatrical, and literary traditions informing Ariosto's comedies, noting, in particular, the importance of the *Decameron* as a model for both comic language and intricacies of plot (*intreccio*). Summary account of Ariosto's theatrical activities and the composition and themes of his comedies.

◆§ 122. ———. *Ariosto.* 2d ed. Palermo: Palumbo, 1974. 268p.
Historical perspective on Ariosto criticism in Italy from the sixteenth century to major trends in modern scholarship. Considers the commentaries of Ariosto's contemporaries in the context of the fluid and evolving nature of early sixteenth-century critical theory and the views on Ariosto among late Renaissance participants in the polemic over the nature of epic poetry. Reviews the major critical perspectives in the seventeenth and eighteenth centuries (Paolo Beni, Galilei; Gravina and Muratori to Baretti). Extensive discussion of Foscolo and De Sanctis; consideration of the historical significance of Croce's view and major critical trends subsequent to him: historico-cultural and philological-linguistic studies. Concludes with a review of selected critical writings in Italy, including those of Bacchelli, Bigi, and Caretti. Selection of critical texts from the sixteenth through the twentieth century; selected bibliography.

◆§ 123. BORSELLINO, NINO. _Lettura dell'"Orlando Furioso."_ Rome: Bulzoni, 1972. 291p.

Introduction to a reading of the _OF_ (pp. 9–47); annotated selections from the text with prose commentary. Prefatory essay considers the Ferrarese cultural, political, and social milieu of Ariosto's literary formation, noting the importance of the urban and courtly perspective to his work. Briefly discusses the evolution of the _OF_ and identifies major thematic elements, including the "motivi inquietanti" (p. 20), "la rappresentazione . . . del mondo naturale ora cosmos ora caos" (p. 21). Analyzes principal structural elements of the poem that assure narrative simultaneity. Argues that the essential vision of the poem is that of humanity longing for a desired object and searching for happiness. Also argues that Ariosto, like Erasmus, celebrates folly as a liberating force from preoccupation. Concludes with an analysis of Ariosto's classically balanced style, which reflects the homogeneity of all elements in a poem that perfectly balances epic and romance.

◆§ 124. ———. _Ludovico Ariosto._ Bari: Laterza, 1973. 159p.

Also in _La Letteratura italiana: storia e testi_, vol. 4, part 1, _Il Cinquecento dal Rinascimento alla Controriforma_, edited by Nino Borsellino and Marcello Aurigemma, pp. 181–326. 9 vols. 2d ed. Bari: Laterza, 1973.

General introduction to the literary formation of the poet and to a reading of Ariosto's works, with annotated selections. Discusses Renaissance culture in Ferrara, noting the importance of an urban consciousness and its especial importance to Ariosto, whose life and works represent an integration of court culture and urban life. Considers the poet's youthful production of verse, noting as important elements its realistic-descriptive and intimate-bourgeois nature (p. 25) and, within it, his evolving "tono medio." Judges Ariosto's comedies as only partially successful in accomplishing their purpose, i.e., "di fare dello spazio scenico, con la prospettiva urbana, familiare e riconoscibile, il centro rituale e festoso di una riproducibilità del reale" (p. 37), and finds the proof of his comic style more evident in his satires, whose unity he sees in the presentation of a moral autobiography. Concludes with a rapid consideration of the _OF_, indicating its major structural elements and its representation of the world as one of illusions. Includes extensive bibliography, pp. 149–54.

◆§ 125. BOSCO, UMBERTO. "Il senso del limite." In his _Saggi sul Rinascimento italiano_, pp. 18–32. Florence: Le Monnier, 1970.

First published in _Atti del III Congresso internazionale sul Rinascimento_ (1952); Fatini, 3514.

◆§ 126. BRAGAGLIA, ANTON GIULIO. "L'Ariosto cineasta." _Bianco e nero_ 26, nos. 5–6 (1965): 88–108.

Discusses as insignificant any reading of the *OF* that attempts a symbolic interpretation, concluding that Ariosto's intention was primarily to entertain and that his aesthetic was purely art for art's sake (p. 91). Agrees with De Sanctis that the Aristotelian concept of unity is alien to the poem and that Ariosto seeks to surprise his audience with constant change (p. 97). Identifies episodes that in their coloring, surrealistic nature, and so on are visual and therefore cinematic. Attributes such techniques (including the passage from one scene to another, "lighting," etc.) to contemporary usage in more popular forms of theater, especially the *sacre rappresentazioni*, or sacred drama.

127. BRAHMER, MIECZYŁAW. "Kilka Uwag O Polskim *Orlandzie*" (Some considerations on the Polish *Orlando*). In *W Kręgu "Gofreda" I "Orlanda"* (entry 913), pp. 131–36. Wrokław-Warsaw-Cracow: Polska Akademia Nauk, 1970.
Concludes that a comparison of Kochanowski's translation and the original of the *OF* reveals a correct reading on the part of the Polish writer. Notes that changes in the Polish version were accommodations to the audience: there is a greater degree of realism, popular expressions, and vivid descriptions of battle scenes. Observes that the Polish stanza, composed of eight tridecasyllables rhyming in pairs, does not equal in its poetic effect the octave of the Italian original.

128. ———. "Entre Shakespeare et l'Arioste. Notes sur *Balladyna* de Słowacki." *Revue de littérature comparée* 50, nos. 1–2 (1976): 116–20.
Notes Juliusz Słowacki's (1809–1849) familiarity with the *OF* and the Ariostean character of his tragedy *Balladyna* (1834), including frequent change of scene, variety of tone, use of irony (p. 117), and the variety of human folly (pp. 118–19).

129. BRAMBILLA AGENO, FRANCA. "Riecheggiamenti e imitazioni nella tradizione letteraria italiana." *Giornale storico della letteratura italiana* 142, fasc. 440 (1965): 550–56.
Points out that in *Il Negromante* Ariosto, in order to achieve a "vivacità toscana" (p. 552), uses expressions from Pulci's *Morgante*, particularly from the Margutte episode.

130. ———. *L'Edizione critica dei testi volgari*. Padua: Antenore, 1975. 289p.
As an example of editorial problems and solutions in preparing a definitive version of a text with several extant editions, briefly describes (pp. 173–77) the critical apparatus of the Debenedetti-Segre edition of the *OF* (entry 25). Also considers the critical editions of the *frammenti autografi* of the *OF*,

containing episodes that the author incorporated into the 1532 edition (pp. 201–2).

131. BRANCA, VITTORE. "Lodovico non della tranquillità." *Il Veltro* 19, nos. 1–2 (1975): 75–81.

Rapid survey of current trends in Ariosto criticism that put the poet in the perspective of a historical moment in crisis—"un Rinascimento turbato e ansioso, sull'orlo di abissi infernali e apocalittici, ossessionato dall'irrazionale e dalla follia, sconvolto dalla coscienza di una civiltà ormai consunta e in rovina" (p. 76)—and, as in the critical writings of Daniela Delcorno Branca and others, in the late Gothic tradition of the medieval romance form.

132. BRAND, C. P. "Ludovico Ariosto—Poet and Poem in the Italian Renaissance." *Forum for Modern Language Studies* 4, no. 1 (1968): 87–101.

Observing that Italian Renaissance poetry is less known than the visual arts of the period, introduces the reader to the court life of the Renaissance poet and to chivalric poetry, focusing on Ariosto and the *OF*. Summarizes the narrative lines of the poem and surveys critical approaches to the text, noting that over the centuries a definition of the poem has eluded critics. Suggests that one of the difficulties in coming to grips with the nature of the poem is its "movement," or its evolution over a period of twenty-five years that saw the maturation of the poet as well as important cultural and social changes. Considers Ariosto's problems with the evolving literary language, his attitude toward chivalric ideals, warfare, and considers the "virtù-Fortuna" topos in the *OF*.

133. ———. "Poet, Poem, and Public in the Italian Renaissance." In *Expression, Communication and Experience in Literature and Language,* edited by Ronald G. Popperwell, pp. 57–71. Proceedings of the 12th Congress of the International Federation for Modern Languages and Literatures. Cambridge, August 20–26, 1972. Leeds: W. S. Maney and Sons Limited, 1973.

Considers the poet-reader relationship in the *OF* and the *GL*. Notes that Ariosto, in the tradition of oral narrative, maintains a familiar rapport with his public and is conscious of its differing tastes; the fiction of a listening audience is preserved throughout the text. In the *GL*, however, there is only an initial formal address, and the narrator refrains from becoming familiar with his audience. Discusses several reasons for these distinctions, including the essentially dissimilar personalities of the two poets and cultural trends that—in both language and style—saw a progressive distancing between poet and audience during the course of the sixteenth century in Italy. Concludes with observations on the modern reader's relationships to the two texts.

୶ 134. ———. "Tasso, Spenser, and the *Orlando Furioso.*" In *Petrarch to Pirandello: Studies in Italian Literature in Honour of Beatrice Corrigan,* edited by Julius A. Molinaro, pp. 95–110. Toronto: University of Toronto Press, 1973.
Discusses the reactions of Tasso and Spenser to the structure, style, and morality of the *OF.* Notes that both poets integrate themes and episodes of the *OF* into the structure of their own epics but that Tasso, striving for structural unity, avoids the multiplicity of episodes found in Ariosto's work. Notes also a "comparative lack of interest in suspense" in Spenser's narrative (p. 99) but a propensity for dramatic suspense in Tasso. Considers Spenser to have achieved structural and stylistic unity in the *FQ,* while Tasso often repeats Ariosto's "mingling of geographical reality with supernatural inventions" (p. 103). States that Spenser does not share Tasso's aversion to the *OF*'s pedestrian and down-to-earth language and to its ironic and mocking tone. Concludes that both Tasso and Spenser, while using the *OF* as the point of departure for their own poems, refashion Italian romance to meet their individual artistic ideals as well as to reflect their particular cultural and historical situations.

୶ 135. ———. "Ariosto and the *Orlando Furioso.*" *The Listener* 91, no. 2356 (23 May 1974): 668–70.
Brief discussion of recent partial or complete translations of the *OF,* including those of Guido Waldman, Barbara Reynolds, and Richard Hodgens.

୶ 136. ———. "The Grand Style: Italy, France, and Spain." In *The Old World: Discovery and Rebirth.* 1974. 3:201–37. *Literature and Western Civilization,* edited by David Daiches and Anthony Thorlby. 5 vols. London: Aldus Books, 1972–1975.
Discusses the development of the "grand style" during the sixteenth century in Italy, observing that the evolution of the epic is symptomatic of its rise, and considers the views of several epic theorists regarding the *OF* (p. 208). Notes that together with the evolution of a noble, grandiose style and a decorous language, "a realistic element persists in various fields in the early Italian Renaissance, that the literary language was opposed for example by the spread of dialect comedy, and the idealization of the Humanists by the essentially pessimistic view of man taken by Machiavelli . . . or by Ludovico Ariosto (1494–1533). Man is not idealized in Ariosto's *Orlando furioso* (1531 [*sic*]): the hero in fact loses his heroism; the brave, Christian, and patriotic Roland of the French *chanson* has here deteriorated into a lovesick knight whose jealousy drives him insane and leads him into stupid and clownish exploits until his friends forcibly restore him to his senses. Throughout the poem we are conscious of Ariosto's doubts about the real nobility, virtue, and dignity of these resplendent knights who think they have the world at their

mercy but who in fact are the victims of their unstable temperaments and the mysterious workings of chance" (pp. 204–5).

◆§ 137. ———. _Ludovico Ariosto: A Preface to the "Orlando Furioso."_ Edinburgh: Edinburgh University Press, 1974. 206p.

General introduction to Ariosto and to his works, with special attention given to the _OF._ Ten chapters: (1) biographical sketch of the poet; (2) brief consideration of the lyric poetry, the satires, and Ariosto's theater; (3) discussion of literary traditions informing the _OF_—surveys epic and chivalric poetry from the _chanson de geste_ and the Arthurian tales to the Italian _cantare_ tradition, Pulci, and Boiardo; (4) considers the treatment of the love motif in the _OF,_ including love as infatuation (Orlando), deception in love (Alcina, Olimpia-Bireno), romantic love (Isabella-Zerbino); (5) discussion of the arms motif, focusing on the poet's tribute to his patrons, on the allusions to important battles of his times, and on the horrors of modern military techniques (p. 91); (6) considers other major themes in the poem, including dynastic and political motifs—especially the encomia of the Este family line, the theme of the battle between the sexes, and the role of Fortune in the narrative; (7) analysis of the narrative devices linking characters and incidents into a coherent structure; (8) Ariosto's role in the perfection of the _ottava_ and its function in the _OF;_ (9) maintains that the contemporary _questione della lingua_ promoted by Pietro Bembo influenced Ariosto's revisions of the poem, touching on the problematic nature of the _CC;_ (10) survey of criticism of the _OF_ from the Renaissance to the present. Includes bibliography, pp. 197–201.

◆§ 138. ———. "Ginevra and Ariodante: A Deception Motif from Ariosto to Shakespeare." In _Essays in Honour of John Humphreys Whitfield,_ edited by H. C. Davis, J. M. Hatwell, D. G. Rees, and G. W. Slowey, pp. 120–36. London: St. George's Press, 1975.

Two part essay: relates the Ginevra-Ariodante episode (_OF,_ 4–6) to its sources (especially Johanot Martorell's _Tirante el blanco_ [1490]) and to its use by Bandello, Spenser, and Shakespeare in _Much Ado About Nothing,_ which develops both Ariosto's deception motif and employs his double-plot structure; considers both the narrative method in Ariosto's episode and the leitmotif of deception as components of the structural technique and thematic texture of the entire poem.

◆§ 139. ———. "Ariosto's Continuation of the _Orlando Innamorato._" In _Cultural Aspects of the Italian Renaissance: Essays in Honour of Paul Oskar Kristeller,_ edited by Cecil H. Clough, pp. 377–85. New York: Alfred F. Zambelli; Manchester: Manchester University Press, 1976.

Surveys and discusses Ariosto's treatment of Boiardo's undeveloped episodes in the *OI* and their effect on the structure of the *OF*. Insists that the *OF*, though autonomous, is a continuation of Boiardo's poem, which, surprisingly, Ariosto never explicitly acknowledged as one of his sources.

⚜ 140. ———. "L'entrelacement nell'*Orlando Furioso*." *Giornale storico della letteratura italiana* 154 (1977): 509–32.
Suggests that the *OF* is characterized by a rational structure based on three main narrative threads (Orlando's love for Angelica; the relationship between Ruggiero and Bradamante; the war) interwoven with six secondary narrative sequences, including Orlando's and Bradamante's pursuit of Angelica and Ruggiero, respectively, and Orlando's madness. Notes that these structural elements are connected by the technique of *entrelacement*, which provides variety, chronological uniformity, and thematic and/or moral unity.

⚜ 141. ———. "Ariosto's Ricciardetto and Fiordispina." In *Stimmen der Romania. Festschrift für W. Theodor Elwert zum 70. Geburtstag*, edited by Gerhard Schmidt and Manfred Tietz, pp. 121–33. Wiesbaden: B. Heymann Verlag, 1980.
Discusses the genesis of the Ricciardetto-Fiordispina episode in the *OF* (22 and 25) and its function to the structure of the central cantos, 22 through 25. Suggests as possible sources for the conclusion of the episode, left unfinished by Boiardo, Bibbiena's *La Calandria*, and Ovid's *Metamporphoses*, the former for the identity intrigue and the latter for the sexual transformation motif (p. 125). Notes the importance of sexual disguise and transformation in sixteenth-century literature and explores Ariosto's use of the themes in the episodes situated around the center of the poem, concluding that in the Ricciardetto-Fiordispina episode in particular, the poet's intent is to raise the "question of the nature of sex itself" (p. 128). Explores other possible reasons for Ariosto's having situated the Ricciardetto story in a central position, noting that it, like the Zerbino-Isabella episode, is split to bracket the madness episode (cantos 23–24) and to provide "contrasting effects" (p. 132).

⚜ 142. BRAY, RENÉ. *La formation de la doctrine classique en France*. Paris: Nizet, 1974. 389p.
First edition 1927; Fatini, 2489. Passim consideration of Ariosto's role in the formation of poetic theory during the classical age in France.

⚜ 143. BRESCIANI, EDDA. "Il *Libro* dei Conti dei balestrieri di messer Ludovico Ariosto commissario ducale in Garfagnana, nell'Archivio Statale di Modena." In *Ludovico Ariosto*, pp. 175–225. Convegno internazionale (entry 475). Rome: Accademia Nazionale dei Lincei, 1975.
Transcription of Ariosto's ledger containing the records of payment to cavalrymen (*balestrieri*) in the employ of the Este family during the poet's com-

mission in the Garfagnana (1522–1525). Extensive commentary on the handwritten entries and the degree to which they reveal Ariosto's attitude toward his appointment, his concern for his charges, and his appreciation for the realities of life and its difficulties in the provinces.

◆§ 144. BRODWIN, LEONORA LEET. "Milton and the Renaissance Circe." *Milton Studies* 6 (1974): 21–83.
Argues that Milton's treatment of the Circe figure "is heir to a Renaissance literary tradition, begun by Ariosto and further developed by Tasso and Spenser, which is grounded in the Homeric text" (p. 23). Notes that Ariosto's episode of Ruggiero and Alcina is the "first major poetic treatment of Circean temptation in the Renaissance" (p. 26). Analyzes the condition of Ruggiero as a reflection of the three temptations of Circe—oblivion, sexual pleasure, and idleness; concludes that the three forms of the temptation of Circe in this episode reflect "the direct influence of the Homeric original while . . . influencing the later depictions in Renaissance epic" (p. 28). See especially pp. 26–28.

◆§ 145. BRONZINI, GIOVANNI B. *Tradizione di stile aedico dai cantari al "Furioso."* Florence: Olschki, 1966. 131p.
Revised and expanded version of "*L'Orlando Furioso* e la tradizione dei cantari." *Convivium* no. 1 (1951): 74–86; Fatini, 3468.
Noting that the Italian *cantare* differs from its medieval French sources in its essentially popular nature and "human" dimensions (p. 12), discusses the elements of the fourteenth- and fifteenth-century *cantari* that are incorporated in the *Morgante* (pp. 19–31), the *OI* (pp. 33–48), and the *OF*, in which the popular tradition assumes a function in a new aesthetic perspective on the real versus the ideal, the human versus the fantastic (pp. 50–51). Documents Ariosto's use of narrative and stylistic techniques common to the *cantari*, including the insistence on creating a dimension of credibility in the narrative by citing "historical" sources for the text, methods of opening and closing cantos, and means of interrupting and continuing episodes. Concludes: "la materia rozza dei cantari . . . in questo elevarsi si esaurisce man mano che si fa innanzi la coscienza del poeta, e si spegne addirittura nell'umanesimo classico del quale è fatto il sorriso ariostesco" (p. 123).

◆§ 146. BROWN, JACK DAVIS. "Hans Carvel's Ring: Elements, Literary Tradition, Rabelais's Source." *Romance Notes* 13, no. 3 (1972): 515–22.
Discusses the literary predecessors of the tale of Hans Carvel's ring in Rabelais, *Tiers Livre*, chapter 28, including Ariosto's tale of Galasso, *Satira V*, ll. 298–328. (pp. 518–19). Through a structural analysis, excludes Ariosto as a source for Rabelais and concludes that the only source is Poggio Bracciolini's *Facetiae*.

⋘ 147. BROWN, PETER M. "The Historical Significance of the Polemics over Tasso's *Gerusalemme Liberata*." *Studi secenteschi* 11 (1970): 3–23. Biblioteca dell'*Archivum Romanicum*, 1st ser., vol. 110.

Discusses Lionardo Salviati's contribution to sixteenth-century polemics over the merits of the *OF* and the *GL*. Refutes the long-held view that Salviati's attacks on the *GL* in his *Stacciata prima* (1584) are prompted by personal or "parochial animosities" (p.8), and shows that the polemist was actually attacking Camillo Pellegrino who, in his *Il Carrafa* (1584), had argued that the *OF* was not an epic in the Aristotelian sense. Explains that according to Salviati, Aristotle, correctly interpreted, was followed more closely by Ariosto than by Tasso. Places the scope of Salviati's polemics in a much wider context by pointing out that the critic adopts Aristotle in the defense of romance in an attempt to promote a national literary tradition free from the restrictions of antiquity. See also on this subject, Peter M. Brown, *Lionardo Salviati, A Critical Biography* (London: Oxford University Press, 1974), chapter 14.

⋘ 148. ———. "In Defence of Ariosto: Giovanni de' Bardi and Lionardo Salviati." *Studi secenteschi* 12 (1971): 3–27. Biblioteca dell'*Archivum Romanicum*, 1st ser., vol. 115.

Defends Salviati's position on the *GL* as essentially a defense of Ariosto against the academic Aristotelianism of Camillo Pellegrino (*Il Carrafa*, 1584) and not a hostile condemnation of Tasso. Reproduces a letter of Salviati to Giovanni de' Bardi (28 September 1582), which documents his fully matured ideas on the vernacular epic and which, by predating the polemical stance of his reply to Pellegrino (*Stacciata prima*, 1584), proves that the basis of his disagreement was an already developed view of epic poetry and not personal animus against the author of the *GL*. See also on this subject, Peter M. Brown, *Lionardo Salviati, A Critical Biography* (London: Oxford University Press, 1974), chapter 14.

⋘ 149. ———. *Prose or Verse in Comedy: A Florentine Treatment of a Sixteenth-Century Controversy*. (An Inaugural Lecture Delivered in the University of Hull on 15th November 1972.) Hull, Yorkshire: The University of Hull, 1973. 31p.

Brief discussion of Ariosto's role in the adaptation of classical comedy to the vernacular and his use of verse, the proparoxytone hendecasyllable (*endecasillabo sdrucciolo*), as a means of "adhering more faithfully to the features of the 'genre' as represented by antiquity" (p. 16).

⋘ 150. BRUNO, PIERA. "L'Ultimo Ariosto e le Satire." *Italyan Filolojisi (Filologia italiana)* (Rivista della Cattedra di Lingua e Letteratura Italiana della Facoltà di Lettere dell'Università di Ankara) 8, no. 9 (1976): 51–63.

Notes that Ariosto's satires have been given considerable attention by recent critics for a better understanding of the mature poet. Argues that they document a crisis in the life of the poet and a passage to a more mature poetic expression attained after a period of reflection on means of refining his style and language: "Il passaggio alle Satire . . . va considerato come un'operazione di techniche e di strutture, attraverso le quali, dopo l'approdo all'oggettività, tanto più distaccata, quanto più attenta alle sfumature impercettibili alla complessa esistenza umana, e dopo la tenuta costante di una forma narrativa indiretta . . . Ariosto assume il suo io e la sua coscienza morale come punto di riferimento per ricondurre all'unità registri linguistici differenti o come filtro per decantare momenti di vita interiore sfoghi rimpianti malumori memorie esortazioni . . . sollevandoli al piano della letteratura" (p. 53). In this context, gives particular attention to the several images of cities and similar locations in the satires as references for treating his own experiences, often linking them to a classical allusion, as well as his perspectives on politics and on political figures: "E tutto ciò è, alla fine, estremamente positivo, in quanto, le medesime variazioni di struttura e reminiscenze classiche sfumanti in una espressione di rancore moderato o approdanti alla lezione di lucida saggezza assolvono contemporaneamente la doppia funzione di relegare a un ruolo subordinato i 'disvalori' e 'non valori' che sorreggono gli spaccati negativi dell'esistenza e di richiamare in un continuo confronto, sia esplicito che sottinteso, i valori reali: onore, cara libertà, amore" (p. 60), adding that love equals the poet's defense of his own individual space.

⁓§ 151. BRUSCAGLI, RICCARDO. *"Ventura e inchiesta* fra Boiardo e Ariosto." In *Ludovico Ariosto: lingua, stile e tradizione*, edited by Cesare Segre (entry 789), pp. 107–36. Milan: Feltrinelli, 1976.
Also in *Filologia e critica* 1, no. 1 (1976): 80–114.

Considers the role of two traditional chivalric topoi—*ventura* (the "prova gentile e ardimentosa, momento emblematico di reincarnazione della *courtoisie* medievale," p. 120) and *inchiesta* (medieval romance quest)—and the way they function in Boiardo's *OI*, in the continuations of his unfinished poem by Niccolò degli Agostini and Raffaele da Verona, in Cieco da Ferrara's *Il Mambriano*, and in the *OF*. Defines the use of these topoi by Boiardo as vehicles for proving the worth of chivalrous heroes and shows that the followers of Boiardo, more concerned with the contemporaneity and topicality of their poems, frequently abandon the significance given them by tradition. Ariosto, on the other hand, takes up again the significant structural charge of these topoi, altering it, however, so that they become circular rather than linear and metaphors of frustration and delusion rather than of accomplishment and realization of a desired goal.

୫ 152. CAGNOLATI, GIORGIO, ed. *Mostra di edizioni ariostesche.* Ottobre 1974–Marzo 1975. Reggio Emilia. Biblioteca Antonio Panizzi. Reggio Emilia: La Biblioteca, 1974. 310p., with 14 leaves of plates.
Exhibit catalog with 673 entries of editions and translations of Ariosto's works: 164 entries of selected critical works from 1517 to 1974; 23 entries of bibliographies, catalogs, and miscellanea from 1730 to 1974.

୫ 153. CAIRNCROSS, ANDREW S. "Shakespeare and Ariosto: *Much Ado About Nothing, King Lear,* and *Othello.*" *Renaissance Quarterly* 29, no. 2 (1976): 178–82.
Argues that Shakespeare had at least a reading knowledge of Italian by demonstrating that he incorporated into several of his plays elements from the Ginevra-Ariodante episode of the *OF* 4–6, which he could not have known from translations or from other Ariostean sources.

୫ 154. CALDARINI, ERNESTA. "A propos du sonnet CVIII de Ronsard." *Bibliothèque d'Humanisme et Renaissance* 27 (1965): 653–54.
Argues that Ariosto's sonnet "Felice stella, sotto ch'il sol nacque," is the source of Ronsard's sonnet 108 of the first book of the *Amours.*

୫ 155. ČALE, FRANCO. "Ancora su uno stilema in funzione umoristica." *Studia Romanica et Anglica Zagrabiensia,* nos. 15–16 (1963), pp. 125–32.
Article devoted mainly to some stylistic observations on Pirandello. Notes the frequency in the *OF* of the syntactical inversion of the subject-protagonist and verb to highlight the former's tragicomic dimensions and to underscore the poet's ironic commentary on the plight of the protagonist.

୫ 156. CALORE, MARINA. "Il Teatro ferrarese tra Ariosto e Giraldi: commedie di Alfonso Battista Guarino, Parte I." *Atti dell'Istituto Veneto di Scienze, Lettere ed Arti* 138 (1979–1980): 65–80; "Parte II: Le Commedie a stampa," ibid., pp. 147–60.
The first of a two-part essay discusses theatrical activity in Ferrara during the first decades of the sixteenth century and Ariosto's role therein; considers the plays of Ariosto's compatriot Alfonso Guarino and their significance to the history of Ferrarese dramatic forms; examines in a comparative way Ariosto and Guarino as "nuovi comici" (p. 75). Considers the nature of Ferrarese theater during the period of Alfonso I d'Este, the extent of Ariosto's influence and activities, especially between 1528 and 1532, and the importance of the presence in Ferrara of playwrights such as Ruzante to the evo-

lution of comic language. Briefly analyzes the three extant plays of Guarino (*Milesia*, "l'unico esempio di commedia umanistica composto a Ferrara da un ferrarese" [p. 73], *Lo Sponsalitio*, and *Il Pratico*) and discusses their dating. Concludes by noting several problematic issues of dramatic composition common to both Ariosto and Guarino and the subject of several prologues of their plays, noting, for example, that both comedy writers "si troveranno di fronte al medesimo dilemma: se vi sia una comicità universale insita nel vario atteggiarsi della natura umana o se essa non vada 'modernamente' cercata piuttosto nella mentalità e nelle convenienze che regolano la società contemporanea" (p. 76). Notes that Guarino is the first to follow Ariosto in the use of *endecasillabi sdruccioli* in his verse plays. Second part of essay analyzes *Lo Sponsalitio* and *Il Pratico*, with occasional references to Ariosto's theater and the satires.

✒ 157. CALVINO, ITALO. "Main Currents in Italian Fiction Today." *Italian Quarterly* 4, nos. 13–14 (1960): 3–14.
In discussing his position vis-à-vis the main currents of modern Italian fiction admits his debt to Ariosto, noting that, albeit unconsciously, he approached the novel of action and political engagement (e.g., Hemingway and Malraux) with the same attitude and narrative modes—veil of irony and fantastic transfiguration—with which Ariosto viewed and transformed the romances of chivalry.

✒ 158. ———. Introduction. In *"Orlando Furioso" di Ludovico Ariosto*, pp. ix–xxvi. Raccontato da Italo Calvino, con una scelta del poema. Turin: Einaudi, 1970.
Prose narrative based on the major episodes of the *OF*. Introduction briefly traces the evolution of the chivalric romance and its impact on Italian culture. Maintains that the *OF* could and should be read without reference to earlier romances such as the *OI* because it is a self-contained universe in which "si può viaggiare in lungo e in largo, entrare, uscire, perdercisi" (p. xix).

✒ 159. ———. "Ariosto geometrico." In *Per L'Ariosto* (entry 623). Special 1976 issue of *Italianistica* 3, no. 3 (1974): 167–68.
Alludes to Ariosto's presence in his own (Calvino's) novels and notes the geometric structure and movement of the *OF*.

✒ 160. ———. "La Struttura del *Furioso*." *Terzoprogramma*, nos. 2–3 (1974): 51–58.
Considers devices used by Ariosto in structuring the *OF*, including the technique of breaking the narrative line with a rhyming couplet serving as an envoi. Notes the significance to the structure of centrifugal movement,

along "zigzag" lines, termed "movimento *errante*" (p. 54). Sees the structural technique of the octave as representative of Ariosto's art in the poem, particularly the discontinuity of the rhythm and the complete freedom of form and tone (p. 55). On the narrative plane, sees Paris and the Castle of Atlante as the major focal points—or centers of gravity (p. 56)—the latter in a negative sense, representing a vortex that removes the characters from the action of the poem (p. 56) and thus provides a means for the poet to keep certain episodes in suspension until the opportune moment.

161. ———. "Piccola antologia di ottave." *La Rassegna della letteratura italiana*, 7th ser., vol. 79, nos. 1–2 (1975): 6–9.
Declares his preference for octaves in the *OF* that introduce new adventures and for those dealing with toponymic references, especially in regard to the British Isles. Points out that in the erotic octaves, the central moment is not in the realization of desire but in the anticipation of fulfillment (p. 8). Brief discussion of the "ottava truculenta," *CC* 4.7.

162. CAMERON, ALICE V. *The Influence of Ariosto's Epic and Lyric Poetry on Ronsard and his Group.* New York: Johnson Reprint Corp., 1973.
Reprint of 1930 edition; Fatini, 2491.

163. CAPACCHI, GUGLIELMO. "L'Ariosto in Ungheria." In *Lodovico Ariosto: il suo tempo la sua terra la sua gente* (entry 468). Estratto dal *Bollettino storico reggiano* 7, no. 25 (1974): 55–59.
Notes that despite the lively interest in Hungary in Italian literature, there has been relatively little interest in Ariosto and only anthological translations; ascribes this attitude to the fact that Hungarian literature has always had a civic character and readers find little sympathy with Ariosto's world of fantasy.

164. CAPPUCCIO, CARMELO. Introduction to Ludovico Ariosto and Torquato Tasso. In *L'Orlando Furioso e La Gerusalemme Liberata: episodi*, selected and annotated by Carmelo Cappuccio, pp. 3–9. Florence: Sansoni, 1969.
First edition 1956; Fatini, 3602.

165. CAPRA, LUCIANO, ed. *Antologia ariostesca.* Catalog of the "Mostra promossa dal Comitato Ferrarese per le celebrazioni ariostesche del 1974." Ferrara: [1974]. 30p., unnumbered, with two color plates.
Catalog listing of 194 items displayed at the Biblioteca Comunale Ariostea, Ferrara (1974) in commemoration of anniversary. Some items annotated. Includes "Il genere letterario del *Furioso*," fifteen entries concerning the romance genre (Renaissance and modern commentaries); "*Orlando Fu-*

rioso," fifty-seven entries of editions and commentaries on the *OF;* "Lirica latina," twelve entries of editions and commentaries on lyrics; "Lirica italiana," fourteen entries of editions and commentaries on Italian lyrics; *"Cinque Canti,"* eight entries of editions and commentaries on the *CC;* "Commedie," eighteen entries of editions and commentaries on the comedies; "Satire," thirteen entries of editions and commentaries on the satires; "Lettere e altri momenti domestici," eleven items; "Celebrazioni funebri del 1612 e del 1801," eleven items; "Di qualche ritratto," nine items; fourteen miscellaneous entries, including bibliographies and items on Ariosto outside Italy.

◄§ 166. CAPRA, LUCIANO. "Per la datazione dei *Cinque Canti* dell'Ariosto." *Giornale storico della letteratura italiana* 151, fasc. 474 (1974): 278–95.
Considers characters, episodes, and linguistic and stylistic elements common to both the *OF* and the *CC* in order to show that the *CC*, contrary to a commonly held view, is antecedent to the 1516 *OF*: "I *Cinque canti* sono stati scritti e lasciati prima dell'apparire del *Furioso*" (p. 278). Argues that revisions of the *CC* were not undertaken by Ariosto alone.

◄§ 167. ———. "Per il testo delle *Satire* di Ludovico Ariosto." *Studi e problemi di critica testuale* 11 (1975): 51–73.
Examines Ferrarese manuscript of Ariosto's satires (Biblioteca Comunale Ariostea, ms. I B), calling attention to selected passages and their respective revisions. Dismisses the possibility that the corrections were made by Ariosto himself, arguing that the changes not only produce mediocre results but fail to preserve the original meaning suggested by the text or to reflect linguistic forms that Ariosto had come to adopt in his revisions of the *OF*. Also faults the Gioliti edition of 1550 for having taken too many liberties with the original text.

◄§ 168. ———. "Qualche nota su un insigne manoscritto ariostesco." *Bollettino di notizie e ricerche da archivi e biblioteche* (Comune di Ferrara), no. 1 (1980): 11–24.
Analysis of ms. I B of the seven satires in the Biblioteca Comunale Ariostea, Ferrara. Argues on linguistic and stylistic evidence and contrary to the thesis of both Debenedetti and Segre that the emendations are not Ariosto's. Concludes with a history of the disposition of the manuscript.

◄§ 169. CARDONA, ANGEL CHICLANA. "Diferencias en el tratamiento de los elementos constitutivos del *Orlando Furioso* de Ariosto, y de *La hermosura de Angélica* de Lope de Vega." *Filología Moderna* (Madrid) 12, nos. 43–44 (1971–1972): 35–70.
Detailed discussion of the major differences between the *OF* and Lope de

Vega's "continuation," *La hermosura de Angélica* (1602), concluding that the Spanish poem is of essentially inferior quality because it imitates a work that evolved from and expressed the character and ideologies of a culture that was both culturally and historically alien to Lope's world.

✍ 170. CARETTI, LANFRANCO. "Ariosto e la critica." *Ferrara viva: rivista storica e di attualità* 3, nos. 7–8 (1961): 3–11.

Discusses the major contributions to Ariosto criticism since the first critical observations of Ugo Foscolo, underscoring the significance of Francesco De Sanctis and Benedetto Croce to the direction of modern critical approaches. Notes the importance, among others, of Walter Binni, Riccardo Bacchelli, and biographers such as Michele Catalano, who have given modern critics the basis for understanding Ariosto and his work. Concludes that we now can see Ariosto as a man of his period, quiet rather than intensively active and one whose moral ethics and profound understanding of human nature are reflected in what has been called the harmonious world of his poetry.

✍ 171. ———. "Ludovico Ariosto." In *Storia della letteratura italiana*, 3:787–895. 8 vols. General directors: Emilio Cecchi and Natalino Sapegno. Milan: Garzanti, 1966.

General introduction to Ariosto's life and works, divided into six parts. "Fortuna dell'Ariosto" (pp. 787–96) reviews the major trends in Ariosto criticism from Ugo Foscolo to Cesare Segre; "Una vita 'sedentaria'" (pp. 796–810) provides a short biography, often citing the poet's own account of his activities; "Interpretazione di una vita" (pp. 811–13) views Ariosto's sense of privacy and choice of life without heroic gestures as a mature choice based on a sense of discretion and pragmatism; "Rime, Satire, Commedie" (pp. 813–36) considers the minor works, noting that they "acquistano valore quando siano considerate non per sé sole, ma in funzione del *Furioso*" (p. 836); "L'ordito del poema" (pp. 837–82) reviews the chronology of the poem's composition, stresses the difficulty of reducing the poem to a simple structure, and explicates selected passages; "L'arte del *Furioso*" (pp. 882–91) points out that the *materia* of the poem is not the chivalric tradition but a modern perspective on life in all of its many psychological manifestations. Briefly discusses Ariosto's style and the narrative rhythm of his poetry, concluding with a consideration of the CC, which betrays Ariosto's awareness "del declino di quel mondo incontaminato e forte di cui egli aveva . . . celebrato la vitalità" (p. 891). Includes bibliography (pp. 892–95).

✍ 172. ———. Introduction. In *Boiardo, Ariosto, Tasso: le tre corone estensi*, edited by Lanfranco Caretti, pp. v–xii. Turin: Loescher, 1974.

Observations extracted from his "Ludovico Ariosto," in *Storia della letteratura italiana*. See entry 171.

⇜§ 173. ———. "Il Generale Miollis e le feste ariostesche del 1801." *La Rassegna della letteratura italiana*, 7th ser., vol. 79, nos. 1–2 (1975): 305–9.

Also in *Notiziario culturale italiano* (entry 573) 15, no. 3 (1974): 37–41.

Describes the festivities accompanying the transfer of Ariosto's remains from the church of S. Benedetto in Ferrara to a room of the communal library in Via delle Scienze in 1801. Notes that the transfer was organized by a French general and patron of the arts, Sextius-Alexandre-François Miollis, and that it offered an opportunity for a public manifestation of patriotism and civic solidarity at a moment of intense internal strife. Notes that the source of information for the ceremony proper is a collection of writings composed for the occasion and entitled *Prose e rime per il transporto del monumento e delle ceneri di Ludovico Ariosto*. (For a description of the collection, see Fatini, 716.)

⇜§ 174. ———. *Antichi e moderni. Studi di letteratura italiana.* Turin: Einaudi, 1976. 497p.

The essays on Ariosto contained in this volume have all appeared in earlier publications; several have been published on numerous occasions. The first essay, "L'opera dell'Ariosto," has been adopted as an introductory essay to a number of editions of Ariosto's works; only the most important have been cited.

Includes "L'opera dell'Ariosto" (entry 177); "Codicillo" to "L'opera dell'Ariosto" (entry 176); "Autoritratto ariostesco" (entry 175); "Storia dei *Cinque canti*" (entry 178).

⇜§ 175. ———. "Autoritratto ariostesco." In his *Antichi e moderni. Studi di letteratura italiana*, pp. 109–19. Turin: Einaudi, 1976.

Also with title "Per un autoritratto di Ludovico Ariosto," in *Terzoprogramma*, nos. 2–3 (1974): 5–14, and in *Il Ponte* 30, no. 10 (1974): 1142–50.

Through an analysis of the satires and especially of Ariosto's correspondence, concludes that the traditional portrayal of the poet as a sedentary ascetic, anxious to withdraw into a fantasy world far from the grim realities of his day, is invalid; argues that Ariosto had a strong moral sense and, like his contemporary Machiavelli, was an attentive, perceptive critic of his world and was interested in and understood human psychology. Maintains that a close reading of his satires, penetrating the surface representation of a distanced persona, and a study of the letters is important to an understanding of the *OF*, which mirrors "una saggezza dolorosamente sperimentata, e una conoscenza lucida e profonda del mondo, del mondo storico degli uomini contemporanei . . . e del mondo universale delle umane passioni" (p. 119).

⚜ 176. ———. "Codicillo" (to "L'opera dell'Ariosto"). In his *Antichi e moderni. Studi di letteratura italiana*, pp. 103–8. Turin: Einaudi, 1976.

Also with title "Invito all'Ariosto," in *Annali del Liceo-Ginnasio 'Ariosto'* (Ferrara, 1974), pp. 77–84.

Denies the legitimacy of viewing the three editions of the OF as moments in an evolution toward creative perfection, but argues for the need of viewing the 1516 and 1532 editions, particularly, as two complete works reflecting differing cultural moments and perspectives: the first, "un'opera splendidamente 'municipale' perché ha ancora dietro di sé una fiorente cultura locale e una forte realtà sociale e politica" (p. 105); the second reflecting "il tramonto d'ogni municipalità, culturale e linguistica, e la dilatazione della letteratura entro dimensioni nazionali proprio nel momento in cui appare definitivamente caduta ogni civile aspirazione italiana" (p. 107).

⚜ 177. ———. "L'opera dell'Ariosto." In his *Antichi e moderni. Studi di letteratura italiana*, pp. 85–103. Turin: Einaudi, 1976.

This essay has been adopted as an introductory essay to a number of editions of Ariosto's works; only the most important have been cited.

First published as the introduction to Ludovico Ariosto, *Opere minori* (Milan-Naples: Ricciardi, 1954), pp. vii–xxv, with a bibliography of criticism; see Fatini, 3539. Republished in his *Ariosto e Tasso* (Turin: Einaudi, first edition 1961), pp. 17–44; included with slight revisions in *Problemi dell'umanesimo*, edited by Marta Bruscia, Ugo Dotti, and Gianfranco Mariani (Rome: Edizioni dell'Ateneo, 1972), pp. 103–24; and adopted as the introductory essay to Ludovico Ariosto, *Commedie*, edited by Cesare Segre (Turin: Einaudi, 1976), pp. 263–81, and to Ludovico Ariosto, *Orlando furioso* (Turin: Loescher, first edition 1968), pp. 1–14.

⚜ 178. ———. "Storia dei *Cinque canti*." In his *Antichi e moderni. Studi di letteratura italiana*, pp. 121–31. Turin: Einaudi, 1976.

Also published as introduction to his editions of the CC (Venice: Corbo & Fiore, 1974, pp. xiii–xxviii, and Turin: Einaudi, 1977, pp. v–xv) and in *Per l'Ariosto* (entry 623), special 1976 issue of *Italianistica* 3, no. 3 (1974): 87–96.

Briefly profiles the history of the dating of the CC (noting that it has been established that the first version dates c. 1518–1519 and no later than 1521, with a revision c. 1526), including the reasons for its composition and for its exclusion from the OF. Discusses the tone of the work (essentially lugubrious, pessimistic; a portrayal of a world in which evil dominates) and the relation of its composition and tone to particularly difficult moments in the poet's life and in Italy's political situation.

179. CARINI, ANNA MARIA. "L'iterazione aggettivale nell'*Orlando Furioso*." *Convivium* 31 (1963): 19–34.

By means of numerous examples shows that through repetition and/or parallelism of synonyms, quasi synonyms, or simply terms made synonymous by the narrative context, Ariosto succeeds in conferring psychological and semantic freshness on linguistic elements that had become restricted in meaning and weakened through use. Argues that this is especially true of adjectives common to the *cantare* tradition, e.g., "gentile," "iniquo," "fello," and "mesto."

180. CARLINI, ANNA. "Progetto di edizione critica delle liriche di Ludovico Ariosto." *Giornale storico della letteratura italiana* 135, fasc. 409 (1958): 1–40.

Examines variations in the three principal sources of Ariosto's lyrics: two manuscripts from the Biblioteca Civica in Ferrara labeled by Giuseppe Antonelli as CL,I,n.64 (F') and CL,I,n.365 (F"), and Jacopo Coppa's 1546 edition (Cp). Notes that the sources differ in that the manuscripts of copyists, which postdate the edition, contain two poems not included in Cp, which, in turn, features seven lyrics not present in F' and F". Points to appropriate revisions in the editions of the OF to show that F' and F" follow revisions made by Ariosto himself and suggests that F' is preferable for the basis of a critical edition since it contains fewer errors than F".

181. CARLO, C. "Fiction and Reality in *Orlando Innamorato* and *Orlando Furioso*." M. Litt. thesis, Trinity College (Dublin), academic year 1967–1968.

Unavailable; cited without additional information in *Index to Theses Accepted for Higher Degrees by the Universities of Great Britain and Ireland and the Council for National Academic Awards* 18 (1967–1968): 26, entry 604.

182. CARNE-ROSS, D. S. "The One and the Many: A Reading of the *Orlando Furioso*, Cantos 1 and 8." *Arion* 5, no. 2 (1966): 195–234.

Two-part essay. "Angelica: the Image of Flight" analyzes OF 1, focusing on the figure of Angelica as an image or as a multiplicity of images that elude pursuing paladins. Argues that the failure of the knights to realize individual goals or to attain the object of their pursuit reveals "the comic formula [of the OF] at work"; central to the poem is "the failed expectation: everything goes wrong for everyone and always in the way they least expect" (p. 214). "Orlando: Single Visionary in a World of Plurals" discusses the paradox and irony that characterize the wise Orlando of epic tradition who goes mad for love. Suggests that the oxymoron of the mad Orlando, "expanded to the point where it becomes a structural device, is in a sense the governing figure of the *Furioso*" (p. 222). Notes that although in the *OF* characters are not endowed with "larger meanings" and "matter much less than the scenes in which they appear" (p. 225), Orlando is the "supreme exponent of single vision in a universe where only multiple vision will serve" (p. 232).

183. ———. "The One and the Many: A Reading of the *Orlando Furioso*." *Arion*, n.s. 3, no. 2 (1976): 146–219.
Argues that the numerous characters and episodes in the *OF* are reflections of the multifaceted aspects of major themes such as love, illusion, and the quest. Considers these variations on themes through a discussion of several characters, underscoring thematic and stylistic analogies. Focuses on Ariosto's repeated variations on phrases such as "di qua di là" and "di su di giù" as stylistic indicators of the poet's celebration of the "unpredictable heartbeat of the universe" (p. 202). Suggests that the *OF* represents a world of multiple perspectives in which "the mental structure Western man had inhabited for centuries was coming apart" (p. 210). Admits that this view does not find support in the last third of the poem in which Ariosto moves from his realm of "vital instability" (p. 204) toward a more conventional world. Considers Ariosto to have weakened the ending of his narrative by concluding the poem with the celebration of political, religious, and social values, all represented by the marriage of Ruggiero and Bradamante.

184. ———. "Ariosto, Lodovico." In *Colliers Encyclopedia*, 2:594–96. 24 vols. New York: Macmillan Educational Company; P. F. Collier, 1982.
Succinct biography of the poet and history of the composition of his works. Focuses on the *OF* and its narrative structure and notes that the theme of Orlando's madness is "the central story to which almost everything in the poem stands in some sort of qualifying relation" (p. 595). Concludes that the central themes of the poem are "deeply serious" (p. 595) although "the characteristic note of [the] poetry is a kind of brilliant gaiety" (p. 596). Includes brief bibliographical note.

185. CARRARA, ENRICO. *Studi petrarcheschi ed altri saggi, raccolti a cura di amici e discepoli*. Turin: Bottega d'Erasmo, 1959. 372p.
Includes "Dall'*Innamorato* al *Furioso* (Niccolò degli Agostini)"; "Alcune 'storie' del *Furioso*"; "La storia di Olimpia"; "La storia di Isabella." All previously published in his *I Due Orlandi*, 1934; Fatini, 3018.

186. CASELLA, ANGELA. Presentazione. In *Commedie*, Ludovico Ariosto, edited by Angela Casella, Gabriella Ronchi, and Elena Varasi, pp. ix–xlix. Milan: Mondadori, 1974. Vol. 4. *Tutte le opere*, Ludovico Ariosto, edited by Cesare Segre. Milan: Mondadori, 1964–.

Stating that the literary quality of Ariosto's comedies is modest and that his only intention in writing for the theater was to please a court audience, discusses each of the comedies and, in particular, their sources. Details Ariosto's borrowings from classical sources and from Boccaccio, as well as the reciprocal influences vis-à-vis his contemporaries, especially Bibbiena and Machiavelli. States that corruption is the dominant theme in Ariosto's theater and of particular importance to *La Lena*, noting, however, that the theme is intended to mirror a social reality and that moralizing is purely external and not "impegnato." Concludes with a discussion of the culinary theme in Ariosto, consonant with the essentially hedonistic world of his theater, considering also the importance and originality of Ariosto's use of Ferrara and its environs as the background of his plays.

◈ 187. CASELLA, ANGELA. "Le *Commedie* e i loro stampatori." See Ronchi, Gabriella, entry 702.

◈ 188. CASES, CESARE. "Le Prime traduzioni tedesche dell'*Orlando Furioso.*" In *Premio Città Monselice per una traduzione letteraria. Atti del Quinto Convegno sui problemi della traduzione letteraria: Le Prime traduzioni dell'Ariosto*, no. 6, pp. 89–106. Monselice: A Cura dell'Amministrazione Comunale, 1977.
Surveys the German translations of the *OF*, beginning with Diederich von dem Werder's unfinished version (1636), noting the generally negative reception of Ariosto among German writers.

◈ 189. CAVALCHINI, MARIELLA. "A Re-evaluation of the Italian Sources of *Much Ado About Nothing.*" *English Miscellany* 14 (1963): 45–56.
Brief discussion of the extent of Shakespeare's indebtedness to Ariosto's tale of Ginevra and Ariodante.

◈ 190. CERISOLA, PIER LUIGI. "Il problema critico dei *Cinque Canti.*" In *Studi sull'Ariosto*, presentazione di Enzo Noè Girardi, pp. 147–86. Milan: Vita e Pensiero (Pubblicazioni dell'Università Cattolica del Sacro Cuore), 1977.
Reviews critical fortune of Ariosto's *CC*, giving particular attention to the two major concerns of criticism to date: the poem's purpose or function and its date of composition. Concludes that available evidence makes it impossible to do more than hypothesize on the author's intentions in composing the work. Reviews three of the most authoritative discussions of the poem's dating (Cesare Segre, "Studi sui *Cinque Canti*," most recently in his *Esperienze ariostesche*, 1966 [entry 783]; Carlo Dionisotti, "Per la data dei *Cinque Canti*" [entry 264]; Luciano Capra, "Per la datazione dei *Cinque Canti* dell'Ariosto" [entry 166]), representing, respectively, linguistic, historico-

documentary, and literary approaches to establishing the period of composition. Final part of essay deals with critical judgments on the work's aesthetic merit, which have been made, explicity or implicitly, as a result of comparisons with the *OF*. Argues that such an approach is invalid because the *CC* results from the author having based the work on the minor cycle of Doon de Mayence, explaining the internal need for a pessimistic seriousness, which cannot be explained as a reflection of any one particularly unfortunate moment in the poet's life.

⏩ 191. CERRI, ANGELO. "L'Ariosto e la battaglia di Pavia." *Giornale storico della letteratura italiana* 152 (1975): 551–56.

Finds that Ariosto, in describing the battle of Pavia (*OF* 33.49–53), follows closely the historical chain of events and identifies the actual causes of the battle: Francis I having placed too much trust in his foreign captains, leading to the defeat of the French army and to the humiliating capture of its king.

⏩ 192. CERULLI, ENRICO. "L'*Orlando Furioso* nella storia culturale." In *Ludovico Ariosto*, pp. 11–21. Convegno internazionale (entry 475). Rome: Accademia Nazionale dei Lincei, 1975.

Discusses the sources of three episodes in the *OF* and, in a limited way, Ariosto's adaptations of the sources: the flight of the Hippogriff (based on the routes of Genoese merchants as documented on fourteenth-century maps found in the Este library); the episode of Isabella's suicide to preserve her chastity; the theme of the whale mistaken for an island, frequently used as symbolic of the deceitfulness of worldly pleasures. Notes that such episodes are couched in the courtly language of Ferrara, giving them more complex cultural dimensions.

⏩ 193. C[ESERANI], R[EMO]. "Annunzi." *Giornale storico della letteratura italiana* 141, fasc. 435 (1964): 469–70.

Notes the importance of Eugenio Garin's discovery of forty-two *Intercoenales* of Leon Battista Alberti ("Venticinque Intercenali inedite e sconosciute di Leon Battista Alberti," *Belfagor* 19 [1964]: 377–96). Suggests that the *intercenale* "Somnium" was an important source for the episode of Astolfo's visit to the Valley of the Moon (*OF* 34) and that it is particularly significant as it provides additional proof of the importance of the humanistic basis of the poem, "riportando sempre di più la concezione dell'opera, dal terreno medievale e cavalleresco, a quello culturale e storico del Rinascimento" (p. 470).

⏩ 194. ———. "Ariosto, Ludovico." In *Grande dizionario enciclopedico UTET*, 2:157–63. 3d ed. 20 vols. Turin: UTET, 1966.

General introduction to life and works of Ariosto, with focus on the *OF*, its sources and aesthetics. Includes short bibliography (pp. 162–63).

⛫ 195. ————. Introduzione. Nota biografica; nota bibliografica. In *Orlando furioso*, by Ludovico Ariosto, edited by Remo Ceserani, 1:9–32. 2 vols. Turin: UTET, 1969.
Notes that the history of Ariosto criticism has been an attempt to clarify the *diletto* that the author claimed to be his main purpose in writing the *OF* and points to De Sanctis and Croce as having more precisely defined *diletto* as "gioia di narrare" and "amore dell'armonia" (p. 10). States that the only true theme of the poem is, in fact, "la gioia stessa di sviluppare [narrative threads], il desiderio di trattarli tutti con uguale simpatia e distacco, con uguale affetto e indulgenza, con uguale serenità e disincantato senso della misura" (p. 10). Examines Ariosto as narrator, noting his constant but unobstrusive presence, his "compostezza" and "discrezione" (p. 12). Discusses the literary heritage informing the composition of the poem and Ariosto's genius in fusing the various threads of poetic tradition. Concludes by including Ariosto among the major artists of the high Renaissance who had in common the ability to express "la sottile vita di relazione che c'è fra le più diverse azioni e i più diversi personaggi" (p. 16).

⛫ 196. ————. "Studi ariosteschi, I: Dietro i ritratti di Ludovico Ariosto." *Giornale storico della letteratura italiana* 153 (1976): 243–95.
Reviews physical descriptions and biographical accounts of Ariosto, from immediately after his death to the present. Mentions various portraits of the poet that were included in early editions of the *OF*, particularly Titian's. Accepts the view that, notwithstanding alleged portraits in the London National Gallery, the John Herron Art Institute (Indianapolis), and the Biblioteca Comunale (Ferrara), all portraits have been lost. Suggests that most literary *ritratti*, such as De Sanctis's, Carducci's, and Michele Catalano's, are based largely on Virginio Ariosto's description of his father or on early biographers, such as Pigna. Notes that after World War II there was an attempt to revise the image of Ariosto the man, especially along the lines of the Marxist-existentialist views of Roberto Battaglia and Antonio Piromalli and with the aid of socio-historical studies of Renaissance Ferrara. Supports Caretti's assertion that Ariosto is a realist in the vein of Machiavelli (see entry 175), but has reservations about Giorgio Resta's psychoanalytical study (in *Rivista di psicoanalisi*, entry 681). Concludes by summarizing acceptable data "della realtà biografica ariostesca" (p. 286).

⛫ 197. CHAMBERLAIN, ROBERTA SIMONE. *"La Lena* by Ludovico Ariosto, Translated from the Italian, with an Introduction to the Comedies of

Ariosto." *DAI* 26, no. 5 (1965): 2724. (University of Illinois, 1965. 188p.)

General introduction to Ariosto's place in the evolution of Renaissance comic theater and to the composition of his plays. Provides first English translation of *La Lena*.

◄§ 198. CHASTEL, ANDRÉ. "Titien et les humanistes." In his *Fables, Formes, Figures,* 1:341–61. 2 vols. Paris: Flammarion, 1978.

Brief remarks on the importance of the relationship between Ariosto and Titian and its significance to Titian's development (pp. 357–59).

◄§ 199. CHENEY, DONALD. *Spenser's Image of Nature: Wild Man and Shepherd in "The Faerie Queene."* New Haven and London: Yale University Press, 1966. 262p.

Argues that Spenser found in the *OF* "a precedent for the ironic evaluation of the chivalric ethic" (p. 78). Analyzes instances of Spenser's use of Ariosto's perspective on and poetic representation of the ambiguous nature of the tradition of quest romance. Concludes: "Ultimately, Ariosto's chief contribution to the tradition of the chivalric romance lies in just this area of ironic ventilation of the conventional ideals, exposing their contradictory insistence on both love and honor stimultaneously. In the *Orlando Furioso* this contradiction becomes a pretext for comic situations, whereby the exalted capabilities of heroes, their supernatural strength, their enchanted weapons, their emotions larger than life, are associated with the undirected frenzies and blindness of romantic love, while the demands of the social order, the claims of a religious and military conflict and the dynastic destiny of Bradamante, are symbols of control and subordination to the larger pattern of things, of coming to one's senses. Where Pulci and Boiardo had emphasized the ribald gigantism or the ingenious variety of the old tales, with a certain amount of nostalgic admiration for the ideals which they embodied, Ariosto provides a far more thorough examination of their points of relevance to contemporary life and to the humbler motivations of everyday men. For him the chivalric milieu becomes a means of confronting the ideal with the actual; and in this respect it is impossible to disregard his influence when one is speaking of the 'Neoplatonism' of Spenser" (p. 88). See especially pp. 75–88.

◄§ 200. CHESNEY, ELIZABETH ANNE. "The Counter-Voyage of Rabelais and Ariosto: Myth, Madness, and Multiplicity." *DAI* 37, no. 6 (1976): 3668A. (Duke University, 1976. 242p.)

Considers the similar internal structures of the *OF* and *Pantagruel*, which share a "coincidence of themes and forms" putting into question the myths and commonly accepted truths of humanist tradition. Studies, for example, the motif of the voyage, "its signs and symbolism" in the two works, concluding that its various dimensions "question the true stature of Renaissance man." Notes in the final chapter that "madness is the most perfect expression of [their shared] antipodal world view," all figures of reason "juxtaposed with and infected by their mirror opposites." In their critical attitudes toward the humanistic world view, these works are representative of the heterogeneous tendencies of a critical period of change from the early to the late Renaissance.

Revision of thesis published with title *The Countervoyage of Rabelais and Ariosto: A Comparative Reading of Two Renaissance Mock Epics*. Durham: Duke University Press, 1982. 232p.

◆§ 201. ———. "The Theme of Folly in Rabelais and Ariosto." *The Journal of Medieval and Renaissance Studies* 7, no. 1 (1977): 67–93.

Discusses the Renaissance concept of madness, or *follia* and *folie*, as represented in both the *OF* and in Rabelais's Pantagrueline tales. Examines the literary representation of abnormality, senselessness, and derangement as in the use of the monster motif (said to externalize man's inner madness) or of thinking horses and animated objects, noting that both writers equate "the humanistic voyage with that of the ship of fools" (p. 74) and that they portray in their works "the rise and fall of men, civilizations and philosophies" (p. 75). Argues that the development of the madness motifs relates to a shared perception of the relativity of wisdom and folly as well as to the poet's realization that nothing is all. Suggests that in their treatment of folly both Rabelais and Ariosto open the doors to "relativism of values and establish a more authentic *modus vivendi*" (p. 93).

◆§ 202. CHEVALIER, MAXIME. *L'Arioste en Espagne (1530–1650): recherches sur l'influence du "Roland Furieux."* Bordeaux: Institut d'études iberiques et ibéro-américaines de l'Université de Bordeaux, 1966. 537p.

Lengthy study of Ariosto's influence on sixteenth- and seventeenth-century Spanish literature. Two parts. Part 1 surveys Italian criticism on Ariosto to 1584, comments on various Spanish translations of the *OF*, on its popularity in Spain, and on its critical interpretations, which tend to follow the moral and allegorical readings established by early Italian critics. Discusses Ariosto's strong influence on the Spanish epic, such as *La segunta parte de Orlando, Los famosos y heroycos hechos del Cid*, and *Carlo famoso*. Maintains that Ariosto's influence on the *romancero*, on the novel, and on the short story is rather slight. Labels the *Lyrae heroycae libri quatordecim* an *OF* "spiritualisé" (p. 214). Part 2 reviews both Italian and Spanish criticism of the *OF* from 1584 to 1640, noting that the Spanish, at first alarmed by Ariosto's lack of moral intent and "indécence" (p. 325), by the beginning of the seventeenth century showed appreciation of the poet's erudition and creative imagination. Observes that by the first quarter of the seventeenth century, Ariosto's influence on the Spanish erudite poem appears to decline, suggesting, for example, that Lope de Vega's *La Hermosura de Angélica* only slightly resembles the *OF* (p. 361). Adds that the *romancero*, the theater, and poetry use Ariosto's themes as pretexts and that the *DQ*, despite its many parallels with the *OF*, gives little evidence that Cervantes's work imitates Ariosto's (p. 457). Includes bibliography (pp. 499–523).

⤙§ 203. CHIAMPI, JAMES THOMAS. "Angelica's Flight and the Reduction of the Quest in the *Orlando Furioso*." *Canadian Journal of Italian Studies* 4, nos. 1–2 (1980–1981): 1–25.

States that in the *OF* knights never find the object of their desire because no created object can satisfy the promises of the imagination. Suggests that horses, helmets, and women, especially Angelica, are not mere objects of a quest but signs of a code that confers identity upon an errant knight. Notes that the Ariostean knights live in a world of signs and in constant "movement toward an ephemeral goal" (p. 23).

⤙§ 204. CHIAPPELLI, FREDI. "Sul linguaggio dell'Ariosto." In *Ludovico Ariosto*, pp. 33–48. Convegno internazionale (entry 475). Rome: Accademia Nazionale dei Lincei, 1975.

Through a detailed linguistic and structural analysis of *OF* 5.23 and the scene of Olimpia's abandonment (10.19–26), illustrates the significant changes that occurred in the definitive edition of the poem and that, through attentive syntactic and lexical study, will reveal the evolutionary process of Ariosto's poetry toward "la magnificazione interna dell'episodio [toward what happens *in* Angelica and Olimpia rather than *to* them], l'adozione di un gusto compositivo, la determinazione della catena narrativa in base a ragioni intrinsiche, le dimensioni interpretate del linguaggio" (p. 47).

⤙§ 205. CHIODAROLI, GIAN FRANCO. Introduzione. In *Orlando Furioso*, by Ludovico Ariosto, pp. 7–23. Novara: Istituto Geografico De Agostini, 1966.

Biography of poet and a summary account of the major narrative lines of the *OF*.

⤙§ 206. CHITTOLINA, ROBERTO. "Sulle rime dell'Ariosto. Problemi di attribuzione." *Studia Ghisleriana*, 2d ser., 3 (1967): 296–311.

Notes the lack of a reliable critical edition of Ariosto's lyric poetry, including Giuseppe Fatini's (Ludovico Ariosto, *Lirica*. Bari: Laterza, 1924); argues for the exclusion of several poems from those considered authentic by Fatini and for the inclusion of the *capitolo* "Lasso, come potrò chiuder in versi," which Fatini considered of dubious authorship. Concludes with a discussion of the autographed and hand-copied *capitolo* "Rime disposte a lamentarvi sempre," included in a collection of *fogli volanti* entitled *Alcune rime itali-ane di Mr. Lodovico Ariosto* in the Biblioteca Comunale of Ferrara and considered by Michele Catalano as falsely attributed to Ariosto. Argues for its authenticity through a comparative analysis of the calligraphy. Includes nine photographs of autograph manuscripts.

☙ 207. CIORANESCU, AL[EXANDRE]. *L'Arioste en France des origines à la fin du XVIIIe siècle.* 2 vols. Turin: Bottega d'Erasmo, 1970.
Reprint of 1939 edition (Paris: Les Presses Modernes); Fatini, 3233.

☙ 208. CITRONI MARCHETTI, SANDRA. "'Quid Romae faciam? Mentiri nescio . . .': il motivo giovenaliano del rifiuto delle arti indegne nella tradizione della satira regolare italiana e francese." *Rivista di letterature moderne e comparate* 33, no. 2 (1980): 85–121, and 34, no. 1 (1981): 5–36. Discussion of Ariosto in volume 33: 92–100.
Notes the importance of the Horatian model to Renaissance satire, particularly as an expression of personal ideals. Argues, however, that the Horatian ideal and the realities of court life inveighed against in most Renaissance satires are irreconcilable (in a satire "si può avvertire l'incrinatura fra il modello letterario e la realtà della propria vita," p. 85), resulting in the frequent incorporation of a fundamental Juvenalian theme: the indignant renunciation of corruption by the honest man who, maligned and sacrificed, leaves society. Attempts to show "come il modificarsi dell'equilibrio fra la concezione oraziana della satira e l'assunzione di questo atteggiamento di rifiuto giovenaliano possa implicare, nei singoli poeti, una diversa concezione della propria posizione di intellettuale nei rapporti coi grandi" (pp. 85–86) and how, from the sixteenth to the seventeenth century, the motif evolves from individual renunciation to become an instrument of social criticism. Analysis of Ariosto's first and third satires as models of the Horatian form with significant echoes of Juvenalian attitudes toward court corruption and social realities. Argues that whereas in the first satire there is an affirmation of the poet's personal and professional freedom, in the third "La personale esperienza conduce l'Ariosto verso una delusione, e la satira III è appunto la satira della delusione" (p. 99).

☙ 209. CLERKE, E[LLEN] M[ARY]. "Verse Letters of Ariosto." In her *Fable and Song in Italy*, pp. 153–69. London: Grant Richards, 1899. Reprint. Folcroft, Pa.: Folcroft Library Editions, 1974.
General discussion of the satires. Notes the importance of Horace as a model but argues that Ariosto's satires "are more truly letters than either the Satires or Epistles of Horace, inasmuch as they are more exclusively personal either to the writer or his correspondent" (p. 156). Briefly discusses the content of each satire and concludes, "Invaluable as a luminous exposition of

the inner workings of [Ariosto's] mind, they furnish also a vivid reflected image of the society in which he moved, and it is scarcely too much to say that we learn more about the Renaissance from these semi-jocular epistles than from any other single set of writings handed down to us" (p. 169).

᪾ 210. CLOUET, DOMINIQUE. "Empirisme ou égotisme: la politique dans la *Cassaria* et les *Suppositi* de l'Arioste." In *Les écrivains et le pouvoir en Italie à l'époque de la Renaissance* (Centre de Recherche sur la Renaissance Italienne), 2d ser., no. 3, pp. 7–44. Paris: Université de la Sorbonne Nouvelle, 1974.
   Describes cultural and historical circumstances surrounding the composition and original productions of the two plays, detailing such aspects as seating arrangements, attendance, scenic decor, and the interludes. Considers elements of contemporary Ferrarese life in the texts, identifying Crisobolo in *La Cassaria* with Alfonso I and underscoring the parallels between Erofilo's (*La Cassaria*) and Erostrato's (*I Suppositi*) revolts against their masters with the conspiracy of Don Giulio d'Este. Notes the encomiastic elements in the plays, including the praise of Alfonso I as the most perfect lord, the glorification of the Este military complex (through the theme of the hunt), and the parody of Ferrara's enemies. Argues, however, that a close scrutiny of the text reveals the apologia of the Este to be a veiled satirical attack on the financial and judicial institutions of the state, especially the burdensome taxation system and the plethora of official agents. Concludes that Ariosto's satire of the government was intended as an admonishment to the Este of the hidden menace arising from dissatisfied subjects. (See also entry 349, Dominique Gaudin-Clouet, "Le Théâtre de l'Arioste.")

᪾ 211. CLOUGH, CECIL H. "More Light on Pandolfo and Ludovico Ariosto." *Italica* 39, no. 3 (1962): 195–96.
   From a Latin note on a manuscript of Cicero's *Epistolae ad Familiares* concludes that Ludovico Ariosto's cousin, Pandolfo, was in the service of Ippolito d'Este before 1498 and that the poet's ode "Dum te prompte," addressed to Pandolfo, should be dated 1494, not 1499 as suggested by Ariosto's biographer, Michele Catalano. Argues in a later note ("A Further Note on Pandolfo and Ariosto," *Italica* 40, no. 2 [1963]: 167–69) that the d[ominus] *Pandolphus* mentioned in the manuscript note is Pandolfo Ariosto rather than Pandolfo Collenuccio as one might logically conclude.

᪾ 212. COLEMAN, ARTHUR. "*Orlando Furioso.*" In his *Epic and Romance Criticism: A Checklist of Interpretations*, 1940–1972, 2:266–69. 2 vols. New York: Watermill Publishers, 1973–1974.
   Checklist of interpretations between 1940 and 1973 of classical and continental epics and metrical romances (volume 2). Seventy entries of compar-

ative studies on the *OF*, including monographs, articles, and dissertations. Incomplete and inaccurate bibliographical information.

〜§ 213. COLUCCIA, GIUSEPPE. "Intorno al 'Valerio' ariostesco del *Furioso.*" *Quaderno n.* 1 *(1980)*, pp. 51–73. Istituto di Lingua e Letteratura Italiana. Facoltà di Magistero. Università degli Studi, Lecce. Lecce: Adriatica Ed. Salentina, 1980.
Unavailable. Cited in *Italianistica* 11, no. 1 (1982): 140 and in *Studi e problemi di critica testuale* 23 (1981): 289, with the notice that the author identifies with documentary evidence the Gian Francesco Valerio referred to in OF 27.137, 28.78, and 46.16 [textual references ours], stating that he was a noble Venetian, a man of letters, and an illegitimate son of Carlo Valier. Publishes the text of one of Valerio's odes, contained in ms. 828 (1250) of the Biblioteca Universitaria of Bologna (cc. 53r–54v).

〜§ 214. CONTINI, GIANFRANCO. "Come lavorava l'Ariosto." In his *Esercizî di lettura sopra autori contemporanei con un'appendice su testi non contemporanei*, pp. 232–42. Rev. ed. Turin: Einaudi, 1974.
Article first appeared in *Meridiano*, 18 July 1937, then in first edition of this volume (Florence: Parenti, 1939); Fatini, 3179.

〜§ 215. COPPINI, GIUSEPPE. "La Produzione drammatica dell'Ariosto nella sua storia." *Gazzetta di Reggio* 8, no. 98 (1958).
Brief history of the origins and first performances of Ariosto's comedies. Unavilable; cited without page reference in Medici, 22.

〜§ 216. CORDIÉ, CARLO. "Le Imitazioni ariostee nella *Franciade.*" In his *Saggi e studi di letteratura francese*, pp. 19–23. Padua: Cedam-Casa Editrice Dott. Antonio Milani, 1957. [Noted as written in 1931].
Notes that Ronsard "si rifacesse alle grandi opere degli antichi attraverso le vedute dei maggiori moderni—in questo caso, dell'Ariosto—nella trattazione di alcuni motivi cavallereschi" (p. 22) and that he was significantly indebted to Ariosto for his epic material.

〜§ 217. ———. "Il Boiardo nella critica della Staël, del Ginguené e del Sismondi (1800–1813)." In *Il Boiardo e la critica contemporanea*, edited by Giuseppe Anceschi, pp. 157–69. Atti del Convegno di Studi su Matteo Maria Boiardo. Scandiano-Reggio Emilia, 25–27 aprile 1969. Biblioteca dell'*Archivum Romanicum*, 1st ser., vol. 107. Florence: Leo S. Olschki, 1970.
Occasional comparisons between Ariosto and Boiardo in the critical evaluations of several early nineteenth-century French critics.

218. ———. "L'Ariosto nella critica della Staël, del Ginguené e del Sismondi (1800–1813)." In *Per l'Ariosto* (entry 623). Special 1976 issue of *Italianistica* 3, no. 3 (1974): 172–88.

Discusses the positive critical views of the three French writers and suggests that their perspectives on Ariosto were important for future critics, especially for Francesco De Sanctis, who highly valued their critical judgments.

219. CORGNALI, G. B. "Un testo friulano del Cinquecento. Il travestimento del Iº canto dell'Ariosto secondo un codice vaticano." In *Ce fastu?* (Rivista della Società Filologica Friulana), anno 41–43, nos. 1–6 (1965–1967): 71–94.

Transcription of ms. Biblio. Vaticana, Vat. lat. 13711, cc. 1–14, an anonymous sixteenth-century Friulian version of *OF* 1. Vatican manuscript one of two extant apographs, or copies from the original, which is unknown.

220. CORNACCHIA, G. ANTONIO. Introduction. In *Orlando Furioso*, by Ludovico Ariosto, pp. 7–25. Rocca San Casciano: F. Cappelli, 1962.

Cautions against any attempt to determine the character of Ariosto on the basis of the autobiographical elements of his writings, which tend to portray "la vita grigia d'un povero uomo," whereas his was, in fact, a life "intensa di sentimenti e di affetti, di atteggiamenti coraggiosi e di coerenza interiore" (p. 8). Evaluates the "personalità interiore" (p. 10) of the poet, for which the letters of the Garfagnana period are particularly rich documents; concludes that his was a strong character with a profound sense of the realities of life. Considers the stylistic "tono medio" as a poetic manifestation of Ariosto's own psychological equilibrium. Discusses the Ariostean perspective in the *OF* as a detached but sensitive view of the complexities and vicissitudes of life and of a chivalric world no longer a reality. Considers the inseparability of fantasy and reality in the *OF*. Notes the limitations but importance of the critical perspectives on Ariosto formulated by Croce, Luigi Ambrosini (in *Teocrito, Ariosto, minori e minimi*, 1926), and Momigliano, all of whom provided the basis for later critical evaluations. Comments on the aesthetics of the *OF*, focusing on a harmonious equilibrium as the dominant mood, served by the poet's use of irony to undermine anything that threatens the "ritmo ineffabile di un mondo armonico" (p. 24).

221. CORRIGAN, BEATRICE. "The Opposing Mirrors." *Italica* 33, no. 1 (1956): 165–79.

In discussing the symbolism of mirrors in the *GL*, notes that the episode of Rinaldo and Armida (cantos 14–18) as well as that of Ruggiero and Alcina in *OF* 7 are modelled after classical sources, Statius's *Achilleis*, for example. Observes that Ruggiero's adventures are drawn from those of several classical and medieval heroes, whereas Tasso draws mainly from Homer and Statius for Rinaldo.

222. ———. Introduction to *Il Negromante*. In *Two Renaissance Plays*, edited by Beatrice Corrigan, pp. 1–8. Manchester: Manchester University Press, 1975.

Basic introduction for the English reader to Ariosto's life, times, and theater, focusing on the plot, the characters, and the stylistic and thematic novelty of *Il Negromante*. Notes to the text (pp. 152–61) and a selected vocabulary (pp. 171–84) included.

223. CORRIGAN, BEATRICE M., AND BONNER MITCHELL. "Italian Literature." In *The Present State of Scholarship in Sixteenth-Century Literature*, edited by William M. Jones, pp. 1–43. Columbia and London: University of Missouri Press, 1978.

Briefly notes several important studies on Ariosto, with particular mention (pp. 24–25) given to Robert M. Durling, *The Figure of the Poet in Renaissance Epic* (1965, entry 288); includes selected bibliography of studies on sixteenth-century Italian literature (pp. 30–43).

224. CORSARO, ANTONIO. "'In questo rincrescevol labirinto': le satire garfagnine di Ludovico Ariosto." *Filologia e critica* 4, nos. 2–3 (1979): 188–211.

Analysis of the so-called "Garfagnana satires," addressed to Sigismondo Malaguzzi, Bonaventura Pistofilo, and Pietro Bembo. Argues that in the satires of the period of Ariosto's assignment in the Garfagnana, the "concitato incalzante attacco diretto ad uomini e istituzioni [of the earlier satires] cede progressivamente il posto a una forma di critica sociale solitaria e inappellabile, schiva del confronto e della dialettica polemica" (p. 190). Traces the poet's perspective on a reality that seems entirely out of rational control in the fourth satire toward the play in the sixth satire on present and past as grim reality versus an unattainable ideal morality, concluding that the "originalità [of the sixth satire] è . . . nell'indistinta coscienza del venire meno dei valori unitari su cui si fondava la precaria costruzione del Rinascimento italiano" (p. 206).

225. ———. "Sulla satira quinta dell'Ariosto." *Italianistica* 9, no. 3 (1980): 466–77.

Argues against a biographical reading of the satire on matrimony, stating that all historical allusions are merely cultural references in the poet's discourse. Suggests that the theme of man's attitude toward and behavior with women is actually a paradigm of the poet's preoccupations regarding the individual's difficulty in discovering reality and adapting to it. Shows that Ariosto in his arguments and especially in his utilitarian view of marriage draws from Leon Battista Alberti's *I Tre libri della famiglia*. Concludes that Ariosto is fully aware that his views run contrary to the platonic ideals of the time detailed in works such as Castiglione's *Book of the Courtier* and Bembo's *Gli Asolani*.

226. CORSE, LARRY BAILEY. "'A Straunge Kinde of Harmony': The Influence of Lyric Poetry and Music on Prosodic Techniques in the Spenserian Stanza." *DAI* 33, no. 8 (1973): 4404–4405A. (North Texas State University, 1972. 217p.)
In discussing the precedents for Spenser's prosody, focuses on "musical associations of the *Orlando Furioso*, particularly its relations to the tradition of singing narrative poetry to folk melodies."

227. COSTA, GUSTAVO. "Antonio Tebaldeo e Ludovico Ariosto." In his *La Leggenda dei secoli d'oro nella letteratura italiana*, pp. 84–89. Bari: Laterza, 1972.
Notes that the theme of the *Saturnia regna* or the return of the Golden Age pervades Ariosto's works and indicates its presence in the Latin poetry, the sonnets, and especially in *OF* 3.18 and 6.21.

228. COSTANZO, LUIGI. *Ariosto contro Boiardo. Pazzia pagana e pazzia cristiana*. Naples: Federico & Ardia, 1967. 53p.
Written in 1938. Observations on the nature of love, wisdom, and madness in the *OI* and in the *OF*.

229. COTTONE, G. "Donne dell'Ariosto e del Tasso." *Selva* (Turin) 2 (1957): 18–19.
Unavailable; cited in Alessandro Tortoreto, "Ariosto e Tasso: saggio bibliografico (1957–1974)," *Studi tassiani* 24, nos. 1–2 (1974): 71–78, entry 5.

230. CRAIG, CYNTHIA C. "Folly in the *Orlando Furioso*: The Technique of Thematic and Stylistic Build-Up." *Carte italiane: A Journal of Italian Studies* (edited by graduate students, UCLA) 1 (1979–1980): 23–35.
Notes that the opening two verses of the *OF* announce by theme the several underlying structures that anticipate and parallel Orlando's loss of self, or insanity, and his rehabilitation. Briefly discusses each of these structures, illustrating how they serve to build toward the poem's climax, both thematically and semantically, to underscore, for example, the "passage from evil toward good" (p. 27), or to show the impermanence of human achievement. Focuses on the emblematic significance of Astolfo, who regains his wits only to lose them again, and of Rinaldo, whose acceptance of his own limitations

and reestablishment of the value of faith are corollaries to and illuminate the situation of the protagonist, Orlando.

~§ 231. CREMANTE, RENZO. "La memoria della *Commedia* nel-*l'Innamorato* e nella tradizione cavalleresca." In *Il Boiardo e la critica contemporanea*, edited by Giuseppe Anceschi, pp. 171–95. Atti del Convegno di Studi su Matteo Maria Boiardo. Scandiano-Reggio Emilia, 25–27 aprile 1969. Biblioteca dell'*Archivum Romanicum*, 1st ser., vol. 107. Florence: Leo S. Olschki, 1970.

Considers the extent and ways in which the language of the Italian romance tradition was influenced by the *DC*. Notes in particular and as an introduction to a discussion of the *OI* Ariosto's independence from his romance predecessors in adapting Dantesque motifs. Elaborating on earlier observations of Cesare Segre (see entry 781), cites the degree to which Dante's poem affected the "livelli espressivi, l'ambito della tecnica poetica" (p. 181) of the *OF*, as, for example, in Ariosto's favoring of the "rima composta" and in the frequency of "rime aspre e difficili" (p. 182).

~§ 232. ———. Review of *Lodovico Ariosto: il suo tempo la sua terra la sua gente* (1974). In *Studi e problemi di critica testuale* 18 (1979): 229–44.

Review essay with an appended 170-item bibliography (pp. 237–44) of Ariosto criticism (1957–1973) supplementing that of Domenico Medici, "La bibliografia della critica ariostesca dal 'Fatini' ad oggi (1957–1974)," in *Lodovico Ariosto: il suo tempo la sua terra la sua gente* (1974, entry 507). Includes significant reviews; not annotated.

~§ 233. CROCE, BENEDETTO. *Ariosto, Shakespeare e Corneille*. Bari: Laterza, 1968. 263p.

First edition 1920; Fatini, 2143. English translation: *Ariosto, Shakespeare and Corneille*, translated by Douglas Ainslie. New York: Russell and Russell, 1966. 440p.

~§ 234. CROCIONI, GIOVANNI. *Le tradizioni popolari nella letteratura italiana*, edited by Giuseppe Anceschi, pp. 314–25. Florence: Leo S. Olschki, 1970.

These pages first published with title "Le tradizioni popolari nell'*Orlando Furioso*," in *Nuove lettere emiliane*, nos. 9–11 (1965): 47–50.

States that there are relatively few allusions in the *OF* to popular customs, although the poet made frequent use of proverbs and tales, the latter most usually drawn from literary and classical sources. Notes that magic is the most frequently used aspect of popular culture and discusses as a possible source for the character of Gabrina a homonymous historical figure tried and condemned in Reggio in 1375.

❧ 235. CUCCARO, VINCENT. "The Humanism of Ludovico Ariosto (From the *Satire* to the *Orlando Furioso*)." *ADD* 1975–1976: 305. (Harvard University, 1976.)

Not abstracted. Published as *The Humanism of Ludovico Ariosto: From the "Satire" to the "Furioso."* Ravenna: Longo, 1981. 244p.

Dissertation published in 1981 broadly defines Renaissance humanism and proceeds to discuss Ariosto's satires, noting that they are a valuable source for a critical interpretation of the OF and that their artistic, literary, philosophical, spiritual, and religious elements reveal the essence of Ariosto's humanism (p. 73). Second half of study is a humanistic reading of the OF, beginning with a brief survey of past and present critical evaluations of the poem and then examining major themes reflecting humanistic values and ideals. Notes that the poet incorporates into the narration of normal human activity the traditionally antithetical forces of Christianity and paganism; that he measures his characters by the presence of reason and madness in their behavior. Discusses the technique of imitation, as revealed by the Astolfo episode, and the relationship between form and content. Includes bibliography (pp. 239–44).

❧ 236. DALLA PALMA, GIUSEPPE. "Una cifra per la pazzia d'Orlando." *Strumenti critici* 9, no. 3 (1975): 367–79.

Proppian-morphological and psychoanalytic analysis of OF 29.50–74 and 30.1–15. Argues that Orlando's revenge after his discovery of Angelica's betrayal is represented with an equestrian image (29.67.5–8 and 29.69.1–2), anticipated by the association Angelica-mare in preceding cantos; that the verses serve as an "image-bridge" ("immagine-ponte," p. 372) to relate Orlando's fury to other heroes of the poem; and that the image is fundamental to the lexical elements of the several phases of Orlando's madness. Discusses the implications of the equestrian-oriented lexical elements of the episode to a reading of it in the context of the poem.

❧ 237. ⸻. "Dal Secondo al terzo *Furioso*: mutamenti di struttura e moventi ideologici." In *Ludovico Ariosto: lingua, stile e tradizione*, edited by Cesare Segre (entry 789), pp. 95–105. Milan: Feltrinelli, 1976.

Analyzes the structural processes by which Ariosto incorporated into the third edition of the OF new episodes, or "diversioni," and elaborative material, taking as examples of the former the episodes of Olimpia and Marganorre and of the latter the narrative complexities involving Ruggiero and Leone in the final cantos. Identifies two principal means of grafting on new elements: "syntagmatic," whereby the episode becomes integral to the sphere of action of a Christian hero, whose quest for an elusive object is reflected in the plight of a character whom he aids; "paradigmatic," in which the Christian hero intervenes as a means of righting wrongs and reestablishing order. Concludes that additions in the third edition compose a stance against values represented by authority and underscore the mitigating influences of valor and courtesy.

◆§ 238. ———. "Tra *fabula* e intreccio: il legame diversione-segmento nell'*Orlando Furioso*." *Strumenti critici* 13, nos. 2–3 (1979): 406–27.

Proposes a reading of the OF based on the distinction between *fabula* and plot. Groups actions or functions into a fundamental sequence of the hero's assumption of a quest, the quest itself, and the final outcome of the quest, noting that in most cases the sequence is interrupted by "diversioni," or narrative diversions, which may relate to the hero's *fabula* paradigmatically ("diversioni pure," p. 413), syntagmatically ("diversioni miste," p. 413), or both. Suggests that these diversions serve as a "pausa riflessiva" (p. 412) in the functional sequences and are, at the same time, indispensable to both the characterization and the organic construction of the the hero's *fabula*. Proceeds to show that such organic construction can also be observed at the level of plot.

◆§ 239. DALLA VALLE, DANIELA. "Dal Rinascimento al Barocco: un tema ariostesco fonte d'ispirazione per Tristan l'Hermite." *Studi francesci* 25, anno 9, fasc. 1 (1965): 96–100.

Notes that Alexandre Cioranescu's two-volume work on Ariosto in France (*L'Arioste en France des origines à la fin du XVIIIe siècle*, 1939) fails to define the attitude of the French Baroque toward Ariosto. Considers letter 60 of Tristan l'Hermite's *Lettres meslées* (Paris: A. Courbé, 1642, pp. 337–42), which was inspired by the Gabrina and Filandro episode of OF21 and which underscores the baroque interest in the opposition between being and seeming, a theme present in the Italian source and among the most important in seventeenth-century French literature.

◆§ 240. DAL MONTE, MARIA TERESA. *Ariosto in Germania con 'Ariosto e la poesia romantica' di Herbert Frenzel*. Quaderni dell'Istituto di Filologia Germanica 2. Imola: Galeati, 1971. 231p.

Discusses the ambivalent attitude toward Ariosto in Germany, where he has been variously read as both complementary to and alien to the Germanic spirit. Traces the critical reception of Ariosto in Germany from the Reformation and Diederich von dem Werder's important translation of the OF (1632–1636) to the critical perspectives of the neoclassical and romantic periods. Final chapter (pp. 89–124) on nineteenth-century artistic interpretations of the OF, including Julius Schnorr von Carolsfeld's frescoes in Villa

Massimi, Rome. Second part of volume (pp. 145–231) is an Italian translation of Herbert Frenzel's *Ariost und die romantische Dichtung* (1962).

◄§ 241. DAVICO BONINO, GUIDO. "Lo scandalo della *Lena*." In his *Letteratura e teatro. Nove studi, 1966–78*, pp. 3–14. Turin: Tirrenia-Stampatori, 1979.
Earlier versions of essay appeared as "Ariosto uomo di teatro," *Terzoprogramma*, nos. 2–3 (1974): 33–41; as introduction to *La Lena*, edited by Guido Davico Bonino (Turin: Einaudi, 1976), pp. v–xv; and as part of introduction to *Il Teatro italiano*, vol. 2, part 1: *La Commedia del Cinquecento* (Turin: Einaudi, 1977), pp. vii–lxxv, especially pp. viii–xxiv.
An overview of the innovative aspects of Ariosto's theater, which was intended by the author to portray contemporary reality, not by dismissing the classical comic tradition of Plautine and Terentian forms, but by putting imitation in the service of modernity. Traces evolution of theatrical forms from 1507 to 1532, noting the growing sophistication and verisimilitude of characters, the growing maturation of his style with *Il Negromante* (especially in its vision of contemporary society and in its style), and the full maturation of his dramatic art in *La Lena*, in which the city of Ferrara becomes the protagonist and the play represents a world antithetic in its meanness and moral texture to that of its courtly audience.

◄§ 242. DEAN, JOHN. *Restless Wanderers: Shakespeare and the Pattern of Romance*. Salzburg Studies in English Literature. Salzburg: Institut für Anglistik und Amerikanistik, 1979. 360p.
Discussion of romance conventions in classical epic, in Malory, and in the *OF* and their importance for Shakespeare. Cites Ariosto's considerable importance to Elizabethan writers and provides a systematic analysis of romance conventions in the *OF*. Discusses the convention of the female warrior, noting, "For the age of Elizabeth the literary ideals personified by Ariosto's warrior-heroines would have taken on the relevancy of daily politics" (p. 70). Considers Ariosto's double use of recreation, i.e., he "makes a great effort to create an enjoyable story, and, at the same time, the enjoyment is created by invigorating old tales with fresh feelings, by *re*creating, by going over again the pleasurable account of the Charlemagne legends and the struggles of Christianity against the [pagans]" (p. 71). Notes the importance of the expansive time scheme in the *OF* and Ariosto's intent to "capture all aspects of time" (p. 73); notes also the expansiveness of Ariosto's geography and the techniques used to unify the poem's geographical vastness, including "the world-wide value of chivalry" (p. 74). Shows that Ariosto underscores the tradition of narrative disorder when treating the love motif. Argues that unity for the poem's variety is provided through narrative tempo and constant points of reference. Notes Ariosto's analogies for his narrative method, in-

cluding weaving, making instrumental music, and sorcery (p. 81). Argues that Ariosto's method of intertwining moments of the narrative for organization "also serve[s] individually to comment on the nature of human indeterminancy" (p. 82). Concludes with a consideration of the role of the narrator-poet: "The narrator, or authorial figure, provides another form of control over the romance multiverse which the narrator administrates. Since he can bring virtually anything into the narrative, he brings in a bit of himself. This serves as a necessary corrective to meandering tendencies and heightens the mysterious element in the story, heightens mystery without forfeiting narrative control" (pp. 85–86). See especially pp. 68–86.

243. DEBENEDETTI, SANTORRE. *Orlando Furioso*. See Ariosto, Ludovico, entry 25.

244. DE BLASI, GIORGIO. "Problemi critici del Rinascimento." In *Letteratura italiana: le correnti*, 1:202–416. 2 vols. Milan: Marzorati, 1969.
First edition 1956; Fatini, 3604. See especially pp. 283–87.

245. DEDEYAN, CHARLES. "L'Arioste en France au XIXᵉ siècle." In *Notiziario culturale italiano* (entry 573) 15, no. 3 (1974): 49–58.
Overview of the critical fortunes of Ariosto in nineteenth-century France. Notes that in the early part of the century focus was on Ariosto's imagination or fantasy in the *OF*; that Madame de Staël found in Ariosto a lack of true feeling, a "légèreté du sentiment" (p. 52) and that Simonde de Sismondi recognized the significance of the surrealistic in Ariosto but faulted him for a lack of psychological verisimilitude. Remarks on the appreciation of Stendhal, Lamartine (for whom Ariosto represents "un équilibre extraordinaire," p. 56), Victor Hugo, and the particular contribution of Henri Hauvette.

246. ———. "La fortune de l'Arioste en France du XIXᵉ siècle à nos jours." In *Ludovico Ariosto*, pp. 423–87. Convegno internazionale (entry 475). Rome: Accademia Nazionale dei Lincei, 1975.
Briefly reviews the fortune of Ariosto from the seventeenth century through the eighteenth and discusses more fully the reception of Ariosto by or his influence on the following: Delille, Ginguené, Madame de Staël, Sismondi, Chateaubriand, Lamartine, Hugo, Sainte-Beuve, and De Vigny. For the postromantic period, discusses the importance of Ariosto to Gautier, Nerval, and Baudelaire. Notes a variety of nineteenth-century translations and dramatic adaptations of the *OF*. Concludes with a review of the critical reception of Ariosto to the present.

✍ 247. DEGANI, MARIO. "La necropoli di Reggio nei luoghi ariosteschi." In *Lodovico Ariosto: il suo tempo la sua terra la sua gente* (entry 468). Estratto dal *Bollettino storico reggiano* 7, no. 25 (1974): 61–67.

Discusses the extant Roman sepulchral monuments of *Regium Lepidi* (Reggio Emilia) and conjectures on the extent of Ariosto's familiarity with them. Incluldes fifteen photographs and archeological descriptions as well as a map of the Roman necropolis of S. Maurizio in Reggio Emilia.

✍ 248. DE LA FUENTE, PATRICIA ANN. "Mock-Heroic Narrative Techniques in Ariosto and Cervantes." *DAI* 38 no. 5 (1977): 2758A. (University of Texas, 1976. 273p.)

Explores the several narrative techniques by which Ariosto and Cervantes focus on "the simultaneous presence of opposite or conflicting values" in the titular heroes of the *OF* and the *DQ*. Argues that the writers have a similar comic perspective on their heroes and analyzes the artistic components of their comic vision: for example, the discrepancy between ideal heroic action and actual behavior, and the subversion of established codes of chivalry.

✍ 249. DEL BECCARO, FELICE. "Il Cinquecento: Ludovico Ariosto." In his *Guida allo studio della letteratura italiana*, pp. 73–78. Milan: Mursia, 1975.

Brief survey of Ariosto criticism, focusing on the post-Crocean period.

✍ 250. DELCORNO, CARLO. "La tradizione dell'"exemplum' nell'*Orlando Furioso*." *Giornale storico della letteratura italiana* 149, fasc. 468 (1972): 550–64.

Points out that in the *OF*, *esempio* and *istoria*, terms that throughout the Cinquecento had moral connotations, are never purely gratuitous but reflect a moral or psychological situation. Admitting that the exact source of Ariosto's *exempla* is often difficult to identify, as both the classical and medieval traditions became intertwined in the early chivalric genre, finds that selected "esempi," e.g., the stories of Adorno and Anselmo (*OF* 43), reveal strong similarities with *exempla* found in religious writings such as the *Vitae Patrum*, *Liber Miraculis*, and *Speculum Exemplorum*.

✍ 251. DELCORNO BRANCA, DANIELA. *L'"Orlando Furioso" e il romanzo cavalleresco medievale*. Florence: Olschki, 1973. 109p.

Analysis of the *OF* through a study of *entrelacement*, or the narrative technique of interlace. Divided into three parts: "Tradizione e innovazione dei procedimenti narrativi" (pp. 13–56) surveys the use of *entrelacement* in the tradition of chivalric romance, noting Ariosto's innovations in the use of the technique; "Il tema delle armi come fattore di 'entrelacement'" (pp. 57–79) illustrates how episodes in which weapons are the object of a quest or the cause of encounters between contending paladins are unified through *entrelacement* into a single theme that serves as a guiding narrative element ("elemento guida," p. 74) in a reading of the poem; "Armi incantate e cavalleria" (pp. 81–103) argues that enchanted weapons do not guarantee victory as in romance tradition but instead serve as a sign of a paladin's destiny. Concludes that the theme of enchanted weapons, unified through *entrelacement*, reveals Ariosto's opposition to techniques of modern warfare (p. 103).

◆§ 252. ————. "L'Ariosto e la tradizione del romanzo medievale." In *Ludovico Ariosto*, pp. 93–102. Convegno internazionale (entry 475). Rome: Accademia Nazionale dei Lincei, 1975.

Considers a variety of ways in which Ariosto employs elements of the romance tradition, noting a convergence of the figures of the crazed Orlando and the mad Tristan of the Tuscan romance, the *Tavola Rotonda*. States, however, that the narrative mechanics of the fifteenth-century romance tradition are abandoned by Ariosto—due, perhaps, to their overly popular nature (p. 96)—in favor of the more refined techniques of earlier medieval narratives, especially *entrelacement* or interlace. Discusses the use of the arms motif as a connecting device, illustrating its function in the *OI* and its more unified and structurally meaningful use in the *OF* (p. 99). Notes the importance of considering the relationship of the *OF* with the structural devices of the romance genre for understanding the process of allusion, correspondence, and opposition in the narrative threads of the poem.

◆§ 253. DE LISIO, PASQUALE ALBERTO. "Il centenario ariostesco e i *Cinque canti* (note sul *Furioso* e 'dintorni')." *Misure critiche* (Naples) 5, nos. 14–15 (1975): 103–10.

Brief review of Ariosto criticism during the period of the fifth centenary of the poet's birth. Notes in particular the importance of studies on the *CC* for providing a perspective on Ariosto's poetics and for a reading of the *OF*. Identifies the directions of critical perspectives on Ariosto during the late 1960s and early 1970s, especially toward the "immagine di un [Ariosto] più disincantato, con quella sua realistica *Weltanschauung*" (p. 104) and an analysis of the structural elements of the *OF*, for which the studies of Eduardo Saccone and Nino Borsellino are particularly significant. Concludes with a brief discussion of divergent views on the significance of the *CC* and notes the importance of Lanfranco Caretti's views (in *Cinque canti*. Venice: Corbo & Fiore, 1974) on the *CC* for an understanding of the evolution of the *OF*.

◆§ 254. DELLA CASA, ADRIANA. "Tre note ai carmina dell'Ariosto (cc. XII e XVII; VI 20)." In *Studi di letteratura italiana in onore di Fausto Montanari*, pp. 91–96. Genoa: Il Melangolo, 1980.

Notes the lack of a critical edition of Ariosto's Latin lyrics and the problems attendant upon the preparation of one. Focuses on classical reminiscences in the Latin poetry, observing that Ariosto had read and imitated a limited number of Latin poets and preferred Tibullus and Horace "perchè li sentiva sentimentalmente vicini per l'aspirazione alla pace e per l'amore della campagna" (pp. 91–92). Considers classical sources in two poems, "De Nicolao Areosto" and "De Megilla," and concludes that "in queste poesie latine la reminiscenza classica [si nasconde] abilmente più che in precedenti Umanisti . . . : essa è affidata a volte a *iuncturae*, ma anche a singoli termini, a movimenti sintattici che soltanto un classicista di ampie letture può cogliere; e, d'altra parte, se l'Ariosto non è un grande poeta latino, è però più originale di tanti Umanisti nel combinare nuove espressioni con termini attinti a testi diversi di autori classici, poeti e prosatori" (p. 94). Concludes with hypothesizing a correct reading of verse 20 of the *carme*, "Audiet a viridi Dryadum lasciva rubeto."

⋙ 255. De Luca, Antonio. "I prologhi delle commedie ariostesche." In *Ludovico Ariosto*, pp. 577–89. Convegno internazionale (entry 475). Rome: Accademia Nazionale dei Lincei, 1975.
Also in his *Il Teatro di Ludovico Ariosto* (Rome: Bulzoni, 1981), pp. 30–46.
Analyzes the prologues of the comedies as functional components of the dramatic text. Notes that in the first version of *La Cassaria*, the prologue is most programmatic in articulating the rapport between the text ("espressione letteraria," p. 577) and the reality it represents and that Ariosto's maturation as a dramatist is accompanied by an increasingly sophisticated use of the prologue as a transitional space between the audience, reality, and the illusory reality of the stage.

⋙ 256. ———. "La prima redazione della *Cassaria*." *La Rassegna della letteratura italiana*, 7th ser., vol. 79, nos. 1–2 (1975): 215–31.
Also in his *Il Teatro di Ludovico Ariosto* (Rome: Bulzoni, 1981), pp. 47–69.
Through an analysis of the first version of *La Cassaria*, identifies the stylistic and structural elements that indicate "l'avvio di una poetica teatrale" and the creation of a theater that translates chronicle into *fabula*, or contemporary reality into dramatic form (pp. 231, n. 48). Particular attention given to Ariosto's technique in bringing innovation and the burgher world of his time into the weave of traditional, classical forms (pp. 216, 218).

⋙ 257. De Palacio, Jean. "William Godwin, Ariosto, and the Grand Tour; or *Caleb Williams* Reconsidered." *Rivista di letterature moderne e comparate* 23, no. 2 (1970): 111–20.

Considers the importance of Godwin's reading of Italian narrative poetry and of the OF in particular to the writing of Caleb Williams (1794), in which madness and chivalry are leitmotifs and whose hero, Falkland, returns from an Italian journey to become a "Furioso," a "knight run wild as Orlando . . . under the baleful effect of an all-engrossing passion, which in his case is not love . . . but honour" (p. 119).

258. DE RIENZO, GIORGIO. See Getto, Giovanni, Roberto Alonge, Guido Baldi, and Giorgio De Rienzo, *Storia della letteratura italiana*, entry 351.

259. DE RIQUER, MARTIN. "Ariosto y España." In *Ludovico Ariosto*, pp. 319–29. Convegno internazionale (entry 475). Rome: Accademia Nazionale dei Lincei, 1975.
Notes the probable influence on Ariosto of the Catalan romance, *Tirant lo Blanch*, introduced to the poet by Isabella d'Este. Discusses the extensive influence of the OF in Spain, especially after the publication of three important sixteenth-century translations, and attributes its popularity both to Ariosto's art and to his having revived a chivalric tradition long part of the Spanish heritage. Considers the influence of the OF on Spanish Renaissance comedies and especially on Cervantes and the DQ. Discusses the significant difference in the nature of the madness of Orlando and that of Don Quixote.

260. DE ROBERTIS, GIUSEPPE. *Studi II.* Florence: Le Monnier, 1971. 352p.
Includes reprints of the following articles: "Idea dell'*Orlando*," pp. 11–18 (Fatini, 3423); "Lettura sintomatica del primo dell'*Orlando*," pp. 19–25 (Fatini, 3448); "L'Armonia dell'Ariosto," pp. 26–31 (Fatini, 3544).

261. DEVOTO, GIACOMO. *Nuovi studi di stilistica.* Florence: Le Monnier, 1962. 245p.
Notes importance for Italian linguistic history of Ariosto's corrections in the successive editions of the OF: "Le tre tappe percorse dall'Ariosto, nelle edizioni dell'*Orlando furioso* . . . documentano le ultime incertezze di un processo, così individuale come collettivo, ormai vicino alla conclusione. Questa consiste nella unificazione linguistica italiana" (p. 144). Notes that Ariosto tends to purify the text of Lombardisms and Latinisms in favor of Tuscanisms (pp. 144–46).

262. "L'Arioste (L')–Ariosto (Ludovico)." In *Dictionnaire des littératures*, directed by Philippe van Tieghem, 1: 215–17. 3 vols. Paris: Presses Universitaires de France, 1968.
Basic factual account of Ariosto's life and brief notes on all of his works.

Observes that the *OF* is unique for the "liberté souveraine avec laquelle le poète enchaîne les événements, change le ton, domine ses personnages sans jamais les asservir; rien de moins classique, au fond, que cette image si juste de l'humanité" (pp. 216–17).

263. Dɪ Mᴀɪᴏ, Aɴᴛᴏɴɪᴏ. "Il poema di Dante e quello dell'Ariosto: espressioni di due concezioni della vita." In *Miscellanea in onore del Preside Gaspare Caliendo*, pp. 76–79. Naples: Casa Editrice Federico e Ardia, [1960].
Notes that in Dante's *DC* there is a representation of the medieval drama of reconciling the human and the divine, reason and revelation, and that the poet is both narrator and protagonist who lives the laborious drama of existence; the *OF*, on the other hand, signifies the perfect synthesis between man and God and is the objective transfiguration of the harmonious vision of life as perceived by the poet's age.

264. Dɪᴏɴɪsᴏᴛᴛɪ, Cᴀʀʟᴏ. "Per la data dei *Cinque Canti*." *Giornale storico della letteratura italiana* 137, fasc. 417 (1960): 1–40.
Sets the date of composition for the *CC* between the end of 1518 and the beginning of 1519, basing argument on textual references. Discussion centers on three major points: the reference to Bibbiena's mission to the court of Francis I (*CC* 2.52); the allusion to the Oria and Adorno, rival Genoese families (*CC* 3.71); and the relationship between the episode of Ruggiero swallowed by the whale (in canto 4) and a similar episode in Cassio de Narni's *La Morte del Danese*.

265. ———. "Appunti sui *Cinque Canti* e sugli studi ariosteschi." In *Studi e problemi di critica testuale*, pp. 369–82. Bologna: Commissione per i testi di lingua, 1961.
Rejects the claim of Cesare Segre and others that the *CC* was composed after 1526 and reiterates his view that it was written before 1521 (see entry 264). Warns against viewing all Ariosto's works in terms of the 1532 *OF*, noting that the 1516 edition is in itself "un capolavoro assoluto" (p. 375). Discusses the merits as well as the limitations of both Rajna's and Dario Bonomo's work on the sources of the *OF*.

266. ———. "Chierici e laici." In his *Geografia e storia della letteratura italiana*, pp. 47–73. Turin: Einaudi, 1967.
Also in *Italia sacra* 2 (1960): 167–85 and, with the title "Chierici e laici nella letteratura italiana del primo Cinquecento," in *Problemi di vita religiosa in Italia nel Cinquecento*, Atti del Convegno di Storia della Chiesa in Italia, 1958 (Padua: Antenore, 1960), pp. 167–85.
Notes that in the early Cinquecento, men of letters enjoying ecclesiastical

ranks and benefits had an ambiguous status in that they lived as laymen but
were, in fact, clerics. Considers Ariosto, especially as revealed in the satires,
as an example of an individual in the ambiguous situation between "laicato
e stato ecclesiastico" (p. 60).

🍃 267. ————. *Europe in Sixteenth-Century Italian Literature* (The Tay-
lorian Lecture delivered 11 February 1971). Oxford: Clarendon Press,
1971. 19p.
Notes that "the building up of a national literature in [sixteenth-century]
Italy . . . contributed to the development and hardening of a polemical attitude towards other languages and literatures [and that] it also led to a gradual
recognition of what other countries meant to Italy" (p. 11). Cites Ariosto as
an example of an Italian man of letters who expressly preferred his own city
and country to any others but who, in the geographical disposition of the *OF*
toward England, Ireland, Scotland, Denmark, and the Balkans, acknowledged the growing importance of Northern Europe.

🍃 268. Dı PINO, GUIDO. "Ariosto lirico." In his *Stile e umanità*, pp. 121–
24. Messina-Florence: G. D'Anna, 1957.
First published in *La Nazione*, 31 March 1948; Fatini, 3405.

🍃 269. ————. "Bivalenza dell'ottava ariostesca." In *Per l'Ariosto* (entry
623). Special 1976 issue of *Italianistica* 3, no. 3 (1974): 125–45.
Argues that in the *OF* illusion and reality intersect constantly, whereas in
the *DQ* they are distinct and separate. Comments on the Ariostean concepts
of illusion and reality; examines, in this context, the poet's use of the octave,
especially in relation to Boiardo and to the tradition of chivalric poetry.

🍃 270. ————. "Il realismo critico del De Sanctis negli studi sull'Ariosto."
In *De Sanctis e il realismo*, 1: 737–44. 2 vol. Naples: Giannini, 1978.
Notes in De Sanctis's writings on Ariosto a methodological approach that
tends to situate chivalric poetry in the context of the historical Renaissance
and a propensity to analyze in detail both themes and characters. Discusses
these two major aspects of De Sanctis's criticism of Ariosto in both the *Storia
della letteratura italiana* (1870–1871) and in the Zurich lectures (1858–
1859), noting that there is little difference in the two evaluations of Ariosto
although in the later work there is a clear preference for the methodological
approach.

🍃 271. Dı TOMMASO, ANDREA. "*Insania* and *Furor*: A Diagnostic Note on
Orlando's Malady." *Romance Notes* 14, no. 3 (1973): 583–88.
Proposes Cicero's concept of *furor* as another possible source for the title
of the *OF*. Notes that unlike Cicero, Ariosto does not distinguish between

furor and *insania*; in the *OF*, *furor* is an extreme manifestation of *insania*, to which even wise men are susceptible. Suggests that the poet's own susceptibility to *furor* underscores the theme of universal madness in the poem.

◄§ 272. ———. "Ariosto, Ludovico." In *Dictionary of Italian Literature*, edited by Peter Bondanella and Julia Conway Bondanella, pp. 22–25. Westport, Conn.: Greenwood Press, 1979.
Brief biographical sketch and notes on Ariosto's minor works, especially the satires. Focuses on the *OF*, commenting on its visual qualities ("some of the most essential elements of the poem . . . are presented in iconic and figurative terms," p. 23) and the play in the poem of madness and mutability, on the one hand, and reason and stability on the other: "So cleverly has Ariosto constructed the world of Orlando and Angelica, of Ruggiero and Bradamante, that even today critics only hesitatingly assert that there is not some hidden allegory lying dormant in it, waiting to be uncovered" (p. 24). Includes short bibliography.

◄§ 273. DOGLIO, MARIA LUISA. "Lingua e struttura del *Negromante*." In *Ludovico Ariosto: lingua, stile e tradizione*, edited by Cesare Segre (entry 789), pp. 427–43. Milan: Feltrinelli, 1976.
Analysis of the composition and revision of *Il Negromante* over a period of two decades (begun in 1509; completed in 1520; revised in 1528) and as an example of Ariosto's maturation as a dramatist, evolving from the imitation of classical models to the creation of a "new comedy," a dramatic form in which plot becomes secondary to a language rich in theatrical meaning and the classical Terentian-Plautine situation gives way to calculated structural complexities resulting in heightened tension and dramatic potential.

◄§ 274. DONATI, LAMBERTO. "Esemplari eccezionali dell'*Orlando Furioso*." *La Bibliofilia* 76, disp. 1–2 (1974): 241–45.
Briefly discusses printing peculiarities of two copies of the 1584 *OF* at the Biblioteca Vaticana (St. Rossiano 3524; St. Capponi, III, 90).

◄§ 275. DONATO, EUGENIO. "The Shape of Fiction: Notes Toward a Possible Classification of Narrative Discourses." *MLN* 86, no. 6 (1971): 807–22.
Distinguishing between various types of narrative discourse, identifies human desire as the narrative unit that conditions the topology of Western novelistic tradition and allows the narrative voice to distance itself from the narrated world in order to speak the truth about desire and its variants. An exception within this type of narrative discourse is the *OF*, in which the narrative "I" never projects itself outside the narrative and consequently is never privileged enough to speak the truth about desire. Notes that the *OF*,

like other similarly open-ended texts, does not propose to tell the truth about human desire but generates desire and is generated by it, thus internalizing its endless mode of production.

276. ———. "'Per selve e boscherecci labirinti': Desire and Narrative Structure in Ariosto's *Orlando Furioso*." *Barroco* 4 (1972): 17–34.
Considers the characters' desire in the *OF*, whether for glory, for establishing individual superiority, or for sexual conquest, to be independent from the object of desire. Argues that the quest for fulfillment of desire often takes place in a wood, which as a literary commonplace not only mediates desire but also constitutes the "ideal place where desire and literature meet and become conjoined in an inextricable way" (p. 19). Suggests that Ariosto's narrative of human desire, which is, in fact, the desire of "the telling of more tales" about desire, makes desire and literature similar, inasmuch as "desire is the source that generates literature in the first place" (p. 24). Views the Alcina episode as an example of the "mutual interdependency of desire and literature" (p. 29). Concludes that Ariosto's discourse is infinitely deployable, for, being a self-referential narration, it is a "narrative that narrates itself being narrated" (p. 32).

277. ———. "Topographies of Memory." *Sub-Stance* 21 (1978): 37–48.
On the premise that a text "always stages a metaphorical memory" (p. 38), notes that the *OF* represents a boundless, labyrinthine memory in the Hegelian sense: "Ariosto weaves a text which is a labyrinth, in which future texts will lose themselves, describing within the space of the *Orlando Furioso* their own trajectories and their own figures. . . . His heroes and heroines are condemned to err indefinitely through the 'torta via'" (p. 43).

278. DONNELLY, JOHN PATRICK, S.J. "The Moslem Enemy in Renaissance Epic: Ariosto, Tasso and Camoens." *Yale Italian Studies* 1, no. 2 (1977): 162–70.
Considers the poets' attitudes toward various aspects of Islamic culture and religion and asserts that the "shapelessness of Moslem culture in the Italian epics, at least, flows from ignorance" (p. 164). Observes that Ariosto shows the least prejudice toward Moslems and expresses surprise, therefore, that he joins Tasso and Camoës in calling for new crusades against the infidels.

279. DÖRING, RENATE. *Ariostos "Orlando Furioso" im Italienischen Theater des Seicento und Settecento*. Hamburg: Romanistisches Seminar der Universität Hamburg, 1973. 339p.
Discusses dramatic adaptations of the *OF* during the seventeenth and eighteenth centuries: Florentine adaptations during the period of neoclassical melodrama, e.g., Ferdinando Saracinelli's *La liberazione di Ruggiero dal-*

l'Isola d'Alcina; seventeenth-century tragic adaptations, e.g., Fulvio Testi's *L'isola d'Alcina*; seventeenth-century Venetian melodrama, e.g., Prospero Bonarelli's *La pazzia d'Orlando*; adaptations for the Roman stage during the period of the Barberini, e.g., Ottavio Tronsarelli's *Il ritorno d'Angelica nell'India*; Spanish-type adaptations, e.g., Marc'Antonio Perillo's *Orlando forsennato*; early eighteenth-century *opere serie*, e.g., Grazio Braccioli's *Orlando Furioso*; *opera buffa*, e.g., Tertulliano Fonsaconico's *Angelica ed Orlando*; Metastasian adaptations, e.g., *Il Ruggiero ovvero l'eroica gratitudine*. Notes that adaptation to the stage brought modification to both characters and episodes: Orlando is at times transformed into a commedia dell'arte character; new comic elements are introduced; relationships between characters are altered; and the importance or insignificance of a character is altered. In Giovanni Villifranchi's early adaptation of the OF to the stage, the prologue is heavily allegorical; in baroque stagings, supernatural elements are emphasized; in several Florentine and Counter-Reformational versions, the drama has political overtones.

≈§ 280. DOUTENVILLE, H. "Le 'Roland' de l'Arioste en Petite et en Grande Bretagne." *Bulletin. Société de Mythologie Française*, no. 47 (1962): 81–85.

Observations on inaccuracies in a geographical reference in OF 9.15 (1532 edition) and a parallel in French chronicles on Gargantua's itinerary from Mont Saint Michel to Great Britain. Comments on Ariosto's interest in geography, which author characterizes as "arbitraire et confuse" (p. 83).

≈§ 281. DOYLE, NANCY ANN. "The Artist as *Artifex Mundi* in Ariosto's *Orlando Furioso* and Cervantes' *Don Quijote*." *DAI* 40, no. 7 (1980): 4016–17A. (Indiana University, 1979. 219p.)

Analysis of the narrative devices employed by Ariosto and Cervantes in establishing themselves as creators and manipulators of their fictional worlds. Establishes both similarities and differences in their uses of conventional narrative techniques. Argues that the altering point of view of the narrator of the OF "contributes to the sense of instability about his fictional world and its changing appearances, while Cervantes' narrator provides a stable vantage point from which the reader is able to evaluate the characters' interpretations of objects or phenomena." Compares the use of authorial control and disclaimer and the narrators' attitudes toward their audience, concluding that both the OF and DQ are literary games: the former focuses on the shaping of the poem and celebrates the artist as *artifex mundi*; the latter is essentially instructional, shaping the reader who is intended to maintain a detached perspective on a fictional world of literary creation.

≈§ 282. DUCROS, FRANC. "Au sujet de la rhétorique." *Revue des langues romanes* 80, no. 1 (1970): 51–78.

Applying an operational definition of rhetoric as the paradigmatic listing of topoi and figures, which the individual poet chooses (*inventio*) and arranges (*dispositio*) for the production of his text, discusses, together with Du Bellay and Ronsard, Ariosto's exordium to *OF* 3. Notes that the exordium comprises both invocation and proposition and suggests that the introduction of the theme is entrusted to the combination of three topoi: the poet's modesty, the ineffability of the subject matter, and the invocation itself. Identifies the generative process of the text as lying in the amplification of the main theme, an amplification that arises from the use of repetition, of the flight metaphor, and of the justification of the theme.

283. DÜNNHAUPT, GERHARD. "Der *Rasende Roland* 1632: ein komisches Ritterepos." In his *Diederich von dem Werder: Versuch einer Neuwertung seiner Hauptwerke*, pp. 45–75. Frankfurt: Peter Lang, 1973.
History and analysis of Diederich von dem Werder's German translation of the *OF*. Compares episodes of the original text with the translation, noting that the German version is not always faithful to Ariosto's text. Comparative analysis of Ariosto's style and that of the German version. Includes list of German translations of the *OF* (pp. 70–71).

284. ———. "*Historia Vom Rasenden Roland*—The First German Ariosto Translation." *Renaissance and Reformation* 10, no. 1 (1974): 37–42.
Considers whether Diederich von dem Werder's translation of the *OF* is a fragment or a condensed version of Ariosto's poem. Argues that all omissions (including the genealogy of the Este, the catalog of English, Scottish, and Irish nobles, references to Greek mythology, and other learned allusions), as well as the additions borrowed from Boiardo's *OI*, lend support to the argument that von dem Werder's version is a deliberate attempt to reach a wider audience by popularizing the epic.

285. ———. "Die früheste deutsche Dichtung vom Rasenden Roland: ein Beitrag zum 500. Geburtstag Ludovico Ariostos." In *Annali: Sezione Romanza* (Istituto Universitario Orientale, Naples), 17, no. 1 (1975): 113–24.
Discusses the evolution of Diederich von dem Werder's translation of the *OF*, the complete version of which was published in 1636. Notes that von dem Werder renders the Ariostean hendecasyllable with twelve- to fifteen-syllable alexandrines, successfully reproducing the rhythm of the original. Asserts that the German translation maintains the comic tone of the original but is not a literal rendition, often making allegorical passages, for example, much more explicit in their meaning. Concludes that the German version is more "popular" in character than the original.

⊷§ 286. DURÁN, MANUEL. "Cervantes and Ariosto: Once More, with Feeling." In *Estudios literarios de hispanistas norteamericanos dedicados a
Helmut Hatzfeld con motivo de su 80 aniversario*, edited by Josep M.
Sola-Solé, Alessandro Crisafulli, and Bruno Damiani, pp. 87–110. Barcelona: Ediciones Hispam, 1974.
Observations on parallels and differences between Ariosto and Cervantes,
considered as "two facets" of Renaissance culture (pp. 87–88). Notes their
ambiguous approach to the epic tradition, concluding that the *OF* is a Renaissance "soap opera," a "distorted, tongue-in-cheek epic" (pp. 92–93), anticipating the novel form. Summary evaluation of Ariosto's aesthetic. Discussion of differences between the *DQ* and the *OF*, including Ariosto's emphasis
on the "power of illusion" as compared to Cervantes's insistence on the "illusion of power" (p. 98); considers the significance of misunderstanding to
the narrative structure of the *OF* and notes that misunderstanding is basic to
the motivation of Cervantes's hero.

⊷§ 287. DURLING, ROBERT M. "The Divine Analogy in Ariosto." *MLN* 78,
no. 1 (1963): 1–14.
Draws an analogy between Ariosto, the poet, and God, noting that Ariosto's comments on his manipulation of the narrative material reflect the popular view that the artist is analogous to God and that the work of art, in its
variety, harmony, plenitude, and unity, is like the cosmos. Observes, however, that the poet is not an "analogue of the Creator," but "His spokesman,"
not a creator *ex nihilo* but a "craftsman," a "contingent god" (pp. 12–14).

⊷§ 288. ———. *The Figure of the Poet in Renaissance Epic*. Cambridge:
Harvard University Press, 1965. 280p.
Discusses the role of the poet-narrator in the *OF*, noting that there is no
"insistence upon the illusion of public recitation" (p. 112), as there is in the
OI. Considers the poet's control of his narrative as reflected in the transition
from one episode to another, in his feigned forgetfulness, in his invocation
to the aesthetic principle of "varietà," and in his intervention in the narrative
for the purpose of distributing justice among his characters. Suggests that the
absolute control exercised by the poet on his material makes him analogous
to the Creator. Reviews the inconsistency of the poet's roles vis-à-vis historical exordia, moralizing observations, and encomiastic references to the Este
family, which are clearly qualified. Argues that his attitude toward women is
as shifting and contradictory as that of his characters, particularly Rodomonte, whose change, however, from a misogynist to one smitten by love is
the reversal of the poet's, who at first defends women but then calls them
faithless. Detailed analysis of the Isabella-Rodomonte episode, linking the
poet's farewell to the decapitated Isabella as if he were a deity sending her to

Heaven ("vattene in pace alla superna sede," OF 29.27.7) to the analogy of the poet and the Creator. See especially pp. 112–81.

◆§ 289. ———. "The Epic Ideal." In The Old World: Discovery and Rebirth. 1974. 3:105–46. Literature and Western Civilization, edited by David Daiches and Anthony Thorlby. 5 vols. London: Aldus Books, 1972–1975.

Considers the Virgilian tradition in Renaissance epic, noting in particular the use of the Aeneid both as a standard against which Renaissance epics measured themselves and as the source of literary rivalry. Observes that the poems under consideration (OF, GL, FQ, and Paradise Lost) attempt, "to some degree, a total interpretation of experience, and in particular of history. This . . . ambition, with traditional epic style, is the distinguishing mark of Virgilian epic. Like Virgil, these poets raise questions of the teleology of history and of the nature of the collectivities—empire, Church, nation—and universal institutions to which men belong. Each of them takes on a role as interpreter of the European heritage that is similar to the role taken by Virgil himself in the Aeneid" (p. 105). Argues that "Renaissance Virgilian epic reflects a profound crisis in European unity. . . . Ariosto's Orlando furioso reflects the moment just before the Reformation, when the immensely complex and unwieldy institutions of the Church had not yet collapsed before the Lutheran problematic of unmediated selfhood" (p. 106). Considers characteristics of Virgilian Renaissance epics (e.g., "the closeness with which they directly imitate the ancient genre in formal respects," p. 109) and considers the OF in the context of the introductory discussion (pp. 110–15). Observes that the "cyclical totality of Ariosto's poem derives both from the Virgilian conception of a morally determined military plot and from the vision of human life as a totality of quests that characterizes the Grail romances" (p. 110) and describes the structural elements of the poem and its complex interweaving: "In this network each character comes into contact with almost all the others, usually by far-fetched coincidences that are a chief display of the poet's virtuosity. Although chance has seemed to many to be the law of the world of the poem, there is a strong suggestion that chance is an instrument whereby Providence brings order out of the chaotic and destructive variety of men's wills. . . . For the fundamental activity of the poet's consciousness is that of seeing the entire bewildering and disheartening variety of experience with uncompromising clarity, of dominating it by seeing it as sharply as possible, and of forcing the reader to do the same. I will hazard the formula that the artistic totalization of the poem rests precisely on the reader's accepting its manner of not totalizing reality but of being critical of it" (p. 111–12). Concludes discussion of the OF with an analysis of 17.11–13, of Virgilian inspiration, to show that "Ariosto's use of Virgil . . . emphasizes the incongruity of a modern Virgilianism. All the Virgilian allusions and imitations—the encomiastic celebration of the dynasty, the prophecies, the heroics, the military plot, even the elegiac pathos—are circumscribed and modified by Ariosto's elaborate plot and his famous irony, which deprive them of all their authoritative sanctions" (p. 114).

〜§ 290. EDWARDS, ERNEST W. *The "Orlando Furioso" and Its Predecessor.* Philadelphia: R. West, 1977; Cambridge, England: Norwood, 1978. 175p.
Reprint of 1924 edition, Cambridge University Press; Fatini, 2253.

〜§ 291. EDWARDS, GWYNNE. "On Góngora's 'Angélica y Medoro.'" In *Studies of the Spanish and Portuguese Ballad,* edited by N. D. Shergold, pp. 73–94. London: Tamesis Books, 1972.
Stresses the importance of Góngora's "Angélica y Medoro" for anticipating in style and content the poet's later masterpieces; notes that much critical evaluation of the *romance* has failed to acknowledge Góngora's debt to Ariosto who, in the source episode (*OF* 19.16–37), provides both the framework and the predominant themes of the Spanish poem.

〜§ 292. *The New Encyclopaedia Britannica: Macropaedia.* "Ariosto, Ludovico." See A[quilecchia], G[iovanni], entry 22.

〜§ 293. ENTENZA DE SOLARE, BEATRIZ ELENA. "Un nuevo texto ariostesco en la poesía española del siglo de oro." In *Studia Hispanica in Honorem R. Lapesa,* edited by Eugenio de Bustos et al, 2:225–27. 1974. 3 vols. Madrid: Gredos, 1972–1975.
Text of four unpublished octaves in ms. 1. 132 of the Biblioteca Nacional de Madrid as further evidence of Ariosto's importance to Spanish Renaissance poetry. Two are translations of *OF* 16.2 and 16.3; two were possibly influenced by Ariosto.

〜§ 294. ESPOSITO, ENZO. "Situazione editoriale delle opere ariostesche." In *Ariosto 1974 in America,* edited by Aldo Scaglione (entry 760), pp. 179–89. Ravenna: Longo, 1976.
General review of editions of Ariosto's works from the sixteenth century to the present and consideration of editorial undertakings of the texts. Indicates that a group working with Cesare Segre has in preparation a critical edition of Ariosto's *Opera omnia.*

〜§ 295. FACCIOLI, EMILIO. "Il Palazzo Ducale di Révere e un episodio dell'*Orlando Furioso.*" *Civiltà mantovana* 1, no. 1 (1966): 7–12.
Consideration of *OF* 42 and the specific location of Rinaldo's sojourn along the Po. Contends that the description of his travel (43.53–54) places

him in Révere, "che fu castello ben munito ai margini sud-orientali del Ducato dei Gonzaga e luogo di transito obbligato su di un itinerario percorso più d'una volta dall'Ariosto" (p. 8). Argues that the residence of the knight who offers Rinaldo hospitality is inspired by the Gonzaga Palace, still in Révere and fitting much of the poet's description. Draws analogies between the actual place and the description in the _OF_. Suggests that the fountain is imaginary. Concludes: "L'identificazione da noi proposta—'non nuova per i cultori della storia di Révere, ma sfuggita fino ad oggi ai commentatori dell'_Orlando Furioso_—ci sembra pertanto congrua e in tutto rispondente alle idealità ed agli affetti di Ludovico Ariosto: diremmo . . . che essa concorre a documentare il vivo e dinamico contatto che egli mantenne con la natura e con la storia del suo tempo, con quel paesaggio d'acque e di terre che più gli era familiare con quelle regioni concrete dell'esistere che più gli sembravano degne di memoria e di canto" (p. 12).

296. FAHY, CONOR. "L'esemplare già 'Charlemont' dell'_Orlando Furioso_ del 1532." _Lettere italiane_ 14, no. 4 (1962): 441–50.
Traces the history of the so-called Charlemont exemplar, one of the few copies of the _OF_ printed in Ferrara by Francesco Rosso (1532). Observes that the copy, possibly given to Gaspara Stampa by the author, was owned by Giuseppe Valletta and in 1727, after Valletta's death, became part of the Neapolitan Biblioteca Oratoriana. Little is known about the copy until its purchase by Francis Caulfeilf, Count of Charlemont, sometime between 1747 and 1789. Suggests that the exemplar discovered in 1930 by T. W. Koch in the J. Pierpont Morgan Library is perhaps the one owned by Giuseppe Valletta.

297. ———. "Ariosto, Ludovico." In _The Penguin Companion to European Literature_, edited by Anthony Thorlby, pp. 63–64. New York: McGraw-Hill, 1969.
General introduction to Ariosto and to the _OF_. Notes that in the _OF_, "The endless variety of the poem's pattern, together with the continual presence of the author, remind the reader of the finite nature of humanity, and the wisdom of moderation" (p. 63).

298. ———. "The View from Another Planet: Textual Bibliography and the Editing of Sixteenth-Century Italian Texts." _Italian Studies_ 34 (1979): 71–92.
Notes that the 1532 edition of the _OF_ incorporates changes in compliance with Bembo's position on the literary language and that it is the only edition of a major Italian author with authorial press corrections.

🖙 299. FALASCHI, ENID T. "Notes on Some Illustrations of Ariosto's *Orlando Furioso*." *La Bibliofilia*, 75, disp. 1 (1973): 175–88.

Discusses the differences between the illustrations for *OF* 5 and 28 in the 1584 edition, with the engravings of Girolamo Porro, and those prepared for Harington's 1591 translation. Considers whether Harington or the engraver decided upon extra plates for more extensive illustration of the cantos in question. Reproduction of plates from several editions.

🖙 300. ————. "Valvassori's 1553 Illustrations of *Orlando Furioso*: The Development of Multi-Narrative Technique in Venice and Its Links with Cartography." *La Bibliofilia* 77, disp. 2 (1975): 227–51.

Discusses the development of the technique of woodcut design used to illustrate the *OF* from the Zoppino edition of 1530 to the Franceschi edition of 1584. Notes that the 1542 Giolito edition used woodcuts illustrating events separated by time and space; that the 1553 Valvassori edition crowds episodes into small frames to convey the sense of a narrative continuum; and that the 1556 Valgrisi edition introduces full-page woodcuts at the beginning of each canto. Concludes that the Franceschi edition is "the most famous of the sixteenth century . . . the first one where an artist [Girolamo Porro] is named and which has engravings, as opposed to woodcuts, throughout" (p. 248). Includes eleven illustrations.

🖙 301. FANTUZZI GUARRASI, NARDINA. *La Donna nella vita e nelle opere dell'Ariosto*. Special number of *Bollettino storico reggiano* 7, no. 26 (1974): 1–201. Drawings by Anna Cantoni.

Contents: 1) "Daria Malaguzzi," pp. 9–19: documents life of Ariosto's mother (1453–c.1522), noting the poet's particular affection for her side of the family. 2) "L'Ariosto e le più nobili dame della Rinascenza," pp. 20–32: describes the preparations for the wedding of Lucrezia Borgia and Alfonso d'Este (in Rome, 30 December 1501), as well as her entry into Ferrara, described in Ariosto's eclogue "Tirsi e Melibeo" (also notes his epithalamium in Latin and his praise of Lucrezia in *OF* 13.69–71 and 42.83); notes that Ariosto, though at court, had no direct contact with Lucrezia except on the occasion of presenting a gift of Pietro Bembo's poetry; discusses the close relationship between Ariosto and Isabella d'Este (pp. 24–28), their mutual interest in the theater, and quotes from correspondence of Isabella regarding Ariosto; states that a letter to her brother, the Cardinal Ippolito, in 1507, concerning Ariosto's reading of parts of the *OF*, is the first document regarding the poem's composition; concludes with observations on Ariosto's acquaintance or possible acquaintance with several other well-known women, including Veronica Gambara and Vittoria Colonna. 3) " 'De Diversis Amoribus,' " pp. 33–46: notes that in spite of Ariosto's care to keep his personal life private, his broad experiences in love are implicit in the vast production of his love lyrics; conjectures on the specific women in his poems. 4) "Alessandra Benucci," pp. 47–57: recounts Ariosto's meeting of Alessandra Benucci, describes her parentage and first marriage to Tito Strozzi, and draws inferences about the poet's feelings toward her from his poetry. 5) "La donna nelle opere," pp. 59–174: discusses the characteristics, describes the roles, and traces the narrative line of the major female figures in the *OF*, the *CC* and, very summarily, in the comedies and satires. 6) Selection of verses about women and love.

302. FARAONE, LUIGI. "Motivi e caratteri dell'*Orlando Furioso*." *Aretusa* 2, no. 3 (1962): 45–46.
Unavailable; cited in PMLA Bibliography 1963, number 9007.

303. [FARINA, MARIO.] "Ariosto, Ludovico." In *Dai: Dizionario degli autori italiani*, pp. 281–88. Messina-Florence: G. D'Anna, 1973; Ristampa riveduta 1974.
Brief biographical sketch and discussion of Ariosto's writings; short summary of the *OF*.

304. FARRELL, MARY MacLENNAN II. "Mentors and Magic in Ariosto and Rabelais." *DAI* 37, no. 7 (1977): 4395A. (Yale University, 1976. 306p.)
Compares the function of mentors and assorted magi in the *OF* and in Rabelais's five books, concluding that rather than incidental to the narrative, they are frequently figures of the artist, "manipulating, guiding, transforming heroes and their behavior in order, ultimately, to bring about the successful conclusion of the work." Their magic, therefore, is a metaphor for art, revealing the two writers' faith in the powers of art, which, "when properly used, can help bring about a positive, even therapeutic or visionary reconciliation of the conflicts and tensions inherent in the text."

305. FATINI, GIUSEPPE. *Bibliografia della critica ariostea* (1510–1956). Florence: Le Monnier, 1958. 722p.
Annotated bibliography of 3,624 items from 1510 through 1956. Chronological ordering. Indicates some reviews of important entries; reviews of particular interest or critical importance are listed as separate items. Subject and proper name indexes.

306. ———. "Il vero *Furioso* di Messer Ludovico." *Nuova antologia* 480, fasc. 1920 (1960): 467–78.
Concise review of the major editions of the *OF* from that of Lodovico Dolce to the 1960 edition of Debenedetti and Segre. Argues that the poet's linguistic refinement during the course of his stylistic evolution is not to be

attributed to Alessandra Benucci's Florentine nor to the poet's alleged so-journs in Florence, but rather to his long exposure to Tuscan as spoken in the Garfagnana and to the advice of Pietro Bembo and other learned friends.

◆§ 307. ———. Presentazione. In *Le Opere minori di Ludovico Ariosto, scelte e commentate*, edited by Giuseppe Fatini, pp. ix–xxv. Florence: Sansoni, 1961.
Reprint of 1915 edition with a revised preface; Fatini, 2103.

◆§ 308. ———. "Il *Furioso* nella critica dell'ultimo trentennio." *Bollettino del Centro-Studi di Poesia Italiana e Straniera* (Rome) 1, no. 4 (1961–1962): 14–26.
Reviews three decades of criticism, noting the studies linking Ariosto's work to contemporary historical reality (e.g., those of Walter Binni, Lanfranco Caretti, and Mario Marti). Discusses the studies on Ariosto's style conducted by, among others, Emilio Bigi and Raffaello Ramat and, from a Marxist perspective, those by Roberto Battaglia and Antonio Piromalli.

◆§ 309. FAVA, BRUNO. *L'Interpretazione grafica dell' "Orlando furioso."*
See Bellochi, Ugo, and Bruno Fava, entry 79.

◆§ 310. FAVA, BRUNO. "Osservazioni alla biografia di Timoteo Bendedei." In *Lodovico Ariosto: il suo tempo la sua terra la sua gente* (entry 468). Estratto dal *Bollettino storico reggiano* 7, no. 25 (1974): 69–74.
Examines the scarcity of documentary evidence for establishing with any certainty the biography and activities of Timoteo Bendedei, friend of Ariosto, who dedicated to Bendedei a five-distich Latin poem (c.f., *Lirica*, edited by Giuseppe Fatini [1924], pp. 216–17) and mentioned him in OF 42.92. Concludes that he was born after 1478 in Reggio Emilia; held office of *esattore*, requiring frequent travel; died young; and was buried in S. Maria del Carmine.

◆§ 311. FEDI, ROBERTO. "Ludovico Ariosto a Reggio e Ferrara." *Il Ponte* 31, nos. 2–3 (1975): 269–73.
Reports on the fifth centenary of Ariosto's birth celebrated in Reggio Emilia and Ferrara (12–16 October 1974). Briefly notes the several literary topics discussed at the conference and the fact that it was enriched by an exhibit of approximately nine hundred editions of Ariosto's works, a debate on teaching Ariosto in Italian schools, and the announcement of a project to encourage and to fund partially the complete concordance of the three editions of the OF.

⚜ 312. ———. "Petrarchismo prebembesco in alcuni testi lirici del-
l'Ariosto." In *Ludovico Ariosto: lingua, stile e tradizione*, edited by Cesare Segre (entry 789), pp. 283–302. Milan: Feltrinelli, 1976.

Identifies in Ariosto's vernacular poems the Petrarchan elements (for the
most part technical) and their divergency from Petrarch's verse (e.g., absence
of tension resulting from spiritual aspiration and terrestrial binds). Locates
them within the context of a lyrical style in late fifteenth-century Italy, evolving from courtly traditions and already under the influence of Bembo's aesthetic principles. Concludes that the tone of his verse reveals a poet fully
reflective of a bourgeois world, free of the intellectualizing conceits of courtly
verse and still far from the sense of tragic irresolution of the sixteenth-century
Petrarchists.

⚜ 313. FERRARI, TONINO. "Opere d'arte d'ispirazione ariostesca nell'edificio della Cassa di Risparmio di Reggio Emilia." In *Lodovico Ariosto: il
suo tempo la sua terra la sua gente* (entry 468). Estratto dal *Bollettino
storico reggiano* 7, no. 28 (1974): 207–11.

Lists the bronze friezes inspired by Ariosto and molded by Cirillo Manicardi (1856–1925) for the main building of the Cassa di Risparmio on Via
Toschi in Reggio Emilia. With four plates.

⚜ 314. FERRARI, VIRGILIO. "Le case degli Ariosti in Ferrara." In *Ferrara e
l'Ariosto*, by Raffaele Belvederi, Virgilio Ferrari, and Arturo Malagù,
pp. 41–78. (La *Ferrariae Decus* nel V Centenario della nascita del
poeta.) Ferrara: S.A.T.E., 1974.

Photographs and architectural-historical descriptions of houses and other
buildings of importance to the several members of the Ariosto family. Extensively illustrated with photographs.

⚜ 315. FERRERO, GIUSEPPE GUIDO. "Astolfo (storia di un personaggio)."
Convivium 29, no. 5 (1961): 513–30.

Traces the development of the Astolfo figure from his first appearance in
chivalric poetry (in the *Roncevaux*) to the *OI*, in which the development of
the character ends. Views the Ariostean character as mindless and without a
well-developed personality, passing from one adventure to another as if
moved by a magic power, or as personifying one of the great poetic themes
of the *OF*.

⚜ 316. FERRIGUTO, ARNALDO. "Note sull'Ariosto." In his *Abbozzi e frammenti*, pp. 89–97. Verona: Linotipia Veronese Fiorini, 1972.

Briefly analyzes the structure and poetic elements of the lament of Bradamante (*OF* 32), calling it the "episodio gemello di quello d'Orlando non solo
per la costruzione generale e il crescendo di rivelazione, ma perché è dolore

espresso attraverso un dibattito di idee che si succedono, alternano e cancellano" (pp. 95–96).

⚜ 317. FERRONE, SIRO. "Sulle commedie in prosa dell'Ariosto." In *Ludovico Ariosto: lingua, stile e tradizione*, edited by Cesare Segre (entry 789), pp. 391–425. Milan: Feltrinelli, 1976.

Also with title "Le Commedie in prosa dell'Ariosto tra cronaca cittadina e ideologia di corte," in *Il Ponte* 32, nos. 2–3 (1976): 209–42.

Maintains that the concept of authority inherent in the father-son relationship as represented in *I Suppositi* and the intrigues and envies of the servants in *La Cassaria* invite a reading of both plays as microcosms of social and political life in Ferrara during the early sixteenth century. Such a representation of contemporary realities, together with attacks on the taxation and judicial systems and the use of linguistic plays on words ("giochi"), constitute Ariosto's incorporation of the contemporary into comic forms of classical tradition.

⚜ 318. FERRONI, GIULIO. "L'Ariosto e la concezione umanistica della follia." In *Ludovico Ariosto*, pp. 73–92. Convegno internazionale (entry 475). Rome: Accademia Nazionale dei Lincei, 1975.

Comprehensive discussion of the concept of madness in the *OF* and its function in the structure of the poem. Notes the significant parallels between the views on madness of Leon Battista Alberti, Erasmus, and Ariosto, suggesting that the former two could well have provided a basis for Ariosto's own use of the motif, particularly in the concept of madness as a masking device or the creation of an illusory reality and in the Erasmian notion that rational behavior cannot be divorced from folly and that life is constructed upon a complex of illusory realities that, if destroyed, would make existence intolerable. Notes that madness in the *OF*—associated with the key word *errare*—afflicts most characters, of whom Orlando is the prototype: they are victims of life's ambiguities and deceits ("simulacri," p. 83), of which love is the most significant (pp. 85–86). Considers the poet's perspective on his own folly, in both the *OF* and the satires; concludes with a discussion of Rinaldo's refusal to drink a potion guaranteed to reveal whether or not his wife has been unfaithful (*OF* 43), noting the importance of "belief" ("credenza") rather than "certainty" ("certezza") in basic human relationships (p. 90).

⚜ 319. ⸻. "Nota sull'*Erbolato*." *La Rassegna della letteratura italiana*, 7th ser., vol. 79, nos. 1–2 (1975): 202–14.

Analyzes both historically and stylistically Ariosto's prose work on contemporary medicine and its practice; takes issue (p. 202) with the traditional reading, which tends to consider it a satire against medical men and charlatans (e.g., Fatini) or a mere literary exercise (e.g., Segre). Suggests that, in a style and tone that is entirely free of polemical rhetoric, Ariosto presents a "visione policentrica del reale" (p. 204) and a portrayal of man as a complex of contradictions and ambivalences. Notes the affinity in these views with Erasmus, Rabelais, and, in a more radical way, Machiavelli (p. 204). Frequently cites the importance in this regard of the work of Mikhail Bakhtin in *L'oeuvre de François Rabelais et la culture populaire au Moyen Age et sous la Renaissance* (French translation, Paris, 1970).

🐌 320. ————. "Gioco, trucco, illusione: la corte nel corso del tempo." In his *Il Testo e la scena: saggi sul teatro del Cinquecento*, pp. 99–162. Rome: Bulzoni, 1980.

Updated bibliography in article first printed as "Per una storia del teatro dell'Ariosto," *La Rassegna della letteratura italiana*, 7th ser., vol. 79, nos. 1–2 (1975): 85–128.

Denies validity of earlier critical attempts to view Ariosto's theater as a progressive but ultimately unsuccessful attempt to reflect in a dramatic context Renaissance harmony and equilibrium (cites Nino Borsellino, *Ludovico Ariosto*, entry 125); offers a revised perspective on Ariosto's theater, each play representing in its structure and dynamics an important moment in a continuing dialogue between the author and Ferrarese society. Focuses on essential structural or thematic motifs of each play (e.g., the role of the *gioco*, or the practical joke, in the first *Cassaria*; the game of illusion in the *Studenti*; disguise in the *Negromante*; and masking–make-up in the final *Cassaria*), concluding that mutations in the dramatic texture reflect a growing polemical stance in regard to the courtly society of which the author had become such an integral part. Rich with suggestions, both explicit and implicit, for research on Ariosto's theater.

🐌 321. ————. "Percorsi della scena cortegiana." In his *Il Testo e la scena: saggi sul teatro del Cinquecento*, pp. 9–41. Rome: Bulzoni, 1980.

Cites various episodes in the *OF*—"scene di palazzi e di apparati architettonici, dalla grotta di Merlino al castello d'Atlante del canto IV . . . al palazzo incantato di Atlante" (p. 11)—as important paradigms for the study of the illusory stage setting ("simulacro") of sixteenth-century court theaters. See especially pp. 10–13.

🐌 322. ————. "Tecniche del raddoppiamento nella commedia del Cinquecento." In his *Il Testo e la scena: saggi sul teatro del Cinquecento*, pp. 43–64. Rome: Bulzoni, 1980.

Analyzes the exchange of identity or doubling ("raddoppiamento") of characters in the *Suppositi*, noting that such exchanges carry over into the "immagine dello spazio e della città-scena; se il raddoppiamento costitutivo dell'intreccio, (Erostrato) Dulippo↔(Dulippo) Erostrato, dà luogo a quello

marginale e più debole, (Senese) Filogono, quest'ultimo, di fronte all'apparizione del vero Filogono, fa nascere una battuta del servo Lico, un'ipotesi di
raddoppiamento diretto dei personaggi, dei luoghi, e della stessa Ferrara,
luogo reale e luogo fittizio della rappresentazione" (p. 49). See especially pp.
47–49.

◄§ 323. FICHTER, ANDREW JOHN. "Epic and the Vision of Empire: Histo-
    riography in Virgil, Ariosto, and Spenser." *DAI* 36, no. 1 (1975): 271–
    72A. (Yale University, 1974. 308p.)
    See *Poets Historical: Dynastic Epic in the Renaissance*. New Haven: Yale
University Press, 1982. 237p.
    Argues that the *Aeneid*, the *OF*, and the *FQ* reveal "a sense of history
evolving from a passive acceptance of received cultural dogma to an effort on
the part of the epic poet to exert a determinative influence on his culture."
The poet becomes the "agent of prophecy, the mediator of the vision of
imperium," questing for "an image of an idea of authority capable of with-
standing the pressures of historical reality." For both Ariosto and Spenser,
Virgil's *Aeneid* is the "*locus classicus* of the prophecy of empire"; however,
the "literary self-awareness of the Renaissance poet came to be formulated as
a search for a language of sufficient scope to celebrate the renovation of
imperium in its aesthetic as well as its historical aspects."

◄§ 324. FIFER, KEN. "Surface and Reality in Ariosto's *Orlando Furioso*."
    Rackham Literary Studies 1 (1971): 35–45.
    Argues that the *OF* intends to demonstrate that the "truly moral man . . .
must reject all ethical codifications, as experience and observation have repeatedly pointed to their inadequacies. The alternative is self-deception, the
acceptance of mere surfaces" (pp. 44–45). Notes that the ambiguous nature
of the poem's "reality," the constant play between appearance and fact, supports the essentially didactic intent of the poem.

◄§ 325. FINZI, RICCARDO. "Lodovico Ariosto a Correggio." In *Lodovico
    Ariosto: il suo tempo la sua terra la sua gente* (entry 468). Estratto dal
    Bollettino storico reggiano 7, no. 25 (1974): 75–85.
    Discusses the circumstances surrounding the conferral of a pension upon
Ariosto by the Marchese Alfonso del Vasto in Correggio on 18 October 1531.
Considers Ariosto's mention of several *correggesi* in *OF* 46.3–4 of the 1532
edition and in particular the role of the poetess Veronica Gambara at the
court of Correggio during that time.

◄§ 326. FIORONI, ROMOLO. "Filoni ariosteschi nel 'Maggio' del-
    l'Appennino." In *Lodovico Ariosto: il suo tempo la sua terra la sua gente*

(entry 468). Estratto dal *Bollettino storico reggiano* 7, no. 25 (1974): 87–96.

Notes that as the *OF* entered popular culture it became the "sillabario" (p. 88), or basis, of the *maggi* of the Emilian Appenines, in which as a common theme "alla gloria si assurge non per destino, ma per aver amato più di ogni altro, per aver saputo soffrire più di ogni altro con la dignità dei forti" (p. 95). Discusses and provides selections of texts of several *maggi* with Ariostean themes. Illustrated.

≈§ 327. FIRPO, LUIGI. Introduzione. In *Cinque canti di un nuovo libro di M. Lodovico Ariosto*, edited by Luigi Firpo, pp. 7–19. Turin: UTET, 1964.

General introduction to the *CC*, tracing the printing history of the manuscript; briefly relates the sixteenth-century debate over the work's relationship to the *OF* and reviews recent scholarship on the dating of the composition, accepting Dionisotti's dating of 1518–1519. Discusses the tone and thematic content of the *CC*, emphasizing what he calls its Tassian character, with power struggle replacing chivalrous encounters and the dominance of religious and political motifs. Identifies Gano as the protagonist, the "vero simbolo del male che nessuna forza può sradicare dai cuori umani" (p. 17) and the world portrayed as one in crisis.

≈§ 328. FONTANA, PIO. "La balena dei *Cinque canti* e un problema di fonti e di cronologia." *Aevum* 35, fasc. 5–6 (1961): 511–18.

Holds that Ariosto first conceived the *CC* sometime before 1521. Argues against the view that for the episode of the whale (*CC* 4) the poet was inspired by and rivaled a similar episode in Cassio da Narni's *La Morte del danese*, noting strong thematic differences between the two versions.

≈§ 329. ———. *I "Cinque Canti" e la storia della poetica del "Furioso."* Pubblicazioni dell'Università Cattolica del Sacro Cuore, serie terza, no. 4. Milan: Vita e Pensiero, 1962. 89p.

Essay divided into three chapters and a conclusion. First chapter ("I *Cinque Canti* e la conclusione del *Furioso*," pp. 15–33) argues that the *CC* was conceived prior to 1521 as an addition to the *OF* but was eventually substituted in the 1532 edition by the episode of Ruggiero and Leone, which stresses epic dignity and moral rectitude. Second chapter ("Decadenza della cortesia e preannunci di una nuova epica," pp. 35–67) discusses the erosion of chivalric topoi in the *CC*, where the *locus amoenus* becomes a place of deceit and love the occasion of violence and sin. Final chapter ("Astolfo tra Luciano e Giona," pp. 69–81) draws analogies between Astolfo's descent into the belly of the whale and his victimization by Alcina (*OF* 6) and the Dantesque experience of purification. Concludes (pp. 83–84) that the *CC*, intended as a work for later development by the poet, not only reflects his personal crisis but also represents a significant example of the "fermenti precursori dell'età barocca" (p. 83).

⟨⟨⟨ 330. ———. "Ancora sui *Cinque canti* dell'Ariosto." In *Per l'Ariosto* (entry 623). Special 1976 issue of *Italianistica* 3, no. 3 (1974): 97–109.
Takes issue with Luciano Capra's dating of the *CC* at some time prior to the first edition of the *OF* (entry 166). Refutes Capra's textual and extratextual (comparison with Machiavelli's *Prince*) evidence and concludes that the arguments for a later dating of the five-canto fragment are still valid.

⟨⟨⟨ 331. FORCIONE, ALBAN K. *Cervantes, Aristotle and the "Persiles."* Princeton: Princeton University Press, 1970. 365p.
Discussion of the role of the Ariosto-Tasso polemic in the development of Cervantes's own theory of the prose epic and the polemic's importance to both the *DQ* and *Los Trabajos de Persiles y Sigismunda* (passim). Discusses Cervantes's defense of Ariosto (pp. 124–25) and the particular influence of Ariosto on authorial intrusion and the various assertions of mastery over their subject matter and their audiences on the part of Cervantes's narrators (pp. 176–77 and passim).

⟨⟨⟨ 332. FORTI, FIORENZO. "Bacchelli e il Rinascimento." In *Critica e storia letteraria. Studi offerti a Mario Fubini*, 2:626–43. 2 vols. Padua: Liviana, 1970.
Review essay of Riccardo Bacchelli's *La Congiura di Don Giulio d'Este, e altri scritti ariosteschi* (first edition, 1931). Discusses the author's particular contribution to Renaissance studies, especially to the critical perspective on Ariosto. Notes that the book's intent is to explore the dialectic between the real world (in the case of Ariosto, Ferrarese society in the fifteenth and sixteenth centuries) and the world of art, noting that Ariosto's poetry evolves from the experiences of a writer intimately familiar with and sensitive to the cultural shifts of his age (pp. 629ff.). Suggests that Bacchelli's critical views and methodology foreshadow important recent critical developments, including Roman Jakobson on hyperbole and preterition (p. 642): a reexamination of Ariosto's "realism" and growing sense of despair over sociopolitical realities (p. 632); the recognition of the *CC* as an important document of a pre–Counter-Reformation vision of a world in the grips of political and religious absolutism (pp. 632–33); a sophisticated view of Ariosto in the context of literary regionalism (pp. 640–41).

⟨⟨⟨ 333. FORTINI, FRANCO. "I silenzi dell'Ariosto." *La Rassegna della letteratura italiana*, 7th ser., vol. 79, nos. 1–2 (1975): 12–14.
Notes the difficulties in understanding the *OF*, the essence of which often

lies in the unstated. Compares the OF to Adolfo Bioy Casares's novel *Inven-ción de Morel* suggesting that in order to penetrate the structure of Ariosto's poem, one must, like Casares's protagonist, "accettare di farti inghiottire dalla macchina prodigiosa e di penetrare in un universo della ripetizione, dove tutto ha senso a breve, ed è insensato a lungo termine" (p. 13).

◄§ 334. FRANCESCHETTI, ANTONIO. "Appunti sull'Ariosto lettore del-l'*Innamorato*." In *Ludovico Ariosto*, pp. 103–17. Convegno interna-zionale (entry 475). Rome: Accademia Nazionale dei Lincei, 1975.

Reviews the several reasons posited by critics for Ariosto's decision to use the OI as a point of departure for his own poem, noting as especially percep-tive the considerations of Emilio Bigi (see entry 92), who views the OI as the work that "ha portato l'Ariosto al genere cavalleresco, ed è in relazione a quel poema soprattutto che . . . si è determinato e definito il mondo spiri-tuale del *Furioso*" (p. 105). For a sense of how Ariosto uses his principal source, Franceschetti examines in detail several episodes, concluding that whereas in Boiardo characters are motivated and the narrative progresses for external reasons such as ideals or chance, in the OF, characters act and give impetus to the narrative after a rational evaluation of circumstances or an appropriate psychological reaction. Notes as a consequence that Ariosto's characters are humanized and do not reflect an idealized projection of man, as do Boiardo's. In this regard, views the lack of a complex psychology or of a dominant sentiment in the majority of characters as evidence of Ariosto's perception of the human psyche, which, far from heroic and monolithic, manifests itself as ill defined and subject to constant flux (p. 112). Concludes with an analysis of Orlando, exemplary of Northrop Frye's romance hero and intended, in his vicissitudes, as a parody of Boiardo's protagonist, the victim of love rather than a figure ennobled by his passions. Sees in this distinction a reflection of a courtly society and ideal (in Boiardo) and a per-sonal vision of reality (in Ariosto).

◄§ 335. ———. *L'"Orlando Innamorato" e le sue componenti tematiche e strutturali.* Florence: Leo S. Olschki, 1975. 274p., passim.

To distinguish between the "strutturazione psicologica" (p. 156) of the characters in the OI and in the OF, compares parallel episodes (OI 1.3.80 and OF 1.17–22) in which the same characters (Feraguto / Ferraù) react entirely differently to the same situation. States that Ariosto chose to under-score a specific difference between his representation of characters and that of his predecessor by placing the episode at the very beginning of the poem, and concludes that while the characters in the OF "partecipano della 'ra-gionevolezza' che fu una delle più spiccate qualità del suo autore, quelli dell'*Innamorato* agiscono invece sotto l'insegna della loro qualifica fonda-mentale del loro aspetto più evidente: in altre parole, i primi si comportano generalmente come nelle stesse circostanze si comporterebbe il poeta, o meglio come in quelle circostanze si comporterebbe secondo il poeta l'individuo medio; i secondi come per il Boiardo si comporterebbe un uomo o una donna la cui personalità si riassuma in una caratteristica specifica" (p. 157).

◈§ 336. FRANZBACH, MARTIN. "Beiträge zu einem deutschen Ariost (Satiren und *La Cassaria*)." *Germanisch-Romanische Monatsschrift* 15 (1965): 196–202.
Considers the reception in Germany and some early translations of Ariosto's satires. Discusses a variety of problems inherent in translating the Italian texts. Discussion of Otto Gildemeister's (1823–1902) translations of the *OF*, the satires, and parts of *La Cassaria*.

◈§ 337. FRATTAROLO, RENZO. "Ariosto 1974." *Accademie e biblioteche d'Italia* 42, no. 6 (1974): 426–66.
Lengthy survey of Ariosto criticism, from the poet's contemporaries and the Ariosto-Tasso polemics to the modern period. Briefly discusses the contributions of De Sanctis, Croce, and Momigliano, among others, and reviews a selection of important essays of the last half-century. Notes, especially, the writings of Walter Binni, Lanfranco Caretti, and Mario Santoro. Discussion of bibliographies of Ariosto criticism. Extensive selected bibliography of criticism arranged by subject (pp. 459–62).

◈§ 338. FREER, ALAN. "*Amadís de Gaule* e l'*Orlando Furioso* in Francia (1540–1548)." *Revue de littérature comparée* 43 (1969): 505–8.
Points out that the first French translation of the *OF* (1543), contrary to the opinion of Alexandre Cioranescu, caught the attention of several men of letters and, though mediocre, rivaled in popularity Nicolas Herberay des Essarts's *Amadís de Gaule*.

◈§ 339. FRENZEL, HERBERT. "Ariost und Kudrun: Ariost und die Ambraser Handschrift." *Germanisch-Romanische Monatsschrift* 7, no. 1 (1957): 78–84.
Defends his theory of the influence of the Ambraser manuscript on the *OF* against the arguments to the contrary of Otto Grüters (entry 397). Discusses several examples of probable influences, including Ariosto's use of proper names in the German epic. Suggests that many of Ariosto's sources were in the Este library.

◈§ 340. ———. *Ariost und die romantische Dichtung*. Cologne, Graz: Böhlau, 1962. 72p.
Italian translation in Maria Teresa dal Monte, *Ariosto in Germania con*

'*Ariosto e la poesia romantica*' di Herbert Frenzel, pp. 145–231. Imola: Galeati, 1971. See entry 240.

Two-part essay that considers the *OF* in the context of the cultural milieu of Renaissance Ferrara and the significance of Ariosto to the formation of German romantic taste and poetics. Discusses the *OF* in relation to the classical and medieval epic tradition, noting its unique structural qualities and its essentially classical style. Relates courtly tone of the *OF* and its perspective on women to the court culture of Ferrara and sees a strong affinity with the societal and cultural values expressed in Castiglione's *Book of the Courtier*. Discusses the importance of the figurative arts, especially of tapestries, to Ariosto's aesthetic and style, which favors pictorial rhetorical devices (chapter 3). Argues that Ariosto was conscious of living at the end of an epoch and that his poem is a synthesis of medieval culture raised to the level of myth. Final chapter analyzes Ariosto's importance in the creation of a myth of the Middle Ages and, consequently, his importance to the development of European romanticism, especially in Germany, for which he provided the most important access to the medieval world.

◀§ 341. ———. "Der Stammbaum der Este. Ein Beitrag zur genealogischen Trojalegende." In *Wort und Text*, edited by Harri Meier and Hans Sckommodau, pp. 187–99. Frankfurt am Main: Vittorio Klostermann, 1963.

Notes the current interest in rhetorical topoi and, specifically, that of genealogical lines in medieval and Renaissance romance. Discusses the genealogy of the Este family and its eulogy in the Italian romance, especially in the *OF*.

◀§ 342. FRIEDMANN, ANTHONY EDWARD. "The Description of Landscape in Spenser's *Faerie Queene*: A Study of Rhetorical Tradition." *DAI* 26, no. 10 (1966): 6039–40. (Columbia University, 1965. 303p.)

Study of the rhetorical nature of Spenser's landscape descriptions and the conventions and traditions that served as his models. Chapter 8 discusses the description of landscape in Italian pastoral romance and romance epic, including Sannazaro's *Arcadia*, the *OF*, and the *GL*.

◀§ 343. FROSINI, VITTORIO. "*Pinocchio* come satira politica." In his *Intellettuali e politici del Risorgimento*, pp. 147–88. Catania: Bonanno, 1971.

Published in part in the *Corriere della Sera*, 2 April 1970, p. 3, with title "Le Balene dell'oceano letterario."

Argues that Collodi's source for the episode of Pinocchio and the whale is Ariosto's *CC* 4, in which Ruggiero is swallowed (p. 187).

344. FUBINI, MARIO. "Divagazioni metriche." In *Scritti in onore di Luigi Ronga*, edited by Riccardo Ricciardi, pp. 211–23. Milan: Ricciardi, 1973.

The discussion on Ariosto, pp. 213–19, first appeared with title "Poscritto: gli *enjambements* nel *Furioso*," in his *Studi sulla letteratura del Rinascimento* (Florence: La Nuova Italia, 1971), pp. 241–47.

In discussing the *enjambement* in Ariosto and Tasso, points out that in the former the device may have the function of muting or softening the poetic line ("smorzamento"), peculiar to prose style; in other instances, it may be used to put in relief the melodic qualities and the dynamism of the verse; and, finally, it may serve the poet to signal stress and tension in the octave.

345. FUCILLA, JOSEPH G. *Estudios sobre el petrarquismo en España.* Madrid: OGRAMA, 1960. 340p., passim.

Indications of imitations of Ariosto's vernacular lyrics among Spanish Renaissance poets and especially of the sonnet "Chiuso era il sol da un tenebroso velo," which is called "uno de los más copiados del renacimiento italiano" (p. 63).

346. GANDOLFO, FRANCESCO. *Il "Dolce tempo": mistica, ermetismo e sogno nel Cinquecento.* Rome: Bulzoni, 1978. 323p.

Brief analysis of the grotto of Sleep ("grotta del Sonno," *OF* 14. 92–94), noting that the major source is Statius's *Thebais* (10.84–117) and that the description is essentially scenographic. See especially pp. 301–3. Includes forty-six illustrations.

347. G[ARDAIR], J[EAN]-M[ICHEL]. "Arioste (l')." In *La Grande Encyclopédie*, 5:1000. 61 vols. Paris: Librairie Larousse, 1972.

Notes as constant themes in Ariosto the poet's love of his native province and of his personal freedom. Briefly traces Ariosto's service under the Este; notes the minor works and Ariosto's variety of activities as a man of the theater. States that the 1969 production of a dramatization of the *OF* by Sanguineti and Ronconi is proof of the poem's theatricality. Brief discussion of the evolution of the *OF*.

348. GARDNER, EDMUND GARRATT. *The King of Court Poets, a Study of the Work, Life, and Times of Lodovico Ariosto.* New York: Haskell House Publishers, 1968. 395p.

Reprint of 1906 edition; Fatini, 1929.

349. GAUDIN-CLOUET, DOMINIQUE. "Le théâtre de l'Arioste." In *Notiziario culturale italiano* (entry 573) 15, no. 3 (1974): 81–85.

Without making a distinction between the prose and verse versions of the comedies or the chronology of their composition, states that Ariosto's theater remains, in its adherence to tradition, for the most part alien to the audience for which it was intended and unsympathetic in its generally critical, satirical representation of court mores and greed. (See also entry 210, Dominique Clouet, "Empirisme ou égotisme.")

📚 350. GETTO, GIOVANNI. "La Corte estense luogo d'incontro di una civ- iltà letteraria." In his _Letteratura e critica nel tempo_, pp. 325–57. Milan: Marzorati, 1968.
First edition 1954; Fatini, 3547.

📚 351. GETTO, GIOVANNI, ROBERTO ALONGE, GUIDO BALDI, AND GIOR- GIO DE RIENZO. "Ludovico Aristo." In _Storia della letteratura italiana_, pp. 201–24. Milan: Rizzoli, 1972. 664p.
In a brief biographical note observes that there is in Ariosto the coexistence of an active and contemplative personality, representing "un aspetto . . . della più vasta e ricca esistenza umana" (p. 202) rather than an irreconcilable antithesis. Summary analysis of the minor works, noting that in the satires, the "elemento biografico vale piuttosto come occasione, come punto di par- tenza per un discorso che si allarga a considerazioni più vaste, moralistica- mente atteggiate, ora in senso bonario, ora in senso decisamente polemico" (p. 206). Discussion of the _OF_; observes that the knight in the poem "si presenta come individuo libero, teso esclusivamente all'affermazione della propria personalità, alla conquista della gloria e della fama come sanzione di questa eccellenza. . . . Il vero soggetto del poema non è . . . dato dalle isti- tuzioni cavalleresche ma dalla nuova concezione della vita tipica della cos- cienza rinascimentale" (pp. 209–10). Argues that Ariosto is essentially a re- alist, as, for example, in the depiction of the complexity of human psychology (pp. 210–11) and considers each of the major figures in the poem. Brief discussion of major themes, including love, friendship, and fi- delity. Defines the spatial and temporal dimensions of the poem as "open" ("aperti"): "Il _Furioso_ non si inquadra in una struttura precisa, finita, circo- scritta, ma si muove entro una cornice per così dire fluida, mobile, senza centri stabili. Al gusto medievale per le architetture ben precisate . . . si sostituisce un gusto di spazi e di tempi aperti in cui l'unico centro è e resta l'uomo" (p. 220).

📚 352. GETTO, GIOVANNI. "L'_Orlando Furioso_ e la poesia dello spazio." In _Studi di letteratura italiana in onore di Fausto Montanari_, pp. 97– 132. Genoa: Il Melangolo, 1980.
Denies the commonly held view that Ariosto is "un fantasioso poeta dello spazio e che il suo capolavoro si offra, in uno degli aspetti fondamentali, sotto l'apparenza luminosa di una spazialità concretamente disposta in mol-

teplici forme e dimensioni" (p. 97). Comments extensively on elements in the *OF* that provide a geographical dimension to the narrative or that simply produce a sense of spaciousness, such as the description of cities, rivers, roads, the sea, and the flights of the hippogriff. Notes that Ariosto probably felt the influence of Renaissance architecture in his descriptions of palaces and gardens and that he often appears to be rivaling contemporary sculptors and architects (p. 124). Emphasizes the significance of space and of the sense of space ("emozioni spaziali," p. 129) in the poem, but insists that the description of spatial elements is too sporadic, casual, and vague to be seen as a systematic part of the poem's structure.

⚜ 353. GHINASSI, GHINO. "Il volgare mantovano tra il Medioevo e il Rinascimento." In *Ludovico Ariosto: lingua, stile e tradizione*, edited by Cesare Segre (entry 789), pp. 7–28. Milan: Feltrinelli, 1976.

Summary view of the evolution of the Mantuan koiné toward standard Italian. Ariosto mentioned as manifesting in the several revisions of the *OF* the historical moment of linguistic change from "volgari locali e regionali alla lingua comune" (p. 7) and, in his letters, like Castiglione in his, elements of regionalism with a tendency toward standardization.

⚜ 354. GHIRARDINI, LINO LIONELLO. "Ludovico Ariosto Capitano nella Rocca di Canossa." In *Lodovico Ariosto: il suo tempo la sua terra la sua gente* (entry 468). Estratto dal *Bollettino storico reggiano* 7, no. 25 (1974): 97–104.

Considers the period of Ariosto's employment in Canossa as captain of the Rocca di Canossa, apparently in charge of a small group of soliders to oversee the territory and to enforce justice; dates the stay from April 1502 to January 1503, possibly to October 1503, noting that given our knowledge about the earliest dates for the initial octaves of the *OF* (3 February 1507), it is possible the poem was conceived while the poet was in residence at Canossa.

⚜ 355. GIAMATTI, A. BARTLETT. Chapter 3, part 4. In *The Earthly Paradise and the Renaissance Epic*, pp. 137–69. Princeton: Princeton University Press, 1966. 374p.

Focuses on the antithesis illusion/reality, a topos informing the episode of Alcina's garden (*OF* 6–7). Notes that Astolfo, largely because of having lost all illusions about Alcina and because of his humanity is much like the poet himself, "soaring above all creation," omniscient yet never seeming to do much (p. 141). Ruggiero, instead, is human and, driven by his passions and illusions, cannot and does not heed Astolfo's warning about the dangers of Alcina's garden. Observes that Ruggiero, like all men, is restless and in need of illusions and the challenges of danger and deception. Concludes that human nature is such that Alcina's garden of the illusory will always be alluring and attractive while Logistilla's island, representing the "state of soul which has found constancy and peace in a world of change," will seem bland, pale, and dull (p. 162).

⚜ 356. ———. Introduction. In *Orlando Furioso*, by Ludovico Ariosto, translated by William Stewart Rose, edited by Stewart A. Baker and A. Bartlett Giamatti, pp. ix–xliv. Indianapolis and New York: Bobbs-Merrill, 1968.

General introduction to Ariosto and his works, with a critical perspective on the *OF*. Notes that within the ordered universe of the poem lies a vision of a world in constant flux and decay and of man subject to limitations and to the incessant mutability of his fortunes. Views the poem's irony as resulting from Ariosto's "sense of the profound discrepancy between the way things appear and the way things are" (p. xxxv), from expectations that, if exaggerated, can threaten our equilibrium and abilities to survive. Concludes with a discussion of the poem's unifying elements, including the Virgilian model for structural form, and of its epic qualities.

⚜ 357. ———. "Proteus Unbound: Some Versions of the Sea God in the Renaissance." In *The Disciplines of Criticism: Essays in Literary Theory, Interpretation, and History*, edited by Peter Demetz, Thomas Greene, and Lowry Nelson, Jr., pp. 437–75. New Haven and London: Yale University Press, 1968.

Extensive analysis of the Proteus figure in a variety of Renaissance texts. Notes that it not only appropriately "figure[s] the multiple glories of man, but [that] man's Protean ability to adapt and to act many roles is the source of the power that enables him to assume the burdens of civilization" (p. 439). Considers the multiple roles of the Proteus figure in the Renaissance, including that of the poet and *vates*, or seer; the *magus* and sinister manipulator of words; the actor and deceiver; and, in Boccaccio, Ariosto, and others, a figure representative of man's passions. Analyzes the nature of Proteus in *OF* 7, 10, and 11, representing sexual lawlessness and civil discord (p. 469), concluding that in this episode, "noticeably absent is [Ariosto's] habitual ironic preoccupation with the discrepancy between illusion and reality, perhaps because the incidents involving Proteus are part of a more somber theme in the poem, the insanity which is caused by love and, finally, the insanity which is love. . . . we might also suggest that the Proteus episodes lack Ariosto's customary irony because that is what the episodes are about: they deal with that loss of balance, of perspective, of proportion—irony in its largest sense—without which men are doomed and which men seemed forever doomed to lack" (p. 470).

⚜ 358. ———. *Play of Double Senses: Spenser's "Faerie Queene."* Englewood Cliffs, N.J.: Prentice Hall, 1975. 140p.

States that "Spenser knew and loved [the *OF*] and borrowed from it brilliantly, learning from it a radical truth, that we believe only what we need and want to believe, that no one truly deludes a man but himself. The warnings throughout *The Faerie Queene* to be wary, to be wise . . . derive ultimately from lessons learned in the bright, deceptive, conservative world of Ariosto" (p. 31).

◆§ 359. ———. "Headlong Horses, Headless Horsemen: An Essay on the Chivalric Epics of Pulci, Boiardo, and Ariosto." In *Italian Literature, Roots and Branches. Essays in Honor of Thomas Goddard Bergin*, edited by Giose Rimanelli and Kenneth John Atichity, pp. 265–307. New Haven and London: Yale University Press, 1976.

Having traced the metaphor of the curbed and unrestrained horse from Virgil to Boiardo, discusses its use in the *OF*. Argues that a knight's ability to curb his horse symbolizes or "figures control of one's intellective part, and that part of us, for Ariosto, is our destiny" (p. 293), while the unchecked horse reveals one's unrestrained energy and lack of self-control. Compares Astolfo's expert handling of the hippogriff to the artist "who disciplines the imagination by bridling the sheer energy it contains" (p. 293). Views Orlando's madness in terms of the metaphor of the unbridled horse, an image reflecting the "loss of control that invariably results from substituting something else for one's native *senno*" (p. 301).

◆§ 360. ———. "*Sfrenatura*: Restraint and Release in *Orlando Furioso*." In *Ariosto 1974 in America*, edited by Aldo Scaglione (entry 760), pp. 31–39. Ravenna: Longo, 1976.

Suggests that the image of the rein curbing and releasing the horse and associated with the narrative of Orlando's adventures is symbolic of the paladin's restrained and unrestrained behavior, respectively. Views Orlando as rational and in control when dealing with outside forces, but weak and incapacitated in the face of his own needs and emotions (p. 32). Argues that Orlando's loss of his senses, or *senno*, and his eventual repossession of his sanity is a lesson in human despair and hope, "the paradigm for man's excesses and for the self-imposed limitations that will be his salvation" (p. 39).

◆§ 361. GIBALDI, JOSEPH. "Will Ariosto be the Next Tolkien?" *College Literature* 2 (1975): 138–42.

Brief perspective on the teaching of the *OF* in translation in American colleges and universities, noting texts available and suggesting pedagogical approaches to the text.

◆§ 362. ———. "Bibliography of Ariosto in England and America." In *Ariosto 1974 in America*, edited by Aldo Scaglione (entry 760), pp. 159–77. Ravenna: Longo, 1976.

Selected bibliography of 296 entries divided into eight sections and intended to provide a basic list of source materials for "the student of Ariosto interested in the poet's fortunes in England and America" (p. 159). Includes "Studies in Italian"; "Anglo-American Editions of Ariosto's Works"; "Translations"; "Principal Imitations and Allusions"; "Criticism: Books and Pamphlets"; "Criticism: Articles in Periodicals"; "Doctoral Dissertations"; "Ariosto and the Other Arts."

363. ———. "The Fortunes of Ariosto in England and America." In *Ariosto 1974 in America*, edited by Aldo Scaglione (entry 760), pp. 135–58. Ravenna: Longo, 1976.
Surveys translations, editions, and imitations of Ariosto's works, especially of the *OF*. Considers both English and American interest in the poet, noting that he was most popular in the English-speaking world during the Renaissance and throughout the romantic period. Notes that interest in Ariosto is currently on the rise, judging from the many critical studies, translations, and doctoral dissertations devoted to Ariosto in the United States.

364. GIBBONS, FELTON. *Dosso and Battista Dossi: Court Painters at Ferrara*. Princeton: Princeton University Press, 1968. 320p.
Discussion of the Ferrarese court and patronage during the late fifteenth century and the first decades of the sixteenth. Notes the importance of the Este villas and *villeggiatura* to court life and cites the poetry of Ariosto as a "suggestive source for the attitude prevalent in the Ferrarese court toward the outdoors" (p. 10); suggests further that Dosso's landscapes reflect the "pastoral ideality" (p. 10) of Ariosto's poetry. Questions the validity of insisting too strongly on the association between Ariosto and Dosso and, therefore, on the parallels between their art. Remarks, nevertheless, certain similarities in their aesthetic, including an interest in the intimate and human as opposed to the grandiose or monumental; a persistent comic streak in their work; and that Bertoni's dictum that Ariosto "was a pure priest of Beauty" holds true for Dosso as well (pp. 19–20; Giulio Bertoni, *L'"Orlando furioso" e la Rinascenza a Ferrara*, 1919). Discusses the Ariosto-Dossi association in theatrical activities, noting the complete lack of extant set designs by the Dossi but asserting that they were designers and painters of Ariosto's sets (p. 22). Includes extensive bibliography, pp. 296–306, and 237 plates.

365. GILBERT, ALLAN H. "Spenserian Comedy." *Tennessee Studies in Literature* 2 (1957): 95–104.
Notes Spenser's use of the story of Fiammetta (*OF* 28) in *FQ*, 3.7.51–61, in which the "close-packed and varied comedy of the stanzas" (p. 99) outdoes the original in cynicism and humor.

◆§ 366. ———. "*Orlando Furioso* as a Sixteenth-Century Text." *Italica* 37, no. 4 (1960): 239–56.

Review essay of the 1960 edition of the *OF*, edited by Santorre Debenedetti and Cesare Segre (entry 25). Considers Debenedetti's collation of eleven of the twenty-three extant copies of the 1532 edition and the continuation of his editorial work by Segre, noting and commenting on orthographic and other changes. Considers Ariosto's assiduous revisions of his text in the context of linguistic changes during the sixteenth century, observing that he edited his work "in the direction of modernity. But he was a poet rather than a linguistic scholar, and he lived in an age when orthographic uniformity such as ours had not yet come. Bembo dealt with the matter because he realized his age's confusion and lack of guidance. In this confusion Ariosto shared" (p. 253). Cautions against editorial interference: "While Debenedetti's efforts to determine Ariosto's preferences in spelling are excellent for an article, they are annoying when carried into an edition for painstaking students, who wish the book as it was, not as an editor believes it should have been" (p. 255). Argues for the importance to students of "old-spelling" editions (p. 255), since readers interested in orthography and metrics cannot rely on even the most competently revised modernized version.

◆§ 367. GINZBURG, LEONE. "I Frammenti autografi dell'*Orlando Furioso*." In his *Scritti*, pp. 433–37. Turin: Einaudi, 1964.

First published under pseudonym "Aquilante" in *Lavoro* (Genoa), 4 June 1937; Fatini, 3167.

◆§ 368. ———. "Sulla 'toscanità' dell'Ariosto." In his *Scritti*, pp. 471–73. Turin: Einaudi, 1964.

Unpublished notes written while a political prisoner, 1935.

States that Ariosto, even in the first edition of the *OF*, avoids the Lombardisms—or "ferrarismi"—of Boiardo. Suggests linguistic influence of Pulci on the purifying process and suggests need for a study of Pulci's influence. Briefly notes Ariosto's interest in the *questione della lingua* and the influence of Pietro Bembo and, possibly, of the views of Baldassare Castiglione.

◆§ 369. GIRALDI CINTHIO, GIOVAMBATTISTA. *Giraldi Cinthio on Romances; being a translation of the "Discorso intorno al comporre dei romanzi."* With introduction and notes by Henry L. Snuggs. Lexington: University of Kentucky Press, 1968. 194p.

Translation of Giraldi Cintio's theory of the epic poem (1549) and defense of the *OF*. Introduction considers the nature of Giraldi Cintio's theory of the *romanzo* (pp. xiii–xxii).

🥚 370. GIRARDI, ENZO NOÈ. "Ariosto, Shakespeare, Corneille e la definizione crociana del Furioso." In Studi sull'Ariosto, presentazione di Enzo Noè Girardi, pp. 13–38. Milan: Vita e Pensiero (Pubblicazioni dell'Università Cattolica del Sacro Cuore), 1977.

Brief analysis of Croce's formulation of the aesthetics of Corneille's and Shakespeare's theater; extensive discussion of the validity of Croce's analysis of the Ariostean aesthetic of harmony, noting, however, that the critic failed to see it for what it was, "il frutto dell'incontro di una grande personalità di artista con la ricca e varia materia narrativa ed umana che il Boiardo aveva messa insieme nel suo poema" (p. 35). Considers the aesthetics of the OF in relationship to an evolution away from the medieval sense of the distinction between form and content toward a conjoining of the signifier and the signified: "nell'Ariosto intuizione e tecnica sono al servizio di una assolutamente nuova e piena coscienza operativa della serietà e dignità intrinseca dell'arte, della sua sostanziale alterità e libertà dal mondo della necessità economica . . . ma come criterio immediato del bello, indipendentemente dal supporto più o meno pretestuoso di una funzione pratica, cioè edonistico-ricreativa o parenetica" (p. 35).

🥚 371. ———. Studi sull'Ariosto, presentazione di Enzo Noè Girardi. Milan: Vita e Pensiero (Pubblicazioni dell'Università Cattolica del Sacro Cuore), 1977. 191p.

Contents: Enzo Noè Girardi, "Ariosto, Shakespeare, Corneille e la definizione crociana del Furioso" (entry 370); Giovanna Barlusconi, "L'Orlando furioso poema dello spazio" (entry 58); Giuseppina Romagnoli Robuschi, "Lettura del canto XXIII dell'Orlando furioso" (entry 696); Pier Luigi Cerisola, "Il problema critico dei Cinque canti" (entry 190).

🥚 372. GISOLFI, ANTHONY M. "Ariosto's Delightful Prologue to La Cassaria." The Theatre Annual 22 (1965–1966): 41–47.

Calls the prologues to the comedies an art form in themselves, noting that they provide a commentary on social mores and an entertainment for Renaissance theater audiences. Includes an English verse translation of the prologue to La Cassaria.

🥚 373. GIUFFRIDA, AGOSTINO. "'Ciance legali' e codici ariostei." Biologia culturale 9, no. 4 (1974): 169–71.

Cites references in the OF to legal points, suggesting at times a reflection of Ariosto's own moral stance.

🥚 374. GNUDI, CESARE. "L'Ariosto e le arti figurative." In Ludovico Ariosto, pp. 331–401. Convegno internazionale (entry 475). Rome: Accademia Nazionale dei Lincei, 1975.

Also in his *L'ideale classico: saggi sulla tradizione classica nella pittura del Cinquecento e del Seicento* (Bologna: Edizioni Alfa, 1981), pp. 119–60, with thirty-four plates.

Two-part essay examines Ariosto's aesthetic in relation to that of contemporary painters, especially Raphael and Titian, and the influence of Ariosto upon painters subsequent to him, particularly those whose creative spirit was notably stimulated by his poetic vision: Dosso Dossi, Nicolò dell'Abate, and Jean-Honoré Fragonard. Extensive discussion of the affinity between the ideals of classical harmony dominating pictorial art in Tuscany, Urbino, and Rome in the late Quattrocento and early Cinquecento (Leonardo, Bramante, Raphael) and Ariosto's own poetic representation of the harmonious rapport between man and his universe. Considers the influence of Venetian painting, especially Titian, on the late Ariosto, in particular the representation of the "infinito variare di sentimenti e ricchezza di sensi, nel cuore della natura" (p. 370). Interprets the significance of *OF* 33. 2, stating that the catalog of artists is intended as a tribute to artists who most directly influenced him (pp. 379–83). Includes forty-one reproductions.

❦ 375. ———. "Il Ciclo cavalleresco del Pisanello alla corte dei Gonzaga: I. Il Pisanello e la grande scoperta di Mantova." In *Studies in Late Medieval and Renaissance Painting in Honor of Millard Meiss*, edited by Irving Lavin and John Plummer, 1: 192–204. 2 vols. New York: New York University Press, 1977.

Brief observations on the dramatic and melancholic representation of the heroic-chivalric tradition in the frescoes of Pisanello in Mantua and the more distanced, objective perspective on the world of chivalry in the *OF*: "Lo sguardo dell'artista [Ariosto] è al centro di quell'orizzonte infinito. Tutto è veduto da lontano, così che i contorni della realtà si fanno più tenui, e tutto si amalgama e digrada, proprio al contrario che in Pisanello dove tutto è veduto da vicino, dove ogni particolare è esaltato ed evidenziato, dove tutto si ispessisce e si accosta a noi, al nostro occhio, ci prende e ci avvolge" (p. 199).

❦ 376. GOFFIS, CESARE FEDERICO. "I *Cinque Canti* di un nuovo libro di M. Ludovico Ariosto." *La Rassegna della letteratura italiana*, 7th ser., vol. 79, nos. 1–2 (1975): 146–68.

Also published as a monograph (Genoa: Tilgher, 1975), 52p.

Reviews the polemic surrounding the composition and the revision of the CC from Aldo Manuzio (1545) to the present. Focuses on the dates proposed by Carlo Dionisotti and Cesare Segre and gives a detailed summary of Luciano Capra's arguments for dating the CC prior to the first edition of the OF. Suggests that the CC is "un'opera rimasta allo stato acerbo, riletta qualche volta dall'autore con talune sporadiche correzioni; ma in condizioni di sviluppo assai arretrate rispetto al *Furioso* 1516" (pp. 162–63).

377. GOLENISHCHEV-KUTUZOV, I. N. "Ariosto, Lodovico." In *Great Soviet Encyclopedia*, 2: 297. Translation of the third edition. 31 vols. plus indexes. New York: Macmillan; London: Collier Macmillan Publishers, 1973.

Very brief outline of Ariosto's literary production, stating that the *OF* is "a new kind of humanistic narrative poem, independent of its predecessors." Notes Russian translations of the *OF*.

378. GOOSSE, MARIE-THÉRÈSE. "*Du sang, de la volupté et de la mort*: Quelques pages du Tasse et de l'Arioste." *Revue de littérature comparée* 36, no. 1 (1962): 111–18.

Rejects Jacques Bainville's observation (1903) that in the second edition of Maurice Barrès's *Du sang, de la volupté et de la mort* one finds "une fantasie sur les poèmes de l'Arioste et du Tasse" (quoted on p. 111). Shows that, in fact, Barrès had borrowed from Le Brun's translation of the *GL* and from Philipon de la Madelaine's French rendition of the *OF*.

379. GORÒCHOVA, R. M. "La Fortuna dell'Ariosto in Russia." In *Ludovico Ariosto*, pp. 545–62. Convegno internazionale (entry 475). Rome: Accademia Nazionale dei Lincei, 1975.

Notes that Ariosto first became known in Russia in the eighteenth century and principally through French translations. Reviews Ariosto's critical reception during the romantic period and especially the interest of K. N. Batiushkov, whose essay on Ariosto and Tasso (1815) reflects the esteem in which the poet was held in the nineteenth century. Discusses Ariosto's influence on Pushkin, notes the several fragmented translations of the *OF* and the first full-length prose translation (1892). Concludes by noting that there are no significant modern critical studies of Ariosto in Russian. Includes Russian text (pp. 527–43).

380. GOROKHOVA (GORÒCHOVA), R. M. "Ariosto v Rossii (Materialy k istorii ego izucheniia i vospriiatiia)" (Ariosto in Russia [materials on the history of his study and acceptance]). *Russkaia literatura*, no. 4 (1974): 115–26.

Summary of Ariosto's critical fortunes in Russia. Notes that the poet is first mentioned in the eighteenth century and by the end of the century seems to have gained a certain popularity. The *OF* was known in the original but especially through French translations; the first nearly complete Russian translation, based on a French version, was published at the end of the eighteenth century. Ariosto gained popularity in the nineteenth century, and from the 1820s on he figured prominently in literary polemics between the classicists and the romanticists. At the beginning of the century, the *OF* was viewed as a national heroic epic, a view colored by the importance given during the Enlightenment to national epics. K. N. Batiushkov is especially important for the diffusion of interest in Ariosto in Russia: a student of Italian language and literature, he translated fragments of the *OF* and wrote an important critical essay on Ariosto and Tasso. Aleksandr Pushkin's "Ruslan and Ludmilla" (1820) was immediately compared to the *OF*. Contends that Pushkin's poem is an attempt to rival rather than to imitate Ariosto. Discusses early nineteenth-century translations of the *OF*, noting that by the end of the 1830s, with the waning of Russian romanticism, interest in Ariosto diminished and was never revived to any important degree. Observes that there is no complete verse translation of the *OF* into Russian, nor are there significant modern critical evaluations of the poet and his work.

᠊ᢙ 381. GOTTFRIED, RUDOLF. Introduction. In *Orlando Furioso: Selections from the Translation of Sir John Harington*, pp. 9–20. Bloomington and London: Indiana University Press, 1963.
Notes that the liberties taken by Harington with the original text were in line with prevailing views of translation in Renaissance England and that his translation captures the spirit of the original better than other English versions. Finds "ironic disillusionment with the whole of life" (p. 14) as the basis of Ariosto's poem, and discusses the tone and variety of poetic irony in the *OF*, noting by way of example, comic, pathetic, and violent forms of irony.

᠊ᢙ 382. GRABHER, CARLO. "Ariosto, Ludovico." In *Enciclopedia dello spettacolo*, 1: columns 848–56. 9 vols. Rome: Casa Editrice Le Maschere, 1954–1962.
Biography of Ariosto; brief discussion of the *OF*. Considers Ariosto's theatrical activities and interests. Synopsis of each play and a brief critical evaluation. Concludes that plays are inferior to Ariosto's poetry but reveal the same good sense and wisdom resulting from his varied experiences found in the satires.

᠊ᢙ 383. GRACIOTTI, SANTE. "Piotr Kochanowski w Polskim Oświeceniu oraz Przekłady Ariosta i Tassa Pióra Krasickiego i Trembeckiego" (Piotr Kochanowski in the Polish Enlightenment and the translations of Ariosto and Tasso by Krasicki and Trembecki). In *W Kręgu "Gofreda" I "Orlanda"* (entry 913), pp. 85–103. Wrocław-Warszawa-Craków: Polska Akademia Nauk, 1970.
Notes that the eighteenth-century translation by Ignacy Krasicki of parts of

the *OF*, in a renewed interest in chivalric literature, is faithful to the original but lacks the poetic qualities of Kochanowski's version.

◆§ 384. "Arioste (Ludovico Ariosto, dit l')." In *Grand Larousse Encyclopédique*, 1:569. 10 vols. Paris: Librairie Larousse, 1960.
Summary account of Ariosto's life and works. Describes the *OF* as "Oeuvre parfaite par le style, l'imagination souriante, la fine ironie, les peinture des paysages et des amours imaginaires, le merveilleux et la richesse des intrigues, ce poème est le chef-d'oeuvre de la Renaissance parvenue à sa maturité."

◆§ 385. "Ariosto, Ludovico." In *Grande Enciclopedia Vallardi*, 2:78–80. 16 vols. Milan: F. Vallardi, 1968–72.
General and summary introduction to Ariosto's life and work. Calls the *OF* "il poema della bellezza, dell'eroismo, della gioventù" and states that in it "lo spirito rinascimentale sembra raggiungere il suo più perfetto equilibrio e splendore" (p. 80).

◆§ 386. GRAYSON, CECIL. "Appunti sulla lingua delle commedie in prosa e in versi." In *Ludovico Ariosto: lingua, stile e tradizione*, edited by Cesare Segre (entry 789), pp. 379–90. Milan: Feltrinelli, 1976.
Compares the lexical elements of the prose and later verse versions of *La Cassaria* and *I Suppositi* and concludes that, in general, the verse redactions—especially of *La Cassaria*—reveal a loss of picturesque and highly colored vocabulary and a tendency toward a more neutral language. Suggests that the verse versions reveal an interest on the part of Ariosto to eliminate regional elements from the language for a more standard vernacular and to draw less attention to individual lexical elements in an attempt to create a more simple and natural language for the theater.

◆§ 387. GRAZIOSI, MARIA TERESA. "Il 'parasita' nella commedia del Rinascimento." *Atti e memorie dell'Accademia Letteraria Italiana Arcadia*, 3d ser., 6, fasc. 3 (1974, but 1975): 93–107.
Briefly discusses characteristics of the parasite in Plautine comedy ("buffone di professione," p. 95) and Terentian comedy (greater psychological subtlety but without scruples, p. 95) and states that in Renaissance theater the character "acquista maggior rilievo . . . un suo posto preciso nella fastosa vita delle corti; di una società sensibile ai piaceri mondani, il parasita è una componente essenziale per la capacità di aderire allo spirito cortegiano" (p. 97). Notes that the principal characteristic of the parasite is gluttony and that in Renaissance dramatic forms classical elements merge with reality and "la figura del parasita si arricchisce quindi di motivi polemici nuovi, si valorizza nell'esaltazione dell'intelligenza e della furbizia nei suoi molteplici aspetti,

risulta una efficace rappresentazione delle capacità umane" (p. 97). In this context, briefly discusses the role of the parasite Pasifilo in Ariosto's *I Suppositi* (p. 97).

✒ 388. GRECO, AULO. "Capitolo sulla commedia del Rinascimento." In *Essenza-Persistenza-Sviluppi*, pp. 125–43. Vol. 1 of *Interrogativi dell'Umanesimo*, edited by Giovannangiola Tarugi. Atti del IX Convegno Internazionale del Centro di Studi Umanistici, Montepulciano, Palazzo Tarugi, 1972. Florence: Leo S. Olschki, 1976.
With Ariosto as a major example, focuses on the evolution of Renaissance comedy from its Latin origins. Briefly discusses the comic prologues and their subsequent elaboration to show that while Ariosto was at first faithful to his Roman models, he slowly developed his own poetics, revealed in his changing style (testimony to the effect of Bembo's linguistic theories), the reflection of current customs, and the references to contemporary historical personages and events.

✒ 389. ———. "Ludovico Ariosto: modelli per l'istituzione del teatro comico." In his *L'Istituzione del teatro comico nel Rinascimento*, pp. 49–71. Naples: Liguori, 1976.
Also in *Annali della pubblica istruzione* 21 (1975): 147–59.
Places Ariosto's activity as a dramatist in the sociocultural context of Ferrarese society and states that his comedies, while continuing in the Plautine tradition favored by the Este court, are experimental (p. 62) and constantly aim—through language, characters, and themes—at realizing a truly topical theater in close touch with the social realities of his time. Traces the evolution of Ariosto's dramatic experimentation from *La Cassaria*, in which traditional situations and characters constantly recall a contemporary mercantile society (p. 56), to *Il Negromante* and its satire and ironic vision of Ferrarese society (p. 66). Considers several analogies between the comedies and the *OF*, including structural complexities (p. 67), the use of satire, and the use of subtle irony.

✒ 390. GREENE, THOMAS M. "Ariosto and the Earlier Italian Renaissance." Chap. 6 in *The Descent from Heaven: A Study in Epic Continuity*, pp. 104–43. New Haven and London: Yale University Press, 1963. 434p.
In the context of an analysis of the descent of the angel Michele (Archangel Michael) in *OF* 14 and of its relation to the literary convention of the celestial messenger in classical and humanistic epic, considers the particular nature and modernity of the *OF*: "[Ariosto] follows the classical texts with enough fidelity to invite comparison. But once compared, the originals are striking for their simplicity. Ariosto's mercurial artistic sense is alive to all of

the possible vantage points upon a single scene, and he proffers in turn the heroic, the mordant, the melodramatic, the idyllic. . . . In his critical sense, his artistic independence, his freedom from any tradition, Ariosto stands as a more modern figure than any of the men who attempted after him to write epic poetry. . . . Comparing his work to the ancients', we remark the comparative clutter of modern literature, its impurity, its resistance to classification. And in his sensibility we encounter, astonishingly early, the blurred edge of consciousness, the reflexive irony, the unwillingness to see quite whole and clear, the capacity to entertain simultaneously more than one thought" (pp. 128–29).

Observes in the episode of Michele's descent a comic manner and ironic, humorous tone that make it exemplary of Ariosto's perspective on Christianity (it "is not so much disbelieved as made insubstantial," p. 122) and independence of humanist tradition: "For the very reason that Ariosto's Humanistic feeling was deep, the irreverent treatment of Michele's descent bears significance for the *Furioso* and in fact for literary history. The liberties taken with an enshrined epic convention anticipate the mock-heroic or burlesque modes of the seventeenth and eighteenth centuries. Ariosto is less obvious than Scarron or Boileau, and Pope himself is no defter. But the liberty is particularly momentous in reference to the date; it is astonishing to find in the morning glow of Humanism a literary independence which was to emerge as a logical, historically explicable, widely shared spirit only in an age when the most enlightened moderns could quarrel with the ancients. There had been anti-Humanistic movements in Italy well before Ariosto, but not this Olympian toying with a beloved thing" (pp. 124–25). Relates the tone of the episode to Ariosto's "middle style which denies itself the highest effects, broadest gestures. There is almost nothing of the ritualistic in it, beside an occasional formal simile. It is completely subservient and faithful to the demands of the narrative whole, and even where these demands are heavy . . . the language never dramatizes itself, never calls attention to its own compelling force" (p. 117). Discusses, in relation to the episode of Michele's descent, the nature of Ariosto's skepticism and its manifestation in the text; the motif of disillusionment, which has its quintessential representation in the episode of Astolfo's voyage to the moon ("The terrible sadness of the voyage stems from the serene knowledge that nothing on earth truly is as it is supposed to be," p. 131); Ariosto's sense of history in the text and his role as dynastic poet; the moral perspective in the *OF*: "It wavers . . . between a bourgeois impulse to moral judgment and a wearier, more refined inclination to shrug the shoulders. . . . It is plain that the heroic dimensions of the action in the *Furioso* are reduced by the moral ambiguity" (p. 138).

Concludes with a discussion of the *OF*'s failure as epic in its lack of a "pressing moral imperative" (p. 139), though in "certain passages portraying Rodomonte, Ariosto most nearly approaches epic intensity and heroic awe"

(p. 142). Concludes that considerations in discussion "help to mark the limits of Ariosto's imagination, the frontiers of his fictive country. But once we reenter his country they fall away as pedantic foolishness. Ample, bright, labyrinthine, and seductive, that country's peculiar gift is that its visitor wants it to be nothing more than itself. Ariosto's richest achievement was the creation of that fine insidious world where heroism is not necessary" (p. 143).

⚜ 391. ———. "The Flexibility of the Self in Renaissance Literature." In *The Disciplines of Criticism: Essays in Literary Theory, Interpretation, and History*, edited by Peter Demetz, Thomas Greene, and Lowry Nelson, Jr., pp. 241–64. New Haven and London: Yale University Press, 1968.
Notes the importance of Pico della Mirandola's *Oration on the Dignity of Man* for asserting human freedom "to select one's destiny, to mold and transform the self" and compares this strain of humanist thought with medieval doctrines "which held human nature to be unalterably fixed" (p. 243). Discusses Petrarch's importance for having first explicitly challenged the "radical stasis of the medieval personality" (p. 246) and notes that humanist interest in the fashioning of the self gave rise to one of the most important Renaissance genres, the "institute," or didactic tract. Notes that the "fashioning of the pupil by the pedagogue was replaced by the reflexive fashioning of the individual's own mind and soul. Humanist formation first assisted in, then gave way to, metaphysical transformation" (p. 252). Surveys several texts that conclude with meditations on human transcendence, including Castiglione's *Book of the Courtier*. Discusses the position of both Machiavelli and Ariosto in the context of the essay's thesis, noting that for the former "the vertical flexibility of man is very limited" (p. 257) and that in the *OF* the rare instances of human transcendence are seen as deceptive and futile hopes. Concludes with a discussion of "Humanist anthropology" (p. 260) in the English Renaissance, "which fixed much firmer upper limits on human potentiality" (p. 260).

⚜ 392. GRIERSON, HERBERT J. C. *Cross-Currents in 17th Century English Literature: The World, the Flesh, and the Spirit, Their Actions and Reactions*. Gloucester, Mass.: Peter Smith, 1965. 345p.
First edition 1929. In considering the express purpose of the *FQ* and relating it to its romance predecessors, observes: "It would not be unjust to contend that both the *Morte d'Arthur* and the *Orlando Furioso* are more impressive ethical poems than the *Faerie Queene* because they are more human, deal with more realisable characters, their temptations and sins and repentance. Arthur [of the *FQ*] and Artegal are no more than names; Belphoebe and Florimel and Britomart but charming shadows. No one of them is either an individual for whose fate we feel deeply concerned, or, as an abstraction,

assumes the proportions of Everyman face to face with one of the great, elemental temptations or experiences of men" (p. 63).

◄§ 393. GRIFFIN, ROBERT. *Ludovico Ariosto*. New York: Twayne, 1974. 180p.
Introductory critical study of Ariosto's life and works. Divided into seven chapters. Chapter 1 ("Along the Pleasant Shore of Italy," pp. 13–24) relates the poet's life in its cultural and historical contexts. Chapter 2 ("Minor Works," pp. 25–48) considers the comedies, the satires, and the Latin lyrics. Chapter 3 ("Oh, Great Goodness of the Ancient Knights," pp. 49–74) gives a summary review of the epic and chivalric traditions informing the *OF* and states that "Ariosto's attitude toward warfare is ambivalent" (p. 73), noting the reasons. Chapter 4 ("Variety, Which is Usually Pleasing to Many," pp. 75–98) argues against the view that the poem lacks unity. Chapter 5 ("That Paradise Called Earthly," pp. 99–111) links the quest motif of Astolfo's voyage to Asia, the underworld, and to the moon to the topology of medieval journeys to Paradise. Chapter 6 ("Perhaps it was Allowed by God the Avenger," pp. 112–36) analyzes Ariosto's use of numerology, irony, and a variety of forms of ambiguity. Chapter 7 ("Pure and Sweet Speech," pp. 137–56) differentiates between three kinds of rhetorical speech in the *OF* (deliberative, panegyric, and courtly), points out the narrator's inconsistencies in the poem, and concludes with a concise survey of Ariosto criticism. Includes bibliography (pp. 171–73).

◄§ 394. GRILLI, ALFREDO. "L'Ariosto e la critica." *Nuova Antologia* 475, fasc. 1897 (1959): 110–14.
Praises Giuseppe Fatini's annotated bibliography of Ariosto criticism (1958, entry 305) but notes a number of omissions.

◄§ 395. GRIMM, JÜRGEN. *Die Einheit der Ariost'schen Satire*. Analecta Romanica, vol. 25. Frankfurt am Main: Vittorio Klostermann, 1969. 80p.
Analysis of the style, theme, and structure of the satires. Discusses principal motifs (e.g., personal freedom, the poet's love for his studies) and considers Ariosto's ironic perspective on himself. Identifies major stylistic characteristics (e.g., periphrasis, rhythmic changes, structural patterns) and discusses literary allusions (especially the use of Dante and Petrarch), qualities of his portraits of individuals, and the use of fables. Considers the nature of Ariosto's satire and extrapolates the poet's "theory" of the satirical mode.

◄§ 396. GRONDA, GIOVANNA. "L'opera critica di Antonio Conti." *Giornale storico della letteratura italiana* 141, fasc. 433 (1964): 1–37.
Discusses Conti's changing critical views on Ariosto and Tasso. Cites passages from a letter to Madame Ferrant in which Conti considers Ariosto

superior to Tasso, praising his vast imagination and both the seeming simplicity and internal order of the *OF*. Observes that in a later critical evaluation, the *Discorso sopra l'italiana poesia*, the eighteenth-century critic favors
Tasso, lamenting Ariosto's lack of verisimilitude and the introduction into his
work "del comico vile, della lascivia, del vizio" (p. 20). See especially pp.
16–22.

◄§ 397. GRÜTERS, OTTO. "Ariost und Kudrun: Kudrun und *Orlando Furioso.*" *Germanisch-Romanische Monatsschrift* 7, no. 1 (1957): 75–78.
  Takes issue with Herbert Frenzel's hypothesis that Ariosto was familiar with
the Ambraser manuscript and other manuscripts of Middle High German
epics. (Herbert Frenzel, "Von der Olimpia-Episode zu den Parerga des *Orlando Furioso,*" *Germanisch-Romanische Monatsschrift* 5 (1955): 161–79;
Fatini, 3585; see also entry 339). Discusses passages from the *OF* to substan-
tiate his claims.

◄§ 398. GUIDOTTI, ANGELA. "Dall'imitazione all''arroganzia': sviluppo e
maturazione della tecnica teatrale nelle commedie dell'Ariosto." *Rivista
italiana di drammaturgia* 5, nos. 15–16 (1980): 17–38.
  Examines Ariosto's comedies, including the unfinished *I Studenti*, to
show that his dramatic art evolves from a faithful imitation of classical theater
(*La Cassaria*) to the realization of a personal poetics (*La Lena*), namely the
development of a main character consistent with contemporary reality. Attributes this achievement to the playwright's arrogance, that is, his presumption
to manipulate in an ironic key the classical model.

◄§ 399. GÜNTERT, GEORGES. "Per una rivalutazione dell'Ariosto minore:
le *Rime.*" *Lettere italiane* 23, no. 1 (1971): 29–42.
  Suggests that the vernacular lyrics constitute an evolutionary phase in
Ariosto's poetics. Notes that love, portrayed in the Petrarchan tradition as a
dark prison ("carcer tetro," p. 34) through images of knots, snares, and other
constrictions, in Ariosto becomes a refuge from the existential prison of life
that, gladdened by love ("allietata da amore," p. 35), becomes a sweet prison
("carcere soave," p. 35). Maintains that in the *Rime* and in the satires the
poet is a victim of the snares of Fortune but that in the comedies and in the
OF, the poet manipulates them and, as artist, remains in control of them.

◄§ 400. GUYER, FOSTER. *Chrétien de Troyes: Inventor of the Modern Novel.*
New York: Bookman Associates, 1972. 247p.
  First edition 1957. Notes that the infusion of medieval romance elements
("first of all the love element, but also idealization of the hero, all the courtesy of chivalry, generosity, the magnificent and lavish spectacles of tourna-
ments, that nobility of character that made a promise sacred and finally had

its culmination in real life, in the concept of 'nobless [sic] oblige'") into the epic reaches "its highest point of development and exaltation" in the OF (p. 149). The power of love, its symptoms and effects, are essential to the poem's thematics, and the "glamor of romance remains" despite the poet's humorous intrusions (p. 150). Argues that Orlando's madness was suggested by Yvain's madness in Chrétien's romance; notes other elements in the OF reminiscent of Chrétien, including Angelica's magic ring and Rinaldo's rescue of Ginevra. "The portrait of Alcina in the seventh canto is typical of those that Chrétien placed in vogue" (p. 151). Concludes: "High adventure, indomitable courage, invincible strength in the heroes, and passionate love, and nobility of character and purpose are the dominant characteristics of this poem. They reveal it as a romance inspired by romances and carrying on the tradition invented, molded and transmitted by Chrétien de Troyes" (p. 153). See especially pp. 149–53.

⋙ 401. HALE, JOHN R[IGBY]. "Gunpowder and the Renaissance: An Essay in the History of Ideas." In *From the Renaissance to the Counter Reformation*, edited by Charles H. Carter, pp. 113–44. New York: Random House, 1965.

In discussing European reaction and eventual adjustment to the use of gunpowder during the Renaissance, notes that "the most famous and influential of all attacks on gunpowder as unchivalrous came from Ariosto, in cantos nine and eleven of the *Orlando Furioso*" (pp. 120–21).

⋙ 402. HALL, KATHLEEN M. "A Defence of Jean De La Taille as a Translator of Ariosto." *Modern Language Review* 67, no. 3 (1972): 536–42.

Having noted that De La Taille has been harshly criticized for his translation of *Il Negromante*, demonstrates by the use of various examples that the fault lay with the text upon which the translation was based, edition 'Z' published by Zoppino in Venice (1535), "perhaps the worst . . . available" (p. 536).

⋙ 403. HANNING, ROBERT W. "Sources of Illusion: Plot Elements and Their Thematic Uses in Ariosto's Ginevra Episode." *Forum Italicum* 5, no. 4 (1971): 514–35.

Argues that the story of Ginevra, Ariodante, and Polinesso (OF 4–6) is "a self-enclosed episode the central function of which is to demonstrate with much comic irony, the complicating effect of illusion on human values and behavior" (p. 514). Relates the episode's principal motifs to Orlando's love-madness (pp. 524–25) and suggests the importance of its complex consideration of perception to the sixteenth-century interest in both the illusions of art and the art of illusion.

◆§ 404. ———. "Ariosto, Ovid, and the Painters: Mythological Paragone in *Orlando Furioso* X and XI." In *Ariosto 1974 in America*, edited by Aldo Scaglione (entry 760), pp. 99–116. Ravenna: Longo, 1976.

Argues that the theme of abandonment informing the episodes of Olimpia and Bireno and of Alcina and Ruggiero are variations on the Ovidian myths of Ariadne and Theseus and of Andromeda and Perseus. Calls Alcina abandoned by Ruggiero a "tragico-pathetic heroine—a new Dido" (p. 108) and Angelica tied to the rock a "new Andromeda" (p. 109). Notes that Ariosto's variations on these myths, while inviting comparison with Ovid and other mythological sources, betray the poet's "intent to solicit comparisons between himself and mythological painters" (p. 114) of his era, such as Giovanni Bellini and Titian.

◆§ 405. HARDIN, RICHARD F. "Robert Tofte's Translation of Ariosto's Satires." *Satire Newsletter* 7, no. 2 (1970): 104–8.

Notes that Tofte's translation of the satires (1608) reveals his extensive knowledge of Italian culture and that his own ordering of them suggests that his familiarity with Ariosto's life persuaded him to amend the arrangement of the 1550 edition. Suggests that Tofte's interpolations of Ariosto's text were intended to entertain and provide readers with information on Italy. Notes that the translations are more moralizing than the original. Concludes that Tofte's translations had "little effect on the development of verse satire in England"—where "Juvenalian *indignatio* was preferred to Horatian urbanity" (p. 107)—but were received, rather, as "adjuncts to the poet's biography" (p. 108).

◆§ 406. HARMS, PAUL. *Die deutschen Fortunatus-Dramen und ein Kasseler Dichter des 17. Jahrhunderts.* Hamburg: L. Voss, 1892. Reprint. Nendeln, Liechtenstein: Kraus, 1978. 94p.

Consideration of the Fortunatus drama in Germany during the seventeenth century. Discussion of an anonymous manuscript, referred to as the Kassel manuscript, containing the text of two plays, one of which is called a tragicomedy and is based on the Ginevra and Ariodante episode of *OF* 4–6. Considers parallel passages in the German text and in the *OF*, as well as possible sources of the play, such as Diederich von dem Werder's translation of Ariosto. See especially pp. 54–79.

◆§ 407. HARTLEY, K. H. "Some Italian Sources for *La Pucelle d'Orléans.*" *MLN* 72, no. 7 (1957): 512–17.

Analysis of several borrowings from the *OF* in Voltaire's *La Pucelle d'Orléans*, disagreeing with an earlier critical appraisal that declared the French epic closely modelled on Ariosto (Jean Dubled in *Bulletin Italien*

11–13 [1911–1913]) and concluding that although Voltaire's debt to Ariosto was extensive, he used his source freely.

⋙ 408. ———. "Robert Garnier and Ariosto." *Modern Language Review* 56, no. 3 (1961): 389–91.
Concludes that Garnier is least effective ("goes astray," p. 391) in his *Bradamante* when not closely following Ariosto. Briefly discusses the legal and moral validity of the marriage between Ruggiero and Bradamante and the role of Melissa in both the *OF* and in Garnier's play.

⋙ 409. HEIER, EDMUND. "Ariosts *Orlando Furioso* und Nicolays Ritterepen." *Germanisch-Romanische Monatsschrift* 13, no. 2 (1963): 206–9.
Influences of Ariosto on the writings of Ludwig Heinrich von Nicolay (1737–1820), his use of the Alcina episode (in *Vermischten Gedichten* 2:71–174), and his attempt to render the spirit of the original in his translation of the *OF*.

⋙ 410. HELLER, AGNES. *Renaissance Man.* Translated by Richard E. Allen. New York: Schocken Books, 1981. 481p. Originally published as *A Reneszánsz Ember* (Budapest: Akadémiai Kiado, 1967).
In the context of considerations on Renaissance measure and moderation and on the cult of beauty in Italy as the protest against the "tyranny of utility" by the more aristocratic spirit of the late Quattrocento and early Cinquecento (pp. 256–60), briefly discusses the *OF*, calling it a "fable" or a "variety of *parable*" (p. 256). Discussion focuses on Ariosto's attack on the invention and use of gunpowder (*OF* 11.26), noting that if there is an expression of nostalgia in the poem, it is not for the world of chivalry but for the values that characterized the "world of the city-state republics in their prime" (p. 258). States that the poem is a world of beauty in which "terror, despair and the monstrous are all resolved" (p. 259). Concludes that Ariosto's nostalgia is a nostalgia for beauty.

⋙ 411. HEMPFER, KLAUS W. "Textkonstitution und Rezeption: zum dominant komisch-parodistischen Charakter von Pulcis *Morgante*, Boiardos *Orlando Innamorato* und Ariosts *Orlando Furioso*." *Romanistisches Jahrbuch* 27 (1976): 77–99.
Notes that the comic in literature is a reflection of sociocultural variables, making it and the principle of comedy from one historic moment to another difficult to define. Characterizes the principle of composition in the *OF* as "variatio," a mixture of the comic, the tragic, and the epic. Concludes that with Ariosto the comic dimension is essentially parodic and has as its subject the traditional structure of the chivalric epic. Artistic invention to entertain an elite audience replaces the authority of fact of traditional epic poems.

⊸§ 412. HERCZEG, G[IULIO]. "Studi di sintassi ariostesca." *Acta Linguistica. Academiae Scientiarum Hungaricae* 25 (1975): 81–117.
A slightly abridged version of the first part of essay published in *Atti. XIV Congresso internazionale di linguistica e filologia romanza*, edited by Alberto Varvaro, 4: 651–72 (Naples: Macchiaroli; Amsterdam: John Benjamins, 1977); second part of essay published in *Ludovico Ariosto: lingua, stile e tradizione*, edited by Cesare Segre (1976, entry 789), pp. 207–30.
Two-part essay. 1. "Struttura della frase dell'*Orlando Furioso*," pp. 81–103: Concludes that the "ideale stilistico" (p. 82) of Ariosto, present primarily in battle scenes and duels in the *OF*, is an enumerative process: the narrative is based on a succession of actions, each of which is normally self-contained in an independent syntactical clause. Calls the tone of Ariosto's style discursive ("tono discorsivo," pp. 85–89), characterized by brief syntactical units and the avoidance of subordinate clauses. Remarks the linguistic consequences of the narrative technique of interlace (pp. 88–89). Discusses the significant aspects of the infrequent longer syntactical units in the poem, "periodi di lunga estensione" (p. 89), noting their provenance from epic tradition or their importance to the evolution in the *OF* of indirect discourse, "stile indiretto libero." Notes the rarity of rhetorical constructions in the poem in favor of those reflecting discursive, common language. 2. "Stile indiretto libero nella lingua del *Furioso*," pp. 103–17: Extensive analysis of the variety of indirect discourse in the narrative and the violation of certain norms in the *consecutio temporis* for effect. Notes that the use of indirect discourse is a syntactic phenomenon intended to lighten a lengthy clause (p. 116). Briefly discusses the use of indirect discourse in the linguistic context of Ariosto's epoch, noting its disappearance in the later sixteenth century (e.g., with Bandello) where a greater adherence to fourteenth-century linguistic models is found.

⊸§ 413. HERRICK, MARVIN T. *Italian Comedy in the Renaissance*. Urbana and London: University of Illinois Press, 1960. 238p.
First reprint 1966, University of Illinois Press; second reprint 1970, Books for Libraries Press, Freeport, N.Y.
Brief discussion of each of Ariosto's comedies, noting their debt to classical models and the most obvious elements of their modernity. Concludes that *La Lena* is the most successful: the "plot is single and naturally resolved without recourse to the already hackneyed recognition scenes of Terence" (p. 69); satire is an integral part of the play's structure and not reserved for set scenes; and the characters are believable rather than stereotyped. See especially pp. 67–71.

⊸§ 414. HERRON, DALE. "The Focus of Allegory in the Renaissance Epic." *Genre* 3, no. 2 (1970): 176–86.

Summary discussion of the Renaissance attempt to evaluate the Virgilian epic, the confusion regarding the nature of epic, and the problematic nature of allegory, focusing on allegory in the *FQ*. Comments on the sixteenth-century polemics over the poetic nature of the *OF*, "a monstrous put-on" (p. 179), and the allegorical readings of the period.

415. HERVAL, RENÉ. "L'Arioste et le Mont Saint-Michel." In *Millénaire Monastique du Mont Saint-Michel*, edited by R. Foreville, 2: 443–49. 6 vols. Paris: Bibliothèque d'Histoire et d'Archéologie Chrétiennes, 1967.
Notes references to Normandy in the *OF* and suggests that Ariosto's information came from contemporary Italian explorers and cartographers, as well as from Frenchmen visiting the Ferrarese court. Notes as one possible source for the episode of Ruggiero and the Orc of Ebuda the legend of *Bouclier et de l'Epée*.

416. HOPE, GEOFFREY R. "Du Bellay as Mad Orlando: A Forgotten Source for *Regrets* 88." *Bibliothèque d'Humanisme et Renaissance* 40 (1978): 105–8.
Notes in Du Bellay's *Regrets* 88 the reference in verses 6–7 to the episode of Melissa rescuing Ruggiero from Alcina (*OF* 7.45–74) and argues that the last two images of the poem (verses 11–14) are not a direct allusion to Phineus, as is commonly held, but to Astolfo's flight to the moon to find Orlando's lost sanity and to restore Senàpo's sight. Suggests that the loss of mind and sight serves to articulate the sonnet with other types of loss and with madness, or "the disintegration of the self" (p. 108), that characterize the entire collection.

417. HOUGH, GRAHAM. Introduction. In *Sir John Harington's Translation of "Orlando Furioso,"* edited by Graham Hough, pp. vii–x. Carbondale: Southern Illinois University Press, 1962.
Summary introduction to the Italian romance epic, to the *OF* as a continuation of the *OI*, and to their stylistic differences. Allusion to the poem's structure and "moral temper," concluding that its most evident quality is its "sheer luxuriance and fertility of invention" (p. ix). Brief note on Harington's translation.

418. ———. "Ariosto." Chap. 2 in *A Preface to "The Faerie Queene,"* pp. 25–47. New York: W. W. Norton & Company, 1963. 239p.
Study of the *FQ* in relation to the genre to which it belongs, with extensive discussion of the major Italian sources from which Spenser drew. Discusses structural principles, motifs, and the nature and extent of allegory in the *OF*, focusing on their relation to Spenser's reading of the poem and his use of

them in the *FQ*. Regarding the allegorical content of the two poems, concludes: "Ariosto's poem is *mainly* controlled by the needs of pure romance, of incident and adventure; Spenser's is *mainly* controlled by allegorical intention. But it is a difference of emphasis, not a difference of *genre*" (p. 42). Discusses Spenser's reading of the *OF*, noting that he could not read it in the ironic key of much modern criticism; observations on the nature of Ariosto's irony, noting that it is pervasive: "There is a sense in which nothing in the poem is 'real'; it is all a world of artifice. But enter into this world and all its elements are equally real" (p. 46).

◄§ 419. HUGHES, MERRITT Y. "Milton's Limbo of Vanity." In *Th'Upright Heart and Pure: Essays on John Milton Commemorating the Tercentenary of the Publication of Paradise Lost*, edited by Amadeus P. Fiore, O.F.M., pp. 7–24. Pittsburgh: Duquesne University Press, 1967.

Concludes: "In essence Milton's Paradise of Fools is far from being a counterpart of Ariosto's 'mock-heroic, mock Dantesque voyage into disillusion,' which Professor Thomas Greene [*The Descent from Heaven*, entry 390] regards as 'for many readers . . . the quintessence' of the *Orlando Furioso*. In the context of the *Orlando* as a whole and in that of Astolfo's visit to the moon, Milton's Limbo is distinctly antipathetic to Ariosto's tolerant satire of a 'futility [in whose] cool tranquillity of meaninglessness the world of action is folly and the world of poetry appealing only if it admits of being an unreal game'" (p. 18).

◄§ 420. HUTCHINSON, MARY ANNE. "The Devil's Gateway: The Evil Enchantress in Ariosto, Tasso, Spenser, and Milton." *DAI* 36, no. 10 (1976): 6656A. (Syracuse University, 1975. 234p.)

On the narrative function of the temptress in Italian romance and the use of traditional conventions by Milton in the revitalization of the temptress figure.

◄§ 421. IANNUCCI, AMILCARE A. "Ariosto's Satire-Epistle to Bembo: Meditations on Humanism and the Value of a Humanistic Education." *The Humanities Association Review. Revue de l'Association des Humanités* 30, no. 3 (1979): 147–60.

Traces the concept of humanistic education from Petrarch, for whom "the renewal of culture was to be achieved through the study of Latin grammar and literature" (p. 150), to the fifteenth-century theorists of the *studia humanitatis*. Considers Ariosto's sixth satire (c. 1525) in the context of the Ferrarese humanistic tradition of Guarino Veronese and, though ironic in tone, as a serious statement of the "ideals of humanistic education" (p. 152). Considers Ariosto's program for a humanistic education, including training in both Greek and Latin. Notes the significance for Ariosto and the early humanists of language as a "gateway to both learning and virtue" (p. 155). Discusses Ariosto's satirical view of contemporary humanists who betrayed their calling through immorality, irreligion, and pedantry. Concludes, however, that Ariosto saw his as a new golden age, realized "to a large extent because of the power of humanistic education" (p. 157).

꧁ 422. IJSEWIJN, J. "Ariosto, Ludovico." See Van den Bergh, H., entry 873.

꧁ 423. INNAMORATI, GIULIANO. "Ariosto." In *I Protagonisti della storia universale*, vol. 5, no. 30, pp. 309–36. Milan: Compagnia Edizioni Internazionale, 1965–.
Chronology, biography of Ariosto, his life as a court poet; introduction to works and selected bibliography. Illustrated.

꧁ 424. ⸺. Introduzione. In *Orlando furioso e opere minori*, pp. 3–57. Bologna: Zanichelli, 1967.
Identical hardbound edition as part of the series *I Classici italiani*, edited by Walter Binni; abridged version of introductory essay in *Orlando furioso. Scelta con introduzione, note e antologia critica*, edited by Giuliano Innamorati, pp. 9–39. Bergamo: Minerva Italica, 1971.
Profiles the education, professional career, and literary achievements of Ariosto, noting in particular the details and the importance to his own moral stance and intellectual formation of the humanistic and cultural environment of Renaissance Ferrara and the contribution of Battista Guarino; analyzes Ariosto's literary formation and the significance of his experimentation in the early lyrics. Traces the genesis of the OF and notes the major thematic elements. Supplemented with a detailed biographical note (pp. 47–52) and a selected bibliography (pp. 53–57) through the mid-1960s.

꧁ 425. ISELLA, SILVIA. "Ariosto e Folengo: due operazioni convergenti." In *Ludovico Ariosto: lingua, stile e tradizione*, edited by Cesare Segre (entry 789), pp. 39–48. Milan: Feltrinelli, 1976.
Indicates a number of parallels between the OF and Teofilo Folengo's *Baldus* (first edition 1517): similar dates of the several editions of both works and their authors' substantial linguistic redactions; both authors (from the Po Valley) of similar cultural and linguistic orientation; similar treatment of chivalric material—an "aderenza alla realtà contemporanea" (pp. 39–40)—with a demythologizing of the chivalric hero; a similar working toward what is termed a "grammatica" (p. 41) and from a hybrid linguistic tradition, following a similar progression, toward the establishment of a unique poetic voice. Proceeds to examine Folengo's progression, which involves both a movement from Latin toward vernacular and dialect and, inversely, from

dialect to vernacular and Latin: "il risultato . . .è un più studiato effetto della interazione delle singole componenti" (pp. 42–43). Concludes: "è possibile confermare, muovendo dal dialetto, la graduale regolarizzazione del *pastiche*, come disciplina del macaronico. . . . In modo analogo sarebbe da auspicare un esame linguistico anche delle tre redazioni del *Furioso* nel senso sia di rilevarne una sempre più convinta adesione alla grammatica del Bembo, ma sia anche, e soprattutto, per mettere in evidenza quanto della sua dialettalità padana continua a sopravvivere nella redazione definitiva" (p. 48).

ك 426. Istituto Grafologico 'G. Moretti,' Ancona. "Analisi sulla grafia di Lodovico Ariosto." In *Lodovico Ariosto: il suo tempo la sua terra la sua gente* (entry 468). Estratto dal *Bollettino storico reggiano* 7, no. 25 (1974): 105–8.
Attempts to analyze Ariosto's character through his handwriting, concluding that although his writing "denoti una personalità ricca e vivace, non ha fermezza di carattere, può giocare con le situazioni e riderci sopra solo perchè constata l'insuccesso dei tentativi volti a dominarle" (p. 108). A comparison of samples of his maturity (1509) and of his later years (1523) reveals "una flessione di ritmo; nei primi il ritmo è teso, energico, in totale sintonia con il desiderio di affermazione e di espansione del soggetto . . . mentre negli altri esso è più morbido, ondeggiante e quasi cadente, il ritmo di una persona che nutre aspirazioni ma vi rinuncia per adeguarsi a quel poco che è riuscito a ottenere" (p. 108). Includes two photographs of samples of Ariosto's handwritten letters to the Este.

ك 427. JACK, R[ONALD] D. S. *The Italian Influence on Scottish Literature.* Edinburgh: Edinburgh University Press, 1972. 256p.
Discusses the adaptation of the *OF* by John Stewart of Baldynneis and particularly his debt to French versions of the Italian poem, including those of Philippe Desportes and Jean Martin (pp. 57–71). Credits Stewart with opening "to Scottish readers the gate to Ariosto's inspired and vivid realism" (p. 71). Notes that Ariosto was the most favored Italian author in eighteenth-century England and briefly discusses Boswell's appreciation of the *OF* (pp. 146–47). Discusses the influence of Ariosto and the Italian romance tradition on eighteenth- and nineteenth-century English novelists, especially Sir Walter Scott (pp. 216–19), and on Tobias Smollett's *Sir Launcelot Greaves* (pp. 207–11).

ك 428. JACKSON, RICHARD PAUL. "The Approach in Time: A Study of the Romance Epics of Ariosto, Spenser and Byron." *DAI* 37, no. 7 (1977): 4337. (Yale University, 1976. 213p.)
Notes that the romance epics here under consideration, unlike the more

classical epic intent on "establishing stable fictional worlds," are concerned with "analyzing and evaluating continually expanding and altering worlds." Argues that the significance of "these poems is a process of ongoingness where pauses and deflections in time, interpolated episodes and digressive materials continually generate, from apparent discontinuities of vision, newer and larger visions." The first chapter "deals with the problems of romance history and temporization in *Orlando Furioso*, and with the digressive structure of Ariosto's narrative as a unified and coherent temporal strategy."

๔ 429. JAVITCH, DANIEL. "Rescuing Ovid from the Allegorizers." *Comparative Literature* 30, no. 2 (1978): 97–107.

With title "Rescuing Ovid from the Allegorizers: The Liberation of Angelica, *Furioso* X," in *Ariosto 1974 in America*, edited by Aldo Scaglione (entry 760), pp. 85–98. Ravenna: Longo, 1976.

Ruggiero's rescue of Angelica from the Orc (*OF* 10) is modelled after Perseus's rescue of Andromeda (Ovid, *Metamorphoses* 4. 663–764). However, argues that by integrating this episode into the narrative structure of the *OF* as a logical development of events, Ariosto is divesting it of any allegorical significance and implicitly taking a stand against the medieval habit of imposing Christian allegory on Ovid's stories. Ariosto's technique is, throughout the poem, essentially anti-allegorical: characters and events are too contradictory and shifting to allow for allegorical interpretation. It is precisely in his portrayal of the world as one of constant change and in the wry humor elicited by such a situation of uncertainty that Ariosto shares a vision of an unstable, chaotic world, "totally unpredictable except for its constant changes. In both poets, these mixtures aim to challenge single literary representations of reality as well as the reassuring vision of order and permanence often assumed in such constructs. Not that Ovid or Ariosto are finally dismayed by the mutability they perceive and represent. On the contrary, instability inspires both poets; it allows them, paradoxically, to assert the shaping and controlling power of their art. Nevertheless, their fluctuating styles which serve to depict the flux of the world question the validity of fixed symbolic images of reality" (p. 106).

๔ 430. ———. "*Cantus Interruptus* in the *Orlando Furioso*." *MLN* 95, no. 1 (1980): 66–80.

Distinguishes two types of interruptions of the narrative in the *OF*: one in which the narrative is interrupted at the close of the canto and normally continued in the following canto; the other coming before the end of a canto and often not continued for a considerable time. Focuses on the second type, noting that early critics regarded it as a structural flaw that tends to annoy and discourage the reader, frustrating the desire for continuity. Suggests that the deprivation experienced in such instances by the reader is actually anticipated by Ariosto, who uses abrupt interruptions as a device intended "to *duplicate* the similar experience that so often besets various characters in his poem" (p. 78) as well as "to condition the reader for the time when his frustration will not be merely literary" (p. 79).

❧ 431. JENNI, ADOLFO. "Raziocinio dell'Ariosto." In *Studi in onore di Alfredo Schiaffini*, 1: 577–85. Special issue of *Rivista di cultura classica e medievale.* 2 vols. Rome: Ateneo, 1965.
Demonstrates through a summary analysis of *OF* 4.1–50 the absolute control of the poet's rational faculties over his material, noting that Ariosto is always reflective and precise and that he heightens the poem's irony by couching the fantastic and improbable in terms of the concrete and the particular.

❧ 432. JONES, R. O. "Ariosto and Garcilaso." *Bulletin of Hispanic Studies* 39 (1962): 153–64.
Finds Garcilaso de la Vega's second eclogue, like the *OF*, profoundly imbued with Renaissance Neoplatonism. More specifically, argues that the pattern of the *OF*, in its juxtapositioning of Ruggiero's disciplined love and Orlando's unbridled passion leading to madness, all against a backdrop of war and chivalry, suggested to Garcilaso the form of his own poem, the "expression of a private crisis" (p. 164) in which the dutiful Duke of Alba is contrasted with the less than noble courtly lover, Albanio.

❧ 433. JORDAN, CONSTANCE. "Enchanted Ground: Vision and Perspective in Renaissance Romance." *DAI* 37, no. 7 (1977): 4337–38A. (Yale University, 1976. 329p.)
Argues that romance establishes a phenomenology wherein vision is problematic: the questioning knight "must distinguish the apparent from the true, those things which change from those which endure through change." In the *OF*, the figure of the beloved lady, especially Angelica, is the object of a quest, promising perfection and truth but, as a "masked presence," revealing an illusory truth understandable better from the "inverted position of the moon."

❧ 434. KANDUTH, ERIKA. "Bemerkungen zu Dante-Reminiszenzen im *Orlando Furioso*." In *Studien zu Dante und zu anderen Themen der romanischen Literaturen*, edited by Klaus Lichem and Hans Joachim Simon, pp. 59–70. Graz: Universitäts-Buchdruckerei Styria, 1971.
Technical and thematic borrowings from the *DC* in the *OF*. Considers Ariosto's method of elaboration upon motifs in the *DC*, especially the tendency to translate the transcendental into concrete realities. Notes Ariosto's expectation of familiarity with the *DC* to appreciate his ironic use of it.

435. KENNEDY, RUTH WEDGWOOD. "Apelles redivivus." In *Essays in Memory of Karl Lehmann*, edited by Lucy Freeman Sandler, pp. 160–70. New York: Institute of Fine Arts, New York University, 1964.

On the development of Titian's interest in, imitation of, and rivalry with ancient painting. Discusses the association of Titian and Ariosto while in the service of Duke Alfonso d'Este, their mutual interest in the technique of ancient masters and, in particular, the significance to their work of Philostratus's *Imagines*, of which Ariosto, the author suggests, most likely provided a translation for the painter.

436. KENNEDY, WILLIAM J. "Modes of Allegory in Ariosto, Tasso and Spenser." *DAI* 30, no. 8 (1970): 3431–32A. (Yale University, 1969. 386p.)

Notes that tradition had provided Ariosto, Tasso, and Spenser with clearly defined allegorical conventions, but that in the OF Ariosto "inverts and deflates these conventional materials for comic, ironic effect, so that oblique and problematic meanings emerge." Notes that in the Renaissance epics under consideration, allegory is "a versatile, changeful mode that must be read image by image, symbol by symbol, myth by myth for their complex polyphonic meanings."

437. ———. "Ariosto's Ironic Allegory." *MLN* 88, no. 1 (1973): 44–67.

Notes that irony has an integral function in the allegorical episodes of the OF, that it "implements the allegory and modifies it, so that in effect the irony becomes the allegory" (p. 46). Illustrates the links between the ironic and allegorical modes of the poem through a close analysis of the Alcina episode, an exemplary expression of Ariosto's "moral, ironic, and very serious vision of the world" (p. 67). Argues that the episode is controlled by three ironic strategies: literary allusion, the narrator's shifting point of view, and the repetition of key words or phrases that underscore the doubling back of the dramatic action upon itself, "analogically [reflecting] its own image" (p. 47). Identifies three allegorical motifs informing the structure of the episode: the transformation of Astolfo; Ruggiero's fall; Ruggiero's renunciation of Alcina.

438. ———. "Ariosto's *Orlando Furioso*." In chap. 3 of *Rhetorical Norms in Renaissance Literature*, pp. 135–51. New Haven and London: Yale University Press, 1978. 229p.

In chapter entitled "The Epic Genre and Varieties of Form," notes that a constant in late-Roman and Renaissance epics is the speaker's "implicit rhetorical identification with the audience," and states that the OF illustrates most fully the "heightened involvement" (p. 136) of the speaker in the action. Considers the rhetorical strategies used in creating the dynamics between speaker and audience, and identifies five fictive audiences in the OF, the most significant of which is an "impartial observer who construes the relationships among [the several] audiences and assigns each its proper place" (p. 143) and who can adjust his or her perspective with the shifting action of the narrative line. That observer becomes progressively more aware— through the speaker's own admitted unreliability—of the absence of any certainties upon which to judge the fictional action. Concludes that the rhetorical strategies adopted provide an epic dimension to the OF lacking in predecessors of chivalric romance, namely Boiardo and Pulci.

◆§ 439. KIRÁLY, ERZSÉBET. "Egy új és teljes Ariosto-fordítás kísérlete elé." (Introduction to a new and complete translation of Ariosto). *Filológiai Közlöny* (Budapest) 18, nos. 1–2 (1972): 147–48.
   Brief introduction to a new Hungarian translation of the OF (*Örjöngö Orlando*) by Gyula Simon; translation of cantos one and two on the following pages, 148–83.

◆§ 440. KLEIN, ROBERT, AND HENRI ZERNER. "Vitruve et le théâtre de la Renaissance italienne." In *Le lieu théâtrale à la Renaissance*, pp. 49–60. Paris: Centre National de la Recherche Scientifique, 1964.
   Briefly notes the historical importance of the stage designs for the 1508 production of *La Cassaria* and for a production of *I Suppositi* (date uncertain; either 1509 in Ferrara or 1519 in Rome) to the history of perspective stage design (p. 52). Includes four plates.

◆§ 441. KLOPP, CHARLES D. "Narrative Structure in the *Orlando Furioso*." ADD 1969–1970: 215. (Harvard University, 1970.)
   Proposes a division of the OF into five parts as an aid to understanding the poem's structure, noting a debt to Attilio Momigliano in the analytical approach. Suggests that there are specific pivotal points in the poem's action, namely, cantos 13, 19, 29, and 39. Argues that the first part has a cumulative structure and that the movement is one of expansion; part two has an alternating structure; part three, the richest, combines elements from the first two parts in new configurations; the fourth part is characterized by a process of contraction and a more disillusioned tone; the final part sees a resolution of the poem's several episodes. Considers the nature of Ariosto's characters, noting that they function as representatives of common human characteristics and are, therefore, often psychologically unrealized. Notes structural techniques employed to assure a detached perspective on the poem's action and concludes that the poem is intended to foster a disillusioned evaluation of the world of the poem as well as of the world of the reader.

◆§ 442. ———. "The Centaur and the Magpie: Ariosto and Machiavelli's *Prince*." In *Ariosto 1974 in America*, edited by Aldo Scaglione (entry 760), pp. 69–84. Ravenna: Longo, 1976.

Considers the possibility of Ariosto having known Machiavelli's *Prince* at the time he wrote the *CC*. Argues on the basis of the tone of the *CC* and suggests the influence of Machiavelli in Ariosto's condemnation of mercenary troops and in his view of the utility of the study of ancients for contemporary political and military strategies. Further suggests that a lack of sympathy toward Machiavelli's intransigence in his attitude toward issues too complex for simple solutions may have been responsible for Ariosto's rejection of the *CC* in revising the *OF*.

◄§ 443. KOSTIĆ, VESELIN. *Spenser's Sources in Italian Poetry: A Study in Comparative Literature.* Belgrade: (Filološki Fakultet Beogradskog Univerziteta, Monografije, Knjiga 30) Novi Dani, 1969. pp. 109–242.

Revised version, with amplified notes, of "Ariosto and Spenser," *English Miscellany* 17 (1966): 69–174.

First part of discussion (pp. 109–60) traces the development of certain critical ideas in the period from Ariosto to Spenser in order to understand the English poet's use of the Italian romance tradition. Discusses the doctrine of imitation, the particular importance of developing theories of epic poetry, and argues that Spenser began his poem along Ariostean lines, only later tending toward the classical, Aristotelian conception of epic form predominant among the learned. Notes the importance to Spenser of the changing attitudes after Ariosto toward the function of poetry, which was to provide moral instruction; concludes with an extensive discussion of the growing importance in the sixteenth century of allegory and of the particular importance to Spenser of the rich allegorical tradition in England. Second part (pp. 161–242) is a comparative analysis of selected elements of the *OF* and the *FQ* to illustrate Spenser's use of Ariosto. Notes Spenser's debt to Ariosto for narrative methods, and concludes that Ariosto's structural patterns did not always suit Spenser, who was unable to control a complex narrative. Discusses the unsuitability of Ariosto's variety to Spenser's dominant allegorical mode. Conclusion notes that "a comparison of the poetic methods of the two poets develops more in terms of differences than in terms of similarities" (p. 182). In this context, considers the importance of irony to the *OF* and its absence in the *FQ*; simile in the *OF* as functional and illuminating the action as compared to the *FQ*, where it is ornamental and enriching; Spenser's use of Ariosto's finely developed studies in human psychology for purely moral and exemplary purposes. Argues that Spenser's was a programmatic imitation of Ariosto, with no real affinity with him: "The best stimuli which Ariosto could offer to a poet found no response in Spenser. On the other hand, of poetry which could fire Spenser's inspiration there was very little in the *Orlando Furioso*. Therefore almost all borrowings from Ariosto appear in the *Faerie Queene* in a considerably impoverished form" (p. 241).

👋 444. KRAILSHEIMER, A. J., ed. *The Continental Renaissance, 1500–* *1600*. Hassocks, England: The Harvester Press; Atlantic Highlands, N.J.: Humanities Press, 1978. 576p.

Brief analysis of the OF in the context of Renaissance culture. Considers Ariosto's perspective on human nature, cautioning against labeling it ironic, a term that "requires too many qualifications" (p. 114). Summary considerations of major characters and selected episodes, particularly Alcina's magic island as an example of the poet's interest in the interplay of illusion and reality (pp. 110–20). Notes that the satires manifest Ariosto's objective look at life, his bemusement at human follies (pp. 160–62), and that of Ariosto's dramatic writings, *La Lena* is the most successful for its better developed characters and greater unity of plot (pp. 258–59).

👋 445. KREMERS, DIETER. "Versuch einer kritischen Geschichte der Ariostforschung." *Romanische Forschungen* 68, nos. 3–4 (1956): 294–345.

Reviews the critical reception of the OF from Ariosto's contemporaries to the 1950s, particularly the writings of Attilio Momigliano and Walter Binni. Discusses the OF in the context of Renaissance polemics over the definition of epic form; considers the relative importance and influence of Ariosto and Tasso from the sixteenth century to the romantic period; reviews the more important critical views of nineteenth-century writers (Gioberti and De Sanctis) and Pirandello's interest in various motifs of the poem, including madness. Considers a variety of critical perspectives on the OF among modern scholars, including the play between unity and dichotomy.

👋 446. ⸻. *Der "Rasende Roland" des Ludovico Ariosto*. Stuttgart: W. Kohlhammer, 1973. 263p.

General study of major themes and narrative lines in the OF, with analyses and commentary on several important passages of the poem. Traces evolution of epic romance from the Middle Ages to the Italian Renaissance and considers Ariosto's use of the topos of the *cavaliere errante*. Considers the love motif in the context of literary development in Italy from the Dolce Stil Nuovo, or Sweet New Style, particularly love as an irrational passion. Discusses the function of the poet-narrator, the point of view of the narrator, and the intentional distancing between Ariosto and the material of his poem. Considers the tension between the organized world of the poem and the theme of folly. Concludes that Ariosto perceives human judgment as easily subject to error.

👋 447. KRÖMER, WOLFRAM. "Die Rezeption des antiken Dramas in der 'Tragoedia laeta' und der 'Commedia seria' der italienischen Renaissance." *Arcadia* 9 (1974): 225–34.

Discusses the assimilation of ancient Roman theater into the dramatic forms of the Italian Renaissance, with particular attention given to the development of the moral dimensions of the genre. Notes the role of Ariosto in the history of Renaissance comedy and, in particular, cites *La Lena* as an example of a typically Italian comedy of intrigue with a tendency toward moralizing.

448. KRUSE, MARGOT. "Ariost und Cervantes." *Romanistisches Jahrbuch* 12 (1961): 248–64.
Observes that there first appears to be little similarity between the *OF* and the *DQ*, as, for example, in the difference between Ariosto's great variety of protagonists of nearly equal importance to the narrative and Cervantes's focus on a central figure. Notes, however, that Cervantes follows Ariosto's technique in narrative structure (e.g., in the use of sudden interruptions and of interpolated shorter episodes) and in tying interpolated stories to the main narrative thread. Cites as an example of analogous technique in narrative structure Cervantes's episode of Marcella and that of Ginevra in the *OF*.

449. LAPP, JOHN C. "Ariosto and La Fontaine. A Literary Affinity." In *Studies in Seventeenth-Century French Literature. Presented to Morris Bishop*, edited by Jean-Jacques Demorest, pp. 202–30. Ithaca, N.Y.: Cornell University Press, 1962.
Analyzes formal and thematic variations on the motif of women's infidelity in La Fontaine's "Joconde," "La Coupe enchantée," and "Le petit chien qui secoue de l'argent et des pierreries" and in their respective sources: *OF* 28.1–74; 42.70–43.67; 43.72–143. Notes that in La Fontaine the theme is characterized by a skeptical attitude toward marriage and that the betrayed husband, reflecting the prevailing *morale aristocratique*, often manifests the "blasé detachment of the aristocrat" (p. 212). Formally, La Fontaine, like Ariosto, "stresses his position as an omnipresent author" (p. 205) and takes the part of the subservient narrator, pretending "to efface himself before his Italian master, as Ariosto had done before Turpin" (p. 215). Feels that "in imitating Ariosto La Fontaine most resembles him in his aesthetic independence" (p. 230).

450. LARIVAILLE, PAUL. "Personnages, thèmes et structures du *Roland Furieux*." In *Notiziario culturale italiano* (entry 573) 15, no. 3 (1974): 15–26.
Begins with a discussion of the structural-thematic elements of the *OF* in relation to those of the Christian epic tradition and suggests that a structural analysis of the 1516 edition of the poem—a five-part structure analogous to the divisions of a classical dramatic piece—clearly reveals the theatrical experiences of the author and, though chronologically predating the Aristote-

lian theoretical basis of Giraldi Cintio's writings on dramatic form, anticipates the basic divisions of neoclassical theater. Final part of essay includes a
variety of observations based on the structural breakdown, including the conclusion that the poem reveals "le déclin irréversible de l'humanisme et de la
confiance en l'homme dont il s'était bercé" (p. 25).

451. ———. *Syntaxe dramatique et syntaxe narrative dans le "Roland
Furieux."* Nanterre: Université Paris 10, Centre de Recherches de Lan-
gue et Littérature italiennes, 1975. 28p., photoduplicated.
   Argues that the traditional narrative codes of epic tradition—particularly
the Christian-pagan antithesis and its variants—do not fully explain the
complexities of the labyrinthine structures of the *OF.* Suggests that the narrative syntax, or the intricacies of the narrative line, resulted from Ariosto's
familiarity with and growing interest in the contemporary perception of classical norms for the writing of comedy. Discusses the evolution of comic
theory and its impact on Ariosto; suggests that the differences in dramatic
schema from the first edition of the *OF* to the last have a counterpart in the
maturing technique of Ariosto's theatrical pieces. Concludes, "L'important
est de reconnaître qu'une pratique assidue du théâtre a créé chez lui une
sorte d'automatisme: une conception de l'action, du découpage de l'action
. . . qui ne peut qu'interférer plus ou moins fortement dans la composition
de ses oeuvres non théâtrales" (p. 25).

452. LAZZARO, NANCY LEE. "Magia meccanica e realtà magica nel-
l'Ariosto." *DAI* 41, no. 8 (1981): 3603–4A. (UCLA, 1980. 136p.)
   Investigation of the "magical element as a coefficient of Ariosto's inspiration" and, through textual analysis, of "how this coefficient has blended with
the poet's narrative style." Categorizes manifestations of magic in the *OF,*
arguing that they serve as basic elements in Ariosto's depiction of human
nature.

453. LEA, KATHLEEN M. "Harington's *Folly."* In *Elizabethan and Jacobean Studies Presented to Frank Percy Wilson in Honour of His Seven-
tieth Birthday,* edited by Herbert Davis and Helen Gardner, pp. 42–58.
Oxford: Clarendon Press, 1959.
   Detailed description of the manuscripts of Harington's translation of the
OF toward showing how the Englishman worked toward adapting the poem
for his Elizabethan audience.

454. LEE, JUDITH MARY. " 'The Lively Patterne': Sir John Harington's
Translation of the *Orlando Furioso." DAI* 40, no. 8 (1980): 4578A.
(SUNY–Binghamton, 1980. 323p.)
   Study of "the critical principles on which Harington based his treatment

of those elements of Ariosto's poem most obviously inconsistent with the Elizabethan concept of the epic." Argues that Harington's narrator is an attempt to "overgo" Ariosto's poet: "Appearing as an Elizabethan courtier— witty, urbane, and 'plaine speaking'—he imposes a rational point of view on the poem. Assuming the role of poet, editor, critic, and moralist, he presents in effect a parallel text in the marginalia and Annotations."

⚜ 455. LEE, RENSSELAER W. "Adventures of Angelica: Early Frescoes Illustrating the *Orlando Furioso.*" *The Art Bulletin* 59, no. 1 (1977): 39–46.

Points out that despite the numerous editions of the OF published in the Renaissance with woodcuts and engravings, the poem was not a thematic source for painters of the period. Suggests that the OF's lack of appeal to the imagination of figurative artists was due to the rapid movement of the narrative and to the ceaseless shifting of both scenes and characters. After observing that few of the extant visual representations of the text have received attention from art historians (e.g., Dosso Dossi's *Melissa* [1520]; Niccolò dell'Abbate's frescoes; Pietro Dolce of Savignano's monochrome medallions), calls attention to six frescoes in the Osteria della Ferrata—part of the palace of the Marchesi di Ceva at Chiusa di Pesio in the Piedmont—four of which illustrate the adventures of Angelica and her admirers in OF 1. Assigns the frescoes to the school of Defendente de Ferrari and observes striking similarities between them and the illustrations for the Giolito edition of the OF (1542); cannot establish date of their execution.

⚜ 456. ———. "Ariosto's *Roger and Angelica* in Sixteenth-Century Art: Some Facts and Hypotheses." In *Studies in Late Medieval and Renaissance Painting in Honor of Millard Meiss*, edited by Irving Lavin and John Plummer, 1: 302–19. 2 vols. New York: New York University Press, 1977.

Suggests that Ariosto's emphasis on form and color and the plasticity of the description of Angelica's rescue from the rock by Ruggiero on the hippogriff (OF 10) explains the appeal of Angelica to painters throughout the centuries. Brief summary of the hippogriff motif in literary tradition, beginning with Ovid's account of Andromeda's rescue by Perseus riding Pegasus. Notes that the Ovidian tale had been popularized by the publication of Bersuire's *Ovidius moralizatus* shortly before the 1516 edition of the OF and suggests that Ariosto might have also been familiar with fifteenth-century representations of the story. Noting that the first illustration of the rescue of Angelica by Ruggiero appears in the 1542 Giolito edition of the OF, discusses the subsequent portrayals of the episode, including a maiolica dish by Orazio Fontana (1549) and an illustration of Bernard Salomon for *La Métamorphose d'Ovide figurée* (1557), the possible inspiration of which is the illustration in the 1542 Giolito edition of the *OF*.

✒ 457. ———. *Names on Trees: Ariosto into Art.* Princeton: Princeton University Press, 1977. 124p.
Traces the topos of carving names of trees from Greek and Latin literature to the Renaissance and Ariosto. Discusses paintings and engravings of Angelica from the 1542 Giolito edition of the *OF* to Delacroix; reviews Renaissance, baroque, and rococo representations of Angelica and Medoro carving their names into trees in a *locus amoenus*; concludes with an account of variations on the motif in the nineteenth century, focusing on representations such as Fragonard's *Le Chiffre d'amour*, Arthur Hughes's *The Long Engagement*, and Humphry Repton's *Mr. Knight Carving Our Joint Names*. Includes fifty-seven illustrations.

✒ 458. LENTZEN, MANFRED. "Alcina, Armida und die Jüdin von Toledo: drei Verführerinnen bei Ariost, Tasso und Lope de Vega." In *Spanische Literatur im Goldenen Zeitalter: Fritz Schalk zum 70. Geburtstag*, edited by Horst Baader and Erich Loos, pp. 229–68. Frankfurt am Main: Vittorio Klostermann, 1973.
Discussion of the sources and motifs of the Alcina episode in *OF* 6–7. Comparative analysis of the Alcina episode and Tasso's Armida episode, noting the function of the latter in Tasso's observance of the Aristotelian unities. Contrasts the two episodes with that of the Jewess Raquel de Toledo in Lope de Vega's *Jerusalém conquistada* (1609) and suggests the authors' reasons for inserting these particular episodes.

✒ 459. LEO, ULRICH. "Petrarca, Ariost und die Unsterblichkeit. Ein Beitrag zur Motiv-Geschichte." In *Romanistische Aufsätze aus drei Jahrzehnten*, edited by Fritz Schalk, pp. 194–230. Cologne and Graz: Böhlau, 1966.
Ariosto's concept of the function of the poet in the face of man's mortality. Argues that for Ariosto, as for Petrarch, man's nemesis is Time and the threat of oblivion; the poet immortalizes men by making them heroes through poetic language (" 'Dichter machen Helden,' " p. 217). For Ariosto, immortality depends on Fame alone; he does not share Petrarch's Christian-metaphysical sense of eternal glory. See especially pp. 212–30.

✒ 460. LEONE, GIUSEPPE. "Interpretazione delle *Satire* dell'Ariosto." In his *Dal Boccaccio all'Ariosto*, pp. 37–58. Salerno: Grafica Di Giacomo, 1963.
States that a general interpretation of the unity of the satires must take into account the two basic components of Ariosto's ethic: the "autentica e schietta

moralità del poeta" and that which is "gnomica e didascalica" (p. 38). The real morality of Ariosto is in his condemnation of all that offends his conscience as a man "alieno da problemi di alta speculazione etica, ma sorretto da una connaturata sanità e fondamentale rettitudine" (p. 38). Tradition dictates that from this comes "un saggio e illuminato ideale di vita da rappresentare e consigliare al lettore" (p. 41), but characteristic of Ariosto is the relativity of his poetic voice, that of a man ever aware of the "carattere relativo e la fatale insufficienza di ogni forma di catechizzata saggezza" (p. 42). Often, the "intonazione ironica dell'apologo nasce proprio dalla sua precisa funzione logica: che è sempre quella di richiamare alla realtà, un modo di contrapporre i limiti e le leggi del reale ad ogni illusorio vagheggiamento o irrazionale aspirazione" (p. 48). Characteristic of the satires is Ariosto's continual awareness that his is a personal, subjective representation of morality and that others might well differ (p. 50). Agrees with Walter Binni that the style is "discorso poetico medio" and proceeds to illustrate the fact that Ariosto "intende aderire alla materialità della vita vissuta e nel tempo stesso tradurla in forme ed immagini mutuate dalla sfera del mito e della letteratura" (p. 56).

461. LEVAL, NICOLE DE. "Le coppie più rappresentative dell'*Orlando Furioso* e della *Gerusalemme Liberata.*" *Revue des Langues Vivantes* 30, no. 2 (1964): 153–61.

General comparison of Tasso and Ariosto as poets and of the nature of the characters in their epic poems. Concludes: "I personaggi della Gerusalemme hanno una evidenza più interiore che esteriore e che di essa non si ricordano atteggiamenti scultorii, come nel Furioso, ma immagini indefinite. Il modo di sentire del Tasso è più complicato. I sentimenti dell'Ariosto sono semplici, rettilinei. Ma questi personaggi non ci colpiscono privi come sono di concretezze, di profonda umanità" (p. 161).

462. LEVI DELLA VIDA, G[IORGIO]. "Isabella d'Oriente." *Corriere della Sera*, anno 83, no. 98 (24 April 1958): 3.

Observations on the origins of the Isabella episode in the *OF*, noting that the original source, unknown to Pio Rajna, is an Arabic tale, known best through the pictorial representation of Piero della Francesca in the Church of San Francesco, Arezzo. Notes that Ariosto secularizes sources that had a religious or sacred connotation.

463. LEWIS, C. S. *The Allegory of Love: A Study in Medieval Tradition.* New York: Oxford University Press, 1977. 378p.

Discusses Italian epic romance influences on the *FQ*, suggesting that Spenser's continued allegory may have been influenced by a reading of sixteenth-century allegorical interpretations of the *OF* (p. 297). Compares the

OI and *OF*, noting Ariosto's superior character delineation and his genius at invention: "When you are tired of Ariosto, you must be tired of the world" (p. 302). See especially pp. 301–3.

◥§ 464. "ARIOSTO, LUDOVICO." In *Lexikon der Weltliteratur: Fremdsprachige Schriftsteller und anonyme Werke von den Anfängen bis zur Gegenwart,* edited by Gerhard Steiner, pp. 68–69. Leipzig: V. E. B. Bibliographisches Institut, 1966.
Brief note on Ariosto's life and major works, observing that in the *OF,* "Seine reiche Phantasie offenbart sich in der Mannigfaltigkeit der Episodenhandlungen, wobei die einzelnen Situationen treffend und wahrheitsgetren gezeichnet sind" (p. 68).

◥§ 465. LIBERATORE, UMBERTO. "Ludovico Ariosto." In his *Prose e poesie. Profili storici-critica-teatro,* pp. 39–54. Campobasso: Edizioni "il Pungolo Verde," 1972.
Summary account of poet's life and activities; no critical evaluation.

◥§ 466. LILLI, FURIO. "Aeronautas y astronautas del *Orlando Furioso.*" In *Actas de la Semana de Cultura Italiana* (25–30 setiembre de 1972), pp. 63–97. Mendoza, Argentina: Universidad Nacional de Cuyo, 1973.
Consideration of episodes in the *OF* that, though essentially fantastic in nature and allowing the freest reign to the poet's imagination, provide for moments of reflection on the nature of existence. Particular consideration of the hippogriff, Ruggiero's and Astolfo's flights, and the latter's trip to and sojourn in the Earthly Paradise and on the moon.

◥§ 467. LIMENTANI, ALBERTO. "Struttura e storia dell'ottava rima." *Lettere italiane* 13, no. 1 (1961): 20–77.
Having compared octaves from Poliziano's *Stanze per la giostra* and the *OF,* discusses the evolution of the *ottava rima* in the fourteenth and fifteenth centuries. Finds that Ariosto not only masters Poliziano's brief but intense lyricism but develops the *ottava* into an organic, narrative unit.

◥§ 468. *Lodovico Ariosto: il suo tempo la sua terra la sua gente.* Atti del Convegno di studi organizzato dalla Deputazione di Storia Patria per le antiche provincie modenesi, Sezione di Reggio Emilia, nel quinto centenario della nascita del Poeta. Reggio Emilia, 27–28 aprile 1974. Estratto dal *Bollettino storico reggiano* 7, no. 25 (1974).
Contains: Eugenio Ragni, "L'Ariosto a cinquecento anni dalla nascita" (entry 666); Gino Badini, "Reggio al tempo dell'Ariosto dalle relazioni del Guicciardini e da documenti d'archivio" (entry 38); Ugo Bellocchi, "Il fenomeno giornalistico al tempo dell'Ariosto" (entry 78); Guglielmo Capacchi,

"L'Ariosto in Ungheria" (entry 163); Mario Degani, "La necropoli di Reggio nei luoghi ariosteschi" (entry 247); Bruno Fava, "Osservazioni alla biografia di Timoteo Bendedei" (entry 310); Riccardo Finzi, "Lodovico Ariosto a Correggio" (entry 325); Romolo Fioroni, "Filoni ariosteschi nel 'Maggio' dell'Appennino" (entry 326); Lino Lionello Ghirardini, "Ludovico Ariosto Capitano nella Rocca di Canossa" (entry 354); Istituto Grafologico 'G. Moretti'-Ancona, "Analisi sulla grafia di Lodovico Ariosto" (entry 426); Paola Manzini, "Le condizioni sanitarie a Reggio e la relativa legislazione al tempo dell'Ariosto" (entry 490).

Estratto dal *Bollettino storico reggiano* 7, no. 27 (1974).

Contains: Franca Manenti Valli, "Restauri al Mauriziano" (entry 488); Giovanni Marzi, "Musica e strumenti nella poesia ariostesca" (entry 504); Domenico Medici, "La bibliografia della critica ariostesca dal 'Fatini' ad oggi (1957–1974)" (entry 507); Mario Medici, "Presenza e vicende della coordinazione di indicativo con congiuntivo in proposizioni dipendenti nel *Furioso*" (entry 508); Francesco Milani, "Reggio 'ecclesiastica' al tempo dell'Ariosto, parroco fra il 1506 e il 1512 d'una chiesa di Montericco" (entry 519); Marco Cesare Nannini, "Lodovico Ariosto visto da un medico" (entry 557).

Estratto dal *Bollettino storico reggiano* 7, no. 28 (1974).

Contains: Vittorio Nironi, "Tre luoghi ariosteschi nella città di Reggio" (entry 569); Odoardo Rombaldi, "Lodovico Ariosto commissario generale della Garfagnana" (entry 697); Giuseppe Adriano Rossi, "'La nascita di Lodovico Ariosto': poemetto dell'abate Michele Baraldi" (entry 707); Luciano Serra, "Da Tolomeo alla Garfagnana: la geografia dell'Ariosto" (entry 804); Angelo Spaggiari, "Carte relative al commissariato di L. Ariosto in Garfagnana presso l'Archivio di Stato di Modena" (entry 815); Lopez Spagni, "La monetazione estense nel periodo ariostesco" (entry 817); Tonino Ferrari, "Opere d'arte d'ispirazione ariostesca nell'edificio della Cassa di Risparmio di Reggio Emilia" (entry 313).

Estratto dal *Bollettino storico reggiano* 7, no. 26 (1974). See Fantuzzi Guarrasi, Nardina, *La Donna nella vita e nelle opere dell'Ariosto*, entry 301.

✒§ 469. LO GATTO, ETTORE. "L'Ariosto nella letteratura russa." *Nuove lettere emiliane* nos. 9–11 (1965): 5–12.
Noting the limited interest in Ariosto among Russian writers and critics, reviews the poet's reception in Russia and his influence on Mikhail Kheràskov and particularly on Pushkin.

✒§ 470. LOI, FRANCESCO. "Riflessi leopardiani delle letture ariostesche." *Osservatore politico letterario* (Rome) 23, no. 3 (1977): 76–82.

Observations on Leopardi's reference to *OF* 1.65 as an example of Ariosto's use of lexical elements that "destano idee vaste e indefinite" (Leopardi, *Zibaldone* [Milan: Mondadori, 1961], 1:1145–46). Argues that Leopardi's choice of poetic line to illustrate his aesthetic concept of the poetic indefinite was inappropriate as it does not reflect Ariosto's intent in the octave, grounded in the specific and the finite.

471. LONGHI, GIUSEPPE. "Postille autografe di Ludovico Ariosto nel poema: 'I fasti di Ovidio.' " *La Martinella di Milano* 18 (1964): 245–46.
On marginal notes, assumed to be in Ariosto's hand, in a 1520 edition of the poem "I fasti di Ovidio." Unavailable; cited with annotation in Medici, 138.

472. LOPES PEGNA, MARIO. "Tra i monti della Garfagnana ariostea." *L'Universo* (Florence) 36, no. 6 (1956): 963–72.
Historical and geographical description of the Garfagnana region with comments on Ariosto's assignment in the area from 1522 to 1525. Unavailable; cited with annotation in Medici, 3.

473. LOVARINI, EMILIO. "I Prologhi della *Moschetta*." In his *Studi sul Ruzzante e la letteratura pavana*, edited by Gianfranco Folena, pp. 319–41. Padua: Antenore, 1965.
Revision of "Nel centenario del Ruzzante. I prologhi della *Moschetta*," *Rivista italiana del teatro*, no. 6 (1942): 3–20.
Documents a 1528 performance at the court of Ferrara of *La Lena* and of *Il Negromante*, the stage sets of which are referred to in the Manciano edition of Ruzante's *La Moschetta* (pp. 327–30).

474. LOWINSKY, EDWARD E. "The Problem of Mannerism in Music: An Attempt at a Definition." *Studi musicali* 3 (1974): 131–218. Proceedings of the Congresso Internazionale on 'Manierismo in Arte e Musica,' Rome, Accademia Nazionale di Santa Cecilia, 18–23 October 1973.
On Francesco Manara's setting to music of Ariosto's madrigal "Se mai cortese fusti" (pp. 150–51).

475. *Ludovico Ariosto:* Convegno internazionale. Roma-Lucca-Castelnuovo di Garfagnana-Reggio Emilia-Ferrara. 27 settembre–5 ottobre 1974. Rome: Accademia Nazionale dei Lincei, 1975. 589p.
Contains: Enrico Cerulli, "L'*Orlando Furioso* nella storia culturale" (entry 192); Natalino Sapegno, "Ariosto poeta" (entry 752); Fredi Chiappelli, "Sul linguaggio dell'Ariosto" (entry 204); Emilio Bigi, "Le liriche volgari dell'Ariosto" (entry 94); Giulio Ferroni, "L'Ariosto e la concezione umanistica della follia" (entry 318); Daniela Delcorno Branca, "L'Ariosto e la tradizione

del romanzo medievale" (entry 252); Antonio Franceschetti, "Appunti sull'Ariosto lettore dell'*Innamorato*" (entry 334); Gioacchino Paparelli, "Pubblico e poesia dell'*Orlando Furioso*" (entry 606); Walter Binni, "Le *Lettere* e le *Satire* dell'Ariosto" (entry 101); Edda Bresciani, "Il *Libro* dei Conti dei Balestrieri di Messer Ludovico Ariosto Commissario Ducale in Garfagnana, nell'Archivio Statale di Modena" (entry 143); Aurelio Roncaglia, "Nascita e sviluppo della narrativa cavalleresca nella Francia medievale" (entry 699); Bronislaw Bilinski, "Le risonanze ariostee nella poesia romantica polacca" (entry 97); Zlata M. Potapova, "Ariosto e Puŝkin" (entry 652); Martin De Riquer, "Ariosto y España" (entry 259); Cesare Gnudi, "L'Ariosto e le arti figurative" (entry 374); Wanda Roszkowska, "*Orlando Furioso* e il seicento polacco" (entry 710); Charles Dedeyan, "La fortune de l'Arioste en France du XIXᵉ siècle à nos jours" (entry 246); Horst Rüdiger, "Ariosto nel mondo di lingua tedesca" (entry 715); Mario Praz, "Ariosto in Inghilterra" (entry 655); R. M. Goròchova, "La fortuna dell'Ariosto in Russia" (entry 379); Selene Anceschi Bolognesi, "Era nata a Reggio Emilia la figlia del re del Catai?" (entry 15); Antonio De Luca, "I prologhi delle commedie ariostesche" (entry 255).

⊷§ 476. LUGLI, VITTORIO. "Boileau tra l'Ariosto e La Fontaine: la *Dissertation Critique sur Joconde*." *Rendiconto delle sessioni della Accademia delle Scienze dell'Istituto di Bologna*, 5th ser., 10 (1960–1961), 1961, Classe di Scienze Morali, pp. 121–32.
Noting Boileau's mysterious silence regarding La Fontaine's *Fables* in his *Art poétique*, discusses the significance of the critic's appraisal of La Fontaine's style in earlier works, particularly the *conte* based on *OF* 28 and entitled "Joconde." Discusses Boileau's evaluation of the French adaptation, the reasons for his preference for La Fontaine's version to the original, and the significance of the Ariosto–La Fontaine comparison to Boileau's defense of French poetry.

⊷§ 477. MACIEJEWSKI, MARIAN. "Tradycje Epiki Ariostyczno-Wielandowskiej W *Grażynie*" (The Traditions of the epic of Ariosto and Wieland in the *Grażyna*). *Roczniki Humanistyczne* 18, no. 1 (1970): 105–33.
Considers the place of Adam Mickiewicz's *Grażyna* (published in 1822) in the development of the lyric romance in Poland and, in particular, the influence of the Ariostean tradition and that of Wieland's *Obéron* on its composition.

⊷§ 478. MCMURPHY, SUSANNAH JANE. *Spenser's Use of Ariosto for Allegory*. 1924. Reprint. Norwood, Pa.: Norwood Editions, 1978. 54p.
Argues that allegory is part of the poetic variety—the "universal embrace"

(p. 12)—of the *OF* but that authentic examples are few, the most important being the episode of Ruggiero's sojourn on the isle of Alcina and Astolfo's voyage to the moon. Discusses the nature of Ariosto's allegory, the important readings of the poem in the sixteenth century (Fornari's and Toscanella's) and concludes that by Spenser's lifetime a tradition as to how to read Ariosto had been established. Consideration of English Renaissance commentaries on Ariosto (e.g., Harington's preface to his 1591 translation of the *OF*), a brief exposition of some examples of Ariosto's allegory, and a concluding analysis of Spenser's allegorical reading of the poem and his use of it in the *FQ*.

479. McNEIR, WALDO F. "Ariosto's Sospetto, Gascoigne's Suspicion, and Spenser's Malbecco." In *Festschrift für Walther Fischer*, pp. 34–48. Heidelberg: Carl Winter, 1959.
Argues as untenable the thesis that the Malbecco character in the *FQ* 3.9–10 derives either from Gascoigne's version of Ariosto's fable of Suspicion (*CC* 2) in *The Adventures of Master F. J.* or directly from the Italian source.

480. McNULTY, ROBERT. Introduction. In *Orlando Furioso, Translated into English Heroical Verse by Sir John Harington (1591)*, edited with an introduction by Robert McNulty, pp. ix–liv. Oxford: The Clarendon Press, 1972.
Introduces the *OF* by briefly noting selected motifs and similarities with the *Aeneid*. In view of the fact that Ariosto celebrates Christian victory over paganism and urges the Este family and the whole of Italy on to heroic deeds, asserts, "No more sincere Italian patriot than Ariosto exists in Renaissance literature, not even Dante" (p. ix). Includes brief summary of Harington's life and works and a detailed discussion of his translation.

481. MACRÍ, ORESTE. "L'Ariosto e la letteratura spagnola." *Nuove lettere emiliane*, nos. 9–11 (1965): 13–29.
Also in *Letterature moderne* 3, no. 5 (1952): 515–43; Fatini, 3497.

482. MADELAINE, R. E. R. "'When Griffon Saw the Reconciled Quean': Marston, Ariosto and Haydocke." *Notes and Queries* 217 (1972): 453–54.
Notes Richard Haydocke's translation of *OF* 18.1–4 as the source of four verses in Marston's *The Malcontent* (Third Quarto, 1604).

483. MAJOR, VIRGINIA CAROL. "The Course of True Love: The Romance Background of the Love Stories in Spenser's *Faerie Queene*." *DAI* 39, no. 4 (1978): 2294A. (Southern Illinois University, 1978. 305p.)
On conventions from earlier romances used in Spenser's love stories.

Notes that the *OF*, a major Italian influence on Spenser, parodies medieval conventions and that weaknesses in lovers are tolerated more than in earlier epic romances. Argues that, in their virtues, Spenser's heroes and heroines are intended to mirror a harmonious society.

484. MALAGOLI, LUIGI. "La Poesia dell'*Orlando Furioso* e lo spirito e l'arte del Rinascimento." In his *Storia dell'antica poesia dalle origini all'Ariosto*, pp. 255–78. Florence: La Nuova Italia, 1965.
Explores the poetics of harmony and the elements of Ariosto's spiritual and psychological modernity in the *OF*. Identifies major components of his style (e.g., comparison, hyperbole, fullness of description) and their function in Ariosto's poetic vision, which is a representation of the liberation of the spirit and the sense of world harmony: "con lui il senso del dominio sereno sulle cose trionfa e si sviluppa la rappresentazione degli accordi intimi e fusi" (p. 275).

485. ———. "La Duplicità del Rinascimento nel Machiavelli e nell'Ariosto." In his *Le Contraddizioni del Rinascimento*, pp. 25–37. Florence: La Nuova Italia, 1968.
Notes a duplicity ("duplicità") present in the sixteenth century marked by a constant oscillation between a sense of harmony and the idyllic, on the one hand, and, on the other, a sensibility marked by unease and melancholy (mirrored already in the fifteenth century, for example, in Sannazaro). Cites as well the contradiction between the possession of a freedom of spirit and a profoundly medieval sense of a "realtà immota" (p. 25). Discusses in this context the ways in which Machiavelli's thought reflects irreconcilable contradictions and how Ariosto—in the *OF*'s harmonious universe of change and antithesis—poetically represents the essence of the Renaissance *geist* at this time.

486. MALAGÙ, ARTURO. "Appunti sulle fonti pittoriche dell'*Orlando Furioso*." In *Ferrara e l'Ariosto*, by Raffaele Belvederi, Virgilio Ferrari, and Arturo Malagù, pp. 9–40. (La *Ferrariae Decus* nel V Centenario della nascita del poeta.) Ferrara: S.A.T.E., 1974.
Also in *Gazzetta di Ferrara*, 3–5 October 1974.
Discusses the important influence on Ariosto of contemporary figurative arts, focusing on the stimulation given the poet's imagination by the miniatures in the Este collection and the importance of Tura, Dossi, and other contemporary painters for Ariosto's poetic landscapes. Notes in particular the apparent influence on Ariosto of the Trecento frescoes in the house of the Del Sole (now Minerbi) near his own residence and, especially, of the frescoes in the Palazzo Schifanoia and the Sala dei Mesi. Suggests that the Schifanoia frescoes provided him with "concetti generali" (p. 30), a sense of

pictorial realism, "lo spirito di armoniosa bellezza, di sintesi culturale, di gusto del racconto vivace" (p. 31). Also suggests an influence of the monochromatic bas-reliefs painted by Mazzolino and the reciprocal influences with the Dossi brothers. Discusses in particular the two Circes and the relationship with Ariosto's Alcina and Melissa. Includes seven illustrations.

◈§ 487. MALAGÙ, UGO. *Alcune terre di messer Ludovico Ariosto.* Ferrara: Industrie Grafiche Ferrara, 1976. 59p.
Detailed descriptions, drawings, and photographs of properties belonging to Ariosto and his family, with descriptions of documents of ownership and their provenance.

◈§ 488. MANENTI VALLI, FRANCA. "Restauri al Mauriziano." In *Lodovico Ariosto: il suo tempo la sua terra la sua gente* (entry 468). Estratto dal *Bollettino storico reggiano* 7, no. 27 (1974): 5–55.
Details the history of the Mauriziano, a palace belonging to Ariosto's mother's family, the Malaguzzi Valeri, and inhabited for an extensive period of time by the poet, who mentions it in Satire 4. Contains genealogy of the Malaguzzi Valeri, detailed descriptions of the building during the fifteenth century, and a discussion of the modern disposition of the property. Reproduces documents regarding the property, including a sixteenth-century inventory of its contents.

◈§ 489. MANGANELLI, GIORGIO. "Nell'universo degli ippogrifi." *Terzoprogramma*, nos. 2–3 (1974): 58–68.
Discusses the sources and variety of magical elements in the *OF* and their function to the poem's structure; focuses on Astolfo and his associations with magic.

◈§ 490. MANZINI, PAOLA. "Le Condizioni sanitarie a Reggio e la relativa legislazione al tempo dell'Ariosto." In *Lodovico Ariosto: il suo tempo la sua terra la sua gente* (entry 468). Estratto dal *Bollettino storico reggiano* 7, no. 25 (1974): 109–22.
Provides documents recording the outbreak of disease during Ariosto's time and discusses measures taken by civic officials to improve hygiene.

◈§ 491. MARCHI, GIAN PAOLO. "Lessing critico dell'Ariosto." In *Scritti in onore di Antonio Scolari*, pp. 191–207. Verona: Istituto per gli Studi Storici Veronesi, 1976.
Discusses Lessing's criticism of *OF* 7.11–15 (the description of Alcina's beauty): "[Lessing] non poteva apprezzare il 'quadro senza quadro' della descrizione di Alcina, che egli considera come 'la più istruttiva ammonizione' che si possa rivolgere ai poeti affinché non tentino soggetti e argomenti . . .

riservati alle arti figurative" (p. 197). Notes that to Lessing, whose tastes were firmly anchored in Aristotelianism, "rimaneva estraneo il libero gioco fantastico" of the *OF* (p. 206).

492. MARCONI, EMO. "Teatralità dell'Ariosto." In *Per l'Ariosto* (entry 623). Special 1976 issue of *Italianistica* 3, no. 3 (1974): 63–85.
Formulates a theory of theatricality that is applied to a reading of the *OF*. Defines theatricality as that component of the human mind capable of concretizing well-defined images and ideas. In the *OF*, theatricality occurs when an image in movement is sufficiently delimited as to allow its eventual scenic rendition. Such a process is accomplished through an ingenious correspondence between idea and concretizing symbol.

493. MARINELLI, PETER VINCENT. "The Dynastic Romance: A Study in the Evolution of the Romantic Epics of Boiardo, Ariosto and Spenser." *DA* 25, no. 10 (1965): 5931. (Princeton University, 1964. 420p.)
Argues that rather than a continuation of the *OI*, the *OF* is essentially "an allegory of temperance, an allegory which transfers the center of interest from Orlando . . . to Ruggiero and Bradamante, the foredestined mythical forbears [sic] of the d'Este family." The values of reason and temperance are expressed in terms borrowed from both traditional Christian philosophy and iconography, resulting in a poem with "a serious moral intention." Chapter 4 devoted to the sixteenth-century allegorizers of the *OF*, vindicating Simone Fornari's reading of the poem by reference to contemporary thought and iconography. Examines Spenser's debt to Ariosto in the creation of a dynastic romance in praise of the Tudors, affirming "an ascertainable development" from the Italian romance to the *FQ*.

494. ———. "Redemptive Laughter: Comedy in the Italian Romances." In *Versions of Medieval Comedy*, edited by Paul G. Ruggiers, pp. 227–48. Norman: University of Oklahoma Press, 1977.
Also in *Genre* 9, no. 4 (1977): 505–26.
Identifies the comic impulse of the *Morgante*, the *OI*, and the *OF* in order "to assert the unique and essential character of each poem . . . and the increment of meaning and moral and intellectual complexity visible in the [comic] process" (p. 228). Discusses the progression of comedy from Pulci to Ariosto, noting that it is on differing planes and concluding that in the *OF*, with the conflict of human motives and desires, we are "in the presence of a Christian Lucianist, scanning the complexity of human desire with wonder and laughter; and of a Christian Democritus . . . , who watches the spectacle of the unwearying hunt of mortals for earthly satisfaction in terms of a comic hilarity" (p. 229). Argues for the importance of reading the *OF* in the cultural context of fifteenth-century Neoplatonism, the philosophical structure

of which is grafted onto the material of the *OI* and its predecessors, resulting in a humorous juxtapositioning of a popular epic tradition and serious metaphysical considerations. Cites as an example the use of Astolfo, whose traditional character is at odds with Ariosto's portrayal of him as redeemed and worthy of spiritual flight—a Neoplatonic exemplar—and as one who stands in marked contrast to the mad Orlando. Compares Ruggiero's progress toward becoming the model dynast with the course of Astolfo and Orlando, noting that he "fluctuates between the two poles [represented by Orlando and Astolfo], as befits a creature whose life in the world is conceived as the mean between outright hedonism and complete transcendence" (p. 244). Concludes with a discussion of the role of Providence in the direction of the poem's multiple actions, noting the humor that results from the constant contrast between will ("voler divino") and human desire ("voglia").

᪾ᨠ 495. MARIOTTI, SCEVOLA. "Per il riesame di un'ode latina dell'Ariosto." *Italia medioevale e umanistica* 2 (1959): 509–12.
Argues that the lyric poem "De vellere aureo" is a political allegory, primarily because of Ariosto's tendency to base his poems on actual events and because he uses as a model the form of the Horatian ode, traditionally considered the vehicle for political allegory. Proposes a reading of the ode, without attempting to identify the precise historical allusions.

᪾ᨠ 496. ———. "Cronologia di congetture e congetture superflue." In his *Scritti medievali e umanistici*, pp. 221–26. Rome: Edizioni di Storia e Letteratura, 1976.
Also in *Studi e problemi di critica testuale* (Bologna: Commissione per i testi di lingua, 1961), pp. 359–68.
Textual problems in a correct reading of Ariosto's Latin poem traditionally entitled "Ad Alphonsum Ferr. ducem III."

᪾ᨠ 497. MARSH, DAVID. "Horatian Influence and Imitation in Ariosto's Satires." *Comparative Literature* 27, no. 4 (1975): 307–26.
Discusses Ariosto's debt to Horace through a textual comparison of the satires and Horace's *Satires* and *Epistles*. Shows that Ariosto borrows words and entire phrases from the Latin satirist; identifies thematic affinities between the two poets: the antithesis between the poet and his world, the autobiographical mode, and moral pronouncements, for example. Remarks a strong structural similarity between Horace's *Satire* 1.6 and Ariosto's sixth satire and notes that Horace's *Satires* 1.6 and 2.6 and *Epistle* 1.7 exercised "the greatest thematic and structural influence on Ariosto" (p. 325).

᪾ᨠ 498. MARTELLI, MARIO. "Una delle *Intercenali* di Leon Battista Alberti fonte sconosciuta del *Furioso*." *La Bibliofilia* 66, disp. 2 (1964): 163–70.

Notes that Astolfo's sojourn on the moon (*OF* 34.73–85) is in imitation of *Somnium*, one of Alberti's *Intercenali* discovered by Eugenio Garin (see "Venticinque Intercenali inedite e sconosciute di Leon Battista Alberti," *Belfagor* 19 [1964]: 377–96). Defends this claim with a comparison of the central passage of *Somnium*, in which Libripeta talks of having found in dreamland all things lost on earth, to Astolfo's discovery in the lunar valleys of everything that man has lost on earth. Adds that Ariosto, though at times translating literally the Alberti text, enriches his version with new, "felicissimi simboli" (p. 169).

🖙 499. MARTI, MARIO. Introduzione. In *Orlando Furioso*, by Ludovico Ariosto, episodi scelti e commentati da Mario Marti, pp. 3–8. 2d ed. Rome: Signorelli, 1958.
First edition 1954; Fatini, 3551.

🖙 500. ———. "La Poesia del ridere." *Terzoprogramma* 3 (1961): 187–95.
Brief observations on the presence in Ariosto's works of elements derived from the burlesque tradition of Francesco Berni and other popular poets (pp. 193–95).

🖙 501. ———. "Ludovico Ariosto." In *Letteratura italiana: I Maggiori*, 1:307–406. 2 vols. Milan: Marzorati, 1969.
First edition 1956; Fatini, 3609.
Selections from this essay have also appeared in his *Dal certo al vero: studi di filologia e di storia* (Rome: Edizioni dell'Ateneo, 1962), with the following titles: "Indagine sulla formazione di L. Ariosto," pp. 159–69; "Poesia minore dell'Ariosto," pp. 171–87; "Il tono medio dell'*Orlando furioso*," pp. 189–212; the last also in *Convivium* 23, no. 1 (1955): 29–42 (Fatini, 3550).

🖙 502. ———. "L'Ariosto e il *Furioso*." In his *Nuovi contributi dal certo al vero: studi di filologia e di storia*, pp. 193–98. Ravenna: Longo, 1980.
Places the genesis and composition of the first edition of the *OF* in the perspective of Ariosto's years of personal hardship and familial problems (especially 1504–1509), noting that the poem stands as a symbol both of the human condition and of Ferrarese civilization and is, at the same time, a "prepotente compensazione della fantasia nei confronti di una esteriore realtà" (p. 196).

🖙 503. MARTINI, CARLO. "Il 'Conto dei Contadini' di Ludovico Ariosto." *Accademie e biblioteche d'Italia* 40, no. 1 (1972): 44–46.
Brief discussion of a codex in the Biblioteca Pubblica of Ferrara, containing assorted notes by Ariosto on business concerning his farmland; notes the importance of the manuscript for providing a picture of Ariosto in a world of

daily activities and for its examples of administrative terminology and the popular jargon of rustic life.

◆§ 504. MARZI, GIOVANNI. "Musica e strumenti nella poesia ariostesca." In *Lodovico Ariosto: il suo tempo la sua terra la sua gente* (entry 468). Estratto dal *Bollettino storico reggiano* 7, no. 27 (1974): 57–62.
States that the OF reveals no technical or theoretical musical knowledge on the part of Ariosto. Notes that certain instruments or instrumental sounds are referential to particular situations in the narrative. Remarks on the importance of Ariosto's octaves to Renaissance composers as a source of lyrics. Appendix of musical terms and instruments mentioned in the OF.

◆§ 505. MASCIANDARO, FRANCO. "Folly in the *Orlando Furioso*: A Reading of the Gabrina Episode." *Forum Italicum* 14, no. 1 (1980): 56–77.
Relates the Gabrina episode to the central theme of Orlando's madness (especially in OF 23), noting both thematic parallels and analogous topoi, e.g., the association of the rock ("sasso") with folly. Notes that the narrative and episodes adjacent to it concern the folly resulting from an inflexible view of reality and stubborn adherence to chivalric codes of honor (cf. Zerbino and Filandro) and that the carrying out of justice and victory over Gabrina by Odorico is accomplished through an ironic negation of chivalric ideals.

◆§ 506. MAZZAMUTO, PIETRO. "Ludovico Ariosto." In *Rassegna bibliografico-critica della letteratura italiana*, pp. 179–213. 3d ed. Florence: Le Monnier, 1963.
Fatini, 3525, reviews second edition, 1953.
Reviews trends in Ariosto criticism, departing from the position that there have been two basic approaches to the OF, one taking into particular account the moral stance of the author and the other the poem's fantastic and surrealistic elements. Surveys critical positions from the Renaissance to the modern period, highlighting the particular contributions of Bonaventura Zumbini (aesthetical analysis of characters), of Liborio Azzolina (interpretation of the poem as an epic of the human soul), and the influential writings of Croce and Momigliano. Does not consider critical writings after the 1950s, focusing on Binni, Raffaello Ramat, and the Marxist views of Antonio Piromalli. Cursory discussion of the critical reception of Ariosto's minor works.

◆§ 507. MEDICI, DOMENICO. "La bibliografia della critica ariostesca dal 'Fatini' ad oggi (1957–1974)." In *Lodovico Ariosto: il suo tempo la sua terra la sua gente* (entry 468). Estratto dal *Bollettino storico reggiano* 7, no. 27 (1974): 63–150.
Not comprehensive bibliography of 360 entries in chronological order for

period 1957–1974 (pp. 73–150). Summary annotations of items available to compiler; other entries indicate source of citation. Brief introductory essay on mainstreams of Ariosto criticism in the twentieth century, noting especially the increased interest in recent decades in Ariosto's minor works and in linguistic-philological studies of the texts. Concludes with an introduction to the major Italian critics represented in the bibliography and a survey of those critical writings of foreign scholars available to him.

508. MEDICI, MARIO. "Presenza e vicende della coordinazione di indicativo con congiuntivo in proposizioni dipendenti nel *Furioso.*" In *Lodovico Ariosto: il suo tempo la sua terra la sua gente* (entry 468). Estratto dal *Bollettino storico reggiano* 7, no. 27 (1974): 151–57.
Continuing and augmenting an earlier study by Luigi Sorrento (*Sintassi romanza-Ricerche e prospettive*, 1950, especially pp. 304–6), cites examples and briefly indicates the significance of the use of the indicative and subjunctive in syntactic constructions in the *OF*, at times contrary to expected usage but that, to quote Sorrento, "risponde alle esigenze del pensiero e della fantasia creatrice" (pp. 276–77 of Sorrento; quoted on p. 152). Mentions as imminently forthcoming a work of a more extensive nature on this argument.

509. ———. "Varianti di indicativo e congiuntivo nelle tre edizioni dell'*Orlando Furioso.*" *La Rassegna della letteratura italiana*, 7th ser., vol. 79, nos. 1–2 (1975): 279–304.
Detailed analysis with many examples of shift from indicative to subjunctive and vice versa in the three editions of the *OF*. Concludes by assigning to Ariosto an important position in the evolution of literary prose (a position analogous, author suggests, to Alessandro Manzoni's for the nineteenth century) and notes the significant convergence of Ariosto's linguistic evolution and the theoretical basis provided by Pietro Bembo.

510. ———. *Usi alternativi di indicativo e congiuntivo nell'"Orlando Furioso."* Lecce: Edizioni Milella, 1977. 65p.
Analyzes Ariosto's use of the indicative or subjunctive mood in syntactical structures of a comparative nature, including simile, noting in conclusion "l'altezza delle qualità linguistiche del poeta, il grado di perfezione raggiunto" (p. 57). Includes bibliography of studies on Ariosto's language (pp. 59–64).

511. ———. "Aspetti delle varianti dei frammenti autografi dell'*Orlando Furioso.*" *Annali dell'Università di Lecce. Facoltà di Lettere e Filosofia* 8–10, part 1 (1977–1980): 447–58.
Notes that the only extant autographs of the *OF* are fragments of episodes

added for the 1532 edition: "Della primaria importanza di questi autografi non vi è tuttavia dubbio: la loro condizione linguistica ancora più interna, e più immediata, li rende particolarmente significativi per la storia linguistica generale e per quella stilistica ariostesca, oltre che per un quadro di usi e funzioni" (p. 447). Examines changes from indicative to subjunctive and vice versa, systematically by type, providing text of autographs and of the relevant passages of the 1532 edition. Concludes: "I tipi di varianti presentati dagli autografi ariosteschi, le elaborazioni del testo definitivo dai versi messi in carta con immediatezza (sia per quello che si è visto qui, sia per altro che resterebbe da studiare), sono senza dubbio particolarmente interessanti sul piano metrico, stilistico e sintattico . . . , anche al di là di quelle presentate dal raffronto delle parti 'antiche' delle tre edizioni. Se il divario in generale è meno marcato di quello che risulta nel percorso dall'edizione 1516 alla 1532, è allora possibile raccogliere con tutta evidenza il livello formale e stilistico e la tensione espressiva a cui l'Ariosto è pervenuto" (p. 458).

512. ———. "Varianti di indicativo e congiuntivo nei rifacimenti delle *Commedie* ariostesche." *Critica letteraria* 6, no. 3 (1978): 495–508.
Noting that the optional use of the subjunctive or indicative is linked to "una duplice possibilità funzionale o strutturale o di scelta stilistico-tonale secondo cui ci si può spontaneamente esprimere, o operare in modo riflesso" (p. 495), catalogs (with facing texts) a number of changes in verb mood in the two editions of *La Cassaria* (1508; 1529), *I Suppositi* (1509; 1532), and *Il Negromante* (1520; 1528).

513. MENGALDO, PIER VINCENZO. *La lingua del Boiardo lirico*. Biblioteca dell'*Archivum Romanicum*, 2d ser.: Linguistica 30. Florence: Leo S. Olschki, 1963. 382p.
Briefly notes the role of the OF in maintaining alive the interest in Boiardo's OI during the first part of the sixteenth century, indicating that there were eight published editions of the OI between 1530 and 1544. See especially pp. 352–54.

514. MEO ZILIO, GIOVANNI. *Estudio sobre Hernando Domínguez Camargo y su s. Ignacio de Loyola, poema heroyco*. Messina-Florence: G. D'Anna, 1967. 359p.
Passim discussion of Ariostean elements in the religious epic of the Columbian poet Hernando Domínguez Camargo (1606–1659).

515. MEREGALLI, FRANCO. "La literatura italiana en la obra de Cervantes." *Arcadia* 6 (1971): 1–15.
Notes that Cervantes read the OF in the original, deploring the inaccuracies of Urrea's Spanish translation. Comments on Maxime Chevalier's study

on Ariosto's influence on Cervantes (pp. 439–91 in _L'Arioste en Espagne_, entry 202), noting its documentary value but expressing the need for greater clarification of the affinity Cervantes felt with Ariosto. Discusses similarities between their attitudes toward life, their commonly held civic values, and their insistence on personal ethics as the only criteria for making value judgments.

516. MERVYN, LOIS. "_Orlando Furioso._" In _Teaching the Epic_, edited by Margaret Fleming, pp. 42–43. Urbana, Ill.: National Council of Teachers of English, 1974.

Summary information on themes, tone, and narrative line for including the _OF_ in an academic course on epic poetry.

517. MEZZANOTTE, P. ROMEO. _L'Ariosto e il Tasso a raffronto._ Milan: Gastaldi, 1958. 46p.

Explores superficial similarities and differences between Ariosto and Tasso, concluding that Tasso is the superior poet for his deeply moral and religious sentiment.

518. MIGLIORINI, BRUNO. "Sulla lingua dell'Ariosto." In his _Saggi linguistici_, pp. 178–86. Florence: Le Monnier, 1957.

Also in _Italica_ 23, no. 1 (1946): 152–60; Fatini, 3369.

519. MILANI, FRANCESCO. "Reggio 'ecclesiastica' al tempo dell'Ariosto, parroco fra il 1506 e il 1512 d'una chiesa di Montericco." In _Lodovico Ariosto: il suo tempo la sua terra la sua gente_ (entry 468). Estratto dal _Bollettino storico reggiano_ 7, no. 27 (1974): 159–67.

Describes the minor ecclesiastical post (and the attendant responsibilities) held by Ariosto to supplement income needed to support his family after the death of his father.

520. MIRANDA, JOSÉ DA COSTA. "Ludovico Ariosto, _Satire_ e _Rime_: alguns apontamentos e breves considerações sobre a sua presença em Portugal." _Estudos italianos em Portugal_ 40–42 (1977–1979): 3–25.

Considers Ariosto's influence on several Portuguese poets, especially of the sixteenth century. Discusses the interpretation of the satires in Portugal and, in particular, the literary repercussions of what was perceived as Ariostean misogyny, especially in Satire 5. Suggests that several expressions of pessimism and bitterness in Camões's _Os Lusíadas_ were suggested by a reading of both the satires and the _OF_. Gives particular attention to the influence of the satires on Francisco Manuel de Melo and on Sá de Miranda, in whose _cartas_ "encontrariamos influências temáticas provenientes das sátiras . . . e, ocasionalmente, a forma estrófica e a estrutura rímica usadas pelo italiano,

encontrar-nos-íamos . . . con certas poesias mirandinas, com directas refer-
ências ao Ariosto ou a acções realizadas por personagens do *Furioso*" (p. 17).
Briefly considers the nature of Ariosto's Italian lyrics and their influence on
Camões, Pêro de Andrade Caminha, and other Portuguese poets.

📚 521. ———. "Camões / Ariosto: um confronto evidente no percurso do
Orlando Furioso em Portugal." In *Rime scelte, tradotte e commentate*,
by Luíz de Camões, edited by Riccardo Averini. Special issue of *Estu-
dos italianos em Portugal* 41 (1979): 273–90.
Surveys comparative evaluations of Ariosto and Camões in Portuguese
critical writings from the Renaissance to the present, noting the general preference for Camões due to his exaltation of the heroic ideal and the perennial
celebration of the Portuguese poet as a spokesman for patriotic nationalism.

📚 522. MIROLA, GIAN. "Il poeta che per trentasei anni governò la Garga-
gnana [*sic*]." *Notiziario* (Lucca) 9, no. 7 (1969): 3–7.
Unavailable; cited in PMLA (1971): 58.

📚 523. MITCHELL, BONNER. "Italian Literature." See Corrigan, Beatrice
M., entry 223.

📚 524. MODIC, JOHN L. "Gascoigne and Ariosto Again." *Comparative Literature* 14, no. 3 (1962): 317–19.
Notes that in his translation of Ariosto's *I Suppositi*, Gascoigne used both
the original prose version and the revised verse version, accounting for what
had appeared to Karl F. Thompson ("A Note on Ariosto's *I Suppositi*," entry
840) as discrepancies in Gascoigne's portrayal of some characters. Notes that
Thompson compared Gascoigne's translation only to the prose version, fail-
ing to see that his creation of more sympathetic father figures is true to Ariosto's poetic redaction.

📚 525. MOLINARO, JULIUS A. "Ariosto and the Seven Deadly Sins." *Forum
Italicum* 3, no. 2 (1969): 252–69.
Notes that in OF 14.81 cruelty replaces lust in Ariosto's list of the seven
deadly sins. Discusses Ariosto's representation of cruelty in the OF, best represented in the person of Marganorre and placed in antithesis to chivalric
courtesy; argues that the poet's insistence on moral values and his condemnation of cruelty refute De Sanctis's and Croce's refusals to attribute a moral
dimension to the poem. Concludes, after examining the representation of
lust in the OF, that it is a self-punitive vice and a lesser evil than cruelty,
which is perpetrated upon others.

526. ———. "Avarice and Sloth in the *Orlando Furioso.*" *Renaissance and Reformation* 10, no. 2 (1974): 103–15.

Analyzes the figurative representations of avarice and sloth in the *OF*, as well as Ariosto's commentary on the vices (e.g., the extended discourse on avarice introducing canto 43). Notes that although the poem is not a formal allegory with a moral purpose, Ariosto's treatment of the deadly sins enriches a poem intent on representing the frailties of man and the dangers he encounters in his exploits.

527. ———. "Sin and Punishment in the *Orlando Furioso.*" *MLN* 89 (1974): 35–46.

Proposes to reconcile the divergent views of those who see a moral lesson in the *OF* and those who consider Ariosto amoral and irreligious by demonstrating that the theme of sin and punishment pervading the poem reveals that "Ariosto's moral code falls within a system of ethics, sanctioned by time and tradition" (p. 45).

528. ———. "*Superbia, Ira, Invidia* and *Gola* in the *Orlando Furioso.*" *Italica* 53, no. 4 (1976): 475–94.

Examines Ariosto's treatment of four deadly sins. Points out that pride, the cause of all sin, "occupies the most prominent place in the *Orlando Furioso*" (p. 476). Discusses the poet's concept of pride as personified by Rodomonte and Senàpo, with reference to classical, theological, and medieval (particularly Dantesque) sources. Argues that for Ariosto there are two kinds of wrath, "*ira*, the traditional sin which is destructive . . . and righteous anger, which is good" (p. 481). Notes that this distinction is found in some English sermons of the later Middle Ages and in Spenser's *FQ*, concluding that Ariosto's concept seems to stem from a common tradition, also present, for example, in Giotto's representation of the sin in the Arena Chapel, Padua. Notes that gluttony and envy, although less prominent in the poem, are, nevertheless, "precisely defined" (p. 483). Takes issue with Francesco De Sanctis's view that Ariosto is concerned only with form; also takes issue with his statement that in the *OF* there is no "serietà di vita interiore" (*Storia della letteratura italiana* [Milan, 1961], p. 336; quoted on p. 480), stressing that Ariosto is a poet "intrigued by man's frailties" and always probing into "the depths of man's spiritual infirmities" (pp. 491–92).

529. ———. "The Active and the Contemplative Life in the *Orlando Furioso.*" *Esperienze letterarie* 1 (1977): 3–10.

Argues that in the *OF* Astolfo represents the active life and St. John the contemplative life, but that Ariosto, unlike his humanist predecessors, did not enter into debate over their relative merits, celebrating instead the rewards of the active life.

➾ 530. ———. "Ariosto in America." *University of Toronto Quarterly* 48, no. 2 (1978–1979): 172–78.

Discusses three volumes: *Orlando Furioso: The Ring of Angelica* (1), translated by Richard Hodgens (1973); *Ariosto 1974 in America*, edited by Aldo Scaglione (1976, entry 760); *The Satires of Ludovico Ariosto: A Renaissance Autobiography*, translated with an introduction by Peter DeSa Wiggins (1976, entry 909). Expresses reservations about the quality of the Hodgens translation and Lin Carter's observations in the introduction to the volume that the *OF* lacks structure; briefly presents the essays in *Ariosto 1974 in America* and praises Wiggins's prose translation of the satires.

➾ 531. ———. "Ariosto in English." *Quaderni d'italianistica* (Ottawa) 1, no. 2 (1980): 200–207.

Review essay of Barbara Reynolds's translation of the *OF* ("a lively version, the fruit of a fine critical taste and a sensitivity to poetry," p. 203; entry 683), Robert Griffin's *Ludovico Ariosto* (1974, entry 393), and *The Comedies of Ariosto*, translated and edited by Edmond M. Beame and Leonard G. Sbrocchi (1975, entry 26). Briefly discusses the comedies in relationship to the *OF* to indicate areas of potential interest for further study; judges *La Lena* to be a superficial treatment of Renaissance corruption and a play of potentially powerful themes left undeveloped.

➾ 532. ———. "Ariosto's Concept of Virtù." *Esperienze letterarie* 5, no. 2 (1980): 3–16.

Argues that in the *OF* Ariosto uses the word *virtù* in both its traditional meaning and in the meaning given it by his contemporary Machiavelli, i.e., connoting personal ability and perspicacity. Considers the use of the word in several episodes, including its association with the character of Melissa, in which it becomes related to personal glory and the antithesis of slothfulness. Discusses the binary *virtù*-sloth in the *OF* and the variety of meanings given to the word *virtù* by Ariosto who, though possibly influenced by Machiavelli, does not cite him among the illustrious in the last canto of the poem.

➾ 533. MOMIGLIANO, ATTILIO. "La realtà e il sogno nell'*Orlando Furioso*. (Linee per uno studio sul poema dell'Ariosto)." In his *Introduzione ai poeti*, pp. 67–96. Florence: Sansoni, 1964.

Previously published in *Giornale storico della letteratura italiana* 85 (1925): 268–87 and in his *Introduzione ai poeti* (Rome: Tumminelli, 1946), pp. 55–78; Fatini, 2293.

➾ 534. ———. *Saggio sull'"Orlando Furioso."* Bari: Laterza, 1971. 309p.

First published in 1928; Fatini, 2407.

535. MONTANARI, FAUSTO. "La Poesia dell'Ariosto." _Studium_ 71, no. 5 (1975): 717–22.

Identifies Boiardo and Boccaccio as the major influences on the paradoxical world of the _OF_, the former for the mythologizing nature of poetic discourse and the latter for the phenomenological variety of the vicissitudes of love ("varietà fenomenica delle vicende d'amore," p. 719). Argues that Ariosto's sense of paradox continues a basic vision of life established in the _OI_ and manifest in the title of his poem, but makes more explicit the contrast between what is and what should be and the fact that the rational nature of man both defines his essence and is ironically the source of his own undoing. ("Perciò il misterioso motto ariostesco _Pro bono malum_ può anche essere interpretato come generica allusione a quello che si potrebbe chiamare lo scandalo della storia: l'uomo, fatto per il bene, fa invece il male e, qualificato dalla ragione, usa la ragione contro se stessa," p. 720). Sees in Ariosto's sense of the concrete and the specific his capacity for fantasy, for portraying the human paradox as interplay between the real and the illusory.

536. MONTANO, ROCCO. "La follia di Orlando." In his _Saggi di cultura umanistica_, pp. 163–92. Naples: Quaderni di Delta, 1962.

Previously published as a brief monograph (Naples: Ediz. Humanitas, 1942), 78p.; Fatini, 3316.

537. ———. "Ludovico Ariosto: The Sixth Satire." _Umanesimo_ 1, no. 3 (1967): 60–70.

Briefly characterizes Ariosto's satires as a "deeply Catholic expression of humanistic literature" (p. 60) and states that the sixth satire celebrates classical education as "essential to Christian spirituality" and the "basis of religion and humanity" (p. 61). Includes an Elizabethan translation of the satire addressed to Bembo.

538. MONTEVERDI, ANGELO. "A proposito delle 'fonti' dell'_Orlando furioso_." _Cultura neolatina_ 21 (1961): 259–67.

Also in _Atti del II Congresso internazionale della Société Rencesvals_ (Modena: Tipografia Modenese, 1961), pp. 1–9; with title "Lipadusa e Roncisvalle," in _Lettere italiane_ 13 (1961): 401–9; abstracted in _Bulletin bibliographique de la Société Rencesvals_ 3 (1963): 103.

Argues that the Lipadusa episode in the _OF_ is an example of the poet's instinctive return to the most ancient and genuine epic tradition, despite Pio Rajna's inability to find but a modest number of direct influences from the Carolingian romance (_Le fonti dell'"Orlando Furioso_, 1876; 1900).

539. MOORMAN, CHARLES. "The Allegorical Knights of _The Faerie Queene_." _The Southern Quarterly_ 3, no. 2 (1965): 131–50.

Considers the Tudor revival of Arthurian legend in England and argues that knighthood emerged "as a literary framework for allegory, a 'vehicle for moral instruction in a Protestant and Erastian England'" (p. 136; quotes Arthur B. Ferguson, *The Indian Summer of English Chivalry* [1960], p. 97). Notes that in the *FQ*, which owes much to the Italian chivalric romances, Spenser's "knights remain fundamentally different from those of his sources . . . because they are, as the Italian knights are not, essentially and before all else figures in an allegory, and it is finally their allegorical nature that determines their forms and actions" (p. 137). Illustrates this statement by comparing Spenser's Britomart with Ariosto's Bradamante, noting that Bradamante is "an interestingly rounded character" with psychological dimension, whereas the essence of Britomart "lies in her allegorical function"; whereas "Bradamante is chaste, Britomart is Chastity" (p. 138). Briefly considers critical evaluations of Spenser's debt to Ariosto and of the "influence of Ariosto's cynical attitude toward the virtues of chivalry on Spenser," concluding that the most acceptable theory is that Spenser tempered Ariosto's cynicism for his work of ethical instruction (p. 141). Concludes that in contrast with the allegorical structure of the *FQ*, "The literal in Ariosto is all, or very nearly all important, for while there are passages in the *Orlando Furioso*—the Alcena [*sic*]-Logistilla story, for example—which are to a degree allegorical, they seem included more for the sake of variety than for instruction" (p. 141).

540. Mora, Vittorio. "Proposta di lettura del canto primo dell'*Orlando Furioso* alla 'Rustica Bergamasca,'" *Bergomum* (Bollettino della Civica Biblioteca, Bergamo) 68, nos. 3–4 (1974): 27–74.

Discussion and analysis of a seventeenth-century Bergamasc translation of the first eleven cantos of the *OF* (ms. Biblioteca Civica di Bergamo, Salone, Cassap. 1, G.3.68); work of uncertain authorship. Appendix with transcriptions of selected parts of the manuscript.

541. Moretti, Walter. "Tre maestri della tecnica epica tassiana." *Annali della Scuola Normale Superiore di Pisa*, 2d ser., vol. 30, fasc. 1–2 (1961): 1–59.

Considers a variety of influences of the *OF* on the *GL*, noting at the same time significant differences between the poems. Analyzes the structure of the *ottava* in both poems, noting that the only similarity is in the grouping of pairs of verses for a "movimento pendolare" (p. 34); otherwise, the structure of the *ottava* in the *OF* is essentially hypotactic for narrative effectiveness and in the *GL* it is paratactic to assure a solemnity of tone (*gravitas*). Discusses Tasso's evaluation of Ariosto's aesthetic, which he found to consist of a representation of the *bello* and *dilettevole* (p. 39). States that Tasso's hedonistic tone is essentially Ariostean in origin, citing the cantos of Armida and

Rinaldo as examples. Comparative analysis of *GL* 14–16 and *OF* 6–7 to show "la presenza dell'Ariosto nel mondo epico tassiano" (p. 43). See especially pp. 33–47.

🖘 542. ———. "La bontà di cuore nell'*Orlando Furioso*." In his *Cortesia e furore nel Rinascimento italiano*, pp. 19–33. Bologna: Pàtron, 1970. Revision of "La Storia di Cloridano e Medoro: un esempio della umanizzazione ariostesca delle idealità eroiche e cavalleresche," *Convivium* 37, nos. 5–6 (1969): 543–51.

Argues that the episode of Cloridano and Medoro (*OF* 18–19), intended as a polemical contrast to the treachery of contemporary court society, is essentially an episode in which the classical virtue and fidelity of its Virgilian source (*Aeneid* 9) are transformed into the representation of *humanitas* and the highest form of Renaissance courtesy.

🖘 543. ———. "La Fortuna del *Furioso* negli ultimi vent'anni." In *Annali del Liceo-Ginnasio 'Ariosto,'* pp. 85–91. Ferrara, 1974.

Suggests that the publication of the *OF* and of Ariosto's minor works in 1954 (Milan-Naples: Ricciardi, edited by Lanfranco Caretti and Cesare Segre, respectively) marked a turning point in Ariosto studies: "ha proposto un'immagine del poema ariostesco fortemente rinnovata, che si offriva con vigore generoso e stimolante al complesso travaglio metodologico delle indagini ariostesche di questi ultimi vent'anni, recuperando gli esiti migliori della storiografia idealistica dell'Ottocento e del primo Novecento, e proseguendo per la via indicata dalla critica storicistica e dai nuovi studi di poetica" (p. 85). Briefly discusses the writings on Ariosto by Benedetto Croce and Attilio Momigliano and, after commenting on Caretti's introduction to the 1954 edition of the *OF*, concludes that it provides "l'immagine dell'Ariosto interprete del rinascimento estense nel suo momento eticamente più vitale e artisticamente più splendido; saldamente legato alle mura della sua città e nello stesso tempo aperto alla multiforme e dinamica realtà della storia degli uomini" (p. 88). Notes that all the editions of the *OF* since Caretti's in 1954 have "in misura diversa, avvertito l'esigenza, posta dal Caretti . . . di una dialettica relazione fra l'energia dinamica della realtà storica contemporanea e le aperte e cordiali disposizioni psicologiche, fantastiche ed artistiche dell'Ariosto" (p. 88). Notes that critical studies on Ariosto during the 1970s seem directed "verso una puntuale determinazione dei modi ideologici coi quali l'autore del *Furioso* istituisce il suo confronto con la realtà storica, e delle strutture con le quali l'arte del poema ariostesco realizza la sua interna coerenza formale" (p. 89).

🖘 544. ———. *L'ultimo Ariosto*. Bologna: Pàtron, 1977. 117p.

Profiles the 1516 and 1532 editions of the *OF* as reflections of two different historical moments and ideologies. Argues that the several wars between Italy and the great European military powers during the second and third decades of the sixteenth century, marking the end of personal and political freedom on the peninsula, affected Ariosto's perspective on the world and had an impact on the revisions of his poem. Whereas the 1516 OF is a poetic realization of idealized cosmic harmony, the poet later comes to understand that all human activity is subject to blind forces, incomprehensible and outside the sphere of one's control. Therefore, the humanistic ideals of the poet's early period are replaced by the discovery that the true measure of the individual is violence and that the present age cannot be identified with utopian visions of the past. In this context, discusses the madness motif in both editions: in the first, *pazzia* is identified with the perennial quest of the individual paladins; in the third edition, madness becomes a force, a "tragica presenza sulla scena del mondo" (p. 104), and assumes the form of monsters and tyrants or is identified with new social norms, especially power and self-serving behavior. Argues that the protagonists of episodes incorporated into the 1532 edition fight a solitary battle against threats to civilization in a world devoid of the chivalric ideals of an earlier moment. In this edition, the poet takes a stand against authoritarian and oppressive institutions, his heroes serving as noble opponents to evil and as defenders of justice and human dignity. Concludes by calling the 1532 OF a "romanzo moderno, senza idillio e senza favole, [che] diventa l'ideale artistico dell'ultimo Ariosto: egli sostituisce il romanzesco 'entrelacement' con una tecnica fondamentalmente drammatica, che con accenti nudi e scavati celebra la persuasione eroica del vecchio poeta ferrarese" (p. 104).

◄§ 545. MORINI, LUIGINA. "Ruscelli e le pretese varianti ariostesche al *Furioso* del '32." In *In Ricordo di Cesare Angelini: studi di letteratura e filologia*, edited by Franco Alessio and Angelo Stella, pp. 160–84. Milan: Il Saggiatore, 1979.

Extensive analysis of the appendix to Girolamo Ruscelli's 1556 edition of the OF (*Mutationi e miglioramenti, che M. Lodovico Ariosto havea fatti per mettere nell'ultima impressione del Furioso*), which, according to the editor, contained corrections to the 1532 edition made by the author and obtained from his brother, M. Galasso Ariosto in 1543. Discusses the history of the debate over the authenticity of Ruscelli's claim, from Lodovico Dolce to the early twentieth century, analyzes the variants contained in the appendix and Ruscelli's commentary on them, and concludes that evidence, rather than substantiating the editor's claim, manifests that his own corrections of the text conform to his ideals of stylistic decorum, a common editorial practice in the sixteenth century.

⮥ 546. MORREALE, MARGHERITA. "Appunti per uno studio sulle traduzioni spagnole dell'*Orlando Furioso* nel Cinquecento." In *Premio Città
Monselice per una traduzione letteraria. Atti del Quinto Convegno sui
problemi della traduzione letteraria: Le Prime traduzioni dell'Ariosto*,
no. 6, pp. 33–72. Monselice: A Cura dell'Amministrazione Comunale,
1977.

Analysis of the metrical, rhyming, and lexical elements of Jerónimo Ji-
ménez de Urrea's 1549 translation of the *OF*, with comparisons to the original text and to similar linguistic features of a 1550 Spanish version of Hernando Alcocer. Includes bibliography of seventeen complete or partial
sixteenth-century Spanish translations and their locations in Italian libraries.

⮥ 547. MURESU, GABRIELE. "L'*Orlando furioso* nella storia della poesia
melodrammatica di G. B. Casti." *La Rassegna della letteratura italiana*, 7th ser., vol. 72, no. 1 (1968): 3–64.

Discusses the theatrical career of eighteenth-century playwright Giovanni
Battista Casti, noting that in some of his plays, including *Orlando Furioso*
and *Rosmonda*, Casti denounces political and social injustices. Includes text
of Casti's *Orlando Furioso* (pp. 19–64).

⮥ 548. MURILLO, L. A. "*Don Quixote* as Renaissance Epic." In *Cervantes
and the Renaissance*, edited by Michael D. McGaha, pp. 51–70. Eas-
ton, Pa.: Juan de la Cuesta-Hispanic Monographs, 1980.

On the nature of Renaissance epic and how it informs the *DQ*. Defines
Renaissance epic as the assimilation into classical form of "various medieval
materials, popular or learned, Christian or 'barbarian'" (p. 52), noting that
the *OF* is the "major achievement in the long evolution of narrative that
began with the oral tradition of feudal epics and moved by stages toward
written and eventually printed form" (p. 54). Considers the relation of the
OF to the *DQ* "unique, because [the *OF*] is the precedent that is both a
romanzo . . . and an epic poem" (p. 54). Comments particularly on the
"literary myth" (p. 55) of the love madness of the chivalric hero, which con-
nects the two works and their protagonists in that "their elect status of hero
within the work is the condition by virtue of which their respective narratives
attain epical qualities" (p. 55).

⮥ 549. MURTAUGH, KRISTEN OLSON. *Ariosto and the Classical Simile*.
Harvard Studies in Romance Languages, no. 36. Cambridge: Harvard
University Press, 1980. 195p.

Detailed analysis of the structure and use of the epic simile in the *OF*,
concluding that as a rhetorical device it functions to assure a median tone
and unity of the poem. Reviews the assessments of the Ariostean simile from
the Renaissance to the evaluations of Piromalli, Raniolo, and Ramat (pp.

23–35); analyzes the use of extended simile in Ariosto's predecessors (Boiardo, Pulci, and Cieco da Ferrara), noting that with Ariosto it becomes a major structural device in emulation of Virgil (pp. 47–67); and discusses Ariosto's "borrowed" similes, concluding that the poet's intent was not to conceal his sources but to show his virtuosity in the art of Renaissance imitation (pp. 87–116). Final chapters discuss the function of the similes in helping to assure a balance between *fantasia* and *realtà* (pp. 117–34), as well as tonal equilibrium (pp. 135–51), and to give a perspective on the epic and romance material, disclosing Ariosto's "classical ideal of *aurea mediocritas*" (p. 153) and helping the reader to distance himself from the action. Includes bibliography and index of similes in the OF.

🌢 550. MUSACCHIO, E. "*L'Olimpia* dell'Ariosto." *Proceedings of the Pacific Northwest Conference on Foreign Languages* 21 (1970): 102–10.

Argues that the traditional typological view of Olimpia is simplistic and fails either to acknowledge the subtleties of her personality or to place her episode within the context of the poem. Notes the contradictory nature of her personality and suggests that a careful reading of her tripartite episode reveals a figure of complex Oedipal dimensions whose words and preoccupations prefigure the tragedy of her plight.

🌢 551. ———. "I Boschi dell'*Orlando Furioso*." *Proceedings of the Pacific Northwest Conference on Foreign Languages* 30, parts 1–2 (1979): 95–100.

Notes the significance of the woods topos to the structure and thematics of the OF and discusses its sources in literary tradition, arguing that in both the OI and the OF it has its closest association with the French medieval romance tradition rather than with the Latin-Italian tradition, in which the woods is a locus of fear and perdition (p. 96). Notes the frequency of Ariosto's use of the term *bosco*, in preference to either *selva* or *foresta*, concluding that the former is without the negative connotations of the latter two and represents a "dimensione dello spirito" (p. 97). Suggests that the wood, rather than a locus suggesting physical and moral dangers, is emblematic of man's natural state, with a myriad of possibilities and the personal freedom to choose, away from the constraints of a social order.

🌢 552. MUSCETTA, CARLO. Introduzione. In *Orlando furioso, le Satire, i Cinque Canti e una scelta delle altre opere minori*, edited by Carlo Muscetta and Luca Lamberti, 1:vii–xxvi. 2 vols. Turin: Einaudi, 1962.

Examines in both a thematic and structural-stylistic context the OF as a work that demythologizes ("diseroicizzare," p. xiii) the chivalric tradition through an ironic view of a world subject to change and, therefore, in a constant state of flux and uncertainty. Underscores the poem's humanistic representation of the individual in a state of complete liberty and, consequently, subject to the vagaries of life and Fortune. Observations on the modernity of the poem's structure and the importance of the romance structure to the "grandi maestri del realismo, come Cervantes e Stendhal" (p. xx). Extensive discussion of the aesthetics of the OF, including observations on Ariostean echoes of polyphonic technique and analogies with cinematic montage.

🖎 553. MUSIĆ, SRDJAN. "Dragiše Stanojevića prevod Bijesnog Rolanda" (Dragiša Stanojević's translation of the Orlando furioso). Uporedna istraživanja (Belgrade: Inst. za književnost i umetnost) 1 (1975): 587–601.

On Dragiša Stanojević's Serb version of the OF. Notes that Stanojević's translation distorts the spirit of the original, giving it a heroicomic dimension reminiscent of Teofilo Folengo's Baldus or Alessandro Tassoni's mock-heroic La Secchia Rapita. Discusses translator's adaptation of the Italian hendecasyllable. Argues that Stanojević based his version of the poem more on German translations of the original than on the Italian text and that it is essentially a hybrid work. Summary in Italian, pp. 600–601.

🖎 554. MUSUMARRA, CARMELO. "Arioste. Ludovico Ariosto, dit L'." In Dictionnaire biographique des auteurs de tous les temps et de tous les pays, 1:61–62. 2 vols. Paris: Lafont-Bompiani, 1956.

Brief, detailed biographical sketch, focusing on the poet's early education, his service as a courtier and in the Garfagnana, and on his family life.

🖎 555. MUTINI, CLAUDIO. "Ariosto a se stesso." In his L'Autore e l'opera: saggi sulla letteratura del Cinquecento, pp. 13–26. Rome: Bulzoni, 1973.

Revised version of "Nota sull'Epitaphium Ludovici Areosti." Bibliothèque d'Humanisme et Renaissance 25 (1963): 198–206.

Discusses the evolution through revision of Ariosto's youthful Latin epitaph, "Epitaphium Ludovico Areosti" (1498), and its significance in projecting the poetic world of the mature Ariosto.

🖎 556. MYERS, CATHERINE (RODGERS). Time in the Narrative of the "Faerie Queene." Salzburg: Institut für Englische Sprache und Literatur (Universität Salzburg), 1973. 128p.

Argues that the OF served as a model for structural elements and the handling of time in the FQ, books 3–4, although "Spenser differs from Ariosto in the handling of the historical aspect of the narrative. In the Faerie Queene we discover a persistent strain of meditation on the operation of time that is not present in Orlando Furioso" (p. 57). See especially pp. 51–58.

◆§ 557. NANNINI, MARCO CESARE. "Lodovico Ariosto visto da un medico." In *Lodovico Ariosto: il suo tempo la sua terra la sua gente* (entry 468). Estratto dal *Bollettino storico reggiano* 7, no. 27 (1974): 169–75. Describes physiognomy, complexion, personality, and personal habits of Ariosto as documented by his contemporaries, noting his several affairs, his abstemiousness in eating, and his tendency toward melancholy.

◆§ 558. NARDI, PIERO. Introduzione. In *Orlando Furioso, con introduzione e commento di Piero Nardi*, pp. 11–46. 22d rev. ed. Milan: Mondadori, 1970.
First edition 1927; Fatini, 2356.

◆§ 559. NATALI, GIULIO. *Ludovico Ariosto*. Florence: La Nuova Italia, 1966. 163p. plus index.
Introduction to Ariosto: biography, discussion of poet's critical fortune, summary consideration of minor works. Origins of the romance epic and discussion of both classical and medieval sources of the *OF*. Consideration of style and language. Concludes that Ariosto is an "ironico e scherzoso osservatore della realtà e sublime idealista; apertamente ridente o malinconicamente sorridente delle umane debolezze, e delle proprie; delicatamente sentimentale e sensuale senza ipocrisia; ondeggiante, come nell'ebbrezza di un sogno divino, tra una visione ironica della vita, che è soggetta alla Fortuna, e la contemplazione di ciò che rende cara e bella la vita stessa" (p. 151).

◆§ 560. NEGRI, RENZO. *Interpretazione dell'"Orlando Furioso."* Milan: Marzorati, 1971. 147p.
Notes that the complexity of the *OF* has limited the poem's popularity, especially in the classroom, and that even the best criticism usually confines itself to a consideration of specific themes, episodes, and characters rather than to the entire narrative construct. Proposes to identify and define the structure of the poem by dividing it into narrative sequences, arguing that such an approach facilitates a linear reading of the text and allows for the isolation of individual sequences as complete and independent narrative units of the whole. Identifies and discusses twenty-one such sequences.

◆§ 561. ———. "Ipotesi sull'*Orlando Furioso*." In *Per l'Ariosto* (entry 623). Special 1976 issue of *Italianistica* 3, no. 3 (1974): 45–62.
Argues that the serenity and harmony of the *OF* belie the representation of an "ambiguous Utopia," an ugly and hostile reality, a repressed indignation and unvoiced sarcasm (pp. 46–47).

🖙 562. ———. "Manzoni e Ariosto." In his *Manzoni diverso*, pp. 163–
69. Milan: Marzorati, 1976.
Revision of "Manzoni e Ariosto," *Italianistica* 1, no. 2 (1972): 299–304.
Noting that the OF and the *Promessi sposi* are the major examples of narrative in Italian literature and their authors the two major humorists (p.
167), suggests parallels in the two works, including a *tono medio* with ironic overtones and similarities in narratology: "'Punto di vista' demiurgico, ironia,
aria confidenziale, temperatura media, orizzontalità, interruzioni e riprese,
prologhi e cantucci per l'autore, digressioni ritardanti, diaframmi di trascrizione (dall'Anonimo e da Turpino), ritmo inesausto, eclettismo ordinato alla
naturalezza" (p. 164). Discusses similarities in the narrative voice, narrative
technique, and the treatment of certain subjects, narrative perspective and
tone in episodes having to do with crowds of people, for example.

🖙 563. ———. "Pinocchio ariostesco." In *Studi collodiani*, pp. 439–43.
Atti del I Convegno Internazionale. Pescia, 5–7 ottobre 1974. Bologna:
Cassa di Risparmio di Pistoia e Pescia, 1976.
Agrees with the view that common sources for the sea monster in *Pinocchio*, chapter 26, and in *CC* 4, are Jonah and the *True Stories* of Lucian (see,
for example, Allan H. Gilbert, "The Sea-Monster in Ariosto's *Cinque Canti*
and in *Pinocchio*," *Italica* 33, no. 4 [1956]: 260–63). Argues for the probability of much source material in Ariosto for Collodi, "attraverso una serie di
mediazioni culturali" (p. 440). Dynamism and the fantastic, fundamental to
the OF, are also the basis of *Pinocchio*. Notes Ariostean echoes in *Pinocchio*,
the same use of hyperbole and the "straripante potere illusionistico" (p. 441).
Mentions three particular elements common to both works: the wandering
titular character; extreme mobility of the narrative; use of the marvelous.

🖙 564. ———. "Nastagio in un continuatore dell'Ariosto." In *Il Boccaccio
nelle culture e letterature nazionali*, Congresso Internazionale: "La Fortuna del Boccaccio nelle Culture e nelle Letterature Nazionali,"
Firenze-Certaldo, 1975, edited by Francesco Mazzoni, pp. 577–82.
Florence: Leo S. Olschki, 1978.
On the confluence of a Boccaccian motif—the infernal chase of a recalcitrant lover (*Decameron* 5.8)—and Ariostean material in Giambattista Pescatore's *La Morte di Ruggiero continuata a la materia dell'Ariosto . . .*
(1557), canto 5.

🖙 565. NELSON, TIMOTHY G. A. "John Steward of Baldynneis and *Orlando Furioso*." *Studies in Scottish Literature* 6, no. 2 (1968): 105–14.
Brief analysis of Steward's [Stewart is the common spelling] "creative imitation" (p. 106) of the OF, the *Abbregement of Roland Furious* (c. mid-
1580s), noting that it conventionalizes the Italian poem, reduces its complex

weave of genres and narrative threads to a single plot line, and corrects Ariosto's ambivalent characters with the decorum of traditional types.

❧ 566. NENCIONI, GIOVANNI. Presentazione. In *Orlando Furioso*, edited
   by Pietro Papini, pp. vii–xxiii. Florence: Sansoni, 1964.
Introduces reprint of 1903 edition of the *OF*, edited with a commentary
by Pietro Papini; Fatini, 1862.
Evaluates Papini's commentary on the *OF* in the context of the
positivistic-historical school of Italian criticism. Concludes that his major
contribution to a reading of the poem was his linguistic annotations and that
his edition serves as a "*baedeker* . . . che ti conduce davanti all'oggetto storico, ti fornisce mille opportune notizie, ma lì ti lascia, senza introdurti in
nessun aspetto, né formale né sostanziale, della sua storicità" (p. xxii).

❧ 567. NEWBIGIN, NERIDA. "Bradamante and Erostrato: Love's Metamorphosis and the Page Disguise in Comedy." *Lingua bella* (Rivista Culturale dell'Associazione Australiana degli Insegnanti d'Italiano) 7, no. 2
   (1974): 23–26.
Argues for the importance of Ariosto to the development of comic theater
in sixteenth-century Italy and, consequently, to aspects of the genre throughout the European Renaissance. Notes in particular the development in
Ariosto's theater of a romantic dimension that tests presuppositions (most
notably in *I Suppositi*) and the full development of the cyclical pattern in the
action from an interruption of social order to the establishment of a new
order. Attributes to Ariosto the important beginnings of the disguise plot and
the many variations on metamorphosis, of which comic theater is the "living
metaphor" (p. 25).

❧ 568. NEWMAN, J. K. "Orazio, Ariosto and Orazio Ariosto." in *Acta
   Conventus Neo-Latini Amstelodamensis*, Proceedings of the Second International Congress of Neo-Latin Studies, edited by P. Tuynman,
   G. C. Kuiper, and E. Kessler, pp. 820–34. Munich: Wilhelm Fink,
   1979.
Argues that Ariosto's sixteenth-century critics failed to recognize in the *OF*
an epic structure that, rather than denying classical tradition, incorporates it
in such a way as to conform to the historical realities and the ethos of the
moment of its composition. Suggests that his Latin poem "De diversis amoribus" serves to clarify the poet's achievement in the epic, that it makes "explicit the correspondence between unstable life and an unstable heaven,
[and] it places the poet firmly in the Aristotelian / Callimachean tradition as
it really existed, and as it had been grasped by both Virgil and Horace. The
Orlando Furioso, with its lyricism and musicality, its prosaic vocabulary, its
deviousness, its learning, its affected naivety, its seriousness and its irony is a

noble reminder of what the epic poet may still accomplish in a late and distracted age" (p. 827).

❧ 569. NIRONI, VITTORIO. "Tre luoghi ariosteschi nella città di Reggio." In *Lodovico Ariosto: il suo tempo la sua terra la sua gente* (entry 468). Estratto dal *Bollettino storico reggiano* 7, no. 28 (1974): 5–36.

Detailed historical account and description of the following places that were important to Ariosto's experiences during his residence as a young man in Reggio: la Cittadella, site of Ariosto's childhood residence (the Casa del Capitano), which is a quadrangular area including the modern-day public garden and municipal theater; the Casa Valeri, inherited by Ariosto's mother and his possible birthplace (p. 14), and frequently his residence when in Reggio; the Piazza (del Duomo), site of the Malaguzzi house. Includes illustrations of a seventeenth-century woodcut of the Cittadella, a reconstruction of the Cathedral in the period of Ariosto, and a detailed map of Reggio at the end of the fifteenth century.

❧ 570. NOBUMORI, HIROMITSU. "Ariosto's Influence on Milton." *Milton Center of Japan News* 3 (1979): 24–26.

Unavailable; cited in *Milton Quarterly* 14, no. 4 (1980): 137, with the following abstract: "Ariosto's influence on Milton is documented through his many references in his religious treatises and his Commonplace Book. Influenced both by his life and his work, Milton's use of allegorical fables and romances from Italian chivalric epic poetry is frequent in the earlier works, less so in *PL* [*Paradise Lost*]. However, though difficult to tell, in technique and skill Ariosto's *Furioso* does appear to offer parallels to *PL*. Any direct affect [*sic*] came from Milton's total apprehension of the marvellous superposant technique of Ariosto's epic structure. Perhaps inspired by Ariosto, Milton made a conscious attempt to exalt and enhance the English language as well as to establish his poetic diction."

❧ 571. ———. "Meaning and Structure of the *Orlando Furioso*" (in Japanese). *Studi italici* (Kyoto, Japan) 28 (1980): 48–65.

Examines the narrative strategies of the *OF*. Japanese text accompanied by a summary in Italian: "Vale la pena di considerare il significato e la struttura dell'*Orlando Furioso*, in quanto Ariosto è riuscito a realizzarvi una costruzione stratificata a sistema gerarchico, adoperando la tecnica di sovrapposizione con alienazione per mezzo del metodo catalizzatore al fine di mescolare fra loro tanti episodi al livello profondo, e di trasformarli in paradigmi delle formanti superficiali. Fra i personaggi che appaiono nell'*Orlando Furioso*, il modulo paradigmatico di Orlando e Ruggiero-Bradamante è rappresentativo degli aspetti sintagmatici, ma l'Ariosto assegna a Rinaldo un ruolo altrettanto importante nel campo della dispersione. Egli tenta di confondere lo spettro metaforico utilizzando Orlando e Rinaldo alternativamente in una struttura eterogenea con sindeddoche o metonimia; cerca inoltre di costruire una peripezia di storie fluenti fra gli altri molteplici episodi, ricorrendo all'eco lontana di chronos e cairos."

572. NOHRNBERG, JAMES. *The Analogy of "The Faerie Queene."* Princeton: Princeton University Press, 1976. 870p.
  Considers sixteenth-century views on epic form, particularly those of Antonio Minturno and his suggestion that the *OF* contains the materials of two epic structures corresponding to Homeric types, the Iliadic (Orlando) and the Odyssean (Ruggiero) (pp. 13–14). Suggests that the *OF* "creates something like a comprehensive representation of Being; that is, an image of totality, analogous to the creation itself" and that, in the poem, "two large continuities stand out . . . . : a 'matter' of Orlando and a 'matter' of Ruggiero" (p. 14), the first concerned with the theme of distraction and the second "where love implies finding one's identity rather than losing it" (p. 15). Argues that the "continuities" are emphasized by the poem's allegories, especially the isle of Alcina and the Edenic garden, which involve "a loss and recovery of self" (p. 16), respectively: "It might follow that the two paradises, as reserves, function as repositories of potential Being. Ruggiero is urged not to leave his future offspring dormant in Alcina's paradise, and Orlando's wits are kept in a jar on the moon. The latter is particularly suggestive, since Plato refers to a none-too-serious link between the shifting of the desiring soul and a jar" (p. 16). Adds that the poem's "structure shows a departure from, and return to, epic. The epic strength of the distracted Orlando is wasted upon the complexities and errors of romance, and the romantic circuit traced by Ruggiero gradually makes him eligible for epic celebration. If the heroic potential of the cavaliers may be either enhanced or subverted by their romances, then romance itself is subject to two poles of sensibility: a romantic or sympathetic one, and an ironic or critical one" (p. 17). Considers Astolfo as a link between the continuities. Notes that the poem's characters become "increasingly subject to the melancholy fact of mortality" (p. 18). See especially pp. 13–19.

573. *Notiziario culturale italiano* 15, no. 3 (1974). Numero dedicato a Ludovico Ariosto (Quinto centenario della nascita). Proceedings of conference held in Paris, November 1974. Paris: Istituto Italiano di Cultura, 1974. 98p.
  Contents: Alberto Tenenti, "Le monde de l'Arioste: histoire et civilisation" (entry 836); Paul Larivaille, "Personnages, thèmes et structures du *Roland Furieux*" (entry 450); André Rochon, "L'imaginaire et le réel dans le *Roland Furieux*" (entry 691); Lanfranco Caretti, "Il Generale Miollis e le feste ariostesche del 1801" (entry 173); Adriano Seroni, "L'Ariosto e la Francia in due

inserti storici del *Furioso*" (entry 799); Charles Dedeyan, "L'Arioste en France au XIXᵉ siècle" (entry 245); Aurelio Roncaglia, "L'Arioste et la poésie chevaleresque française" (entry 698); Emilio Bigi, "Aspetti stilistici e metrici delle *Rime* dell'Ariosto" (entry 93); Cesare Segre, "Appunti sulla funzione del dialogo nelle satire dell'Ariosto" (entry 791); Dominique Gaudin-Clouet, "Le théâtre de l'Arioste" (entry 349); Liano Petroni, "Un exemple de poétique 'dramatique' et d'une 'politique' de la comédie issu de l'Arioste: la comédie littéraire de Jean de la Taille" (entry 631). Concluding remarks by Lanfranco Caretti briefly describing the state of Ariosto scholarship at the time of the conference (pp. 95–98).

📖 574. OPRANDI, NICOLE. *L'Expression artistique du mouvement dans le "Roland Furieux" de l'Arioste.* 2 vols. Thèse de troisième cycle. Nice: Université de Nice Faculté des Lettres et Sciences Humaines, 1973. 494p.
Argues that movement is the fundamental motif of the *OF* and that it reflects the psychological instability of the characters, who are characterized by change and dissatisfaction and are often victims of an unstable and illusory reality. Develops argument in a two-part study: analysis of the various manifestations of the theme, both in individual characters and in the collective actions of the paladins, concluding that movement is expressed through repetition and progression; detailed stylistic analysis of the techniques used in the representation of movement.

📖 575. ———. "L'énumération dans le *Roland Furieux* de l'Arioste." *Hommage à André Joucla Ruau*, special issue of *Annales de la Faculté des Lettres et Sciences Humaines de Nice*, no. 23 (1975): 71–95.
Analysis of the variety and function of enumeration in the *OF*. Concludes that "l'énumération, qui a souvent d'étroits rapports avec la narration et qui constitue parfois un lien efficace entre le réel et l'imaginaire, est essentiellement un procédé littéraire: elle apparaît comme une figure de style proche de l'hyperbole. Son emploi systématique témoigne d'un choix délibéré d'où l'ironie est absente même si, parfois, l'humour du poète s'exerce sur le référent. Cet emplois sérieux de la figure de style, en tant qu'ornement du discours, s'unit au souci d'équilibre dans le rythme, conformément aux préceptes de l'époque, mais aussi au goût et à la propre poétique de l'Arioste" (p. 95).

📖 576. ORLANDI, MARY-KAY GAMEL. "Ovid True and False in Renaissance Poetry." *Pacific Coast Philology* 13 (1978): 60–70.
Characterizes the Ovidian narrator in Renaissance poetry as one wont to intrude in the fiction and to manipulate the material for purposes of showing the relativity of the poetic truth and the difficulty of perceiving clearly. Iden-

tifies instances of Ovidian narrative technique in the *OF*, especially in the continually shifting tone and level of discourse (p. 62), in the use of abrupt changes to disappoint expectations (p. 64), and in the distancing between "words and action, between how something or someone looks, sounds, acts. In the Ovidian universe of metamorphic flux, words run the risk of being too fixed to be at all accurate. Ambiguity, puns, shifts of tone and perspective, bathos, revelation of the partial view of central and secondary narrators—all are ways to make language more representative of this flux" (p. 66). The Ovidian Ariosto represents a fragmented and diverse world.

ᴥᴥ§ 577. ORR, DAVID. *Italian Renaissance Drama in England before 1625: The Influence of "Erudita" Tragedy, Comedy, and Pastoral on Elizabethan and Jacobean Drama.* University of North Carolina Studies in Comparative Literature, no. 49. Chapel Hill: The University of North Carolina Press, 1970. 141p.
Discusses the importance of Gascoigne's translation of Ariosto's *I Suppositi*, representing the introduction to an English audience of an "Italian comedy in almost unmodified form" (p. 25). See especially pp. 24–26.

ᴥᴥ§ 578. ORVIETO, PAOLO. "Differenze 'retoriche' fra il *Morgante* e il *Furioso* (Per un'interpretazione narratologica del *Furioso*)." In *Ludovico Ariosto: lingua, stile e tradizione*, edited by Cesare Segre (entry 789), pp. 157–73. Milan: Feltrinelli, 1976.
Establishes the essential rhetorical grounding of the *Morgante* to be medieval (*elocutio*) and of the *OF* to be humanistic (*inventio*), demonstrating how the structural elements of the poems manifest two entirely different narrative systems: the *Morgante* is structured "inductively" through a series of essentially unrelated moments, whereas the *OF*, following a "deductive" system, is a rationally organized network of correlatives. Proposes the application of modern anthropological methods (Alan Dundes, Kenneth C. Pike, and, especially, Vladimir Propp) for an understanding of the narratological substructures of the poem.

ᴥᴥ§ 579. OSSOLA, CARLO. "Dantismi metrici nel *Furioso*." In *Ludovico Ariosto: lingua, stile e tradizione*, edited by Cesare Segre (entry 789), pp. 65–94. Milan: Feltrinelli, 1976.
Analysis of how borrowings—especially rhymes—from the DC are incorporated into the structure of the octave in the *OF*, and particularly how they provide, in many instances, a structural basis for the octave, being spatially marginal elements within which the closed structure of the octave evolves. Following the theories of Gérard Genot and Jurij Tynjanov, gives attention to "sursémantisation," or the absorption of the borrowed text in the formation of a new text, and to the use of the original model for an ironic or parodic

text. Compares the consistent reconstruction of Dante's text with the relatively unchanged borrowings from Petrarch. Concludes that the *tono medio* of the *OF* results from the filtering of traditional literary models through Petrarch (e.g., Dante, especially through Petrarch's *Trionfi*), following the prescriptions of Pietro Bembo.

580. ———. "Métaphore et inventaire de la folie dans la littérature italienne du XVIe siècle." In *Folie et déraison à la Renaissance*, pp. 171–96. Brussels: Editions de l'Université de Bruxelles, 1976.

Considers the literary manifestations in sixteenth-century Italy of the folly topos, from the *OF* to Tomaso Garzoni's *Hospidale de' pazzi incurabili* (1589) and *Teatro de' varii e diversi cervelli mondani* (1583). Distinguishes between a medieval ethical representation of folly (as, for example, the voyage of Ulysses, *Inferno* 26) and its Renaissance counterpart, a metaphor of "la régression d'une pensée déjà assouvie qui veut s'oublier" (p. 171). Establishes the Erasmian transfiguration of the earthly Paradise as the locus of folly in works such as the *OF* and the *GL*. Discusses the textual signifiers of the folly topos in Alcina's garden and the implications of the moon as the "*speculum, ex negativo*, de la sagesse" (p. 184). Analysis of Astolfo's voyage toward a contemplation of the absence of reason in human behavior as a parody of the Dantesque voyage toward the contemplation of divine grace. Concluding discussion on Garzoni's Counter-Reformation perspective on the folly topos: argues that in Ariostean terms madness is essentially an absence of reason and is systematized in such terms, whereas Garzoni quantifies the chaos of human insanity.

581. OTTONE, GIUSEPPE. "'Postille' e 'Considerazioni' galileiane." *Aevum* 46, fasc. 1–2 (1972): 312–24.

Brief discussion of Galilei's *Postille all'Ariosto*, noting in particular several types of emendations to the *OF*, including the elimination of Latinisms, infelicitous uses of repetition or assonance, and changes in certain syntactical structures.

582. PABST, WALTER. "Einwirkungen der italienischen auf die deutsche Literatur." See Petriconi, Hellmuth, entry 624.

583. PACE, ELVIRA. "Le Liriche latine dell'Ariosto." *Giornale italiano di filologia* 14 (1961): 104–28.

Situates the composition of the Latin lyrics in the cultural and humanistic context of fifteenth-century Ferrara and speculates on the reasons they were not published during the poet's lifetime. Provides a chronology of the editions of the Latin poems, from the 1553 edition of G. B. Nicolucci, called Il Pigna, and briefly analyzes the critical fortune of the poems, noting the particular importance of the studies of Giosuè Carducci (1875), Francesco Torraca (1920), and Adolfo Gandiglio (1925, 1926). Discusses Ariosto's use of classical sources in the Latin lyrics, concentrating on Horace, with whom the poet felt a particular affinity, Catullus, Tibullus, and Virgil. Considers Ariosto's adaptation of classical motifs and style. Concludes with observations on the images of women and the development of the love motif in these compositions.

⚜ 584. PACIFICI, SERGIO. *A Guide to Contemporary Italian Literature: From Futurism to Realism.* Cleveland and New York: The World Publishing Company, 1962. 352p.

Summary observations on the importance of Ariosto to Italo Calvino: "Calvino, much like Ariosto, abstracts from our historical time certain verities that he weaves into fantastic stories. . . . Like Ariosto, Calvino sits in his laboratory (his study in Turin) and dreams of a world created by the novelist's fantasy. Unlike Ariosto, however, Calvino holds that his fables are not, *in fondo*, flights from reality, but come from the bitter reality of our twentieth century" (pp. 148–49).

⚜ 585. PADOAN, GIORGIO. "Angelo Beolco da Ruzante a Perduoçimo." *Lettere italiane* 20, no. 2 (1968): 121–200.

Noting that Ariosto and Ruzante knew each other and discussed their work, considers the significant influence of the former upon Ruzante's theater. See especially pp. 165–67, 171–72, 177–85.

⚜ 586. ———. "Note Ruzantesche. IV. *L'Anconitana* tra Boccaccio, Bibbiena ed Ariosto." *Lettere italiane* 22, no. 1 (1970): 100–105.

Notes specific debts to Ariosto in Ruzante's plays *La Moscheta* (1529), *La Piovana* (1532), and, especially, *L'Anconitana*.

⚜ 587. ———. "La Raccolta di testi teatrali di Marin Sanudo." *Italia medioevale e umanistica* 13 (1970): 181–203.

Notes as important to historians of Venetian theatrical life in the Renaissance the collection of plays in the library of the chronicler Marin Sanudo and publishes a list of holdings contained in the codex Marciano, ms. it. VII 375 (= 8954) of the Biblioteca Nazionale Marciana, Venice. Notes presence of a copy of Ariosto's *La Cassaria* and *I Suppositi* and provides a history of the editions of all texts contained in the list until Sanudo's death in 1536.

⚜ 588. ———. "*L'Orlando Furioso* e la crisi del Rinascimento." In *Ariosto 1974 in America*, edited by Aldo Scaglione (entry 760), pp. 1–29. Ravenna: Longo, 1976.

Also in *Lettere italiane* 27, no. 3 (1975): 286–307.

Concerned with the close reflection in the *OF*—and later, in the *CC*—of the political realities of the period of composition and of a consequential prevailing sense of frustration and pessimism before an existence seemingly dominated by the blind forces of chance. Views the *OF* as a poem of human illusions in which the various protagonists deny reason and the discomforts of reality for a world of illusory and evanescent desires.

⋙ 589. ———. *"Ut pictura poesis:* le 'pitture' di Ariosto e le 'poesie' di Tiziano."* In his *Momenti del Rinascimento veneto*, pp. 347–70. Padua: Antenore, 1978.

Notes that in spite of Lodovico Dolce's declaration that Ariosto's Alcina could be taken by painters as a perfect rendering into art of feminine beauty (*Dialogo della pittura*, Venice, 1557), Ariosto is in fact following a literary tradition in the descriptive elements and, in the 1516 edition of the *OF*, in particular, reveals little direct influence from the figurative arts. Suggests, however, that in the 1532 edition and after his documented acquaintance with Dossi and Titian, there is a greater (figurative) tonality in his description of feminine beauty (see, for example, the description of Olimpia, *OF* 11), which evokes the eroticism of Titian's art (pp. 359–62).

⋙ 590. PAMPALONI, LEONZIO. "La guerra nel *Furioso."* *Belfagor* 26 (1971): 627–52.

Systematic and exhaustive analysis of war as both an important motif and psychosocial metaphor of human needs and behavior in the *OF*: "territorio privilegiato per la sua [Ariosto's] inchiesta sull'uomo" (p. 652). After analyzing the motivating forces behind war and bellicose actions, concludes that in the poem private interests rather than religious ideology are of greatest significance, so that "la guerra diventa una grande palestra di esercizi comportamentali (dal livello piú spontaneo, vitalistico a quello piú eticamente sublimato)" (p. 630). Considers Ariosto's presentation of war in relation to his ethical stance (e.g., the absence of firearms in a narrative otherwise replete with contemporary realities as a personal commentary with moral dimensions). Concludes with a discussion of Ariosto's use of ludic vocabulary in treating war and the significance in the *OF* of war as a ritual act that contains the ideology of the courtier and defines his social role (pp. 650–51).

⋙ 591. ———. Introduzione alla lettura. In *Orlando Furioso*, by Ludovico Ariosto, pp. v–xxi. Florence: La Nuova Italia, 1971.

Essay in several parts. First intends to identify the "strumenti per comprendere i principi costruttivi" (p. vi) of the *OF*. Notes first that the poem evolves from a particular vision of human behavior, its adjectives often having an ethical dimension, and that it is structured like a series of *novelle*, referential to each other. Notes also that themes are developed in two divergent directions—"polarizzazione" (p. vii), e.g., loyalty and deceit in love; "simmetria" (pp. vii–viii), e.g., analogous behavior of characters presented as opposite types or parallelism of situations. Adds then that themes are developed in three phases: "dal fatto, alla riflessione morale, all'esempio paradigmatico" (p. viii). Discusses Ariosto's technique of interrupting episodes and reconnecting the narrative threads. Notes that characters are always subordinated to their structural function (p. xi) and are never predictable, but act according to the circumstances of the episode. Major episodes have a paradigmatic evolution: development of motif; crisis and upset; reestablishment of equilibrium. Second part of essay discusses Ariosto's use of his sources, in particular Boiardo, who uses the exordium in a traditional way, whereas Ariosto uses it as a crucial point in an episode. Underscores the close ties between the OF and contemporary Ferrarese culture and the need to keep in mind that Ariosto's perspective, like that of his audience, is of the court society of the period: "Quando si afferma che il *Furioso* riflette la vita in tutti i suoi aspetti, o, più modestamente, che è 'quasi un atlante della natura umana', occorre sottointendere che del mondo e dell'uomo, Ariosto vede ciò che vede la corte. La corte è insieme confine e filtro" (p. xvii). Concludes with discussion of the OF as containing the "ritratto di un uomo labirintico, aperto ad infinite vie ma privo di una meta prefissata e visibile. Di qui il senso di estrema libertà dei personaggi ariosteschi, per i quali sembra che tutto sia possibile, e nello stesso tempo nulla sia da loro raggiunto stabilmente. Questi uomini sono soprattutto dei ricercatori, e una delle loro prime scoperte è che esistono delle limitazioni invincibili sul piano dell'agire di quelli che sono i valori e le scelte stabiliti sul piano del conoscere" (p. xx).

592. ———. "Per una analisi narrativa del *Furioso*." *Belfagor* 26 (1971): 133–50.
Notes that the narrative line of the OF is segmented or interrupted in three fundamental ways ("indicatori di trapasso," p. 134): by the ending of a canto, which never coincides with the completion of an episode; by the breaking off of an episode within the frame of the canto; by the imperceptible passage from one narrative line to another. Breaking points have a dual function, the suspension of the narrative and the beginning, or "reprise," of another. Identifies the most frequent and important thematic or tonal elements accompanying the breaking points, including temporal allusions, often serving to distance episodes by switching from one season to another or from one time of day to another. Concludes that an analysis of segmentation reveals a complexity of juxtaposition responsible for a seemingly chaotic structure. Considers the function of characters in the syntagmatic pattern and notes that, lacking any psychological consistency, they are intended to relate to a specific narrative moment and to serve to underscore a specific ethical perspective (p. 146) or to signal, with their actions, a line of development (p. 148). Con-

cludes by identifying within a narrative line fundamental structural phenomena, especially progression from narrative fact to moral reflection and paradigmatic exempla; pairing of narrative lines with similar dramatic situations and antithetical resolutions; and grouping of dissimilar narrative lines with identical resolutions (pp. 148–50).

◆§ 593. ———. "Le *Intercenali* e il *Furioso*: noterella sui rapporti Alberti-Ariosto." *Belfagor* 29 (1974): 317–25.

Discusses the important influence of Alberti's *Intercenali* upon Ariosto and the limited amount of inquiry to date on Ariosto's use of the censored and clandestinely circulated texts. Continues Cesare Segre's discussion (see entry 778) on the Albertian source of the Astolfo on the moon episode and identifies Ariosto's alterations of his sources, namely the *Somnium* and the *Fatum et Fortuna*. Discusses what seem to be important Albertian influences on both the content and narrative modes in the *OF* (for example, the prologues to the cantos) and concludes by identifying several passages in the *OF* that can profitably be compared to the *Intercenali* and are worthy of additional study.

◆§ 594. PANDOLFI, VITO. *Storia universale del teatro drammatico*, 1:254–59. 2 vols. Turin: UTET, 1964.

French translation, *Histoire du théâtre*, 1:293–97. 5 vols. Verviers: Gérard & Co., 1968.

Notes Ariosto's importance to the early developments of sixteenth-century comedy in Italy ("per aver saputo conferire autentico stile ad un certo tipo di composizione, aver assunto dal teatro classico come dalla narrativa i motivi più singolari e sulla base di essi, aver ricreato freschezza di situazioni e di personaggi. . . . Nei lavori comici dell'Ariosto attraverso la tentazione irriducibile della satira si fa luce il vigore dell'attualità, il gusto del costume contemporaneo e della determinazione psicologica, l'adozione di tipi tratti dalla vita di quegli anni," pp. 254–55). Provides essential information on the date of composition and the first performances of each comedy, as well as a brief plot summary.

◆§ 595. ———. Chap. 3 in *Il Teatro del Rinascimento e la commedia dell'arte*, pp. 34–50. Rome: Lerici, 1969.

Discusses the productions of classical comedies at the Este court in the second half of the fifteenth century. Provides contemporary documents describing the number of performances. Considers Ariosto's contributions to the evolution of comedy in the vernacular; in his theater, "si fa luce il vigore dell'attualità, il gusto del costume contemporaneo e della determinazione psicologica, l'adozione di tipi tratti dalla vita" (p. 50).

◆§ 596. PAOLETTI, LAO. "Cronaca e letteratura nei *Carmina*." In *Ludovico Ariosto: lingua, stile e tradizione*, edited by Cesare Segre (entry 789), pp. 265–82. Milan: Feltrinelli, 1976.

Through an analysis of a selected number of Ariosto's early Latin lyrics, concludes that in the nonamatory verse, especially, the poet maintains a balance between the formalist structure of humanist *imitatio* poetics and the need, as a pragmatist in tune with the vagaries of court and political life, to use his verse to exalt the Este dynasty and to urge for peace on the peninsula as a guarantee for the prosperity of his own region.

◆§ 597. PAOLINI, PAOLO. "Situazione della critica ariostesca." In *Per l'Ariosto* (entry 623). Special 1976 issue of *Italianistica* 3, no. 3 (1974): 3–22.

Schematic and comprehensive review of Ariosto criticism from De Sanctis and Crocean idealistic aesthetics to the beginning of structuralist narratology. Touching upon the contributions of major critics and critical methods, including the Marxist views of Roberto Battaglia and the inroads made by the reading of the *OF* of Robert M. Durling or the media interpretation of Edoardo Sanguineti, concludes that the figure of Ariosto has become increasingly problematic and that his work reflects the complexities of a culture in crisis.

◆§ 598. PAOLISSO, ITALO, ed. *Orlando Furioso*, by Ludovico Ariosto. Rome: Ciranna, 1968. 222p.

Guide for students. Detailed analysis of the major characters in the *OF* with extensive quotations from critical writings. Includes an anthology of critical commentaries.

◆§ 599. PAPARELLI, GIOACCHINO. *Feritas, humanitas, divinitas: le componenti dell'Umanesimo*. Messina-Florence: G. D'Anna, 1960. 300p.

In a study whose importance to Ariosto is implied and allusory rather than explicit and direct (see preface, pp. 9–10), considers the relationship between Ariosto and Ippolito d'Este in the context of humanistic ideals of *otium* and civic life (pp. 134–36).

◆§ 600. ———. *Appunti su L. Ariosto*. Istituto Universitario di Magistero 'G. Cuomo.' Salerno. Anno Accademico 1967–1968. Pompei: Tip. I.P.S.I., 1968. 125p.

Collection of essays and an appendix of texts. Contains: 1) "La vita di L. Ariosto (dal 1474 al 1512)," pp. 5–16. Summary account of Ariosto's early education and cultural experiences, including a discussion of his early Latin compositions, his involvement with theater in Ferrara, and his service in the house of Ippolito d'Este; 2) "Il Casato," pp. 17–18. On origins of family name, most likely from Riosto, in the *comune* of Pianoso (Bologna); 3) "La Questione della gioventù 'tutta latina' dell'Ariosto," pp. 19–28. Concludes that Carducci's essay on Ariosto's youth ("La Gioventù di Ludovico Ariosto e la poesia latina in Ferrara," 1875) tends to "sopravvalutare la produzione giovanile dell'Ariosto in latino a scapito di quella in volgare" (p. 23)—the thesis, in fact, of Abdelkader Salza ("Intorno alle liriche dell'Ariosto," *Studi su Ludovico Ariosto*, pp. 27–98, 1914), who opposes Carducci and affirms that Ariosto's first activities were in the vernacular. Notes the fortune of the opposing theories. Concludes that the two activities were complementary but that Ariosto preferred writing in the vernacular; 4) "Isabella d'Este," pp. 29–34. As patron of the arts, with comments on her tastes regarding the "poetica del diletto" in the *OF*; 5) "Tra Boiardo e Ariosto: la 'giunta' di Niccolò degli Agostini," pp. 35–39. Discusses the extent of Ariosto's familiarity with the *Giunta* and the degree to which it may have inspired the composition of the *OF*; 6) "L'Ironia dell'Ariosto: come la definí Luigi Pirandello," pp. 40–52. See "Pirandello e Ariosto," in his *Da Ariosto a Quasimodo*, pp. 149–55, entry 605; 7) "Avviamento alla lettura del poema: il canto I," pp. 53–77. Considers the perspectives of Boiardo and Ariosto on chivalric ideals through an analysis of the encounter of Orlando and Agricane in *OI* 1.18 and the encounter of Rinaldo and Ferraù in *OF* 1, noting that the key verse in the *OF* is "Oh gran bontà de' cavalieri antiqui!" in that it is emblematic of Ariosto's ironic stance toward a tradition that, so much a part of court life, was expected to be treated with seriousness by a poet. Notes that the *OF* celebrates *ratio* and *verbum* as peculiar to man (p. 70). Analyzes several elements of *OF* 1 as representative of the author's ironic perspective on the chivalric theme, as, for example, in the frequent images of paladins "a rovescio" (p. 73). Appendix includes a transcription of Ariosto's son Virginio's notes for a biography of his father (pp. 81–84) and a transcription of Gabriele's Latin *epicedio* for his brother Ludovico's death (pp. 85–96).

⁕§ 601. ———. "Il *Furioso* e la poetica del diletto." In his *Da Dante al Seicento*, pp. 139–89. Salerno: Edizione Beta, 1971.

Also as introduction to *Orlando Furioso*, by Ludovico Ariosto, 1:9–42. 2 vols. Milan: Rizzoli, 1974. Revision of "Introduzione al *Furioso*," *Nuova antologia*, anno 106, vol. 512, no. 2046 (1971): 172–95.

Establishes a number of fundamental perspectives for a reading of the *OF*, beginning with the premise that the poem must be understood as a dialectic between the author and his audience—a rapport that is the underlying "grammatica" of the work (p. 145). Through a comparative analysis of episodes from the *OI* (the encounter between Orlando and Agricane) and the *OF* (the duel between Rinaldo and Ferraù), establishes the basic differences in the poets' intent vis-à-vis their audiences: Boiardo elevates courtly society to the world of chivalry; Ariosto "abbassa spesso la cavalleria al rango del pettegolezzo cortigiano" (p. 150). States that parodic and ironic humor in the *OF* is occasioned not by Ariosto's view of the world of chivalry but by his attitude toward a literary tradition that aspired to social and behavioral norms that were idealized rather than realistic—in part the basis in the *OF* for the discord between appearance and reality (pp. 156–58). Sees ambiguity, or "polivalenza," as best characterizing Ariosto's humor (p. 158) and Orlando as an emblematic figure in that he represents the juxtaposition of the ideal and the real (p. 167). Discusses the importance of variety and change in the *OF* as instruments to maintain the audience's interest and attention. Concludes by noting Ariosto's importance as a poetic voice of the High Renaissance, the spokesperson and defender of two Renaissance ideals, *ratio* and *verbum* (p. 178).

◄§ 602. ———. "Una probabile fonte dell'Ariosto: la *gionta* al-l'*Innamorato* di Raffaele da Verona." In *Saggi di letteratura italiana in onore di Gaetano Trombatore*, pp. 343–56. Milan: Istituto Editoriale Cisalpino–La Goliardica, 1973.
Discusses the dating of Raffaele da Verona's continuation of the *OI*, noting the possibility of a 1513 edition but concluding that current evidence provides certainty only for Ariosto's familiarity with the 1518 edition, of which there are extant copies in the British Museum and in the Biblioteca Nazionale Braidense, Milan. Briefly considers the technical and thematic elements of the composition and suggests some influences on Ariosto.

◄§ 603. ———. "L'Ariosto lirico e satirico." In his *Da Ariosto a Quasimodo: saggi*, pp. 15–33. Naples: Società Editrice Napoletana, 1978.
Also in *Per l'Ariosto* (entry 623), special 1976 issue of *Italianistica* 3, no. 3 (1974): 23–43.
Insists that the minor works do not owe their importance to the *OF* and should not be considered as preparatory to it. Discusses the literary value of the minor works by identifying themes not found in the *OF*.

◄§ 604. ———. *Da Ariosto a Quasimodo: saggi*. Naples: Società Editrice Napoletana, 1978. 223p.
Contains: "Pubblico e poesia dell'*Orlando Furioso*" (entry 606); "L'Ariosto lirico e satirico" (entry 603); "Tra Boiardo e Ariosto: le gionte all'*Innamorato* di Niccolò degli Agostini e Raffaele da Verona" (entry 607); "Pirandello e Ariosto" (entry 605).

◄§ 605. ———. "Pirandello e Ariosto." In his *Da Ariosto a Quasimodo: saggi*, pp. 149–55. Naples: Società Editrice Napoletana, 1978.
Also in *Atti del Congresso Internazionale di Studi Pirandelliani* (Florence:

Le Monnier, 1967), pp. 839–46, and in his *Appunti su L. Ariosto* (entry 600).

Analyzes Pirandello's writings on the comic, particularly the essay entitled "L'ironia comica nella poesia cavalleresca," and notes that the pages devoted to Ariosto's comic irony are the most significant of Pirandello's critical observations. States that Pirandello, moving from Frederick Schlegel's concept of irony, defines the essence of Ariosto's style as "duplicità," or the mixture of "immedesimazione" and irony (p. 154). Concludes that for Pirandello, in the OF Ariosto is always conscious of the fictive and real worlds and that, consequently, the comic and tragic remain apart as two aspects of the narrative; in Cervantes, however, the two become one in the character of Don Quixote.

606. ———. "Pubblico e poesia dell'*Orlando Furioso*." In his *Da Ariosto a Quasimodo: saggi*, pp. 5–14. Naples: Società Editrice Napoletana, 1978.

Also in *Ludovico Ariosto*, pp. 119–27. Convegno internazionale (entry 475). Rome: Accademia Nazionale dei Lincei, 1975.

Stating that a reading of the OF must take into account the implicit dynamic between the poet and a public, examines a number of moments in the poem that document Ariosto's continual awareness of an audience or explore the variety of reactions intended by the author. For the latter, assumes a public conversant with the tradition of the epic genre and capable of appreciating the ironic view of a chivalric romance as the mirror of contemporary society.

607. ———. "Tra Boiardo e Ariosto: le gionte all'*Innamorato* di Niccolò degli Agostini e Raffaele da Verona." In his *Da Ariosto a Quasimodo: saggi*, pp. 34–47. Naples: Società Editrice Napoletana, 1978.

Also in his edition of the continuation ("gionta") of Raffaele da Verona (Salerno: Beta, 1971).

Discusses the dating of both Agostini's and da Verona's continuations of the OI, both known to and used as a source by Ariosto. Considers certain stylistic and thematic elements of da Verona's addition, noting the various ways and the variety of tones in which the love motif is treated. Notes especially its treatment in the episodes of the death of Ruggiero and Brandimarte, suggesting their importance to a study of Ariosto's sources.

608. PAPINI, GIOVANNI. "Ludovico Ariosto." In his *Scrittori e artisti* ("I Classici contemporanei italiani"), pp. 379–86. Milan: Mondadori, 1959.

First published in *Ritratti italiani* (Florence, 1932); Fatini, 2125.

⋅❧ 609. PAQUES, VIVIANA. *Les sciences occultes d'après les documents littéraires italiens du XVIᵉ siècle*. Paris: Institut d'Ethnologie, 1971. 220p.
Ethnographic rather than literary study. Focuses on sixteenth-century texts dealing with various aspects of the occult sciences, including astrology, divination, and sorcery. Briefly considers Ariosto's use of magic in the *OF* and several minor works, including *I Suppositi* and *Il Negromante* (pp. 40–41; 75–76; 97–100; 132–33; 141–44).

⋅❧ 610. PARATORE, ETTORE. "Nuove prospettive sull'influsso del teatro classico nel '500." In *Il Teatro classico italiano nel '500*, pp. 9–95. Rome: Accademia Nazionale dei Lincei, 1971.
Discusses Ariosto's use of the word *new* ("nova") in the prologue to *La Cassaria* (1508), noting that it only refers to a departure from direct imitation of a specific classical dramatic text but that it does not imply independence from classical models. Notes in the prologue Ariosto's pride in having initiated the writing of comedies in the vernacular. Identifies specific borrowings in *La Cassaria* and *I Suppositi* from classical sources and states that among sixteenth-century comedy writers there was a love-hate relationship with classical models (pp. 81–84).

⋅❧ 611. PARKER, PATRICIA A. *Inescapable Romance: Studies in the Poetics of a Mode*, pp. 16–53. Princeton: Princeton University Press, 1979.
Studies on the nature of romance, from its implications as the structural basis of the *OF* to its presence in the form of suspension and deferral in poets such as Mallarmé, Valéry, and Wallace Stevens. Initial chapter, on Ariosto, considers the significance of the *OF* to an understanding of the nature of all fiction as a deviation from archetypal norms and a challenge to literary authority, articulated in the *OF*—on both the narrative and moral levels—by means of the "erring" topos and the consequent repeated delay in the closure characteristic of epic convention.

⋅❧ 612. PAROTTI, PHILLIP ELLIOTT. "The Female Warrior in the Renaissance Epic." *DAI* 34, no. 1 (1973): 283A. (University of New Mexico, 1972. 458p.)
Notes that the Italian Neoplatonists revived the "harmonious perspective on the union" of Mars and Venus, a union that originated in Greek culture but was abandoned with the advent of Christianity. Argues for the origin of the warrior maiden in Renaissance epic as deriving from the *discordia concors* of the Mars-Venus union. Discusses especially Bradamante and Marfisa as exemplars of feminine harmony and concord.

⋅❧ 613. PASQUAZI, SILVIO. Introduzione. In *Orlando Furioso*, by Ludovico Ariosto, pp. v–xvi. Milan: Bietti, 1969.

Summary biography, discussion of works, and mention of the structural nature and thematics of the *OF*.

≈§ 614. ———. "Umano quotidiano e umano immaginoso nella poesia di Ludovico Ariosto." *Cultura e scuola* 13, no. 52 (1974): 32–38.

Explores the importance of the cultural milieu of fifteenth-century Ferrara—everyday life as well as humanistic tradition—to the inspiration and composition of Ariosto's works, noting in particular the importance of interpersonal relationships that manifest themselves in writings maintaining a constant dialectic with the poet's public, and the characteristic type of humanism in Ferrara ("più esteriore che interiore," p. 34) that explains in Ariosto's writing a creativity evolving from factual occurrence. Notes that the "spirito di concretezza" (p. 36) dominating the cultural milieu imposes certain restraints, limits the sense of freedom, which Ariosto saw as concomitant with the essence of humanity and which is explored in the character of Orlando. Views Orlando as the traditionally perfect and whole human and, as such, intolerant of limitations (p. 37). The figure of the mad Orlando is an expression of this image of man confronting the drama of life but who, the poet is ironically aware, limits his freedom when not in the control of self-imposed restraints.

≈§ 615. ———. "Ariosto minore e la cultura ferrarese." In his *Ariosto minore e l'umanesimo ferrarese; motivi e problemi danteschi*, pp. 243–304. Rome: Elia, 1976.

Dispense (?). Edition contains anthological selections of Ariosto's poetry, comedies, and satires, all briefly annotated. Concludes with general essay on Ariosto's literary formation against Ferrarese culture of the early Renaissance; summary discussion of literary life in Ferrara before the Este and during the period of their control. Briefly discusses Ariosto's early education and his aesthetics. Introductory comments to the minor works; discussion of the comedies is prefaced by a short history of theater in the fifteenth century. Volume also contains an essay on Dante.

≈§ 616. PAVLOCK, BARBARA ROSE. "Epic and Romance: *Genera Mixta* in Vergil, Ovid, Ariosto, and Milton." *DAI* 38, no. 7 (1978): 4148A. (Cornell University, 1977. 168p.)

Argues that the *Aeneid*, the *Heroides*, the *OF*, and *Paradise Lost* are homogeneous texts that "'decompose' a romantic surface; their strategies revolve centrally around literary imitation, the theme of madness, and the poet's relation to his material." In this context, examines the episodes of Olimpia's abandonment and of Cloridano and Medoro.

◆§ 617. PECORARO, MARCO. *Per la storia dei carmi del Bembo: una reda-zione non vulgata.* Venice: Istituto per la Collaborazione Culturale, 1959. 222p.
Argues that Bembo's Latin *carme* "Ad Melinum" was addressed to Ariosto (pp. 143–44).

◆§ 618. PEETERS, L. "Das Kudrunepos und die Olimpiaepisode in Ariosts *Orlando Furioso.*" *Neophilologus* 53 (1969): 273–90; 402–13.
Discusses the similarities and differences between the Olimpia episode (*OF*, 1532 edition) and the Middle High German epic, the *Kudrun.* Notes Otto Grüters's theory regarding a common source in Frankish (alto-franca) tradition, but argues that Ariosto's source was the *Kudrun* itself.

◆§ 619. PENCE, JAMES LEE. "A Critical Edition of Robert Tofte's Transla-tion of Ariosto's *Satires* (1608)." *DAI* 39, no. 7 (1979): 4282A. (Univer-sity of Arizona, 1978. 344p.)
Notes that "Tofte attempted to adapt Ariosto's *Satires* to an audience he assumed to be more interested in Ariosto's biography and Italian customs than in a faithful translation."

◆§ 620. PENZOL, PEDRO. "Angélica y Medoro en el *Orlando Furioso* de Francisco Bances Candamo." *Clavileño* 7, no. 39 (1956): 19–23.
A summary survey of the Angelica-Medoro theme from the Italian Ren-aissance to its use in the *zarzuela,* "Cómo se curan los celos y Orlando Furioso," of the Asturian dramatist Francisco Bances Candamo (1662–1709).

◆§ 621. PERELLA, NICOLAS J. *Midday in Italian Literature: Variations on an Archetypal Theme.* Princeton: Princeton University Press, 1979.
Notes that midday has a negative value in the *OF* and is used to "drama-tize and allegorize the difficulty of the path to virtue" (p. 48). The noonscape becomes a "poetic objectification . . . of a psychological condition and the spiritual struggle of a soul which in order to acquire virtue must pass through the crisis provoked by a hostile power" (p. 49). Briefly discusses the episode of Orlando's madness, the climactic moment of which occurs at noon and, ironically, in an idyllic retreat traditionally reserved as a refuge from life's cares. See pages 47–50.

◆§ 622. PÉREZ, LOUIS C. "The Theme of the Tapestry in Ariosto and Cer-vantes." *Revista de Estudios Hispánicos* 7, no. 2 (1973): 289–98.
Notes that the *OF* "abounds in tapestry references" and that the art of weaving, important in Ferrara during Ariosto's time, suggests metaphors for both the poem and its internal structure (p. 291). Argues that Cervantes, too,

under the direct influence of Ariosto, conceives of the *DQ* as a narrative weave and employs Ariosto's technique.

✍§ 623. *Per l'Ariosto.* Special issue of *Italianistica* 3, no. 3 (1974). Milan: Marzorati, 1976. 201p.

Includes: Paolo Paolini, "Situazione della critica ariostesca" (entry 597); Gioacchino Paparelli, "L'Ariosto lirico e satirico" (entry 603); Renzo Negri, "Ipotesi sull'*Orlando Furioso*" (entry 561); Emo Marconi, "Teatralità dell'Ariosto" (entry 492); Lanfranco Caretti, "Storia dei *Cinque Canti*" (entries 174 and 178); Pio Fontana, "Ancora sui *Cinque canti* dell'Ariosto" (entry 330); Antonio Piromalli, "Società ferrarese e mondo morale dal Pistoia all'Ariosto" (entry 637); Guido Di Pino, "Bivalenza dell'ottava ariostesca" (entry 269); Alessandro Tortoreto, "Ariosto e Tasso, confronto obbligato" (entry 847); Riccardo Bacchelli, "Ariosto 'solstiziale'" (entry 35); Italo Calvino, "Ariosto geometrico" (entry 159); Carlo Cordié, "L'Ariosto nella critica della Staël, del Ginguené e del Sismondi (1800–1813)" (entry 218); Giuseppe Bellini, "L'Ariosto nell'America ispanica" (entry 76).

✍§ 624. Petriconi, Hellmuth, and Walter Pabst. "Einwirkungen der italienischen auf die deutsche Literatur." In *Deutsche Philologie im Aufriss*, edited by Wolfgang Stammler, 3 (1962): 107–46. 3 vols. Berlin: Erich Schmidt, 1957, 1960, 1962.

Also with title "Einwirkung der italienischen auf die deutsche Literatur," in *Deutsche Philologie im Aufriss*, edited by Wolfgang Stammler, 3 vols. (Berlin: Erich Schmidt, 1952, 1954, 1957), 3 (1957): 223–59.

Brief discussion of the interest in the *OF* during the period of German romanticism and of Christoph Wieland's translation of the poem in *ottava rima*. Includes notes on technical aspects of Wieland's German version.

✍§ 625. Petrini, Mario. "Per una storia interna del *Furioso*." In *Studi in memoria di Luigi Russo*, pp. 15–31. Pisa: Nistri-Lischi, 1974.

Focusing on the proems to the cantos of the *OF*, considers occasions in which the poet, "da situazioni analoghe e analoghe mosse di fantasia e di sentimento ricava non solo esiti e riflessioni diverse dal punto di vista più o meno esterno della soluzione e del giudizio eventuale, ma diverse nell'accento, nel tono, nell'armonia, quasi vere e proprie antinomie" (p. 15).

✍§ 626. Petrocchi, Giorgio. *Ludovico Ariosto e la letteratura del Rinascimento.* Corso di lezioni per l'anno accademico 1967–68. Rome: E. De Santis, [1968]. 199p.

Dispense. General discussion of the *OF*; history of criticism on Ariosto; brief reading of the satires.

627. ———. "Lettura dell'*Orlando Furioso*." In his *I Fantasmi di Tancredi: saggi sul Tasso e sul Rinascimento*, pp. 277–92. Caltanissetta-Rome: Salvatore Sciascia, 1972.
Also as the introduction to Ludovico Ariosto, *Orlando Furioso* (Padua: R.A.D.A.R., 1968), pp. 5–17.
Discussion focuses on the *variatio* of the *OF*—"la volontà precisa del poeta di risolvere nei salti e soprassalti dell'intreccio . . . il suo intenso sentimento della varietà e provvisorietà della vita" (p. 278)—and the nature of several of the principal characters in relation to Ariosto's weave and the agitated movement of human sentiments. Sees in Ruggiero and Bradamante the truest reflection of the Ariostean spirit and Ruggiero as the central character in the ethical-psychological structure of the *OF*, one in which there is a certain dramatic tension. Regarding the episode of Orlando's madness, states: "Ed è questo il segno del grande progresso che l'arte del *Furioso* realizza rispetto ai poemi precedenti: di conservare i toni irreali e smisurati (come nella scena centrale della follia) senza scadere nel grottesco e nel sarcasmo eccessivi, ma discoprendo l'umanità di Orlando in un sottile giuoco di trapassi psicologici" (p. 286).

628. ———. "Orazio e Ariosto." In his *I Fantasmi di Tancredi: saggi sul Tasso e sul Rinascimento*, pp. 261–75. Caltanissetta-Rome: Salvatore Sciascia, 1972.
Also in *Giornale italiano di filologia*, n.s. 1, vol. 22 (1970): 3–13.
Discusses Ariosto's affinity with Horace's ethic and the influence of the Roman poet on Ariosto's Latin works, the Horatian tone and sobriety of the satires, and the little-studied but significant Horatian echoes in the *OF*.

629. ———. "Riprese di giudizio sulla poesia del *Furioso*." In his *I Fantasmi di Tancredi: saggi sul Tasso e sul Rinascimento*, pp. 293–312. Caltanissetta-Rome: Salvatore Sciascia, 1972.
Also in *Cultura e scuola* 5, no. 20 (1966): 16–24 and the second part in *La Fiera letteraria* 42, no. 6 (1967): 20.
Review of some of the most important critical essays on Ariosto in the post-Crocean period, with particular attention given to Walter Binni and Cesare Segre.

630. PETRONI, GUGLIELMO. "Ariosto e Tasso." *La Rassegna della letteratura italiana*, 7th ser., vol. 79, nos. 1–2 (1975): 15.
Notwithstanding his enthusiasm for Tasso, finds in Ariosto the "espressione di completezza di vita e libertà spirituale."

631. PETRONI, LIANO. "Un example de poétique 'dramatique' et d'une 'politique' de la comédie issu de l'Arioste: la comédie littéraire de Jean de la Taille." In *Notiziario culturale italiano* (entry 573) 15, no. 3 (1974): 87–94.

After highlighting Ariosto's particular contributions to the development of Renaissance comedy and dramaturgy, and especially his attempted fusion of an ideal poetic harmony and historical verisimilitude (p. 90), considers the influence of Ariosto on Jean de la Taille. Cites in particular his comedy, *Les Corrivaux* (1562), which thematically, structurally, and in its comic dialogue is indebted to Ariosto, whom de la Taille included with Terence and Plautus for his historical importance.

632. PETRONIO, GIUSEPPE. "Ludovico Ariosto." In his *L'attività letteraria in Italia*, pp. 245–59. Rev. ed. Palermo: Palumbo, 1979.

Brief biographical sketch and summary comments on Ariosto's minor works. Focuses, however, on the *OF*, noting that Ariosto chose as a basis for his work the medieval chivalric tradition because it offered a richness and variety of characters and motifs appropriate for the representation of "la favola varia della vita dell'uomo" (p. 251). Discusses the reflection of the Renaissance ethos in the *OF*, especially in its secular concept of the world ("I personaggi del *Furioso* si muovono e agiscono incuriosi di Dio, senza chiedersi mai se le loro azioni rispondano a leggi deducibili da una rivelazione divina," p. 251); in its representation of man, who has "un carattere naturalistico" (p. 252); in the emphasis given to individualism; and in the representation of women, who, in the integral part they played in Renaissance culture, can be said to represent in the poem "il femminile dell'uomo" (p. 253). Argues that the *OF* reflects the contradictory nature of early sixteenth-century culture and society and that it presents "una concezione del mondo, non tragica o triste, ma certo inquieta" (pp. 253–54): the recurrent "myths" are of the illusory, of delusion, and of the vanity of things. Defines the poem's harmony as "la traduzione in termini di lingua e di stile di quella medietà che il poeta e il suo mondo ritenevano virtú suprema dell'uomo" (p. 257).

633. PETTINELLI ALHAIQUE, ROSANNA. "Tra il Boiardo e l'Ariosto." See Alhaique, Rosanna Pettinelli, entry 7.

634. PFLUG, GÜNTHER. "Bibliothekarische Lesefrüchte im Rasenden Roland." In *Bibliothekswelt und Kulturgeschichte: Eine internationale Festgabe für Joachim Wieder zum. 65. Geburtstag dargebracht von seinen Freunden*, edited by Peter Schwiegler, pp. 49–72. Munich: Verlag Dokumentation, 1977.

On classical and medieval literary traditions used in the composition of the *OF* and its predecessors, particularly the *OI* and Pulci's *Morgante*. Discusses in particular the importance in the *OF* and the *OI* of certain topoi, including those of prophecy, magic, and the protection of individuals from danger.

᪥ 635. PIERANTOZZI, DECIO. *Indicazioni per una lettura dell'Ariosto.* Quaderni del Liceo Classico C. Colombo, Genova 7. Genoa: Arti Grafiche San Giorgio, 1966. 18p.
Unavailable; cited in *Bibliografia Nazionale Italiana* 9 (1966): 682 and *PMLA Bibliography*, 1967, p. 247, entry 13662.

᪥ 636. PIROMALLI, ANTONIO. *Ariosto.* Padua: R.A.D.A.R., 1969. 101p.
Reviews in a selective way Ariosto's critical reception in Italy from his contemporaries to the 1960s. Major divisions of essay: "Dai contemporanei ai romantici," pp. 7–27; "La critica di Francesco De Sanctis e dei positivisti," pp. 29–40; "L'Ariosto visto dal Croce e dai crociani," pp. 41–53; "Gli studi di poetica di Walter Binni," pp. 55–65; "Storicismo integrale e gramsciano," pp. 67–86; "Le recenti tendenze stilistiche e filologiche," pp. 87–94. Includes selected bibliography, pp. 95–98.

᪥ 637. ———. "Società ferrarese e mondo morale dal Pistoia all'Ariosto." In *Per l'Ariosto* (entry 623). Special 1976 issue of *Italianistica* 3, no. 3 (1974): 111–23.
Considers Ariosto's views on society and morality against the background of Antonio Cammelli's (known as "Il Pistoia," 1430–1502) experiences and observations, which, as recorded in his *Dialogo*, manifest a realistic perspective undermining Renaissance myths and institutions. Demonstrates that Ariosto's own attacks on myths and institutions are largely entrusted to his ironic mode, which manifests artistic·maturity while destroying feudal and medieval myths.

᪥ 638. ———. *La Cultura a Ferrara al tempo di Ludovico Ariosto.* 2d ed. Rome: Bulzoni, 1975. 213p.
First edition 1953; Fatini, 3529.

᪥ 639. PISCHEDDA, GIOVANNI. "Conclusioni sul classicismo ariosteo." In his *Classicità provinciale*, pp. 195–210. L'Aquila: La Bodoniana Tipografica, 1956.
States that the most authentic classicism in Ariosto is to be found in the OF rather than in the minor works and discusses the process by which classical motifs, filtered through the vernacular tradition, are interpreted by Ariosto to illuminate his narrative, resulting in a complete fusion of the classical and modern worlds. Cites the episode of the "Virgilian" Cloridano and Medoro (OF 28–29) as a model of this fusion: "ha in sè una precisione

tecnica, una *concinnitas* strutturale, che rivela pienamente il gusto di un '500 proteso verso l'armonia" (p. 201).

◄§ 640. *La Poesia del "Furioso."* Messina: Delf, 1957.
Unavailable; cited without additional information in *Zeitschrift für Romanische Philologie*, bibliography for 1956–1960, p. 489.

◄§ 641. POLLAK, ROMAN. Introduction. In *Orland Szalony*, by Ludovico Ariosto, translated into Polish by Piotr Kochanowski, pp. iii–lxxxiv. Wrocław-Warsaw-Kraków: Zakład Narodowy Imienia Ossolińskich, 1965.
General introduction to a reading of the *OF*. Discussion of the cultural background of the poem and the epic tradition in Italy. Survey of Ariosto's writings. General evaluation of major aspects of the *OF*, including irony and types of characters. Extensive discussion of Kochanowski's Polish version of the poem.

◄§ 642. ———. "Spolszczenia w staropolskim przekładzie Ariosta." *Zagadnienia rodzajów literackich* 7, no. 2 (1965): 43–49.
Discusses Kochanowski's translation of the *OF* (1620) and its adaptation to Polish cultural traditions, such as the use of a traditional verse and stanza form in place of the Italian *ottava rima* and the modification of elements in the original to assure greater appeal to Polish readers.

◄§ 643. ———. "Wątki romansowe e staropolskim przekładzie *Orlanda Szalonego*" (Threads of romance in an old Polish translation of *Orlando Furioso*). *Pamiętnik Literacki* 56, nos. 1–2 (1965): 348–60.
Analysis of Piotr Kochanowski's (1566–1620) translation of the *OF*.

◄§ 644. ———. "*L'Orlando furioso* nella traduzione di Piotr Kochanowski." In *Italia, Venezia e Polonia tra umanesimo e rinascimento*, edited by Mieczysław Brahmer, pp. 58–67. Warsaw: Zakład Narodowy Imienia Ossolińskich Wydawnictwo Polskiej Akademii Nauk, 1967.
Observations on the nature of Piotr Kochanowski's (1566–1620) translation of the *OF*, with particular attention given to the linguistic context in which the Polish version evolved and to the problem of adapting Ariosto's metrical structure. Considers the historical significance of a Polish version of a work whose cultural antecedents were completely alien to Polish society.

◄§ 645. POLT, J. H. R. "Una fuente del soneto de Acuña 'Al rey nuestro señor,'" *Bulletin Hispanique* (Annales de la Faculté des Lettres de Bordeaux) 64, nos. 3–4 (1962): 220–27.

Establishes *OF* 15.21–26—an elaboration of the Empire topos—as the primary source for Hernando de Acuña's sonnet.

◆§ 646. PONTE, GIOVANNI. "Nota sull'Ariosto imitatore del Boiardo lirico." In his *La Personalità e l'opera del Boiardo*, pp. 139–42. Genoa: Tilgher, 1972.
Also in *La Rassegna della letteratura italiana*, 7th ser., vol. 66, no. 1 (1962): 81–84.
Notes that Ariosto's youthful *capitolo* "Or che la terra di bei fiori è piena" echoes expressions of Boiardo's, "i cui 'Amorum libri' dimostra di conoscere e di riprendere in aspetti caratteristici" (p. 139).

◆§ 647. ———. "Boiardo e Ariosto." *La Rassegna della letteratura italiana*, 7th ser., vol. 79, nos. 1–2 (1975): 169–82.
Notes that for Ariosto, the *OI* was essentially "un vasto repertorio di suggerimenti tematici o stilistici" (p. 171), whose influence is most apparent in the first half of the *OF*, in which a gradual breaking away from Boiardesque models is apparent (p. 178). Analyzes a selected number of borrowings from the *OI* and concludes that "la tensione, il senso di vitalità e di vigore" (p. 181) so characteristic of the *OI* find a resolution in Ariosto's poem that reveals an entirely different personality and vision of life: rather than a dream fantasy of an idealized chivalric world, Ariosto's poem constantly juxtaposes the dream-ideal with a rational meditation on reality, resulting in a representation of a world of constant flux, of human folly, of the relativity of all reality. Places Ariosto in this regard in the cultural and psychological context of Guicciardini and Erasmus.

◆§ 648. ———. "La Personalità e l'arte dell'Ariosto nei *Carmina*." *La Rassegna della letteratura italiana*, 7th ser., vol. 79, nos. 1–2 (1975): 34–45.
Study of Ariosto's early Latin lyrics (c. 1491–1503), useful principally "per comprendere gli orientamenti dell'Ariosto in un periodo ancora di formazione" (p. 34); cautions, however, that conclusions must be drawn with care due to the considerable number of early compositions that have not survived. Notes that Ariosto follows the humanistic tradition of imitation of and competition with classical poets. Contends that the basis of the Latin lyrics is not essentially experiential and that "realism" is of literary origin. Of particular importance are the influences of Virgil, Catullus, and Horace, from whom Ariosto learned poetic control, as well as detachment from active life, from emotional involvement, and from immediacy for a celebration of idyllic peace and moralizing reflection. Concludes that the lyrics reveal a profound understanding of man and of both the fascination and perils of the earthly life.

◆§ 649. ————. "Un Esercizio stilistico dell'Ariosto: la tempesta di mare nel canto XLI del *Furioso*." In *Ludovico Ariosto: lingua, stile e tradizione*, edited by Cesare Segre (entry 789), pp. 195–206. Milan: Feltrinelli, 1976.
Analyzes Ariosto's use of literary sources for the storm episode in *OF* 41 (especially Ovid, Virgil, Boiardo, Boccaccio, and Pulci) and concludes that the episode "è costruito . . . nel confluire d'un'ispirazione che è colpita . . . dall'impeto pauroso del mare in tempesta e dal dramma dei naviganti, e di una riflessione vigile che fa evitare ogni emozione troppo appariscente, considera il potere della fortuna con l'imprevedibilità dei casi e la precarietà della condizione umana, sceglie e ordina le espressioni che ritiene efficaci. Nessuno slancio appassionato: la scena fantastica è materiata di esperienza umana, ma si costruisce e si articola alla presenza della ragione che osserva e commenta" (p. 205).

◆§ 650. POOL, FRANCO. *Interpretazione dell'"Orlando Furioso."* Florence: La Nuova Italia, 1968. 241p.
Analyzes major characters and episodes of the *OF*, focusing on irony, especially as revealed through hyperbole, and on Ariosto's use of simile as a prosodic means of linking the fantastic with the real. Fourteen chapters: 1) "L'avvio del poema," pp. 1–24; 2) "L'ippogrifo," pp. 25–34; 3) "L'isola d'Alcina," pp. 35–48; 4) "L'episodio d'Olimpia," pp. 49–63; 5) "Il palazzo d'Atlante," pp. 65–74; 6) "La battaglia di Parigi," pp. 75–103; 7) "'L'audaci imprese,'" pp. 105–19; 8) "La pazzia d'Orlando e la morte di Zerbino," pp. 121–37; 9) "Guerrieri pagani e guerrieri cristiani," pp. 139–49; 10) "Il grande viaggio d'Astolfo," pp. 151–73; 11) "Ruggiero e Bradamante," pp. 175–92; 12) "Rodomonte," pp. 193–205; 13) "Il duello di Lipadusa," pp. 207–20; 14) "Il Nappo incantato," pp. 221–37. Extensive quotations from the poem, little documentation, and no bibliography.

◆§ 651. PORTNER, IRVING ALAN. "The Comedies of Ludovico Ariosto." *ADD* 1969–1970: 215. (Harvard University, 1970.)
Ph.D. dissertation, not abstracted.

◆§ 652. POTAPOVA, ZLATA M. "Ariosto e Puškin." In *Ludovico Ariosto*, pp. 303–16. Convegno internazionale (entry 475). Rome: Accademia Nazionale dei Lincei, 1975.
Notes that Ariosto first became known in Russia in the eighteenth century and briefly traces the fortunes of the *OF* to the present. Considers the significant influence Ariosto had on Pushkin, especially on the composition of his poem *Ruslan and Ludmilla* (1817–1820). Citing Mikhail Rozanov's comparative study of Pushkin and Ariosto (*Izvestija Akademij Nauk SSSR*, 1937), notes specific aspects of Pushkin's poem in which Ariosto's influence

can be seen: lyrical digressions, techniques of transition from one episode to another, use of irony and parody, frequency of animal and nature imagery, and function of fantasy. Notes the importance of Ariosto for Pushkin's aesthetic vision.

◆§ 653. POVOLEDO, ELENA. "La Sala teatrale a Ferrara: da Pellegrino Prisciani a Ludovico Ariosto." *L'Architettura teatrale dall'epoca greca al Palladio* (Bollettino del Centro Internazionale di Studi di Architettura Andrea Palladio) 16 (1974): 105–38.
Traces the development of theatrical space in Renaissance Ferrara, especially after 1486 and the first production of a classical comedy documented in that city. Notes the historical importance of the 1508 production of Ariosto's *La Cassaria* and the scenography of Pellegrino da Udine to the growing sophistication of perspective stage design (pp. 126–28).

◆§ 654. ———. "La Commedia regolare e la scena prospettica." In Nino Pirrotta, *Li Due Orfei: da Poliziano a Monteverdi*, pp. 372–400. Turin: Einaudi, 1975.
Brief discussion of the perspective set designed by Pellegrino da Udine for a production of *La Cassaria* and mentioned in a letter written by Bernardino Prosperi to Isabella d'Este in 1508. Notes that Prosperi's is the first documented use of the term "perspective" in regard to scenic design and suggests that Ariosto himself was responsible for the innovative aspects of Pellegrino da Udine's design.

◆§ 655. PRAZ, MARIO. "Ariosto in Inghilterra." In *Ludovico Ariosto*, pp. 511–25. Convegno internazionale (entry 475). Rome: Accademia Nazionale dei Lincei, 1975.
Earlier versions of this essay: "L'Ariosto in Inghilterra," in his *Machiavelli in Inghilterra ed altri saggi sui rapporti anglo-italiani* (Florence: Sansoni, 1962), pp. 277–96; "L'Ariosto e l'Inghilterra," *Il Veltro* 1, nos. 3–4 (1957): 19–31; "L'Ariosto e la letteratura inglese," *Nuove lettere emiliane*, nos. 9–11 (1965): 31–38; "Ariosto in England," in his *The Flaming Heart. Essays on Crashaw, Machiavelli and Other Studies in the Relations between Italian and English Literature from Chaucer to T. S. Eliot*, 1st ed. (Garden City, N.Y.: Doubleday, 1958), pp. 287–307.
States that Ariosto's influence in Elizabethan England was analogous to that of Dante, Boccaccio, and Petrarch on Chaucer in that it provided a major stimulus to literary creativity. Considers, in particular, the way in which the *OF* was read in Renaissance England—as a collection of moral tales—and the consequent effect on the *FQ*, in which the romance epic tradition is used as a basis for moral allegory. Notes that in spirit A *Midsummer Night's Dream* is closer to the *OF*, although there is no certainty that

Shakespeare was familiar with Harington's translation. Concludes by considering the importance of the *OF* to Sir Walter Scott, who adapted narrative techniques employed in the romance form.

◄§ 656. PULEIO, MARIA TERESA. "Il 'Giocondo' dell'Ariosto e la 'Vagabonde Inconstance' di Estienne Durand." *Le ragioni critiche* (Catania), n.s. 1–2 (1980): 51–72.

Notes Ariosto's critical fortune in France in the sixteenth century and the failure of French imitators to appreciate the irony and the fantastic elements of his poetry (p. 54); considers four imitations-translations in French of the Giocondo episode (*OF* 28): those of Nicolas Rapin (1572), Etienne Durand (1611), Monsieur de Bouillon (1663), and La Fontaine (1665). Cites the differences in the four French versions and the superiority of La Fontaine's "Joconde ou l'infidélité des femmes." Comments on the particular appeal to the baroque sensibility of aspects of Ariosto's episode, particularly such themes as inconstancy and deceit ("feinte," p. 64).

◄§ 657. PUPPO, MARIO. *Manuale critico-bibliografico per lo studio della letteratura italiana.* 13th ed. Turin: Società Editrice Internazionale, 1980. pp. 239–46.

First edition 1954; Fatini, 3558.

◄§ 658. QUAGLINO, MASSIMO. *Dodici litografie ispirate all'"Orlando Furioso."* Turin, 1972.

Contains twelve lithographs, measuring 50 cm. × 70 cm., all autographed. Introductory comment states, "Per arrivare a una legittima interpretazione dell'Orlando, Quaglino si è posto nella stessa condizione di Delacroix . . . , riducendo la complessità dell'opera a poche scene essenziali, che ne rappresentavano simbolicamente lo spirito."

◄§ 659. QUINT, DAVID. "Astolfo's Voyage to the Moon." *Yale Italian Studies* 1, no. 4 (1977): 398–408.

Argues that the moon, the other "face" of the earth (Ariosto: "diversa faccia"), is the "repository not of meaning but of unmeaning," or of lies (p. 398). Suggests that Ariosto intends to discredit the intertextual principles and the literary authority on which his lunar allegory is based; notes that for Ariosto literature has its origins not in "historical fact but in patronage" (p. 402). Points out that Ariosto's charge implicates John the Baptist, thus threatening to reduce the apostle's "testimony to the status of literary fiction" (p. 403). Concludes that Ariosto's encomium of the Este family is actually a lie and that "the 'higher' truth delivered from Ariosto's moon is merely that poet's lie" (p. 407).

👓 660. ———. "The Figure of Atlante: Ariosto and Boiardo's Poem."
    MLN 94, no. 1 (1979): 77–91.
Two-part article. First discusses the function of the figure of Atlante in the
OF. Argues that in Boiardo's *OI*, the magician, like the fairies, attempts to
defer the fate of the poem's hero by stalling the action and is thus seen as
competing with the poet for control of the poem. Atlante is viewed as a
surrogate of Boiardo, with whom Ariosto must compete, and in destroying
the figure of Atlante, Ariosto removes Boiardo's presence from his narrative:
"The death of Atlante-Boiardo is simultaneous with the destruction of his
palace-poem" (p. 81). Second part focuses on Tasso's distinction between
romance (*romanzo*) and epic; notes that "the *Innamorato* is the *romanzo* of
copia," whereas the *OF* begins as a romance but proceeds to an "epic closure"
after the destruction of Atlante's palace (p. 87).

👓 661. ———. "The Source as a Renaissance Metaphor: Imitations of the
    Fourth Georgic in Renaissance Literature." *DAI* 38, 1 (1979): 249A.
    (Yale University, 1976. 215p.)
Revised and published as *Origin and Originality in Renaissance Literature: Versions of the Source* (New Haven: Yale University Press, 1983), 263p.
    Examines the source topos at the end of Virgil's *Fourth Georgic* and its use
in the *OF* and other Renaissance texts: "The source, the confluent origin of
the rivers of the earth, is treated as an epistemological symbol, as a gauge of
each writer's 'source' of literary authority. . . . In the competing claims of
the author's autonomy or originality and of an authoritative source or origin,
the study attempts to define an intrinsically Renaissance debate over the nature of the literary text."

👓 662. QUONDAM, AMEDEO. "'Favola' non 'romansa': la partita di scacchi
    del *Furioso*: un episodio della critica ariostesca del Seicento." *La Ras-
    segna della letteratura italiana*, 7th ser., vol. 79, nos. 1–2 (1975):
    310–21.
Discusses Aurelio Severino's *La filosofia degli scacchi* (1690), a tract that
praises chess as a means of sharpening the intellectual faculties and that
draws important analogies between the strategies of the game and the processes of poetic creation: "Il processo essenziale della facoltà poetica, come
pure del gioco degli scacchi, consiste pertanto nella produzione (*invenzione*),
nella *mente*, di *immagini*, disposte in un insieme organico che è la *favola*"
(p. 312). Notes that chapter 6 of the tract is devoted to a discussion of the
OF as exemplary of Severino's notion of poetic invention, of *favola* ("aderenza ai processi propri della 'mente'") rather than *romansa* ("simmetrica disposizione dei . . . segmenti narrativi," p. 320). Severino's praise of the *OF*
constitutes a rejection of the "romanzesco barocco" (p. 317) and anticipates
important eighteenth-century theorists such as Gravina and Vico, for whom

favola, mente, and *fantasia* become basic to a definition of what constitutes poetry.

◆§ 663. RADCLIFF-UMSTEAD, DOUGLAS. *The Birth of Modern Comedy in Renaissance Italy.* Chicago and London: The University of Chicago Press, 1969. 285p.
Expository discussion of each of Ariosto's comedies and their revisions. Considers the classical influence of Plautine and Terentian models, thematic and other borrowings from the *novella* tradition, Ariosto's representation of contemporary mores, and his introduction of new elements into vernacular theater. See especially pp. 64–110.

◆§ 664. RAGGHIANTI, CARLO L. "Fabrizio Clerici, fantasia e civiltà." *Critica d'arte,* n.s., 15(33), fasc. 97 (1968): 3–22.
Sees Fabrizio Clerici's illustrations for the *OF* (edited by Riccardo Bacchelli; see entry 34) as inspired by the poem but in a completely different imaginative key. Briefly traces the evolution of styles in Clerici's work and how they influence his Ariosto illustrations. Stresses the influence on the artist of Leonardo da Vinci's drawings and his selection of episodes from the *OF* for illustrations that lend themselves to the spirit and energetic force of Leonardesque style. Illustrated with reproductions from the volume.

◆§ 665. ———. "Per una nuova illustrazione dell'*Orlando Furioso.*" *Lettere italiane* 20, no. 3 (1968): 382–91.
Reprints the preface to the exhibition catalog published for a showing of Fabrizio Clerici's drawings inspired by the *OF* held at the Fondazione Giorgio Cini in Venice. Notes that the drawings are a gloss on the artist's own complex work and artistic development and in no way serve to illustrate or illuminate Ariosto's text.

◆§ 666. RAGNI, EUGENIO. "L'Ariosto a cinquecento anni dalla nascita." In *Lodovico Ariosto: il suo tempo la sua terra la sua gente* (entry 468). Estratto dal *Bollettino storico reggiano* 7, no. 25 (1974): 17–32.
Considers fundamental thematic elements of the *OF* in light of modern criticism, noting areas that could profit by further extensive critical reading of the poem. Discusses Ariosto as a poet supremely representative of the cultural and historical moment in which he lived and, consequently, one who reflects in his writings the spirit of his age, most notably the tension between the ideals of the past and the awareness of present realities, the world of man as poised between the negative forces of human nature and fortune, and the positive elements of virtue and goodness. Suggests that the action of the *OF* is, in fact, a "rappresentazione parabolica del mondo umano, sempre lo stesso nel tempo . . . e sempre uguale nelle aspirazioni ad una felicità

ideale che ha nel tempo diversi mezzi di realizzazione, ma che rappresenta pur sempre il fine ultimo d'ogni uomo" (p. 27). Gives particular attention to Ariosto's use of the *cantastorie* tradition and its function in the structure of the poem, as well as to the nature of irony, which he views as directed toward the phenomenological and the outward show of chivalry, the essence of which—valor, *virtù*—are the ideals of his own age and celebrated as such.

~§ 667. ———. "Ariosto e Roma." *Studi romani* 23, no. 3 (1975): 311–29.

Also published as a monograph in the series *Quaderni di studi romani*, 1st ser., no. 40 (Rome: Istituto di studi romani, 1975), 25p.

Considers the frequency of Ariosto's visits to Rome while in the service of Ippolito d'Este (1503–1517) and documents his familiarity with and dislike of the city. Notes that in his writings Rome is either portrayed in the grandeur of its historic past or as a city of moral corruption and decay. Suggests that the poet's attitude toward Rome can serve to delineate more clearly his character and personality, for the city comes to be symbolic of urban corruption and takes an antithetical position to the author's representation of Ferrara, the image of social and moral strength. Notes that in the satires, autobiographical fact takes on the function of an *exemplum* and, as in the case of the representation of Rome and the poet's experiences in that city, is universalized; states that "la ricerca dell'universale nel particolare della verità effettuale" is characteristic of Renaissance culture (p. 326).

~§ 668. RAIMONDI, EZIO. "Una Lettura ariostesca di Renato Serra." In *Critica e storia letteraria. Studi offerti a Mario Fubini*, 2: 203–25. 2 vols. Padua: Liviana, 1970.

Discusses the critical perspectives of Renato Serra, with particular attention given to an exchange of views with Giuseppe De Robertis (in the years 1914–1915) on the *OF* and Manzoni's *I Promessi sposi*.

~§ 669. RAJNA, PIO. *Lodovico Ariosto. Discorso inedito di Pio Rajna letto al Liceo Parini di Milano il 16 marzo 1873*, edited with a preface by Giorgio Gibaldi. Milan: Istituto Lombardo di Scienze e Lettere, 1973. 190p.

Text of a commemorative lecture. Appendix includes an account of Rajna's writing and the publication of *Le fonti dell'"Orlando Furioso"* (first edition, 1876) and the *Origini dell'epopea francese*; also includes several letters by Rajna to Alessandro d'Ancona and four letters to Rajna from Ernesto Monaci, Giosué Carducci (1874, inviting him to prepare a volume on the sources of the *OF*), Gaston Paris, and the editor of the Le Monnier publishing house, respectively.

Lecture briefly touches on Ariosto's life and minor works, noting in his theater a "continuo avvicinarsi alla vita e alla natura" (p. 136), the most characteristic element of his comedies. General remarks on the *OF*, which is judged inferior to the *OI*, a work richer in fantasy and less consciously structured for effect—conclusions that anticipate his study on Ariosto's sources, *Le fonti dell'"Orlando Furioso"* (1876; 1900). Editor's preface (pp. 95–116) discusses the major points of Rajna's discourse, notes the analytical and deductive force of his thought, and briefly analyzes his prose style.

◆§ 670. ――――. *Le fonti dell'"Orlando Furioso,"* edited with an introduction by Francesco Mazzoni. 2d ed. 1900. Reprint. Florence: Sansoni, 1975. 683p.
Fatini, 1790; first edition 1876.

◆§ 671. RAMAT, RAFFAELLO. Introduzione. In *Orlando Furioso e scelta delle opere minori,* by Ludovico Ariosto, edited by Raffaello Ramat. 2d ed. Naples, 1960.
Cited in Eduardo Saccone, "Cloridano e Medoro, con alcuni argomenti per una lettura del primo *Furioso,*" in his *Il "soggetto" del 'Furioso' e altri saggi tra Quattro e Cinquecento* (Naples: Liguori, 1974), note 23, without additional information. Unavailable; Fatini cites no first edition with this title; however, entry 3592 lists Raffaello Ramat's introduction to *Orlando Furioso di Ludovico Ariosto, con introduzione, commento e storia della critica ariostesca,* edited by Raffaello Ramat (Naples: Glaux, 1955).

◆§ 672. ――――. "Ludovico Ariosto." In *I Classici italiani nella storia della critica,* edited by Walter Binni, 1 (1960): 349–407. 2 vols. 2d ed. Florence: La Nuova Italia, 1960, 1962.
Revision of his *La Critica ariostesca dal secolo XVI ad oggi* (Florence: La Nuova Italia, 1954), 261p.; Fatini, 3559.

◆§ 673. RANIOLO, GIUSEPPE. "Lo spirito e l'arte del *Furioso*" (preface). In *Orlando Furioso,* by Ludovico Ariosto, pp. vii–xviii. Florence: Le Monnier, 1969.
First edition 1933; Fatini, 2941.

◆§ 674. RAPIN, DANIEL. "Valore emblematico e figurativo delle fontane dell'amore e dell'odio (*Orl. fur.,* c. I)." *Capitoli. Revue littéraire franco-
italienne.* Numero unico dedicato all'Associazione Scrittori Centro Italia, pp. 111–15. Perugia, 1959.
Argues that the classical nature of the *OF* has a leveling effect so that specific characters and specific symbols, while part of the poet's overall conception of the cosmic structure and of human nature, cannot be considered as having a particular significance in their individuality. Noting that the

fountains of love and hate are first mentioned in *OF* 1.78, and then not again until canto 42, states that they are used to underscore the role of chance in the lives of men, who have only an illusory control over their destiny and to emphasize the proximity of emotions such as love and hate and the theme of contraries; cautions against attributing too much of a symbolic sense to the image of the fountain, which is only a small element in a multitude of episodes that combine to represent the profound unity of life.

675. RAVEGNANI, GIUSEPPE. "Le disgrazie dell'Ariosto." *Osservatore politico letterario* 7 (1961): 69–71.

Notes inaccuracies in Antonio Viscardi's *Storia della letteratura italiana dalle origini al Rinascimento* (see entry 889) regarding Ariosto's home in Via Mirasole (Ferrara), including the false attribution to the poet of the epigraph on the house's façade.

676. RAYA, GINO. "Fisiologia dell'Ariosto." *Biologia culturale* 9, no. 3 (1974): 117–18.

Profile of Ariosto's attitudes toward his age and his skepticism before the humanistic faith in reason and human wisdom.

677. REES, D. G. "Italian and Italianate Poetry." In *Elizabethan Poetry*, pp. 53–69. Stratford-upon-Avon Studies, 2. London: Edward Arnold, 1960.

Notes that the "serene irony which pervades the *Orlando Furioso* has nothing to do with history or morality, but is an aesthetic attitude. The creator is at once of his world and detached from it. The processes of participation and projection hold each other in balance, producing that unique Ariostesque harmony which . . . can symbolize the spirit of the Italian Renaissance" (p. 56). Considers the importance of the Italian Cinquecento to the development of English Renaissance poetry and, in particular, of the *OF* to Spenser, whose *FQ* is essentially different in spirit, replacing "Ariosto's world of romance" with a "sense of moral seriousness and purpose" (pp. 68–69).

678. REICHENBACH, GIULIO. "L'eroe mal fortunato: Sacripante." *Atti e memorie dell'Accademia Patavina di Scienze Lettere ed Arti* (Padua) 75 (1962–1963): 159–74.

Discusses the nature of Sacripante's fate in the *OF*, noting that he is destined to remain an unfortunate victim of Fortune, subject to disillusionment and to disappear in canto 35 after very few appearances. Notes Ariosto's interest in the character in canto 1, his creation of a potentially well-defined personality, but a subsequent loss of interest—characteristic of the poet's greater interest in the weave of the narrative than in the exploration of the psyche of his protagonists.

679. R[ENUCCI], P. "Arioste (L')." In *Encyclopaedia Universalis*, 2:382–85. 20 vols., plus 2 supplementary vols. Paris: Encyclopaedia Universalis France S.A., 1968.

Extensive introductory essay to Ariosto's life and works. Considers the poet's literary formation and education in fifteenth-century Ferrara, his service to the Este court and his minor works. Focuses on the *OF*; states that the poem "peut passer pour le chef-d'oeuvre littéraire du discontinu. La liberté d'invention de l'Arioste refuse les préceptes ou les axiomes des 'arts poétiques'" (p. 384). Proceeds to discuss themes, character types, variety in the narrative discourse, and the poet's point of view and ideas. Limited bibliographical information.

680. RESTA, GIANVITO. "Ariosto, Ludovico." In *Enciclopedia dantesca*, 1: 370–71. 5 vols. Rome: Istituto della Enciclopedia Italiana, 1970.

Notes the profound influence of Dante on Ariosto and cites several thematic echoes and linguistic borrowings from the *DC* in the *OF*. Includes selected bibliography.

681. RESTA, G[IORGIO]. "Ariosto e i suoi personaggi." *Rivista di psicoanalisi* (Florence) 3 (1957): 59–83.

Pages 62–68 republished with title "Il sogno di Orlando," in *I Metodi attuali della critica in Italia*, edited by Maria Corti and Cesare Segre (Turin: ERI, 1970), pp. 144–53.

Psychoanalytical interpretation of the *OF*, largely along Freudian lines. Considers the characters of the poem as representative of varying aspects of the poet's id, with Orlando as a projection of the neurotic and irrational and Rodomonte of the aggressive elements. Views poetic creativity as a "rielaborazione del materiale psichico infantile" (p. 62) and the poetic representation of dreams as particularly significant in the analysis of the psychological bases of a work of art. Analyzes Orlando's dream (canto 8) and relates its major components (the mother figure, loss of being the primary recipient of maternal affection, resultant jealousy, and defense mechanisms to counter emotional instability, p. 63) to the poem's central narrative line and to its secondary episodes. States that Ariosto is a precursor of some psychoanalytic theories, especially regarding amnesia and defense mechanisms (pp. 63, 65).

682. REYNOLDS, BARBARA. "Ariosto, Ludovico." In *Cassell's Encyclopedia of World Literature*, edited by J. Buchanan-Brown, 2:66. Rev. ed. in 3 vols. London: Cassell & Company, 1973.

Brief biographical sketch. Focuses on the *OF* and notes its debt to the *OI*. Suggests that the "creation of the character of Bradamante, especially the fusion of the masculine and feminine sides of her nature, and the growth of her love for Ruggiero with its attendant doubts and conflicts, is perhaps the most remarkable achievement of the whole work." Comments on Ariosto's art as a narrator and on his style, noting that "when he adorns his narration he does so by similes rather than by metaphor or imagery." Includes brief bibliographical note.

❧ 683. ———. Introduction. *Orlando Furioso,* by Ludovico Ariosto, translated by Barbara Reynolds, 1: 11–97 and 2: 7–21. 2 vols. London: Penguin Books, 1975 and 1977.
Volume 1: General introduction, focusing on the first half of the *OF.* Affirms that "what gives the work its fundamental unity is the concept of Europe, seen by Ariosto as the fount of the creative and civilizing forces of the world" (p. 12). Discusses Ariosto's perspective on contemporary civilization and mores, concluding that he intended to "awaken response to ideals of Christendom and chivalry" (p. 24). Summary discussion of aesthetic (the use of contrast) and structural (the incorporation of fantasy into a framework of verisimilitude) aspects of the poem and brief consideration of selected themes, such as the portrayal of love and women. Describes the literary origins of the poem, noting the important integration into the character of Orlando of its Carolingian, Arthurian, and Classical components. Includes a biography of the poet in a cultural-historical context and a survey both of Ariosto's influence on English literature and of English translations of the poem. Volume 2: On structural components of the poem. Identifies three major "patterns" governing the poem's structure: balance through juxtaposition of similar or contrasting episodes; totality or the representation of the multitude of aspects and perspectives on a theme; and resolution of narrative intricacies. Suggests that the poem's development reveals a growing awareness of life and art, manifested in a "heightening of style" (p. 18). Concludes with summary observations on the precision and detail of the real world in which Ariosto located his own world of legend and fantasy.

❧ 684. ———. "Ariosto in English: Prose or Verse?" In *Ariosto 1974 in America,* edited by Aldo Scaglione (entry 760), pp. 117–34. Ravenna: Longo, 1976.
While acknowledging that translations of literary texts lose much of the original, compares the prose versions of the *OF* by Allan Gilbert (1954), Richard Hodgens (1973), and Guido Waldman (1974) with the verse translations of Sir John Harington (1591) and William Stewart Rose (1823–1831). Argues that in prose renditions the form and much of the content is distorted and that the shortcomings of verse translations should be attributed to the "limitations of an individual versifier" and not blamed on "the constraints of English verse" (p. 126). Supports her claim of the efficacy of verse translations in rendering the style and tone of the original by quoting examples of her own translation (1975).

◄§ 685. ———. "I Primi traduttori inglesi dell'*Orlando Furioso*." In *Premio Città Monselice per una traduzione letteraria*. *Atti del Quinto Convegno sui problemi della traduzione letteraria: Le Prime traduzioni dell'Ariosto*, no. 6, pp. 73–87. Monselice: A Cura dell'Amministrazione Comunale, 1977.

Briefly reviews English translations of the *OF*, from that of Sir John Harington (1591) to the version of William Stewart Rose (1823–1831). Notes that the early translators selected passages and incorporated them in works for their motif value (e.g., Christopher Marlowe's use of the death of Isabella in *Tamburlaine* for the theme of innocence betrayed). Counter-Reformation versions of the poem underscored its allegorical and moralizing elements. Briefly discusses the merits of Harington's translation, the failure of John Hoole's version in distichs, and the essentially uninspired version of Rose. Considers Ariosto, of all Italian poets, to be the one closest in nature to the English character in his "amore dell'incongruo, . . . capacità di ridere, soprattutto di ridere di sé stesso" (p. 86).

◄§ 686. RHODES, DENNIS E. "The Printer of Ariosto's Early Plays." *Italian Studies* 18 (1963): 13–18.

Establishes the place of publication of the early prose redactions of *La Cassaria* and *I Suppositi* as Florence and dates the first printings between 1509 and 1511.

◄§ 687. RIDOLFI, ROBERTO. "La Seconda edizione della *Mandragola* e un codicillo sopra la prima." In his *Studi sulle commedie del Machiavelli*, pp. 37–61. Pisa: Nistri-Lischi, 1968.

Also in *La Bibliofilia* 66, no. 1 (1964): 49–62.

Argues that a comparative analysis of the type of the first edition of Ariosto's *I Suppositi* (Florence: Bernardo Zucchetta, c. 1510) and the first edition of the *Mandragola* further supports his argument elsewhere in this volume ("Composizione, rappresentazione e prima edizione della *Mandragola*," pp. 11–35) that Machiavelli's comedy was first published in Florence, probably in 1518 for the marriage of Lorenzo de' Medici (1492–1519).

◄§ 688. *Il Rinascimento nelle corti padane: società e cultura*, ed. Paolo Rossi et al. Bari: De Donato, 1977. 618p.

Proceedings of congress, Società e cultura al tempo di Ludovico Ariosto, held in Reggio Emilia and Ferrara, 22–26 October 1975. Includes: Luigi Balsamo, "L'industria tipografico-editoriale nel ducato estense all'epoca dell'Ariosto" (entry 50); Albano Biondi, "Streghe ed eretici nei domini estensi all'epoca dell'Ariosto" (entry 103); Cesare Vasoli, "L'astrologia a Ferrara tra la metà del Quattrocento e la metà del Cinquecento" (entry 878); and Gianni Venturi, "Scena e giardini a Ferrara" (entry 882).

≈§ 689. RIVERS, J. E. "Sacripant and Sacripante." See Bondanella, Peter E., entry 116.

≈§ 690. ROBINSON, LILLIAN SARA. "Monstrous Regiment: The Lady Knight in Sixteenth-Century Epic." *DAI* 35, no. 9 (1975): 6107–6108A. (University of Maryland, 1974. 439p.)
Argues that unlike the Virgilian epic, in which sexual expression and empire are incompatible, the Renaissance epic views sexuality and the world of war and statecraft as complementary and mutually enriching. Considers the lady knight in the *OF*, *GL*, and *FQ* and the implications of the representation of sexual equality in a traditionally male sphere: "The political issues that are central to these poems are not concerned with sex equality or the institution of the family. Rather, they are concerned with the emerging definition of the bourgeois secular state and the use it makes of qualities perceived as feminine or identified with the realm of sexuality."

≈§ 691. ROCHON, ANDRÉ. "L'imaginaire et le réel dans le *Roland Furieux*." In *Notiziario culturale italiano* (entry 573) 15, no. 3 (1974): 27–35.
Exposition of how the "naturel merveilleux" and the "tono medio" are obtained by tempering reality with fantasy (e.g., human passion couched in Petrarchan terms, p. 29) and putting at the base of fantastic creations the human experience (dreams as a reflection of human sentiment, p. 31).

≈§ 692. ROFFI, MARIO. "Stendhal, Ferrara, l'Ariosto e il Tasso." In *Stendhal e Bologna*. Atti del IX Congresso Internazionale Stendhaliano, 14–19 May, 1972. Estratto da *L'Archiginnasio* (Bollettino della Biblioteca Comunale di Bologna) 66–68 (1971–1973): 231–64.
Extensive discussion of Stendhal's visit to Ferrara in 1827 and of his readings of Tasso and Ariosto, noting his preference for the former and his appreciation for Ariosto's technical perfection but his undervaluation and lack of understanding of the poet's universe.

≈§ 693. ROLFS, DANIEL. "Sleep, Dreams and Insomnia in the *Orlando Furioso*." *Italica* 53, no. 4 (1976): 453–74.
Studies Ariosto's perspective on human folly through an analysis of situations in which characters sleep, have the opportunity to sleep, or in which they dream. Argues that sleeplessness reflects an excess of the passions, often leading to a temporary loss of the senses, as in the case of Bradamante's threatened suicide (canto 32) or Orlando's madness (23). Notes that sound sleep is associated with error or overconfidence and, thus, with human folly: both Zerbino and Ruggiero are captured while asleep (23; 45) and a sleeping Christian camp is massacred by Cloridano and Medoro (18). Dreams are often related to "some misconception of reality" (p. 465): Fiordispina believes

in her dream of Bradamante's change of sex (25) and Orlando accepts as real his dream of Angelica's love (8). Points out that, at times, sleep may be a "prod to conscience" (p. 469), as in the case of Ruggiero, who makes the proper decision to fulfill his duties before marrying Bradamante (25).

♨ 694. ———. "Sound and Silence in Ariosto's Narrative." *Renaissance and Reformation*, o.s., 14, no. 2; n.s., 2, no. 2 (1978): 151–69.
Concludes that throughout the OF, "Ariosto enhances the portrayal of numerous scenes and episodes by means of a wide variety of appeals to the ear. In the many passages enhanced by variations in sound . . . one often notes what could be termed the poet's sense of orchestration, particularly throughout the entire first canto of his work. Ariosto also appeals to the ear by creating moments of relative or total silence, whether as an environmental condition . . . or as a subjective one, as seen in the frequent speechlessness of his characters, particularly Orlando" (p. 166).

♨ 695. ROMAGNOLI, SERGIO, ed. *Antologia della critica ariostesca*. Milan: Fabbri, 1978. 199p.
Selection of critical writings on Ariosto; several are excerpted.

♨ 696. ROMAGNOLI ROBUSCHI, GIUSEPPINA. "Lettura del canto XXIII dell'*Orlando furioso*." In *Studi sull'Ariosto*, presentazione di Enzo Noè Girardi, pp. 131–46. Milan: Vita e Pensiero (Pubblicazioni dell'Università Cattolica del Sacro Cuore), 1977.
Focuses on the structural centrality of the madness episode, which occurs in a canto seen as bringing the preceding action to a type of conclusion before opening it up to new developments, citing Attilio Momigliano's idea of "'irradiazione e . . . concentramento,'" (*Saggio sull'Orlando Furioso*,' first edition 1928). Considers, in particular, the use in OF 23 of classical sources, which remove the action to a level of fablelike quality, saving it from becoming too immediate ("restituendo [il personaggio] alla favola da cui pareva voler uscire, col rischio di sfogare sospiri veri," p. 137); discusses elements of *entrelacement* and the internal structure of Orlando's frenzy, which breaks down into units analogous to parallel scansions in significantly related episodes.

♨ 697. ROMBALDI, ODOARDO. "Lodovico Ariosto commissario generale della Garfagnana." In *Lodovico Ariosto: il suo tempo la sua terra la sua gente* (entry 468). Estratto dal *Bollettino storico reggiano* 7, no. 28 (1974): 37–72.
Extensive history of the Garfagnana region, its possession by the Este family and its administration, particularly during the governorship of Guicciardini. "Per illustrare il governo dell'Ariosto in Garfagnana parrà eccessivo aver

ricordato eventi e personaggi che con quella provincia non hanno evidente connessione, quali i casi dell'Emilia e di Reggio in particolare, e la personalità e l'azione del Guicciardini. Ma a connettere la Garfagnana a Reggio ci invita la Satira IV; si tratta certo di un collegamento personale e privato che l'Ariosto stabilisce tra la città natia e il Mauriziano, ma il luogo della poesia, per l'Ariosto, è il luogo di tutte le sue esperienze. Infatti, la satira, proprio in ragione della tensione che la governa: confronto tra il passato e il presente, rimanda al drammatico conflitto tra la vita privata e quella pubblica del suo autore" (p. 69). Concludes with a brief discussion of Ariosto's experiences in the Garfagnana.

◆§ 698. RONCAGLIA, AURELIO. "L'Arioste et la poésie chevaleresque française." In *Notiziario culturale italiano* (entry 573) 15, no. 3 (1974): 59–67.
Concludes that the French chivalric *roman*, rather than a genre of evasion into a world of fantasy and fable, has a metaphorical structure wherein the personal quest can readily be identified with the perennial search for structure and meaning in the human condition, with the dialectic between the opposing values of life. States that the *OF* is, despite recent attempts to minimize Ariosto's debt to his French predecessors, essentially analogous to the French medieval tradition in that it, too, reflects a search for the significance of life in a world of folly and illusions.

◆§ 699. ———. "Nascita e sviluppo della narrativa cavalleresca nella Francia medievale." *Ludovico Ariosto*, pp. 229–50. Convegno internazionale (entry 475). Rome: Accademia Nazionale dei Lincei, 1975.
Discusses the medieval French romance as a source for the *OF*, emphasizing its importance as a grounding for or as the origin of the *OF*'s "spazio fantastico-narrativo" (p. 231) rather than identifying specific narrative or rhetorical borrowings. Notes that for Ariosto, the world of chivalry has become a mythology, bourgeois civilization of Renaissance Ferrara having substantially distanced the material of the poem from its audience. Ariosto uses the mythology as a basis for his representation and contemplation of "la varietà e la mobile dialettica dei casi e degli affetti umani" (p. 236). Of the important dimensions of the medieval romance tradition incorporated into the *OF*, notes the significant use of visual representation (pp. 236–38); the use of verse for rhetorical dignity (pp. 238–39); a secular spirit, in which the metaphysical preoccupatons of late medieval romance are replaced by a Renaissance contemplation of human sentiments, especially the power of love (pp. 239–41); the use of the text for mirroring the universe, of adventure and the quest as symbolic attempts to comprehend (often futilely) the sense of the world and the meaning of life (pp. 241–50).

≈§ 700. RONCAGLIA CIMINO, MARISA. Introduzione. *Orlando Furioso*, by Ludovico Ariosto, edited by Marisa Roncaglia Cimino, 1:v–xxiii. 2 vols. Rome: Cremonese, 1957.

Brief biographical sketch, concluding that Ariosto was by nature "desideroso di quiete e di tranquillità" (p. viii). Summary account of minor works. Discussion of medieval chivalric tradition and its influence on Pulci, Boiardo, and Ariosto. Notes the policentric nature of the *OF*, which, at the same time, is structurally unified.

≈§ 701. RONCHI, GABRIELLA. "Note sull'*Erbolato*." In *In Ricordo di Cesare Angelini: studi di letteratura e filologia*, edited by Franco Alessio and Angelo Stella, pp. 185–94. Milan: Il Saggiatore, 1979.

Notes the difficulty in definitively attributing the *Erbolato* to Ariosto but suggests that its affinity with the *Negromante* in satirizing the common belief in astrology and magic and its lexical, stylistic, and syntactical parallels with Ariosto's minor works evoke an "atmosfera ariostesca" (p. 192) that supports the view that Ariosto wrote the work or suggests an attempt at imitating Ariosto's language and style.

≈§ 702. RONCHI, GABRIELLA, AND ANGELA CASELLA. "Le *Commedie* e i loro stampatori." In *Ludovico Ariosto: lingua, stile e tradizione*, edited by Cesare Segre (entry 789), pp. 331–45. Milan: Feltrinelli, 1976.

Studies the editorial liberties taken by printers with the comedies, both during Ariosto's lifetime and after his death. Suggests that Ariosto's concern with the revision of the *OF* prevented his giving adequate attention to the editing of his minor works but that his adherence late in life to Bembo's linguistic and stylistic precepts was taken into account by subsequent sixteenth-century editors of the comedies.

≈§ 703. RONCONI, ALESSANDRO. "Prologhi 'plautini' e prologhi 'terenziani' nella commedia italiana del '500." In *Il Teatro classico italiano nel '500*, pp. 197–214. Rome: Accademia Nazionale dei Lincei, 1971.

General discussion of the content and function of the prologues of sixteenth-century comedies, inspired by Plautine and Terentian models and falling into three fundamental categories: those intended to capture the attention of the audience; those of a polemical and/or apologetic nature; those used to describe the plot, or *argomento*. Frequent references to Ariosto's use of tradition in his prologues; notes in particular that his most mature comedy, *La Lena*, is representative of a conflict in sixteenth-century comedy writers between a necessary observance of dramatic conventions and desire to emulate the classics and the aspiration toward innovation.

704. ROSAND, DAVID. "*Ut Pictor Poeta*: Meaning in Titian's *Poesie*." *New Literary History* 3, no. 3 (1972): 527–46.
Notes that *OF* 33.1–3 both equates the artistic achievements of the Renaissance with those of antiquity and proclaims the poet's intention of outdoing painting with his own poetic art (p. 532).

705. ROSE, CONSTANCE HUBBARD. "Spanish Renaissance Translators." *Revue de littérature comparée* 45 (1971): 554–72.
Two-part essay. First compares two Spanish versions of a passage from *OF*, arguing that Alfonso Núñez de Reinoso chose not to use the already extant translation of Jéronimo de Urrea for a gloss on *OF* 44.61–62 for specific personal and aesthetic reasons. Second discusses Alfonso de Ulloa's commentary on the Spanish word *marano* (*marrano*, *OF* 1.26) in his 1553 edition of Urrea's translation, published by Giolito in Ferrara.

706. ROSSETTINI-TRTNIK, OLGA. *Les influences anciennes & italiennes sur la satire en France au XVIᵉ siècle.* Florence: Institut Français de Florence, 1958. 422p.
Notes the Horatian form of Ariosto's satires and his originality in depicting contemporary mores. Remarks on the influences of the burlesque tradition on the humor and movement ("mouvement") in the satires; underscores the autobiographical elements in the satires, more important than in Horace (pp. 31–32; p. 348). Extensive discussion of Ariosto's influence on the satires of Jean Vauquelin de la Fresnaye (pp. 242–44; 258–62; 289–91; 303–4).

707. ROSSI, GIUSEPPE ADRIANO. "'La Nascita di Lodovico Ariosto': poemetto dell'abate Michele Baraldi." In *Lodovico Ariosto: il suo tempo la sua terra la sua gente* (entry 468). Estratto dal *Bollettino storico reggiano* 7, no. 28 (1974): 73–90.
Analysis of Michele Baraldi's 179-octave poem, "La Nascita di Lodovico Ariosto" (Ferrara: Bianchi e Negri, 1802; located in the Archivio di Stato, Reggio Emilia and in the Biblioteca Comunale in Ferrara), written upon the occasion of the transfer of the poet's remains from the church of San Benedetto to the library of the University of Ferrara in 1801. Notes that the poem is a description "del viaggio immaginario che il Genio della poesia, personificato, compie alla ricerca della Natura, . . . per poter realizzare la sua ardita impresa: dare all'Italia un poeta che primeggi su tutti gli altri: Lodovico Ariosto" (p. 78). Notes and lists the frequent borrowings in the poem from the *OF* and the *CC*.

708. ROSSI, LEA. "Sui *Cinque Canti* di Lodovico Ariosto." In *Lodovico Ariosto: il suo tempo la sua terra la sua gente* (entry 468). Estratto dal *Bollettino storico reggiano* 7, no. 28 (1974): 91–150.

Revision of *Saggio sui "Cinque Canti"* (1923); Fatini, 2242.
Lengthy essay divided into nine subheadings, or chapters. Discusses in detail the 1545 (Manuzio) and 1548 (Giolito) editions of the CC and their lacunae. Considers early and inconclusive commentaries on the author's purpose in composing the CC and discusses Antonio Cappelli's edition of variants of the fragment, "tolte da un ms. sincrono che sta presso gli eredi del dott. don. Giacomo Rossi" (Appendix to *Lettere di L. Ariosto*, Bologna, 1866)—the only extant *codice sincrono* of the work (p. 104). On the relationship of the CC to the OF, argues that there is a strict poetic unity in the CC, making it independent from, though inspired by, the OF. Comparing editions of the CC, concludes that it is the fragment of an entirely new poem conceived by Ariosto in the literary tradition of the OF but intended to be substantially different, as can be inferred from its subject and the roles of the characters (p. 113). Discusses at length the arguments and conclusions of critics regarding the period of composition, concluding that the work was composed "nell'apparente 'vacanza' di attività che sta fra il I e il II *Furioso*. Troppi sono gli indizi, storici, cronologici, che li fanno assegnare a questo periodo, troppo numerose le allusioni ad avvenimenti del 1519–1521. Ma soprattutto per la questione della lingua—che nel '21 non era ancora quale la troviamo in quest'opera—e per le numerose varianti riscontrate dal Segre, è evidente che il frammento continuò a interessare il poeta ancora per anni" (p. 123). In considering the nature of the inspiration behind the CC, sees a return to an epic type reminiscent of popular French medieval tradition. Cites the differences between the protagonists in the CC and those in the OF, and the absence in the CC of all but one (Bianca) important female figure. On the style and language of the CC, notes that it was written by one who had already assimilated "non solo la morfologia, ma anche il lessico toscano. . . . Se l'ispirazione è popolare, l'espressione è colta" (p. 136). Proceeds to illustrate the latter statement with examples of Latin and classical linguistic forms. Concluding chapter on pessimism and politics discusses the manner in which the incomplete poem reflects the period of its composition. Includes appended bibliography of editions and critical studies.

🔊 709. Rossi, Luciano. "Considerações sobre Ariosto e Camões." *Brotéria* (Lisbon) 3, no. 4 (1980): 378–92.
    Noting that Camões intended to surpass Ariosto in the composition of his epic *Os Lusíadas*, observes that, unlike the OF, which is largely fictional in nature, the Portuguese poem is based on historical events, namely the voyage of Vasco da Gama and the heroic struggles of the Portuguese against the Indians. Argues that despite Camões's polemical stance against Ariosto and his admirers, his octave form, usually rigidly structured and archaic in the manner of Poliziano's *Stanze*, becomes free and plastic ("livre e dúctil," p. 392) when in imitation of Ariosto. Compares Camões's portrait of Venus and

Ariosto's description of Olimpia and concludes that the Portuguese poet is one of the few Renaissance epic poets to have assimilated successfully Ariosto's innovative technique of visual representation in verse.

◆§ 710. ROSZKOWSKA, WANDA. "*Orlando Furioso* e il seicento polacco." In *Ludovico Ariosto*, pp. 405–21. Convegno internazionale (entry 475). Rome: Accademia Nazionale dei Lincei, 1975.
Discusses the *OF* as the basis of two seventeenth-century Polish works, the translation of Piotr Kochanowski and an anonymous poem entitled "The Seige of Mount Chiaro of Częstochowa." Notes that the former, in particular, emphasizes (by influence from Tasso) the heroic and that the Renaissance spirit of Ariosto gives way to the patriotic exaltation of the Sarmatian people.

◆§ 711. ROTA, DANIELE. "I bergamaschi e l'Ariosto." *L'Eco di Bergamo*, 21 August 1974.
Unavailable; cited without additional information in Vittorio Mora, "Proposta di lettura del canto primo dell'*Orlando Furioso* alla 'Rustica Bergamasca,'" *Bergomum* 68, nos. 3–4 (1974): 27–74.

◆§ 712. ROTH, TH[OMAS]. *Der Einfluss von Ariost's Orlando Furioso auf das französische Theater*. 1905. Reprint. Geneva: Slatkine Reprints, 1971. 263p.
Original publication listed in Fatini, 1920.

◆§ 713. ROTKOVIC, RADOSLAV. "Ljubišini prevodi Horacija, Dantea, i Ariosta" (Translations of works of Horace, Dante and Ariosto by Ljubiša). *Ovdje* (Titograd) 7, no. 72 (1975): 24.
Brief note on the translations of a number of texts by the Montenegrin poet Stjepan Ljubiša (1824–1878).

◆§ 714. ROWES, BARBARA GAIL. "The Subtle Searching: A Theory of the Renaissance Epic." *DAI* 34, no. 8 (1974): 5121A (SUNY, Buffalo, 1973. 174p.)
Considers the structure of the *OF* "in terms of the historical, psychological, and philosophical implications of its operation."

◆§ 715. RÜDIGER, HORST. "Ariosto nel mondo di lingua tedesca." In *Ludovico Ariosto*, pp. 489–509. Convegno internazionale (entry 475). Rome: Accademia Nazionale dei Lincei, 1975.
German translation ("Ariost in der deutschen Literatur") in Horst Rüdiger and Willi Hirdt, *Studien über Petrarca, Boccaccio und Ariost in der*

deutschen Literatur (Heidelberg: Carl Winter-Universitatsverlag, 1976), pp. 56–84.

Noting that Ariosto enjoyed the greatest critical fortune in Germany during the seventeenth century and then during the romantic period, observes that to date there has been relatively slight interest in Ariosto among modern German critics and only three studies of significance in the last four decades, including those of Herbert Frenzel and Dieter Kremers. Provides summary view of Ariosto's reception by, among others, Lessing, Goethe, and Schlegel, concluding that Ariosto's work contributed to German literature by making the romance tradition better known in a classically oriented culture and by helping liberate German art from a moralizing narrowness.

716. ———. "Humor und Ironie in Ariosts *Orlando Furioso.*" *Schweizer Monatshefte* 54, no. 12 (1975): 914–29.

Biographical and literary sources of Ariosto's ironic humor, with discussion of its various manifestations in episodes and narrative techniques in the *OF*.

717. ———. "Eine Episode aus dem *Orlando Furioso*: Rinaldos Rede für Ginevra und ihr moralischer Gehalt." *Italienische Studien* (Vienna) 3 (1980): 35–44.

Consideration of the Ginevra episode (*OF* 4–5), noting that the essentially medieval context of the narrative has a modern perspective. Discusses the parallels between this episode and Boccaccio's tale of Madonna Filippa (*Decameron* 6.7); observes that both Ariosto and Boccaccio condemn unjust laws against women but that Ariosto's view is informed by a humanistic perspective that defends the individual's instinctual nature and the equality of both sexes before laws on morality. Argues the importance of Rinaldo's defense of women in this context, stating that it provides an entirely new view on the rights of women.

718. RUGGIERI, RUGGERO M. "I 'nomi parlanti' nel *Morgante*, nell'*Innamorato* e nel *Furioso.*" In his *Saggi di linguistica italiana e italo romanza.* Biblioteca dell'*Archivum Romanicum*: Linguistica 29, pp. 169–81. Florence: Leo S. Olschki, 1962.

Considers the function of proper names in the three epic romances under consideration (e.g., as a label revealing a dominant characteristic of an individual), notes the frequency of allegorical names in the *OF*, and characterizes the proper names preferred by the three writers: Pulci, "estroso e 'vocabulistico'" (p. 176), is partial to bizarre names; Boiardo's names underscore the *OI*'s romance heritage; and Ariosto's names are those of a humanist, of largely classical derivation and, in the richness of toponymy, for example, reveal the poet's vast culture and interests.

◄§ 719. RUIZ DE ELVIRA, ANTONIO. "Céfalo y Procris: elegía y épica." *Cuadernos de filología clásica* 2 (1971): 97–123.
Discusses Ariosto's adaptation of the Cephalus and Procris motif (*OF* 43), citing Ovid and Gaius Iulius Hyginus as the principal sources. Considers Cervantes's use in the *DQ* of Ariosto as a source for his incorporation of the classical motif.

◄§ 720. RUIZ DIAZ, ADOLFO. "'Ariosto y los Arabes.'" In *Actas de la Semana de Cultura Italiana* (25–30 setiembre de 1972), pp. 99–108. Mendoza, Argentina: Universidad Nacional de Cuyo, 1973.
Discussion on how to read Jorge Luis Borges's poem "Ariosto y los Arabes." States that the poem reveals a conception of the *OF* as the representation, in its structure and motifs, of a specific moment in European history.

◄§ 721. RUPPRECHT, CAROL SCHREIER. "The Martial Maid: Androgyny in Epic from Virgil to the Poets of the Italian Renaissance." *DAI* 38, no. 7 (1978): 4148A. (Yale University, 1977. 263p.)
Notes the relatively slight attention given to the martial maid in epic poetry from Virgil to Tasso and argues for the importance of the figure as a "force of androgyny—a human condition in which each person is free to move among characteristics, attitudes, and functions which have previously been ascribed on the basis of sexual identity." In the Renaissance epic, "She comes to embody a balance of all opposites where the poise at the center is maintained as a dynamic process and not as a fixed state, a balance recognized in Renaissance literature as a form of perfection."

◄§ 722. RUSSO, LUIGI. *L'Orlando furioso*. Pisa: Libreria Goliardica, 1956–1957. 355p.
Dispense. General introduction to the *OF*, analysis of major episodes and summary discussion of language, sources, and Ariosto's use of allegory.

◄§ 723. ———. "Ariosto minore e maggiore." In his *Ritratti e disegni storici*, 2d ser., 2 (*Dall'Ariosto al Parini*): 1–25. Florence: Sansoni, 1961. Also in *Belfagor* 13, no. 6 (1958): 629–46.
Considers the autobiographical dimension of the satires, concluding that "non bisogna considerare le satire come un documento veritiero della vita dell'Ariosto, ma come un'immagine che alquanto fantasticamente il poeta creava a se stesso" (p. 6). Notes the importance of Ariosto's moral perspective in the satires, as well as in the *OF*, suggesting a reading of the many fables in Ariosto's writings as humanistic *exempla*. Observations on Croce's ill-defined Ariostean cosmic harmony, suggesting that it consists of "quella continua volubilità e unità del ritmo delle ottave ariostesche: fughe, selve profonde, trascorrere di cavalieri, mutamento improvviso di scene, l'impennarsi

per il cielo dell'ippogrifo, [che] al lettore si rivelano come un'armonia celeste trasferita su questa terra" (p. 23).

724. RYDING, WILLIAM W. *Structure in Medieval Narrative*. The Hague and Paris: Mouton, 1971. 177p.
Passim discussion of Tasso's views on the OF in the context of the development of Aristotelian narrative structure in the late sixteenth century. See especially pp. 9–18.

725. SACCONE, EDUARDO. "Note ariostesche." *Annali della Scuola Normale Superiore di Pisa* 28, fasc. 1–4 (1959): 193–242.
Two-part essay: First, discussion of the "stratifications" of the OF, i.e., the nature of the additions to the third edition and of the perspective and style of the CC. Characterizes the world of the 1516 edition (pp. 198–99) and notes that political crises during the 1520s are reflected in the revisions incorporated in the last edition and in the CC. Identifies, for example, in the CC an allegory of the Italian political situation (p. 200) and, in the narrative, a recognition of the omnipresence of evil and the disappearance of illusions. In the narrative additions to the last edition, notes the intrusion of tragedy, resulting from a view of life in which individuals are confronted with moral and physical limitations; sees this perspective revealed in the frequent use of parataxis and the new interest in the psychological. Suggests foreshadowings of the baroque in the relatively frequent use of conceits and the poet's obvious sense of inquietude. Second part on metrics and style in OF^1 and the revisions. Notes importance of considering OF^1 in the context of the Renaissance concept of grace and artistic decorum. Extensive discussion characterizing the Ariostean *ottava*, noting the elements of its internal rhythm and its structural relationship to the poet's representation of the interrelationship of all phenomena and of the perpetual movement of life's forces. Observations on linguistic changes in OF^3 and, in general, the importance of Ariosto's use of the relative clause, which functions to maintain a balance between parataxis and hypotaxis. Concludes with a refutation of Antonio Piromalli's interpretation of change from OF^1 to OF^3 (*Motivi e forme della poesia di Ludovico Ariosto*, 1954), arguing that the changes reveal, in fact, a desire for linguistic emendations and that for a change of vision one must refer to the CC.

726. ———. "Appunti per una definizione dei *Cinque canti*." In his *Il "soggetto" del 'Furioso' e altri saggi tra Quattro e Cinquecento*, pp. 119–56. Naples: Liguori, 1974.
Also in *Belfagor* 20 (1965): 381–410.
Concludes that the CC, with its ambiguities and images of a chaotic world of uncontrolled and uncontrollable passions, represents a vision of life that

is the reverse of that in the *OF*: chivalric values have been replaced by per-versions and fraud; moral certainties and the humanistic sense of man's limits by dark, infernal powers and abandonment to the irrational. Suggests that the *CC* represents a crisis in the Renaissance concept of poetry as an ordering force: here it serves to mirror "una visione . . . perplessa della vita interiore" (p. 133).

727. ———. "Cloridano e Medoro, con alcuni argomenti per una let-tura del primo *Furioso.*" In his *Il "soggetto" del 'Furioso' e altri saggi tra Quattro e Cinquecento,* pp. 161–200. Naples: Liguori, 1974.
Also in *MLN* 83, no. 1 (1968): 67–99.
Noting the general inadequacy of critical attention given to the structural system of the *OF*, cites Robert M. Durling's *The Figure of the Poet in Ren-aissance Epic* (entry 288) as one of the most suggestive and valid readings of the poem to date. Argues, however, that Durling's apparent thesis regarding the thematic statement of the poem—man's inconsistency, understood in the broadest sense and incorporating the various manifestations of madness—is a distorted and anachronistic view of the poet's ideology (p. 168). Affirms, instead, the importance to the poem's structure of the potential for good and, therefore, the fundamental nature of reason and rational behavior to the narrative discourse. Discusses two episodes in this context: Rodomonte and Isabella (canto 29) as the exemplification and juxtaposition of madness and faith, i.e., the affirmation of valor through self-sacrifice; Cloridano and Me-doro (cantos 18–19) as emblematic of commitment and human virtue.

728. ———. "Il 'soggetto' del *Furioso.*" In his *Il "soggetto" del 'Furioso' e altri saggi tra Quattro e Cinquecento,* pp. 201–47. Naples: Liguori, 1974.
Discusses the metaphorical nature of the poem's title that, as an oxymo-ron, informs the entire structure of a narrative based on doubling, juxtapo-sition, and irreconcilable contraries, symbolized by the mutant figure of Or-rilo. Analyzes in this context the narrative trajectories of Orlando and Ruggiero, whose significance lies in the analogy of their roles and in their differences; the metaphorical function of the forest and the castle of Atlante, one as emblematic of the possibilities of communication and the other as its contrary, the impossibility of communication; the movement of the poem (called "andirvieni," p. 234) based on constant loss and discovery or acquisi-tion, opening the narrative space to infinite possibilities. Denies the possibil-ity of reading the poem as a perspective on cosmic harmony, but affirms in it the representation of incessant change at a remove from wholeness and unity, which exist only as myths.

729. ———. *Il "soggetto" del 'Furioso' e altri saggi tra Quattro e Cin-quecento.* Naples: Liguori, 1974. 255p.

202 Ludovico Ariosto

Includes: "Appunti per una definizione dei *Cinque canti*" (entry 726); "Cloridano e Medoro, con alcuni argomenti per una lettura del primo *Furioso*" (entry 727); and "Il 'soggetto' del *Furioso*" (entry 728).

⋙ 730. SALINARI, CARLO. "Ludovico Ariosto." In *Sommario di storia della letteratura italiana*, 2:55–77. 3 vols. Rome: Riuniti, 1977.
Also in his *Profilo storico della letteratura italiana*, 2d ed., 3 vols. (Rome: Riuniti, 1962), 2:67–89, and, in a slightly different version, in *Antologia della letteratura italiana* (entry 893).
General discussion of Ariosto and his works. Agrees with Lanfranco Caretti that the poet's so-called sedentary life was actually a mature choice and observes that Ariosto, while attracted to court life, especially for the intellectual activities that it fostered, was at the same time repelled by the corruption it bred. Notes that the poet learned from his age a respect for human sentiments and for the rational efforts that control them. Sees this lesson as the basis for the *OF*, whose ideological platform is identified with the episodes of Atlante's castle and Astolfo's voyage. Argues that both episodes are intended to signify the constant pursuit stimulated by human passions and the impossibility of satisfying human desires—in short, the representation of life in its continuous, dynamic flow. Underscores the poem's open structure and the resultant multiplicity of themes. Notes that the interlacing of the varied themes allows the poet to balance his narrative by alternating the dramatic with the idyllic, the pathetic with the fantastic. Considers this dialectical form of narration as defining the poem's true unity. Concludes by briefly mentioning the minor works.

⋙ 731. SALINARI, GIAMBATTISTA. "Preistoria di Ludovico Ariosto." In his *Dante e altri saggi*, edited by Achille Tartaro, pp. 179–84. Rome: Riuniti, 1975.
Previously published with title "Preistoria della formazione letteraria di Ludovico Ariosto," *Rassegna di cultura e vita scolastica* (Rome) 24, nos. 7–8 (1970): 3–4, and reprinted in the series *Bibliotechina della "Rassegna di cultura e vita scolastica,"* no. 67 (1971).
States that the Latin period (during which Ariosto composed Latin lyrics still extant) was preceded by another, the period of his university years, when he most likely experimented with both Latin and vernacular verse forms. Speculates on Ariosto's early life as a student, citing passages from his comedies that perhaps reflect aspects of his own experiences as a student.

⋙ 732. SAMMUT, ALFONSO. *La fortuna dell'Ariosto nell'Inghilterra elisabettiana*. Milan: Vita e Pensiero (Pubblicazioni dell'Università Cattolica del Sacro Cuore), 1971. 146p.
The influence of Ariosto on Elizabethan and Jacobean literature, 1566–

1625. Considers the reasons for Ariosto's popularity, concluding that it was primarily due to the "aspetto dilettevole ed al presunto contenuto etico" of the *OF* (p. 21). Discusses Ariosto's influence on English Renaissance poetry, with particular attention given to Edmund Spenser (pp. 45–77). Concludes that the spiritual and aesthetic affinity between the *OF* and the *FQ* is greater than most comparative studies have indicated. Examines Elizabethan translations of Ariosto's poetry, concluding with chapters on Ariosto's influence on theater (especially Shakespeare) and on the narrative. Includes selected bibliography (pp. 3–8), not extending beyond 1960.

📚 733. SANGUINETI, EDOARDO. "Ariosto nostro contemporaneo." *Terzo-programma*, nos. 2–3 (1974): 68–76.

Notes the unique metaphorical nature of the structure of the *OF*, referential to all human experience and paradigmatic—a "modello ideologico" (p. 72)—of the variety of all human motivation. Discusses Ariosto's system of oppositions in relation to Italo Calvino's *Il Castello dei destini incrociati* and notes Galilei's perception of the poem's significance as a vision of the human condition.

📚 734. ———. "La Macchina narrativa dell'Ariosto." In *Orlando Furioso*, by Ludovico Ariosto. 4th ed. 1:li–lvii. 2 vols. Milan: Garzanti, 1980.

Argues for the importance of the structure of the *OF* as archetypal to modern romance form and reflected both in the structuralist theories defined by Roland Barthes and in the images of human destiny represented, for one, in the complexities of Italo Calvino's *Il Castello dei destini incrociati*. Discusses the significance of the *OI* to the structure of the poem, whose ironic perspective, for example, results primarily from a movement away from the poem of chivalric ideals toward the adventure novel. Notes the particular importance of the *Decameron* to the structure of the *OF*, in which the chivalric poem serves as a frame for an adventure romance and in which the complexity of human destinies foreshadows the modern European novel.

📚 735. SANSONE, MARIO. "Francesco De Sanctis dal Tasso all'Ariosto." In *Scritti in onore di Cleto Carbonara*, pp. 794–805. Naples: Giannini, 1976.

Traces the development of De Sanctis's study of the Italian Renaissance from his early devotion to Tasso and the *GL* to a growing sensitivity and appreciation for Ariosto, principally through his reading of Galilei's commentaries: Galilei "rappresenta l'anello di congiunzione, il momento di passaggio tra la formazione critica dei primi anni e la concreta analisi della poesia epica" (p. 801).

⋘§ 736. SANTANGELO, GIORGIO. *Il Petrarchismo del Bembo e di altri poeti del '500.* Rome-Palermo: IECE, 1967.
Brief observations on the nature of Petrarchan influence and imitation in the Italian lyrics of Ariosto. Notes that Petrarchan spiritual tension, or *dissidio*, is only sporadic in Ariosto's verse and that the traditional motif of the evanescent nature of beauty and human accomplishments appears only in Ariosto's two *canzoni* on the death of Giuliano de' Medici (p. 199). Suggests that Ariosto's best poetry is of realistic or sensual inspiration, noting that it is often expressed with Petrarchan language and imagery. Affirms that "rifluisce nell'arte ariostesca non già quel che sarà il Petrarca dei romantici, vale a dire il poeta dell'insanabile dissidio fra lo spirito e la carne, fra il cielo e la terra, ma quell'altro Petrarca . . . che quel dissidio aveva saputo risolvere nello *stile* armonioso in cui si componevano le disarmonie della sua contradditoria umanità" (p. 198). Cites in support of his interpretation the critical writings of Cesare Segre and Walter Binni, noting that he does not accept Luigi Baldacci's view that the lyrics reveal more the presence of Horace than of Petrarch (see entry 42). Includes text of selected poems. See pages 197–217.

⋘§ 737. SANTARELLI, GIUSEPPE. "Contributo allo studio del teatro sacro del Seicento: un dramma sconosciuto di P. Girolamo da Mondolfo." *Studi secenteschi* 12 (1971): 207–51. Biblioteca dell'*Archivum Romanicum*, 1st ser., vol. 115.
Notes borrowings from the OF in Girolamo da Mondolfo's sacred drama *La Santa Casa visitata* (mid-seventeenth century; date uncertain): the dream of Eustachio (4.6) was inspired by OF 23.102 ff., and the description of the rose in 2.2 is probably based on the description in OF 1.42–43.

⋘§ 738. SANTINI, EMILIO. "Cavalli savi e cavalli volanti nell'*Orlando Furioso*." *Letterature moderne* 6, 1 (1956): 41–54.
Notes the importance of horses to Renaissance culture and the number of writings on horses available to Ariosto. Discusses the major horses in the OF, concluding that the "reasoning horses" ("cavalli savi") and flying horses aided the poet in reproducing "il sorridente spettacolo dei labili avvenimenti umani" (p. 54).

⋘§ 739. SANTO, LUIGI. "Una *crux* ariostea." *Quaderni dell'Istituto di Filologia Latina* (Padua), no. 4 (1976): 133–56.
Paleographic analysis of *carme* 12 and the Latin ode "Ad Philiroen," to illustrate the editorial inaccuracies of the *editio princeps* of the Latin verses (edited by G. B. Nicolucci [il Pigna], 1553) and of the most recent critical edition of Ezio Bolaffi (Rome, 1934).

740. SANTORO, MARIO. "L'Astolfo ariostesco: *homo fortunatus.*" In his *Letture ariostesche*, pp. 137–214. Naples: Liguori, 1973.

Revision of article by same title in *Filologia e letteratura* 9, fasc. 3, no. 35 (1963): 236–87.

Considers the complementary topoi of *fortuna* and *prudentia* in humanistic writings, especially in Giovanni Pontano's *De prudentia*. Notes in particular Pontano's discussion of the *homo fortunatus*, successful in spite of impulsive behavior and irrational desires, belonging to a category of inferior humanity and at the opposite pole from the prudent individual in possession of humanistic *virtù*. Argues that Ariosto uses Astolfo to represent the *homo fortunatus* and traces the evolution of the character from one traditionally possessed of courage and prowess in the French chivalric tradition to an essentially comic figure or a weak womanizer in the Italian romance (Pulci, Boiardo, and in Cieco da Ferrara's *Il Mambriano*), appearing in the OF as an individual alien to prudent action and representing the *homo fortunatus* in a humorous key, a player in the poet's human comedy and, though unguided by reason, charged with the providential mission of retrieving Orlando's sanity.

741. ———. "'Ecco il giudicio uman come spesso erra . . .'." In his *Letture ariostesche*, pp. 53–80. Naples: Liguori, 1973.

Examines Ariosto's multiple perspectives on human judgment. Notes its relativity and the semantic code through which it becomes a recurrent motif in the OF (the frequency of the verbs *parere*, *credere*, and the substantive, *errore*). Cites the difference between being (*essere*) and seeming (*parere*), and the attendant motif of hypocrisy. Points out the *divario* or dichotomy between intentions and results, stemming from erroneous judgment. Briefly discusses the emblematic nature of Atlante's palace with regard to Ariosto's vision of the fallibility of human judgment; considers Ariosto's vision in the context of sixteenth-century skepticism on the powers of human reason in controlling the forces of reality.

742. ———. *Letture ariostesche*. Naples: Liguori, 1973. 214p.

Contains "Il *proemio*" (entry 743); "'Ecco il giudicio uman come spesso erra . . .'" (entry 741); "'Rinaldo ebbe il consenso universale . . .' (*Fur.*, IV, 51–67)" (entry 744); "L'Astolfo ariostesco: *homo fortunatus*" (entry 740).

743. ———. "Il *proemio*." In his *Letture ariostesche*, pp. 9–49. Naples: Liguori, 1973.

Analysis of the *proemio*, or first four octaves of the OF, noting in their symmetry a paradigm for the poem as a whole. Considers the significance of Ariosto's introduction of the war theme, preannouncing a vision of world chaos, and the emblematic nature of Agramante, whose *ira* and *furore* foreshadow the irrational nature of human behavior portrayed in the poem. Notes that Ariosto established in the *proemio* the important relationship between narrator and protagonist and that the second half of each of the introductory octaves preannounces the ambiguity and polysemous structure of the poem.

≈§ 744. ———. "'Rinaldo ebbe il consenso universale . . .' (*Fur.*, IV, 51–67)." In his *Letture ariostesche*, pp. 83–133. Naples: Liguori, 1973.

Extensive discussion of the importance to the *OF* of the defense of women, particularly in the context of the evolution of commentaries on women and their social roles from the Middle Ages to the sixteenth century. Considers the establishment of the theme during the course of Rinaldo's discussion with the monks in *OF* 4, anticipating the Ginevra episode, and notes the particular importance of Rinaldo to the theme, both in his discourse on women's rights and in his show of prudence in *OF* 43, when, in refusing to test his wife's fidelity, he underscores the fallibility of all human nature, women's as well as men's. Discusses Ariosto's source for the onset of Rinaldo's voyage in *OF* 4, noting how the poet uses the Tristan legend, sets the scene in the locus of romance tradition and then demythifies the hero, Rinaldo, whose concerns remain entirely pragmatic and who reflects carefully before any undertaking, unlike the archetypal romance hero and his own cousin, Orlando.

≈§ 745. ———. "Il 'nuovo corso' della critica ariostesca." *Cultura e scuola* 13, no. 52 (1974): 20–31.

Reviews the critical literature in Italian on Ariosto from 1960, noting that the tendency is toward a "recupero di una più concreta e articolata misura della personalità del poeta e ad una lettura più rigorosa e puntuale della sua opera" (p. 20). Observes that criticism of the period in question results from new critical methods and from new perspectives on the Renaissance, especially on the early Cinquecento. Discusses the interest, in post-Crocean criticism, in the sociohistorical context of Ariosto's writings and, in the 1960s in particular, the important new interest in Ariosto's sources, in his cultural preparation, and in the structure of the *OF*. Considers important research areas to be explored.

≈§ 746. ———. "La Sequenza lunare nel *Furioso*: una società allo specchio." *Atti della Accademia Pontaniana* 23 (1974): 327–50. Naples: Giannini, 1975.

Analyzes the thematic structure of Astolfo's voyage to the moon in search of Orlando's sanity (*OF* 34.70–92; 35.1–30), an episode seen as "una versione laica e rinascimentale dello schema medievale dell'itinerario dell'uomo dalla condizione di miseria terrena alla morte, all'eternità. Lo schema ariostesco si iscrive interamente nell'ambito dell'esperienza terrena: non a caso alla fine, al posto dell'eternità, assicurata dalla vita soprannaturale, troviamo l'immortalità, la sopravvivenza nella società umana, assicurata da un'attività umana, la poesia" (p. 328). Notes that the episode can be seen from a double perspective: as reflective of the human condition and the vagaries of life (fallibility of human judgment, p. 339; universality of "madness," p. 342) and as a commentary, ironic and satirical, on court society. Discusses the influences upon this episode of Leon Battista Alberti's *Somnium* and of Erasmus's *Praise of Folly*.

747. ———. "Polivalenza semantica e 'funzione' dell'apologo della zucca nella satira VII dell'Ariosto." In *Scritti in onore di Cleto Carbonara*, pp. 818–31. Naples: Giannini, 1976.

Noting that the satires are structured on two principal perspectives—meditation on human folly and on vain desires and the condemnation of vice—analyzes Satire 7 on the basis of two fundamental and complementary parts: the examination and demythologizing of illusory promises and the desire of the poet to return to Ferrara. Focuses on the apologue of the gourd (*zucca*) and the pear, the source of which is Leon Battista Alberti's dialogue "Hedera," in the *Intercenali*, and particularly on Pier Crinito's "Disputatio de republica habita, ac de imperio Venetum, et apologus elegans de pinu et cucurbita" in his *De honesta disciplina* (Rome, 1955, 2:14, 98–99) (p. 826). States that the function of the apologue differs from Crinito's: Ariosto's, "assuntò come codice emblematico del 'rapido successo', decodificabile in modi diversi, secondo la diversa ottica degli interessati, o secondo la distanza del tempo, . . . si prospetta come misura della relatività e della fallacia delle opinioni e delle illusioni umane, e nel tempo stesso, come verifica di una segreta illuminante conquista morale" (p. 827). Concludes that the poet identifies with both the gourd and the pear and projects in them two different moments of his own personal experiences: "quello [moment] della 'sciocca speme' . . . e quello, più distaccato e maturo, del sicuro e stabile possesso della propria libertà interiore, della propria vita sentimentale, dei beni inalienabili della coscienza morale. La polisemia dell'apologo, nel contesto della satira, raccoglie e raffigura emblematicamente, sul registro dell'antitesi (che costituisce la struttura interna della satira) tra provvisorietà e certezza, tra varietà e stabilità, tra 'sciocca speme' e coscienza, i motivi essenziali del componimento: dal riconoscimento . . . delle vane speranze, alla cognizione della labilità e della provvisorietà dei beni acquistati col favore della 'fortuna', alla lucida e autoironica accettazione del proprio destino, all'idoleggiamento della serena libertà" (p. 831).

748. ———. "La Prova del 'nappo' e la cognizione del reale." *Esperienze letterarie* 1, no. 1 (1976): 5–24.

Extensive analysis of the structure and motifs of Rinaldo's voyage in the closing cantos of the *OF* (42. 28–43. 150), a sequence of narrative moments that "si configura come una storia esemplare dell'errore delle passioni e del riscatto della 'ragione'" (p. 5). Argues that Rinaldo, though essentially symbolic of prudence and of "un controllo razionale nei confronti della fluida e sfuggente realtà" (p. 24), is subject to the weaknesses of human nature and that only after the loss of rational control and its reattainment can he participate in the testing of the *nappo*, or cup: "una esemplare lezione di tolleranza, di moderazione, di misura, a specchio della cognizione della condizione umana" (p. 24).

⌘§ 749. ———. "L'Angelica del *Furioso*: fuga dalla storia." *Esperienze letterarie* 3, no. 3 (1978): 3–28.

Contrasts the function of Angelica in the narrative structure of the *OI* (the animating source of a series of adventures) to her role in the *OF*, in which she becomes the object of desire ("donna-oggetto," p. 7) to be conquered. Views her role in the *OF* as the narrator's intent "non solo a sperimentare la condizione della donna veduta dall'esterno con un'ottica 'maschilista' . . . ma anche . . . a saggiare nel suo comportamento una crescente ribellione al codice convenzionale della donna-oggetto" (p. 10). Angelica's flight is from male oppression and is a metaphorical representation of a rejection of a reality "segnata dalla violenza e dalla 'pazzia'" (p. 10). It is a conscious estrangement from a world in which she has no independence or control, an estrangement from history. Considers the complementary theme of Angelica's return to her country of origin and, metaphorically, to a utopian world of innocence. Notes the irony arising from the dual perspective of the paladins in pursuit, projections of a conventional moral code, and of Angelica, whose behavior is one of protest against convention and an integral part of the theme of the defense of women. Notes that in her marriage to Medoro, Angelica-woman becomes protagonist rather than object and assumes a nonconformist position in a world controlled by the aristocratic code of courtly values: "Con la scelta di Medoro, Angelica non tradisce irrazionalmente il codice etico, ma contrappone un altro codice, in cui si privilegiano le qualità individuali, a quello convenzionale, in cui si accampavano dominanti il potere, la nobiltà, le ricchezze, le virtù guerriere" (p. 23). The idyllic motif associated with Angelica and Medoro is a metaphorical return to an Edenic world (p. 28).

⌘§ 750. SAPEGNO, N[ATALINO]. "Ariosto, Ludovico." In *Dizionario biografico degli italiani*, 4:172–88. 1962. Rome: Istituto dell'Enciclopedia Italiana, 1960–.

Fundamental introduction to Ariosto's life and work. Considers the several critical evaluations of Ariosto's temperament, concluding that his true personality—his wisdom, his morality, and his judiciousness—is reflected in his work. Brief discussion of the minor works and of the development, structure, and thematics of the *OF*: "Nella forma come nella sostanza dell'ispirazione, il poema dell'Ariosto è l'espressione più completa degli spiriti, della moralità, delle tendenze artistiche del primo Cinquecento" (p. 185). Includes bibliography, pp. 187–88.

✍ 751. ———. Introduzione. *Orlando furioso. Scelta e commentato da Natalino Sapegno*, pp. v–xi. 2d ed. Milan: G. Principato, 1972.
First edition 1941; second edition first published 1943; Fatini, 3338.

✍ 752. ———. "Ariosto poeta." In *Ludovico Ariosto*, pp. 23–31. Convegno internazionale (entry 475). Rome: Accademia Nazionale dei Lincei, 1975.
Beginning with a consideration of the characteristic ways in which Ariosto has been read by critics from Montaigne and Galilei to Benedetto Croce, traces the major areas of concern in modern critical inquiry, noting the major problems in a study of Ariosto and the areas that require more extensive investigation, including a reconstruction of the cultural environment that inspired the *OF* and a closer study of the minor works in relation to the *OF*. Comments on certain aspects of the writer that have been the subject of recent study: the ideology of Ariosto; the structure and thematics of the *OF*; and the lack of a predominant sentiment but a constant alternation of emotions and human feelings (pp. 27–28). Concludes with a recommendation for further study, including a closer examination, first, of the *OF* as poetry that constantly juxtaposes literary ideal and stark reality and, second, of the unique way in which tradition and myth are used as paradigms of human behavior and not, as in Poliziano and Sannazaro, as means of ennobling a grim reality.

✍ 753. SAVARESE, GENNARO. "Le *Considerazioni al Tasso* del Galilei nell'opera di F. De Sanctis." *La Rassegna della letteratura italiana*, 7th ser., vol. 69, no. 1 (1965): 92–111.
Compares and discusses passages from Galilei's *Considerazioni al Tasso* and from Francesco De Sanctis's *Storia della letteratura italiana*, emphasizing the nineteenth-century critic's debt to Galilei. Finds that De Sanctis owes his initial appreciation of Galilei's views on Ariosto to Vincenzo Gioberti's *Saggio sul bello* (1845).

✍ 754. ———. "Ariosto al bivio tra Marsilio Ficino e 'adescatrici galliche.'" *Filologia moderna*, pp. 21–39. (Annali dell'Istituto di Filologia Moderna all'Università di Roma.) Rome, 1978.
Notes that the portrait of Ariosto that results from a reading of Celio Cal-

cagnini's *Equitatio* (1506–1507?) has long been misinterpreted and is important for understanding Ariosto's early humanistic and literary formation and
especially the significance to it of Ficino, whose Neoplatonism owes its diffusion in Ferrara in part to Ariosto and whose influence on the *OF* has not
been adequately studied.

📣 755. ———. "Il *Furioso* e le arti visive." *La Rassegna della letteratura
     italiana*, 7th ser., vol. 83, nos. 1–3 (1979): 28–39.
The significance of the visual arts, both painting and architecture, to
Ariosto's aesthetic. Argues that contemporary painting influenced the *OF*
and cites, in particular, the affinity in taste with Titian. Considers reflections
in the *OF* of contemporary interest in Vitruvian architecture, concluding
that "la mimèsi letteraria del fatto artistico-figurativo è stata riassorbita total-
mente . . . nelle leggi generali dell'immaginario ariostesco" (p. 39).

📣 756. SBROCCHI, LEONARD C. See Ariosto, Ludovico, *The Comedies of
     Ariosto*, entry 26.

📣 757. SCAGLIONE, ALDO. "Shahryar, Giocondo, Kote̲rviky: Three Ver-
     sions of the Motif of the Faithless Woman." *Oriens* 11, nos. 1–2 (1958):
     151–61.
Analyzes Arabic, Italian (*OF* 28, the Giocondo story), and Kota versions
of the motif of the faithless woman, noting that they are products of "relatively independent growth" (pp. 155–56) and that each reflects the particular
spirit of the culture in which it developed. Observes that the severity toward
women in the Arabic tale "is changed into the lighthearted, skeptical, and
malicious smile of Ariosto" (p. 158), who is accepting of the ways of the
world.

📣 758. ———. *Nature and Love in the Late Middle Ages*. Berkeley and
     Los Angeles: University of California Press, 1963. 250p.
Notes the importance of the Renaissance "naturalistic spirit" in the *OF*:
"Beneath and beyond the idealistic convention of a chivalric structure, the
forces which move this human world are those of 'real' sentiments and affections" (p. 133). Cites the fate of Angelica as a "definitive refutation of all the
courtly prejudices" and states that Orlando's madness derives from what he
perceives as the absurdity of her love for a humble soldier. Notes that situations are dominated by "unreason and the unexpected" (p. 133): "Ariosto
may well be the poet of Cosmos and Harmony, provided we do not lose sight
of the fact that the matter of his harmonious representation is the Chaos of
the Irrational of which true life is made" (p. 134). Passim discussion. See
especially pp. 133–34.

✥ 759. ——. "Cinquecento Mannerism and the Uses of Petrarch." In *Medieval and Renaissance Studies* 5 (1971): 122–55.

Suggests aspects of the *OF* that may be related to mannerism, in particular the representation of a cosmic harmony consisting of moral and social chaos. Argues for the importance of Rodomonte and his story ("the most intriguing, the most puzzling, the most 'human' in the poem," p. 125) in conveying this perspective on the *OF*.

✥ 760. SCAGLIONE, ALDO, ed. *Ariosto 1974 in America*. Atti del Congresso Ariostesco. Dicembre 1974, Casa Italiana della Columbia University. Ravenna: Longo, 1976. 189p.

Contents: Giorgio Padoan, "L'*Orlando Furioso* e la crisi del Rinascimento" (entry 588); A. Bartlett Giamatti, "*Sfrenatura*: Restraint and Release in the *Orlando Furioso*" (entry 360); Cesare Segre, "Struttura dialogica delle *Satire* ariostesche" (entry 791); Peter DeSa Wiggins, "A Defense of the *Satires*" (entry 908); Charles D. Klopp, "The Centaur and the Magpie: Ariosto and Machiavelli's *Prince*" (entry 442); Daniel Javitch, "Rescuing Ovid from the Allegorizers: The Liberation of Angelica, *Furioso* X" (entry 429); R. W. Hanning, "Ariosto, Ovid, and the Painters: Mythological Paragone in *Orlando Furioso* X and XI" (entry 404); Barbara Reynolds, "Ariosto in English: Prose or Verse?" (entry 684); Joseph Gibaldi, "The Fortunes of Ariosto in England and America" (entry 363); Joseph Gibaldi, "Bibliography of Ariosto in England and America" (entry 362); Enzo Esposito, "Situazione editoriale delle opere ariostesche" (entry 294).

✥ 761. SCALIA, GIANNI. "Lettere da lontano di Ludovico Ariosto." In *Lettere dalla Garfagnana*, by Ludovico Ariosto, edited by Gianni Scalia, pp. 7–27. Bologna: Cappelli, 1977.

Detailed factual account of Ariosto's tenure as governor in the Garfagnana, quoting extensively the text of his letters by way of documentation. Concludes that Ariosto's letter to Obizio Remo, secretary to the Duke of Ferrara (2 October 1522) reveals his true nature: Ariosto states that he is not a "homo da governare altri homini" and that he desires to return to the comfort and leisure of Ferrara to write poetry.

✥ 762. SCANLON, PAUL A. "Whetstone's 'Rinaldo and Giletta': The First Elizabethan Prose Romance." *Cahiers Elisabéthains* 14 (1978): 3–8.

Argues that the second section of George Whetstone's "Discourse of Rinaldo and Giletta" (in *The Rocke of Regard*, 1576) is based on the episode of Ginevra and Ariodante (*OF* 5–6). Notes that Whetstone has simplified Ariosto's tale, given greater prominence to the couple by reducing other roles, and shifted the emphasis from the deception motif to the lovers' plight.

763. SCHAB, FREDERICK G., ed. *Catalogue of Books, Manuscripts, and Drawings Exhibited to Commemorate the 500th Anniversary of the Birth of Ludovico Ariosto (1474–1533)*. In the Rotunda of the Low Memorial Library, Columbia University. 9 December 1974–29 January 1975. Rare Books and Drawings Lent by American libraries and private collectors. New York: N.p., 1974. 31p.

Brief introductory note (pp. 1–8) observes that Ariosto was the first poet to achieve world fame during his lifetime through the printed book. Gives an account of the important collections of Ariosto materials in American libraries, particularly the holdings of the Houghton Library at Harvard University ("As the Ariosto collection stands now, only two or three editions of some significance [1521–1524], all known in only two or three copies, are wanting from the Harvard collection," p. 5) and the Plimpton Collection at Wellesley College, Massachusetts. Catalog contains forty-six descriptive entries of items exhibited, including an autograph document (lent by the University of North Carolina, Chapel Hill), first and early editions of Ariosto's works, and wash and crayon drawings of Jean-Honoré de Fragonard.

764. SCHUNCK, PETER. "Die Stellung Ariosts in der Tradition der klassischen Satire." *Zeitschrift für Romanische Philologie* 86 (1970): 49–82.

General discussion of the style and tone of the satires. Comparison with classical satires of Juvenal and Horace, especially in the use of the moral and the fable. On subjects treated in the satires. Concludes with a comparison of Ariosto's satires and those of Antonio Cammelli and Antonio Vinciguerra.

765. SCIROCCO, GIOVANNI. "I Saggi su Dante e sull'Ariosto." In his *Croce, la vita l'itinerario il pensiero*, pp. 203–16. Milan: Edizioni Accademia, 1973.

On the theoretical basis of Croce's aesthetics of "harmony" in his critique of the *OF*.

766. SCOGLIO, EGIDIO. *Il Teatro alla Corte Estense*. Lodi: Biancardi, 1965. 135p.

Brief history of court theater, 1486–1597, under the Este family; summary description of dramatic genres developed during the period and a chronology of productions in Ferrara with occasional commentary and incomplete documentation. Appendix with texts of selected relevant documents and an index of sources without complete bibliographical information.

767. SCORRANO, LUIGI. "Dante, Ariosto e il gioco della zara." *L'Alighieri* 13, no. 2 (1972): 62–67.

Comparative analysis of the gambling simile in Dante (*Purgatory* 6.1–9) and in Ariosto's *I Suppositi*. Concludes that "mentre per Ariosto il gioco della zara non costituisce che un'elegante variazione sul tema della fortuna attratto entro la dimensione della quotidianità, in Dante esso riflette l'inquieta situazione del poeta, la cui posta in gioco non è amore o denaro, ma carne e sangue e anima, un ideale per il quale si è combattuto e che si vede tramontare ineluttabilmente e per sempre" (p. 67).

🖎 768. ———. "La *gran confidenzia* di mastro Iachelino e altre osservazioni sul *Negromante*." In *Annali* 1 (1970–1971): 37–71 (Facoltà di Magistero, Lecce). Bari: Adriatica, 1972.
Analysis of the titular character of *Il Negromante*, said to possess "gran confidenzia" (2.1). Argues that Iachelino's self-confidence is the basis for his success in manipulating a world populated by individuals bent on chasing the illusory and too involved in their own selfish pursuits to use their wits and escape the web of the necromancer's plots. To determine the outcome of events, Iachelino appeals to the vanity of others and possesses the ability to urge them on to undertakings they would otherwise eschew. Notes the richness of animal imagery in the play, arguing that it is part of a language emblematic of the subhuman and degraded world represented. Iachelino's morality is subsumed under Temolo's epithet, "una volpaccia vecchia" (1.3); and the necromancer refers to others in terms of animals, underscoring their inferior intelligence. Considers in the context of Iachelino's manipulative ways the significance of magic in the play: it serves as an instrument of deceit, whereas in the *OF*, it is used to underscore the fantastic and the illusory.

🖎 769. ———. "La *Commedia* dantesca nelle commedie dell'Ariosto." *L'Alighieri* 14, no. 2 (1973): 53–65.
Notes a variety of linguistic borrowings from the *DC* in Ariosto's comedies, with a discussion of their adaptation. Hypothesizes several borrowings of Dantesque characters, images, and similes (pp. 64–65, note 21).

🖎 770. ———. "Lettura della *Lena*." *Annali* 2 (1972–1973): 331–74 (Facoltà di Magistero, Lecce). Bari: Adriatica, 1973.
Extensive analysis, thematic and linguistic, of *La Lena* on the premise that the comedy represents "l'affermarsi della categoria dell'utile come sentimento predominante e dell'amaritudine come segreto rovello che s'insinua in quel mondo a turbarne, sia pure momentaneamente, certezza o indifferenza" (p. 333). All characters are motivated by the *utile*, their drive for personal gain; the titular character alone views herself as superior to the corrupt world in which she moves because she is not subject to illusions. Notes as a constant in this world of vice and evil the feeling of bitterness and, as a leitmotif of the play, the statement, "Vorrebbe il dolce senza amar": "A Lena tutto è costato e costa amaritudine. . . . Quel che importa è non rimaner delusa di se stessa" (p. 337). Detailed consideration of the themes of *utile*

and money. Discussion of the originality and importance to the evolution of comic dramaturgy of the trio Lena-Pacifico-Fazio, noting in particular their antagonistic relationships and the originality of their character types, with special consideration given to the creation of Corbolo. Extensive discussion of language: how it is used for realistic effect; importance of verb proliferation and the play's focus on particular verbs; and the use of anadiplosis. Concluding discussion of temporal references: "tutta la commedia sembra colorarsi della luce alacre e allegra e operosa della mattina, e l'incontrarsi e incrociarsi di personaggi e vicende è colto anche nella dimensione più giusta. Il tempo che, però, veramente conta è l'altro: quello entro il quale la vita degli uomini è approdata da certe soluzioni e si è come pietrificata. Questa luce mattinale si riflette su quel tempo e ne discopre l'immobilità, la fissa dannazione quotidiana" (pp. 373–74).

◄§ 771. SCOTT, JOHN A. "De Sanctis, Ariosto and *La Poesia Cavalleresca.*" *Italica* 45, no. 4 (1968): 428–61.
Compares De Sanctis's evaluation of Ariosto in his *Storia della letteratura italiana* (1870–1871) and in his earlier Zurich lectures (1858–1859), concluding that the critic's judgment on the *OF* in the latter "is more detailed, better balanced, and generally more positive than that expressed in the *Storia della letteratura italiana,* where the poem is forced into the general scheme of the political and moral decadence of the Italian Renaissance, its indifference towards content in art and preoccupation with form. Indicative of the two works is the fact that in the Zürich lectures Ariosto and Machiavelli are coupled together and praised as the two great exceptions who resisted the flood of rhetoric that tended to submerge the literature of the Renaissance, whereas in the *Storia* they are opposed to the detriment of the creator of the *Orlando Furioso*" (pp. 454–55).

◄§ 772. SCOTT-GILES, C. W. "Ariosto's Heraldry." *The Coat of Arms,* n.s. 1, no. 95 (1975): 203–7.
Discusses the extent of Ariosto's familiarity with English, Scottish, and Irish heraldry, noting that he is at times historically correct in his descriptions but that for the most part, "He drew on his own imagination, sometimes giving a noble an ensign that played on the Italian form of his title, and sometimes choosing one for the sake of a rhyme" (p. 204). Analyzes and comments on the historic accuracy of each of the ensigns in the heraldic octaves of *OF* 10.

◄§ 773. SCRIVANO, RICCARDO. "Croce e il Cinquecento: note sui concetti di storia e di letteratura nella critica crociana intorno al Cinquecento italiano." *La Rassegna della letteratura italiana,* 7th ser., vol. 71, nos. 1–2 (1967): 58–79.

In an attempt to establish whether Croce's interest in the Cinquecento was spurred by critical or theoretical considerations, notes that the critic's view of Ariosto proceeds from both critical and theoretical formulations (pp. 59–60).

⋙ 774. SCRIVANO, RICCARDO. "Ludovico Ariosto." See Binni, Walter, entry 102.

⋙ 775. SEGRE, CESARE. "Appunti sulle fonti dei *Cinque Canti*." In his *Esperienze ariostesche*, pp. 97–109. Pisa: Nistri-Lischi, 1966.

Revision of article first published in *La Rassegna della letteratura italiana* 58 (1954): 413–20; Fatini, 3564.

States that additions were made to the third edition of the OF when Ariosto realized that attempting to incorporate the CC into the text of the poem would have created contradictions in the narrative and a poetically incompatible tone, the two works having been inspired by different moral climates. Identifies several classical sources in the CC, including Claudian and Pliny, and suggests that Ariosto also used some Greek sources, known through Latin translations. Notes the importance of direct borrowings and translations of sources to a stylistic and philological study of Ariosto's poetry. Concludes by noting the importance of *Morgante* 28 to the battle episodes in the CC and to the change in Ariosto's moral perspectives.

⋙ 776. ———. "La Biblioteca dell'Ariosto." In his *Esperienze ariostesche*, pp. 45–50. Pisa: Nistri-Lischi, 1966.

Revision of article first published in *La Scuola* (Bellinzona) 52 (1955): 29–31; see Fatini, 3595, which cites it as appearing in *Biblioteche di Scrittori* (Lugano: La Scuola, 1955), pp. 25–37.

Declaring it unlikely that Ariosto had a very extensive library but that his reading of both classical and medieval texts was broad, briefly discusses some of the most influential authors in the poet's formation, notably Cicero and Horace for their "equilibrio" (p. 46), Petrarch as a model of lyrical purity, Dante, Boccaccio, and, of particular significance for the OF, the texts of a popular nature and the vernacular epics, including the OI.

⋙ 777. ———. *Esperienze ariostesche.* Pisa: Nistri-Lischi, 1966. 189p.

All essays but the fourth are revisions of articles published earlier, as indicated in individual entries. Contents: "La Poesia dell'Ariosto" (entry 780); "Storia interna dell'*Orlando Furioso*" (entry 782); "La Biblioteca dell'Ariosto" (entry 776); "Un Repertorio linguistico e stilistico dell'Ariosto: la *Commedia*" (entry 781); "Leon Battista Alberti e Ludovico Ariosto" (entry 778); "Appunti sulle fonti dei *Cinque Canti*" (entry 775); "Negromanzia e ingratitudine (Juan Manuel, il *Novellino*, Ludovico Ariosto)" (entry 779); "Studi sui *Cinque Canti*" (entry 783).

◄§ 778. ———. "Leon Battista Alberti e Ludovico Ariosto." In his *Esperienze ariostesche*, pp. 85–95. Pisa: Nistri-Lischi, 1966.
First published with title "Nel mondo della luna ovvero L. B. Alberti e L. Ariosto." In *Rivista di cultura classica e medioevale* 7 (1965): 1025–33 (Studi in onore di A. Schiaffini).
Cites Leon Battista Alberti's *Intercenali*—discovered and published by Eugenio Garin (*Belfagor* 19 [1964]: 377–96)—as the source of two episodes concerning the moon: in Satire 3.208–31, the meditation on fortune in the form of a *favola*, and *OF* 34.72–82, in which a portion of an *intercenale* entitled *Somnium* provides images that Ariosto makes bitterly comic (p. 93). Contends that Alberti was one of the few humanists to have influenced Ariosto and that the relationship merits a systematic study.

◄§ 779. ———. "Negromanzia e ingratitudine (Juan Manuel, il *Novellino*, Ludovico Ariosto)." In his *Esperienze ariostesche*, p. 111–18. Pisa: Nistri-Lischi, 1966.
First published in *Mélanges de linguistique et de philologie médiévale offerts à M. Delbouille* (Gembloux, 1964), 2:653–58.
Brief comparative study of the eleventh *exemplo* of Juan Manuel's *Conde Lucanor*, *novella* 21 of the anonymous *Novellino* and a passage from the *Promptuarium exemplorum*. Concludes with a suggestion that one source for Ariosto's third satire was a story of Lorenzo Abstemio (*Hecatomythium primum* 23, of 1495).

◄§ 780. ———. "La Poesia dell'Ariosto." In his *Esperienze ariostesche*, pp. 9–27. Pisa: Nistri-Lischi, 1966.
First published as "Introduzione all'Ariosto," in *Tutte le opere*, by Ludovico Ariosto, edited by Cesare Segre (Milan: Mondadori, 1964), 1:xv–xxxii, and then revised and published as "Introduzione," in *Orlando Furioso*, by Ludovico Ariosto, edited by Cesare Segre (Milan: Mondadori, 1976, 1979), pp. xv–xxx).
Introduction to a reading of the *OF*, beginning with some fundamental aspects of the minor works that relate to the epic poem, particularly the binomial action-contemplation, which Segre sees as basic to the nature and morality of Ariosto as man and poet and which is often poetically transformed as a juxtaposition of the analytical with the purely fantastic. Briefly discusses major traditions, stylistic elements, and topoi in the *OF*, including the role of irony and the function of the characters, whom he defines as an "atlante della natura umana" or the epitome of the discovery of man in his "libertà e nelle sue determinazioni causali" (p. 19).

◄§ 781. ———. "Un Repertorio linguistico e stilistico dell'Ariosto: la *Commedia*." In his *Esperienze ariostesche*, pp. 51–83. Pisa: Nistri-Lischi, 1966.

Noting the subtlety of Ariosto's use of Dante (cites as only six the episodes or extensive passages in the OF in direct imitation of Dante, as compared to twenty-nine directly taken from Ovid), catalogs and analyzes borrowings from the DC—statistically heavier from the *Inferno*, with a preference for cantos the author calls pre-Ariostean, e.g., those with a fantastic dimension and an allegorical charge (p. 82). Discusses, among other Dantesque elements in Ariosto's works, lexical borrowings and Ariosto's preference for words with a strong semantic concentration; syntagmatic borrowings; and the use of Dante's rhyming technique. Catalogs, with examples, more complex echoes of the DC in the OF, as, for example, landscape description for allegorical connotation. Extensively illustrated with examples.

◆§ 782. ———. "Storia interna dell'*Orlando Furioso*." In his *Esperienze ariostesche*, pp. 29–41. Pisa: Nistri-Lischi, 1966.
Revision of "Le Correzioni dell'Ariosto all'*Orlando Furioso*: lingua, stile, poesia," *Terzoprogramma*, no. 3 (1961): 140–48.
Notes the possibility of tracing the linguistic and structural evolutions of the OF through a comparative study of the first and third editions, especially, and focuses on a number of additions and emendations in the third edition that, though documenting Ariosto's interest in the topicality of the work, reveal a continuing effort toward maintaining a harmonious balance and tonal equilibrium. Notes, too, the linguistic and syntactic refinements in the third edition as evidence of Ariosto's participation in the progression toward a standardized vernacular.

◆§ 783. ———. "Studi sui *Cinque Canti*." In his *Esperienze ariostesche*, pp. 121–77. Pisa: Nistri-Lischi, 1966.
Substantially the same as article first published in *Studi di filologia italiana* 12 (1954): 23–75; Fatini, 3563.

◆§ 784. ———. *Orlando Furioso*. See Ariosto, Ludovico, entry 25.

◆§ 785. ———. "Santorre Debenedetti." In *I Critici. Per la storia della filologia e della critica moderna in Italia*, 4:2645–64. 4 vols. Milan: Marzorati, 1969.
Evaluates Debenedetti's editorial work for the three-volume 1928 edition of the OF (Bari: Laterza), citing its importance as both a critical reading of the text and as a "nuovo tipo di operazione filologica: l'edizione interpretativa di autografi con varianti" (pp. 2655–56). Reviews the progress of Debenedetti's philological analysis of Ariosto's writings, concluding that his determination of a poetic process through an examination of editions and variants became a model for later analytical methods.

⋘ 786. ———. "La Prima redazione inedita di due satire dell'Ariosto." In *Tra latino e volgare*. *Per Carlo Dionisotti*, edited by Gabriella Bernardoni Trezzini, Ottavio Besomi, Luigi Bianchi, Nicola Casella, Valentina Ferrini Cavalleri, Giulia Gianella, and Lorenza Simona, 2:675–708. 2 vols. Padua: Antenore, 1974.

Transcription of satires one and three contained in ms. I. VI. 41 of the Biblioteca Comunale degli Intronati of Siena. Discusses their position in the manuscript tradition of the satires and, through philological analysis, demonstrates that the manuscript contains "un bel mazzo di varianti ariostee, da riportare sull'imponente tabellone delle trasformazioni linguistiche accertate o accertabili nei vari stati redazionali di opere dell'Ariosto" (p. 698).

⋘ 787. ———. "Ariosto, Ludovico." In *Enciclopedia Europea*, edited by Giorgio Cusatelli, 1:618–21. 11 vols. to date. Milan: Garzanti, 1976–.

Succinct biographical sketch and a brief history of the composition of Ariosto's works. Consideration of his theatrical activities. Major factual information about the evolution of the three editions of the *OF* and a discussion of the poem's structure, brief note on principal characters, and a consideration of Ariosto's perfection of the *ottava*: "[Ariosto] rielabora l'ottava tradizionale, superando l'elementare allineamento dei versi non più, come nella prima redazione, con un faticoso carico di *enjambements* e di spostamenti sintattici, ma con la creazione di unità strutturali ampie e fluide nel medesimo tempo, conciliando la prospettiva e il dominio delle situazioni col senso del movimento e della variabilità del reale" (p. 620). Appended summary of the *OF*, *Il Negromante*, and *La Lena*.

⋘ 788. ———. "Le Concordanze diacroniche dell'*Orlando Furioso*: concezione e vicende dell'opera." In *Ludovico Ariosto: lingua, stile e tradizione*, edited by Cesare Segre (entry 789), pp. 231–35. Milan: Feltrinelli, 1976.

Describes the programming of a computerized diachronic concordance of the three editions—1516, 1521, 1532—of the *OF*. Conceived in 1965; first phase completion originally projected for 1975. To include variants in verses and both rhyme and word frequency indexes. See also Zampolli, Antonio, entry 921.

⋘ 789. ———, ed. *Ludovico Ariosto: lingua, stile e tradizione*. Atti del Congresso organizzato dai comuni di Reggio Emilia e Ferrara, 12–16 ottobre 1974. Milan: Feltrinelli, 1976. 446p.

Includes: Ghino Ghinassi, "Il volgare mantovano tra il Medioevo e il Rinascimento" (entry 353); Silvia Isella, "Ariosto e Folengo: due operazioni convergenti" (entry 425); Angelo Stella, "Note sull'evoluzione linguistica dell'Ariosto" (entry 828); Carlo Ossola, "Dantismi metrici nel *Furioso*" (entry

579); Giuseppe Dalla Palma, "Dal Secondo al terzo *Furioso*: mutamenti di struttura e moventi ideologici" (entry 237); Riccardo Bruscagli, "*Ventura e inchiesta* fra Boiardo e Ariosto" (entry 151); Luigi Blasucci, "Riprese linguistico-stilistiche del *Morgante* nell'*Orlando Furioso*" (entry 110); Paolo Orvieto, "Differenze 'retoriche' fra il *Morgante* e il *Furioso* (Per un'interpretazione narratologica del *Furioso*)" (entry 578); Guido Almansi, "Tattica del meraviglioso ariostesco" (entry 10); Giovanni Ponte, "Un Esercizio stilistico dell'Ariosto: la tempesta di mare nel canto XLI del *Furioso*" (entry 649); Giulio Herczeg, "Stile indiretto libero nella lingua del *Furioso*" (entry 412); Cesare Segre, "Le Concordanze diacroniche dell'*Orlando Furioso*: concezione e vicende dell'opera" (entry 788); Antonio Zampolli, "Le Concordanze diacroniche dell'*Orlando Furioso*: procedura per l'elaborazione automatica" (entry 921); Lao Paoletti, "Cronaca e letteratura nei *Carmina*" (entry 596); Roberto Fedi, "Petrarchismo prebembesco in alcuni testi lirici dell'Ariosto" (entry 312); Antonia Tissoni Benvenuti, "La Tradizione della terza rima e l'Aristo" (entry 842); Cesare Segre, "Storia testuale e linguistica delle *Satire*" (entry 790); Gabriella Ronchi and Angela Casella, "Le *Commedie* e i loro stampatori" (entry 702); Pier Marco Bertinetto, "Il Ritmo della prosa e del verso nelle commedie dell'Ariosto" (entry 85); Cecil Grayson, "Appunti sulla lingua delle commedie in prosa e in versi" (entry 386); Siro Ferrone, "Sulle commedie in prosa dell'Ariosto" (entry 317); Maria Luisa Doglio, "Lingua e struttura del *Negromante*" (entry 273).

๙ 790. ———. "Storia testuale e linguistica delle *Satire*." In *Ludovico Ariosto: lingua, stile e tradizione*, edited by Cesare Segre (entry 789), pp. 315–30. Milan: Feltrinelli, 1976.
Paleographic and linguistic analysis of the Ferrarese manuscript of the satires (Biblioteca Comunale Ariostea Cl. I, B) to establish the respective roles of Ariosto and a copyist in the emendations; compares manuscript with known extant transcriptions to establish their diachronic ordering and to trace the history of the manuscripts to 1534.

๙ 791. ———. "Struttura dialogica delle satire ariostesche." In his *Semiotica filologica: testo e modelli culturali*, pp. 117–30. Turin: Einaudi, 1979.
Also in *Ariosto 1974 in America*, edited by Aldo Scaglione (entry 760) (Ravenna: Longo, 1976), pp. 41–54. Another version of this essay, entitled "Appunti sulla funzione del dialogo nelle *Satire* dell'Ariosto" is in *Notiziario culturale italiano* (entry 573) 15, no. 3 (1974): 77–80.
Semiological-structural examination of the satires and their epistolary form, seen as a continual dialogue between the poet (*io*) and another individual (*tu*), whose persona varies from that of the epistle's addressee to the anonymous voice of the interlocutors of the fictitious *favole*. Examining other

levels of discourse and their varying natures, or registers, concludes that in the satires we have, in their immediacy, evidence of the author's most penetrating meditation upon the realities of his age.

◄§ 792. SELIG, KARL-LUDWIG. "A Note on Ariosto in the Netherlands." *Italica* 40, no. 2 (1963): 164–66.

In addition to the two translations of the OF mentioned by Giuseppe Agnelli and Giuseppe Ravegnani in *Annali delle edizioni ariostee* (1933), notes quotations from the poem by Dutch poets such as Johan de Brune and Zacharias Heyns that further attest to Ariosto's popularity and importance among Dutch writers of the seventeenth century.

◄§ 793. ―――. "Cervantes / Ariosto: 'Forse altri cantera con miglior plettro.'" *Revista Hispánica Moderna* 39, nos. 1–2 (1976–1977): 69–72.

On the significance of the Ariosto quotation at the conclusion of Cervantes's *DQ*, part 1 and repeated in part 2.1, both as it relates to Cervantes's debt to Ariosto as a vatic poet and for its function in the structural system of the Spanish text.

◄§ 794. SELLS, ARTHUR LYTTON. *The Italian Influence in English Poetry, from Chaucer to Southwell.* London: Allen & Unwin, 1955. 346p.; Bloomington: Indiana University Press, 1955. 346p. Reprint. Westport, Conn.: Greenwood Press, 1971. 346p.

On pp. 162–75 compares and contrasts aspects of the *FQ* and the OF, noting that Ariosto was Spenser's "general model" and that, like most Renaissance readers, the English poet read "more of allegory into the *Orlando* than Ariosto intended" (p. 172).

◄§ 795. SERENI, VITTORIO. "Un'Idea per il *Furioso*." *La Rassegna della letteratura italiana*, 7th ser., vol. 79, nos. 1–2 (1975): 15–18.

Contends that the OF continues to fascinate readers and critics alike because of the constant movement of its characters, representing the passing and renewal of life forces.

◄§ 796. SERONI, ADRIANO. Introduzione. *Opere*, by Ludovico Ariosto, edited by Adriano Seroni, pp. ix–xviii. Milan: Mursia, 1970.

Notes that the process of revising the OF till shortly before the death of the author makes it a "lavoro in movimento": "La cognizione . . . del *Furioso* come opera in movimento è da ritenersi essenziale all'intendimento del poema come libro che, insieme a pochi altri, esprime pienamente la civiltà, o meglio, la realtà, del Rinascimento: e rende ragione anche, visto l'ampio ventaglio di anni che il lavoro attorno al *Furioso* occupa, di un divenire che non è soltanto il passaggio dall'età giovane alla maturità piena dell'autore, ma anche dalle illusioni del Rinascimento ancor giovane alle malinconie del Rinascimento maturo, che già preannuncia . . . ombre inquietanti, delle quali troviamo un riflesso nei *Cinque Canti*" (p. x). Noting that the OF is firmly anchored in contemporary reality, that the "dilettevole" is interwoven with an awareness or intuition of sociopolitical evolution, calls the OF a "romanzo-saggio," a "*summa* di un complesso momento storico" (p. xiii). Briefly discusses the satires as autobiography and the sixth satire to Bembo in particular as a basis for understanding Ariosto's humanity and humanism. Bio-bibliographical note appended, pp. xix–xxiii.

⚜ 797. ———. "Bacchelli e l'intelligenza dell'Ariosto." In his *Da Dante al Verga. Momenti e ipotesi di storia letteraria*, pp. 148–55. Rome: Riuniti, 1972.
Also in *L'Approdo letterario* 4, no. 4 (1958): 41–49.
Discusses Riccardo Bacchelli's writings on Ariosto and their significance for having put Ariosto into a historical, antiromantic perspective. Briefly considers the evolution of Bacchelli's ideas and the state of his work by 1958, the date of this essay.

⚜ 798. ———. "Introduzione alla lettura del *Furioso*." In his *Da Dante al Verga. Momenti e ipotesi di storia letteraria*, pp. 133–47. Rome: Riuniti, 1972.
Also in *L'Approdo letterario* 6, no. 9 (1960): 63–75.
Noting that the OF is a poetic sublimation of the complex reality of the High Renaissance in Italy (p. 134), discusses the manner in which the structural and thematic elements of the poem function to portray a world in constant change, a reality in continual transformation (pp. 135–36). Identifies movement as the unifying element of the poem, both in the narrative line and as part of the internal structure of the octave. Establishes similarities between Ariosto's "poetic eye" and perspective on the natural world with those of Leonardo da Vinci. Concludes that the subject of the OF is contemporary reality, that its portrayal is as finely tuned as Machiavelli's, and that its moral and spiritual substructure is perceptible in the minor works, especially in the satires, in which the "eye of the poet" ("occhio del poeta") is particularly evident (p. 147).

⚜ 799. ———. "Temi ariosteschi in occasione di un centenario." *Paragone* 25, no. 298 (1974): 3–16.
Abbreviated version, "L'Ariosto e la Francia in due inserti storici del *Furioso*," in *Notiziario culturale italiano* (entry 573) 15, no. 3 (1974): 43–47.
Reviews the critical reconsideration of Ariosto in recent years as a poet who, if by nature ill disposed to the business of court life or to the exigencies of the political world, was intent upon the representation of social and polit-

ical realities. Considers several areas of Ariosto criticism requiring further study, including the evolution of the OF toward the final edition and the particular nature of each of the editions, "opere fra loro diverse" (p. 9). Concludes with a perspective on the coexistence in the OF of reality and fantasy, "entro un complesso organismo nel quale realtà e invenzione fantastica non sono mai disgiunte" (p. 15).

✒ 800. ———. "Favola, storia e realtà nell'*Orlando furioso.*" *Rinascita* 32, no. 13 (28 March 1975): 22–23.

Reviews the activities held in 1974–1975 to celebrate the fifth centenary of Ariosto's birth. Considers the sociopolitical climate in which the 1516 edition of the OF was written, noting that it was a moment of relative peace after the wars following the descent of Charles VIII into Italy (1494); briefly discusses the CC as reflecting a growing pessimism, "l'angoscia del tradimento, la sfiducia dell'uomo" (p. 23), and speculates on Ariosto's reasons for not including them in the 1532 edition, which does, nevertheless, reflect to a certain degree the somber climate of the 1520s.

✒ 801. SERRA, LUCIANO. "La Sublimazione del grottesco: Brunello." In *Il Boiardo e la critica contemporanea,* edited by Giuseppe Anceschi, pp. 489–97. Atti del Convegno di Studi su Matteo Maria Boiardo. Scandiano–Reggio Emilia. 25–27 aprile 1969. Biblioteca dell'*Archivum Romanicum*, 1st ser., vol. 107. Florence: Leo S. Olschki, 1970.

Comparative analysis of the nature of the dwarf Brunello in the OI and the OF: his physical appearance and maliciousness are sublimated into a heroic dimension in the OI, his abilities becoming a creative act as he passes from his grotesque nature to an aerial figure ("'aeriforme,'" p. 495) of unique abilities or *virtù*; in the OF, the figure degenerates into a deceitful thief, suggesting the several motifs of man's darker side common to the poem. Suggests the importance of the essentially opposite treatments of the character to an understanding of the differing perspectives of the two epic romances.

✒ 802. ———. "La satira VII dell'Ariosto: una recente interpretazione." *Bollettino storico reggiano* 5, no. 16 (1972): 32–34.

Discussion of Jürgen Grimm, *Die Einheit der Ariost'schen Satire* (entry 395), and especially of the analysis of Ariosto's seventh satire as an illustration of the unity of the satires. Finds Grimm's study to be an important first step toward a "sistemazione non ancora cercata" (p. 32).

✒ 803. ———. "Dal Boiardo all'Ariosto, grottesco e diroccamento: Orrilo." *Bollettino storico reggiano* 7, no. 24 (1974): 55–63.

Argues that Ariosto, in making use of the characters of Boiardo's OI and giving them new dimensions, creating a new aesthetic perspective and concept of reality, had to reduce them to their skeletal elements and build upon essentials. In the context of this process, discusses the nature of Orrilo: "Nell'Ariosto Orrilo è soggetto / oggetto caricato di fatalità mitologica e di magia alchimica, giuoco comico rovesciato in brivido tragico, dall'assurdo (decreazione = nascita) al reale (distruzione = decreazione)" (p. 55). Examines the grotesque nature of Orrilo in Boiardo and Ariosto, the significance of Ariosto, particularly, in the evolution of the grotesque, of which Orrilo is the "ipotesi surreale" (p. 56), the literary tradition from which the character evolves, and concludes: "Il divertimento, essenziale per capire il poema nel suo tessuto di incanto/disincanto, anche attraverso il grottesco e il riso . . . , anche attraverso Orrilo e la sua ambiguità vitalistica e trascolorante, riporta sempre al perenne conflitto fra essere e nulla, durata e attimo" (p. 63).

804. ———. "Da Tolomeo alla Garfagnana: la geografia dell'Ariosto." in *Lodovico Ariosto: il suo tempo la sua terra la sua gente* (entry 468). Estratto dal *Bollettino storico reggiano* 7, no. 28 (1974): 151–84.
Two-part essay: first, discusses the rich collection of maps and atlases in the Este library and their importance to both Boiardo and Ariosto in writing their poems. Notes the particular significance of several works for Ariosto, including Pietrobono dall'Avogaro's list of cities with the astrological signs or planets governing them (pp. 155–56) and *Le Septe Giornate de la Geographia*, a translation of the Ptolemaic cosmography. Second, considers Ariosto's use of geography, noting that from "cartografia e dal suo evidente mutare, dalla visione del mondo come ipotesi in equilibrio tra il reale e il favoloso, l'Ariosto trasse il suo mondo in bilico tra verità e immaginazione" (p. 158). States that some topoi are suggested by geography and poetically articulated through it: contrast between the Occident and the Orient; poetry of spatial dimensions; geography as paradigmatic of instability ("La geografia stessa è instabilità, carte che mutano, isole sempre nuove che vengono scoperte . . . topografia delle sorti umane," p. 159). Explores in detail Ariosto's fantasy-reality geography of France, England, Spain, Africa, and, most important, the Orient, "il grande spazio geografico dei poemi e romanzi cavallereschi e il rapporto itinerale continuo del *Furioso* in una dispersione e raccolta continue" (p. 169); notes that Northern Europe, on the other hand, becomes the scene of the "cupo" and "orrore" (p. 172). Concludes with a discussion of the literary use of local geography, the exaltation and critique of Ferrara and the Estense through idealization in both the *OF* and the minor works (pp. 181–83). Includes six illustrations.

805. SERRA, RENATO. "De Robertis, Ariosto e Manzoni." *Nuova Antologia*, anno 103, vol. 504 (1968): 495–98.
Summary observations on the nature of Ariosto's poetry.

806. Sestan, Ernesto. "Gli Estensi e il loro stato al tempo del-l'Ariosto." *La Rassegna della letteratura italiana,* 7th ser., vol. 79, nos. 1–2 (1975): 19–33.

Territories under Este control, which included Modena, Reggio, and the Garfagnana, were centralized only in the area of Ferrara and Polisene di Rovigo. Este politics were dominated, therefore, by the interests of Ferrara and by the movements of neighboring powers (Republic of San Marino and the Church State) and the expansionist policies of Venice, which acquired Polisene in 1484 and thus deprived the Este of river routes in the Po Valley. Considers the complex relationship between the Este and the French after the invasion of Charles VIII, examines the Este lineage, and concludes with a discussion of the social structure of the state and the support by all classes given to the extravagant court life of the Este family.

807. Severi, Mario. "Gli studi di Giuseppe Picciola sull'opera di Ludovico Ariosto." *Pagine istriane* (Trieste) 37 (1975): 25–33.

Brief discussion of Giuseppe Picciola's (1859–1912) interest in Ariosto and his affinity with the poet's ideals and the spirit of the *OF*. Considers in a summary fashion Picciola's various writings on Ariosto and on the Renaissance in general.

808. Shumaker, Wayne. "*Paradise Lost* and the Italian Epic Tradition." In *Th'Upright Heart and Pure: Essays on John Milton Commemorating the Tercentenary of the Publication of Paradise Lost,* edited by Amadeus P. Fiore, O.F.M., pp. 87–100. Pittsburgh: Duquesne University Press, 1967.

Considers Milton's achievement in *Paradise Lost* in light of the elements in the Italian "romantic" epic tradition that he rejected. Considers the repudiation of narrative complexity; the use of magic; the central thematics of valor, honor, and romantic love; and, finally, *ottava rima* in favor of blank verse.

809. Simon, Gyula. "Ariosto fordítása közben . . ." (While translating Ariosto . . .). *Filológiai Közlöny* (Budapest) 22 (1976): 169–89.

Considerations on the problems attendant on a translation into Hungarian of the *OF*; includes the text of his translation of canto 29.

810. Simone, Alberto. "Le Lettere di Ludovico Ariosto." *Giornale italiano di filologia* 20 (1967–1968): 299–302.

Review essay of Ludovico Ariosto, *Le Lettere,* edited by Angelo Stella (entry 827). Concludes that Ariosto's personality is remarkably apparent in his correspondence and that one can perceive the same angry reaction yet understanding acceptance before human folly that one finds in the satires and in the detached but acute awareness of the *OF*. Praises Stella's edition and critical apparatus; expresses reservations on the turgid style of the introduction.

◆§ 811. SINGLETON, CHARLES S. "Italian Literature: Three Masters, Three Epochs." In *World Literatures: Arabic, Chinese, Czechoslovak, French, German, Greek, Hungarian, Italian, Lithuanian, Norwegian, Polish, Romanian, Russian, Scottish, Swedish, Yugoslav*, edited by Joseph Remenyi et al, pp. 154–69. Pittsburgh: University of Pittsburgh Press, 1956.
Distinguishes three epochs in the course of Italian literature, arguing that each is characterized by the absence of "any real principle of progress in the development of a literature" (p. 154). Argues that, for all the furious movement in the *OF*, the dominant mood is that of "going nowhere" (pp. 166–68).

◆§ 812. SPADARO, GIUSEPPE. "Epidrasis tu Ariosto ston Erotokrito o Tasso agnostos ston Kornaro" (Influences of Ariosto and Tasso on Kornaros's *Erotokritos*). *O Eraristis* (Athens) 4 (1966): 222–29.
Text in Greek. Influences of Ariosto and Tasso on the Cretan poet Vitzentzos Kornaros's romance epic of the first half of the seventeenth century, *Erotokritos*. Notes in particular the borrowing of Ariosto's similes.

◆§ 813. ――――. "Sulle fonti dell'*Assedio di Malta* di Antonio Achelis." *O Eraristis* (Athens) 4 (1966): 80–116.
On a little-known work by the sixteenth-century Cretan poet Achelis and dedicated to a Venetian resident of Crete, Francesco Barozzi. Notes that the composition is in rhymed verse (2541 lines), in twenty *capitoli*, with a forty-verse prologue. Its main argument is the seige of Malta in 1565, with the Knights of St. George against the Turks. Considers the composition of the poem, the author's sources, and the important influence of the *OF*, which Achelis imitates in structure and from which he takes various poetic elements, particularly similes. Notes Ariosto's presence in the culture of Crete by the late sixteenth century and concludes with selections from the Greek text and the *OF* to show Achelis's debt to the Italian poet.

◆§ 814. ――――. "Ariosto fonte di un passo dello Στάθης." *Byzantinische Zeitschrift* 60 (1967): 273–76.
On the Cretan play *Stathis* and the imitation in 3 4.231–42 of *OF* 19.1; notes use of first two verses of Ariosto's octave and a paraphrase of the rest.

◆§ 815. SPAGGIARI, ALCIDE. "Ariosto e Bologna cinque secoli dopo." *Gazzetta di Reggio*, 2 March 1974, p. 5.

Notes that Ariosto's family was originally from Bologna, comments on Ariosto's sojourns in Bologna, and reviews landmarks in the city with which the family can be associated. Briefly discusses the early members of the Ariosto family who resided in Bologna.

⋙ 816. SPAGGIARI, ANGELO. "Carte relative al commissariato di L. Ariosto in Garfagnana presso l'Archivio di Stato di Modena." In *Lodovico Ariosto: il suo tempo la sua terra la sua gente* (entry 468). Estratto dal *Bollettino storico reggiano* 7, no. 28 (1974): 185–93.

Provides the texts of five documents (*minute*) of 1524 relative to Ariosto's appointment in the Garfagnana and not contained in Giovanni Sforza, *Documenti inediti per servire alla vita di L. Ariosto* (in the collection *Monumenti di Storia Patria per le provincie modenesi*, 1928, appendix, pp. 192–93). Discusses a number of dispatches and documents in the State Archives of Modena, "di affiancare quella fondamentale documentazione [i.e., Sforza's] e di fornire notizie complementari provenienti da fonti diverse da quella del ben noto binomio Ariosto-Alfonso I" (p. 187).

⋙ 817. SPAGNI, LOPEZ. "La Monetazione estense nel periodo ariostesco." In *Lodovico Ariosto: il suo tempo la sua terra la sua gente* (entry 468). Estratto dal *Bollettino storico reggiano* 7, no. 28 (1974): 195–206.

Briefly describes the monetary system during the Este period and provides illustrations and commentary on coins minted in the three mints (Ferrara, Modena, Reggio) during the reigns of Ercole I (1471–1505) and Alfonso I (1505–1534). Also provides an illustration of Pastorino Pastorini's medallion of Ariosto: "Al diritto si vede il busto del poeta girato a sinistra con la testa nuda laureata, lo sguardo un poco assente, ed il bel volto sereno e mite ad un tempo. Al rovescio si vede un'arnia in fiamme da cui sciamano le api, e il motto, abbastanza trasparente, 'Pro bono malum'" (p. 206).

⋙ 818. SPERONI, CHARLES. "More on the Sea-Monsters." *Italica* 35, no. 1 (1958): 21–24.

Acknowledges Allan Gilbert's parallel between the sea monsters in the *CC* and in Collodi's *Pinocchio* ("The Sea-Monsters in Ariosto's *Cinque Canti* and in *Pinocchio*," *Italica* 33 (1956): 260–63; Fatini, 3608). Briefly discusses other whale motifs in literature, specifically in the *Gesta romanorum*, in Cassio da Narni's *La morte del Danese*, and in Giambattista Basile's *Pentameron*.

⋙ 819. SPEVAK, JOHN ANTHONY. "Sir John Harington's Theoretical and Practical Criticism: The Sources and Originality of His Apparatus to the *Orlando Furioso*." ADD (1978–1979): 306. (University of Chicago, 1978.)

Ph.D. dissertation, not abstracted.

820. SPINELLA, MARIO. "Arzigogolo sulla 'r' ariostesca." *Il Piccolo Hans* (Bari) 12 (1977): 5–14.
Speculations on Ariosto's reasons for revising the first line of the OF for the 1532 edition. Suggests that the inclusion of *arme* was to introduce the poem's epic motifs, although by means of the line's structure the love theme continues to have a privileged significance. Notes the frequency of the consonant *r* in the first octave of the OF and in the opening three tercets of the DC, arguing that positioning produces significantly different phonetic effects in each work.

821. STAGG, GEOFFREY. "Tmesis in the Verse of Fray Luis de León and Others: A Western Romance Mannerism." In *Linguistic and Literary Studies in Honor of Helmut A. Hatzfeld*, edited by Alessandro S. Crisafulli, pp. 385–92. Washington, D.C.: The Catholic University of America Press, 1964.
Briefly notes the use of tmesis, or broken rhyme, in the OF and the frequency of adverbial caesura in Ariosto's dramatic works.

822. STÄUBLE, ANTONIO. "Scenografia ed architettura teatrale nel Rinascimento." In *Letteratura e critica: studi in onore di Natalino Sapegno*, edited by Walter Binni et al, 2 (1975): 391–415. 5 vols. Rome: Bulzoni, 1974–1979.
Survey of major lines of development in stage design and theater architecture, with brief observations on the ducal theater constructed under the supervision of Ariosto in 1531 and destroyed by fire in the following year (pp. 407–8). Includes 22 plates.

823. STEADMAN, JOHN M. "Sources of the 'Fountain-of-Oblivion' Episode in the English Wagner Book." *Archiv für das Studium der neueren Sprachen* 196 (1960): 145–46.
Parallels between "The Second Report of Doctor John Faustus" in the English Wagner Book and Astolfo's expedition to the Earthly Paradise (OF 34–35).

824. ———. "A Milton-Ariosto Parallel: Satan and Rodomonte (*Paradise Lost*, IV, 181)." *Zeitschrift für Romanische Philologie* 77, nos. 5–6 (1961): 514–16.
Notes the ethical similarity between Satan and Rodomonte, who, in "their combination of valor and impiety . . . display a marked resemblance to the *contemptor divum* of classical epic" (p. 515). Indicates as evidence of Milton's

ties to the tradition of epic and romance a specific allusion to Ariosto in
Paradise Lost 4.181.

✎ 825. STEFANI, LUIGINA. "Un manoscritto mutilo della *Cassaria* finora
    sconosciuto." *Filologia e critica* 2, no. 3 (1977): 444–52.
Considers the relatively minor variants between the three extant manuscripts of *La Cassaria* (the *princeps*; magliabechiano VII, 44; and the recently
discovered Fondo Nazionale II VIII 28), noting, however, their significance
in establishing the integral text.

✎ 826. STELLA, ANGELO. "Per una nuova edizione delle *Lettere* di L.
    Ariosto (Con lettere e manoscritti inediti)." *Giornale storico della letter-
    atura italiana* 140, fasc. 432 (1963): 566–601.
Noting that Cappelli's edition of the letters (latest edition, Milan, 1887) is
now outdated, provides a chronological list of 214 extant letters known to
date, with the provenance and relative bibliographical references. Discusses
his discovery of two short letters in the State Archives of Modena and reproduces the texts; also reproduces with corrections the entire text of the "Libro
di m. Ludovico Ariosto," a twenty-page record of salaries paid by Ariosto to
his military charges in the Garfagnana for the period 1522–1525.

✎ 827. ———. Introduzione. In *Le Lettere*, Ludovico Ariosto, edited by
    Angelo Stella, pp. vii–xxviii. Milan: Mondadori, 1965.
Brief discussion of the fortune, both editorial and critical, of Ariosto's correspondence, noting that the letters are not in the rhetorical-literary tradition
but in the "ambito cancelleresco e diplomatico" (p. ix). Though he argues
that the letters provide the interior "fisionomia" of Ariosto (p. viii), states that
his true self tends to be hidden behind the veil of his official style and tone.
Discusses most extensively the Garfagnana letters, their polemical tone and
meditative quality, and notes that the style combines the linear, excursive
style of diplomatic correspondence with "forzature, assimmetrie, strutture
parlate, spie che ci riportano a condizioni espressive instabili, dove la re-
azione emotiva dello scrittore eccede gli schemi sintattici consueti e la pagina
diviene registrazione immediata di un comportamento personale" (p. xxvii).

✎ 828. ———. "Note sull'evoluzione linguistica dell'Ariosto." In *Ludo-
    vico Ariosto: lingua, stile e tradizione*, edited by Cesare Segre (entry
    789), pp. 49–64. Milan: Feltrinelli, 1976.
Analyzes selected linguistic changes in the *OF*, especially from the first to
the second edition, as well as in the evolving style of Ariosto's letters. Gives
particular attention to the variations in diphthongs and comments on the
several influences upon Ariosto's phonological and morphological peculiarities, including the Po Valley koiné and the vernacular tradition of Dante,

Boccaccio, and Petrarch. Concludes that phonetic and morphological changes can serve as a basis for dating Ariosto's writings.

829. STONE, DONALD. "The Place of Garnier's *Bradamante* in Dramatic History." *AUMLA. Journal of the Australasian Universities Language and Literature Association* 26 (1966): 260–71.
Analysis of the nature of Robert Garnier's borrowings from the Bradamante-Ruggiero plot in the *OF*.

830. STURROCK, J. "Wordsworth's Translations of Ariosto." *Notes and Queries* 26, no. 3 (1979): 227–28.
Notes Wordsworth's "anxiety to keep close to the meaning of the original Italian and to express that meaning well" (p. 228) in his translations of several *ottave* of the *OF*.

831. STYCH, F. S. "Two Later Versions of the Brazilla / Isabella Theme." *Revue de littérature comparée* 51, no. 4 (1977): 553–56.
On a seventeenth-century Latin version (Vincenzio Guinigi's "Carmen V") and an eighteenth-century German version (Alois Schreiber's "Adeline") of the Brazilla-Isabella theme, noting the superior treatment in *OF* 29.

832. SULLIVAN, EDWIN D. S. "The English Ariosto." *ADD*, 1966– 1967, p. 164. (University of California, Santa Barbara, 1967.)
Ph.D. dissertation, not abstracted.

833. SZMYDTOWA, ZOFIA. "Ariostyczna droga Słowackiego" (Słowacki's Ariostean Path). *Pamiętnik Literacki* 51, no. 4 (1960): 351–87.
On echoes of Ariosto in several works of the Polish romantic poet Juliusz Słowacki (1809–1849).

834. ———. "Jeszcze o Telimenie. Echa Ariosto" (Once more on Telimena. Echoes of Ariosto). *Kwartalnik Prasoznawczy* (1961), pp. 323–25.
Unavailable. Cited in *Years Work in Modern Language Studies* (1961), p. 508. On the possible influence of the *OF* on Adam Mickiewicz's *Pan Tadeusz*.

835. ———. "Lament Sakrypanta W Oryginale I Spolszczeniu Piotra Kochanowskiego Na Tle Renesansowych Przetworzeń Motywu" (The lament of Sacripante in the original and in the version of Piotr Kochanowski against the background of the Renaissance versions of the theme). In *W Kręgu "Gofreda" I "Orlanda,"* (entry 913), pp. 137–50. Wrocław-Warsaw-Cracow: Polska Akademia Nauk, 1970.

Comparing several versions of the motif of Sacripante's lament, concludes that Kochanowski's lacks the lyricism and psychological subtleties of the original.

◄§ 836. TENENTI, ALBERTO. "Le monde de l'Arioste: histoire et civilisation." In *Notiziario culturale italiano* (entry 573) 15, no. 3 (1974): 5–13.
Examines the social and psychological position of Ariosto vis-à-vis his presence in Ferrara during a cultural shift from courtly fifteenth-century traditions, in which the artist's role was to enhance the prince and his court, to its involvement in the chaotic aftermath of Charles VIII's invasion. Sees in all of Ariosto's artistic expression the bitterness over a lost dream and a country fallen victim to the inefficacies of its leaders.

◄§ 837. TERRANOVA, GIOVANNI. "Ludovico Ariosto non riuscì a diventare
   cardinale." In his *Poeti in Roma (Petrarca-Ariosto-Leopardi)*, pp. 10–
   13. Rome: Edizioni Eurostampa, 1966.
Suggests that Ariosto was denied a cardinalate by his old friend Leo X because he was too closely allied with the Este family, who were hostile to the Medici, and because he would have been unwilling to move to Rome and undertake the responsibilities required.

◄§ 838. TESTA, ANTONIO. *La Critica letteraria calabrese nel Novecento.*
   Cosenza: Luigi Pellegrini, 1968.
A discussion and positive evaluation of Antonio Piromalli's *Motivi e forme della poesia di Ludovico Ariosto* (1954), noting that he clarifies the limits of both the historical and Crocean methods of Ariosto criticism. See pp. 153–61.

◄§ 839. TESTA, CORRADO. Introduzione. In *Ariosto e Tasso: antologia
   dell'Orlando furioso' e della 'Gerusalemme liberata,'* pp. v–xvi. Turin:
   Società Editrice Internazionale, 1972.
Considers the diverse critical perspectives on the comic tone of the *OF*, and in particular on Ariosto's irony. Notes that irony implies a judgmental stance and that, consequently, a more appropriate term in Ariosto's case would be *umorismo*: "all'umorismo si suole attribuire una naturale disposizione alla simpatia e, proprio per questo, la proprietà di esprimere comicamente sentimenti e pensieri anche serissimi" (p. vii). States that Ariosto's humor stems from the author's view of the world and "un senso sofferto e consapevole dell'esistenza umana" (p. viii). Considers Ariosto in the context of the Renaissance, noting his aesthetic idealism and his realistic spirit akin to those of Machiavelli and Guicciardini; states that the dominant quality of his art is "grazia" (p. ix). Brief discussion of Ariosto's classicism.

840. THOMPSON, KARL F. "A Note on Ariosto's *I Suppositi.*" *Comparative Literature* 12 (1960): 42–46.
Challenges H. B. Charlton's claim that *I Suppositi* has romantic elements (*Shakesperian Comedy*, 1949, pp. 78–81), noting that the critic made use of Gascoigne's 1566 translation of the comedy to support his argument and therefore mistakenly attributed to Ariosto romantic elements (e.g., "a sympathetic attitude toward the heroine resulting in the depiction of a modest, morally resolute maiden, and a more generous view of the conventional types than is evident in Roman comedy," p. 43) that, indeed, are present in the English version.

841. THOMSON, PATRICIA. "Wyatt's Debt to Dante and Ariosto." *English Miscellany: A Symposium of History, Literature and the Arts* 15 (1964): 47–59.
Argues that Sir Thomas Wyatt's debt to Ariosto, claimed by George Puttenham (*The Arte of English Poesie*, 1589), is minimal and that images reminiscent of Ariosto more likely have their source in other Italian poets, most notably Petrarch and Serafino Aquilano.

842. TISSONI BENVENUTI, ANTONIA. "La Tradizione della terza rima e l'Ariosto." In *Ludovico Ariosto: lingua, stile e tradizione*, edited by Cesare Segre (entry 789), pp. 303–13. Milan: Feltrinelli, 1976.
Documents the popularity of *terza rima* in the second half of the fifteenth century, especially in the *capitolo*, which the author calls the most typical form of courtly poetry during the period. Brief discussion of some characteristics of Ariosto's twenty-six *capitoli* (e.g., the frequency of anaphora); concludes with observations on the historical importance of Ariosto's satires, written in *terza rima*, to the evolution of the genre in the Renaissance.

843. TOFFANIN, GIUSEPPE. *La Vita e le opere di Ludovico Ariosto.* Naples: Libreria Scientifica Editrice, 1959. 167p.
Dispense; reproduction of typescript. General introduction to Ariosto's life and work for students.

844. TOMALIN, MARGARET. "Bradamante and Marfisa: An Analysis of the 'Guerriere' of the *Orlando Furioso.*" *Modern Language Review* 71, no. 3 (1976): 540–52.
Detailed analysis of the two major female warriors in the OF, concluding that Marfisa's character is essentially positive and marked by restraint, courtesy, and rational behavior, whereas Bradamante is often a comic figure, selfish, deceitful, and presented as an ambiguous character unsure of her identity. Discusses the thematic and stylistic elements of the poem that define the nature of the two characters: in the case of Marfisa, simple, paratactic

construction of the verse; in the case of Bradamante, the use of oxymoron and frequent confusion in both the syntax and the narrative line. See also by Tomalin *The Fortunes of the Warrior Heroine in Italian Literature* (Ravenna: Longo, 1982) for a broad discussion of the topic.

◆§ 845. TOMASHEVSKII, BORIS. *Pushkin: Kniga pervaia (1813–1824)*. Moscow and Leningrad: Izd. Akademii nauk, 1956. 743p.

Notes the influence of both the GL and OF on Pushkin's poem, *Ruslan and Ludmilla*. Briefly discusses similarities with Ariosto in Pushkin's use of the fantastic. Observations on structural similarities and differences, including romance techniques; notes that whereas Ariosto's narrative includes multiple plots, Pushkin's narrative is essentially singular. See pp. 357–65.

◆§ 846. TOPAZIO, VIRGIL W. "Voltaire's *Pucelle*: A Study in Burlesque." *Studies on Voltaire and the Eighteenth Century* (ed. Theodore Besterman) 2 (1956): 207–23.

Notes that Voltaire patterned *La Pucelle* upon the OF and considers major differences between the two poems. Unlike Ariosto, Voltaire did not strive for an objective perspective on his burlesque epic because his intention was to produce a satiric work condemning injustice and corruption. States that Voltaire's characters lack the differentiation and delineation of Ariosto's, representing, instead, "ideas or certain philosophic facets" (p. 212). Ariosto's irony lacks the malice and biting quality of Voltaire's. Concludes, "Voltaire succeeded in copying the burlesque pattern of Ariosto without capturing the delicacy and the charm of the Italian" (p. 214).

◆§ 847. TORTORETO, ALESSANDRO. "Ariosto e Tasso, confronto obbligato." In *Per l'Ariosto* (entry 623). Special 1976 issue of *Italianistica* 3, no. 3 (1974): 147–56.

Surveys the Renaissance polemic surrounding the literary superiority of one poet over the other. Focuses on Galileo Galilei's observations, on the critical judgment of Francesco De Sanctis, and on Lanfranco Caretti's analysis (*Ariosto e Tasso*, first edition 1961), which considers the differing cultural and historical periods that informed the lives and creative activity of the two poets (p. 153). Concludes by stressing the validity of De Sanctis's view, which judges Ariosto the superior poet.

◆§ 848. ———. "Ariosto e Tasso: saggio bibliografico (1957–1974)." *Studi tassiani* 24, nos. 1–2 (1974): 71–78.

Annotated but not comprehensive bibliography; entries concern both poets. Twenty-eight entries, plus two references to unpublished (?) lectures. Intended to supplement Fatini for the period 1957–1974.

◄§ 849. TRIOLO, ALFRED ANGELO. "The Boiardo-Ariosto Tradition in *Las Lágrimas de Angélica* of Luis Barahona de Soto (1586)." *DAI* 16, no. 10 (1956): 1909. (University of Chicago, 1956. 376p.)
Argues that Barahona de Soto's poem, only twelve cantos of which are extant, was intended to be modeled structurally after the *OI* and the *OF*. Discusses the influences upon the Spaniard of the Italian romance tradition during the sixteenth century and concludes that the Spanish poem, which grotesquely exaggerates the values of the Italian models, is lacking poetic content.

◄§ 850. ————. "Barahona de Soto's *Las Lágrimas de Angélica* and Ariosto's *Cinque Canti*." *Italica* 35, no. 1 (1958): 11–20.
Argues that the *CC* and not the *OF* is the principal source of Barahona de Soto's twelve-canto fragment.

◄§ 851. ————. "Bernardo del Carpio and Barahona de Soto's *Las Lágrimas de Angélica*." *Kentucky Romance Quarterly* 14, no. 1 (1967): 265–81.
Considering the Ariostean source and elaboration of or borrowings from the *OF* in Spanish Renaissance epics, suggests what the structure of the unfinished *Las Lágrimas de Angélica* was to become.

◄§ 852. TRTNIK-ROSSETTINI, OLGA. See Rossettini-Trtnik, Olga, entry 706.

◄§ 853. TURCHI, MARCELLO. "Fantasia, mimesi e paragoni ariostei." *Sigma* 20 (1968): 42–67.
Discusses the narrative function of animal similes and similar comparisons in the *OF*, noting that their frequency suggests Ariosto's sense of the integral nature of all life forms. Argues that analogies drawn from the animal world serve two purposes: to synthesize in a moment both of tension and of particularly rich expressivity a particular instance in the action; to identify poetic characteristics of particular situations that will then be used in successive developments of the same or of a related theme. Suggests that the mimetic qualities of Ariosto's poetry reflect the poet's sense of the internal rhythm ("ritmo interno") of life (p. 65).

◄§ 854. ————. *Ariosto o della liberazione fantastica*. Ravenna: Longo, 1969. 377p.
Contents: "Immagini di una storia interna dell'*Orlando Furioso*" (entry 857); "Linee d'interpretazione del disegno del poema" (entry 858); "Genesi e sviluppo dei motivi nella prospettiva narrativa del *Furioso*" (entry 856).

◈§ 855. ———. "Una Fonte ariostesca per Pomponio Torelli." *Archivio storico per le province parmensi* 21 (1969): 217–20.

Notes in Torelli's tragedy *Vittoria* (1605) two passages that echo verses of the *OF* and that reflect Torelli's baroque perspective on human destiny and his vision of the world.

◈§ 856. ———. "Genesi e sviluppo dei motivi nella prospettiva narrativa del *Furioso*." In his *Ariosto o della liberazione fantastica*, pp. 179–377. Ravenna: Longo, 1969.

Views the narrative structure of the *OF* as a poetic mimesis of the polymorphous nature of reality and the essence of Ariosto's art as resulting from an analysis of a universal relativism. Canto-by-canto discussion of thematics in their changing perspectives, the coexistence of chivalric ideals and contemporary mores and reality, and the structural significance of recurrent metaphors and motifs.

◈§ 857. ———. "Immagini di una storia interna dell'*Orlando Furioso*." In his *Ariosto o della liberazione fantastica*, pp. 15–83. Ravenna: Longo, 1969.

Also in *La Rassegna della letteratura italiana* 7th ser., vol. 71, no. 3 (1967): 315–40.

Extensive discussion of aspects of the internal unity, or harmony, of the *OF*. Argues that Ariosto's fantasy, rather than existing in and for itself ("vive per sé sola sino a un certo punto," p. 19), has its full realization when juxtaposed with reality and especially when it functions to define human sentiments. Defines the poem as "una liberazione dalla follia, dall'atroce passione" (pp. 35–36) and states that its poetic quality arises from the "incontro tra reale e fantasia" (p. 54) rather than from the traditional conflict of opposing sentiments. Views the poetry of fantasy and harmony as mediated by poetry expressing human feelings (pp. 55–56).

◈§ 858. ———. "Linee d'interpretazione del disegno del poema." In his *Ariosto o della liberazione fantastica*, pp. 85–175. Ravenna: Longo, 1969.

With title "Linee di interpretazione del disegno del *Furioso*," in *La Rassegna della letteratura italiana*, 7th ser., vol. 72, nos. 2–3 (1968): 220–53.

Extensive commentary characterized by generalizations. Views the motif of chivalry in the *OF* as the poetic expression of a dream of freedom and its irony as the manifestation of Ariosto's view of reality. Suggests that the poem is the sum of human adventures, in which magic and fantasy serve to reinforce a particular outlook on life. States that the "disegno," or structure, of the poem corresponds to a conception of life peculiar to the Renaissance. Argues that the poet's relationship with his characters and poetic material constitutes an actual discovery of the invincible, pure beauty of human sentiments—a discovery that, in a world that recognized only the forces of Nature, attests to the innovative spirit of the Renaissance.

⊷§ 859. ———. "Sui personaggi del *Furioso.*" *La Rassegna della letteratura italiana,* 7th ser., vol. 79, nos. 1–2 (1975): 129–45.

Sees in the poem's structure and in the movement of the narrative line a vital dynamism ("dinamismo vitale," p. 135) of which the characters are an integral part, reflecting the variety of human emotion and sentiment in contact with the constant mutations of nature. Cautions against defining the various protagonists in terms of "character," with the "pienezza di una vita drammatica e contrastante degli affetti." (p. 130), or ascribing to them a too rigidly symbolic nature, with a metapoetic significance: does define the characters, however, as representative, or symbolic, of identifiable facets of the human personality, constantly confronting the vagaries of life forces. Analyzes the major characters—Orlando, Angelica, Ruggiero, Bradamante, and Rodomonte—in terms of the human condition and as protagonists in the *epos* of a chivalric image of life. Notes the evolution of critical views on Ariosto's characters, from the nineteenth century (and the insights of Gioberti) to the readings of Walter Binni and Giorgio De Blasi, in particular.

⊷§ 860. ———. Introduzione. In *Orlando Furioso,* by Ludovico Ariosto, 1:vii–l. 4th ed. 2 vols. Milan: Garzanti, 1980.

Suggesting that the OF is a poetic transfiguration of Ferrarese civilization during the High Renaissance (p. xviii), situates the OF thematically and aesthetically within the cultural, political, and literary context of the period. Discusses in a summary way the Renaissance dimensions of the poem: it represents the unifying structure imposed upon a cosmos of infinite multiplicity and complexity; it is an imitation of nature that juxtaposes concrete reality with fantasy; it shows Ariosto's sense of limitation and measure; it demonstrates the importance of illusion, irony, and wisdom, called essential components of the poem. Briefly relates discussion to major narrative lines of the poem. Includes a biographical sketch (pp. vii–xiv), a perspective on the minor works as they relate to the OF (pp. xxx–xxxv), and an overview of Ariosto criticism from the sixteenth century (pp. xxxv–xlv). Includes selected bibliography.

⊷§ 861. TUROLLA, ENZO. "Dittologia e 'enjambement' nell'elaborazione dell'*Orlando Furioso.*" *Lettere italiane* 10, no. 1 (1958): 1–20.

Two-part essay: examines first the tendency from the 1516 to the 1532 edition of the OF toward a growing frequency of synonymic dittology ("dittologia sinonimica"), or the doubling of synonymous words, which serve to enhance the sense of equilibrium and harmony in the poem; second, the progressive elimination or more cautious use in the revisions of the OF of enjambements, symptomatic "d'un itinerario che parte da un mondo sotto certi aspetti potenziale e rudimentale . . . verso una presa di possesso più lucida e consapevole" (p. 20).

◆§ 862. ———. "Rassegna ariostesca." *Lettere italiane* 11, no. 1 (1959): 94–104.
Identifies two fundamental directions of Ariosto criticism in the postwar period: critical inquiry deriving from positions of earlier scholarship (e.g., from the Crocean perspective) and a complete revision of previous critical inquiry (e.g., the Marxist views of Roberto Battaglia). As examples of the most successful exploration of the poetic processes of Ariosto in the OF, cites and discusses the writings of Walter Binni, Giuseppe De Robertis, Raffaello Ramat, and Lanfranco Caretti. Praises the contributions—in what the author calls a neopositivistic vein (p. 101)—of Emilio Bigi and Cesare Segre. Concludes with an evaluation of the Marxist-oriented criticism of Battaglia and Antonio Piromalli and expresses reservations about the position of Leonardo Parrino (*Come sorrideva l'Ariosto*, 1953; Fatini, 3528) and the reading (an "assieme di massime esaltanti la cosidetta *dignitas hominis*," p. 104) of the poem by Giorgio De Blasi ("L'Ariosto e le passioni," *Giornale storico della letteratura italiana* 129 [1952] and 130 [1953]; Fatini, 3518 for both).

◆§ 863. ———. "Rassegna ariosteca: studi sul testo dell'*Orlando Furioso*." *Lettere italiane* 12, no. 3 (1960): 315–22.
Traces the history of the several editions of the OF since the publication in 1532 of the author's revised text; discusses the textual problems encountered by editors and the advances made by Giuseppe Lisio (*Il primo e il secondo canto dell'"Orlando Furioso*," 1909; Fatini, 1982) and by Santorre Debenedetti in his historically significant edition of 1928. Briefly discusses the significance of Cesare Segre's continuation and completion of Debenedetti's critical edition (1960, entry 25).

◆§ 864. UKAS, MICHAEL. "Didactic Purpose in the *Commedia Erudita*." *Italica* 36, no. 3 (1959): 198–205.
In sixteenth-century Italian comedy, distinguishes between plays that portray vice as an end in itself and those that use it as example or illustration. Considers *La Lena, Il Negromante*, and "some of the others by the same author" as belonging to the second group since they "provide a moral purpose by implication" (p. 198).

◆§ 865. ULYSSE, GEORGES. "Notes sur le théâtre de l'Ariosto: les deux versions du *Negromante*." *Annales de la Faculté des Lettres et Sciences Humaines d'Aix* 45 (1968): 421–39.

Compares the 1520 and 1529 versions of *Il Negromante* as a means by which to "juger l'évolution de l'Arioste auteur dramatique" (p. 421) and concludes that although the final version falls short of successfully providing a realistic view of contemporary society, it reveals a greater dramatic efficacy and interest, greater verisimilitude in the portrayal of social ties and character psychology, and the elimination of theatrically insignificant details.

◄§ 866. VALERI, DIEGO. "Poeti di paesaggio." *Osservatore politico lettera-rio*, February 1961, pp. 28–41.
States that in Italian painting and literature, nature and man have always been represented in harmonious accord, "ciascuno al proprio posto, ciascuno nei propri limiti. . . . L'uno complementare dell'altro" (p. 29). Surveys descriptions of landscape in Italian literature. Briefly discusses Ariosto's landscape descriptions as supreme examples of Renaissance aesthetics, comparing them to those of several contemporary painters (p. 35).

◄§ 867. VALESIO, PAOLO. "The Language of Madness in the Renaissance." *Yearbook of Italian Studies* 1 (1971): 199–234.
Posits hypothesis that the representation of madness was essentially iconic in the Middle Ages and before (nudity being the basic feature) and that with the Renaissance, the emphasis was on verbal aspects of madness. Gives particular attention to the folkloric tradition in the verbal expression of madness. Although treated only briefly, Ariosto's representation of Orlando is seen as belonging to the iconic tradition; Shakespeare's Ophelia, on the other hand, is exemplary of the verbal tradition. In an appended note, the author discusses some folkloric elements in the few key words uttered by Ariosto's mad protagonist.

◄§ 868. ———. "Genealogy of a Staged Scene (*Orlando Furioso*, v)." *Yale Italian Studies* 1, no. 1 (1980): 5–31.
Semiotic analysis of the source text for the Ginevra-Ariodante story (an episode from *Tirante el Blanco*), suggesting the significance of its theatrical dimension and exploring the strategy of the Ariostean version. See a brief discussion of the argument delivered as a lecture in "Intervista con Paolo Valesio," *Carte Italiane* 3 (1981–1982): 1–13.

◄§ 869. VALLONE, ALDO. "Lettura delle *Rime* ariostesche (con particolare riguardo ai sonetti)." In *Saggi e ricerche in memoria di Ettore Li Gotti*, 3:362–79. 3 vols. *Bollettino del Centro di Studi Filologici e Linguistici Siciliani*, nos. 6–8. Palermo, 1962.
Considers both the Latin and vernacular poetry in the context of the poet's evolving lyric style, noting that the former reveals an effort to establish a clear personal poetics and the latter, "uno svolgimeto e approfondimento di con-

tenuti e valori morali" (p. 365). Discusses the dual direction taken by the vernacular poetry: lyricism of the love sonnets, *canzoni*, madrigals, and eclogues; the satiric-realistic orientation of the *capitoli* and satires. Discusses the relative importance of both Petrarch and Dante to his Italian verse and indicates certain characteristics, including an objectifying distancing of the poet from his material; the infrequent use of classical myth; the lack of specificity in spatial and temporal references; the cautious use of adjectives; and the importance given substantives.

෫๑ 870. ———. "Ariosto e la magia." In his *Modi e testimonianze di cultura e di stile*, pp. 35–52. Palermo: Palumbo, 1963.
Earlier version in *Italica* 26 (1949): 198–204; (Fatini, 3439); also in *Lo Frutto* (Accademia di Studi "Cielo d'Alcamo") 3 (1952–1954): 174–87.
Noting that magic is a fundamental thematic and structural element in the *OF*—functioning both to complicate and, like a *deus ex machina*, to resolve complications (p. 44)—states that Ariosto is essentially deriding the common belief in magic. Like his contemporary Pomponazzi, whose *De incantationibus* (1520) seeks the rational basis of all phenomena, Ariosto takes to task common belief in the supernatural. Suggests an ironic dimension in the poem: the Christian paladins are more susceptible to magic than the pagans (p. 46).

෫๑ 871. ———. Introduzione. In *Opere minori*, by Ludovico Ariosto, edited by Aldo Vallone, pp. 9–38. Milan: Rizzoli, 1964.
Briefly characterizes Ariosto's minor works, noting that both the Latin and vernacular lyrics were for the most part exercises by which the poet sought to clarify his own poetic ideals. Identifies in the vernacular lyrics two principal types—lyrical-amatory and satirical-realistic—the styles of which converge in the composition of the *OF*. Notes a lack of the personal element in the lyric poetry—oftentimes "un assoluto distacco dalle cose e dagli stessi sentimenti" (p. 16)—and documents this "impression" with a discussion of certain stylistic and thematic aspects of the poetry. In discussing the comedies, underscores the obvious taste for narration, for the lively tone of wit, and especially for the importance of the word, its nuances, and multiple meanings (pp. 21–23). Views the satires as focusing on one central character, the author, to whom all other figures are secondary, and the author's position as one of embracing an antiheroic stance, speaking only for himself and not intending to present his views as exemplary and to be imposed upon others. Includes selected bibliography (pp. 30–37).

෫๑ 872. ———. "Ariosto nell'ultima critica." *Libri e riviste d'Italia* 26 (1974): 779–80.
Summary view of trends in Ariosto criticism from the critical perspectives

of the nineteenth century to recent contributions, especially those of a philological nature.

◄§ 873. VAN DEN BERGH, H., AND J. IJSEWIJN. "Ariosto, Ludovico." In *Moderne Encyclopedie der Wereldliteratuur*, edited by J. Aerts et al, 1:173–75. 9 vols. Hilversum, Netherlands: P. Brand, 1963–1977.
Biographical sketch and summary history of the composition of Ariosto's works. Focuses on the *OF* and its influences and provides essential information regarding the satires and the comedies. Includes selected bibliography.

◄§ 874. VAN ELDEN, W. "Lodovico Ariosto." *Gids* (Amsterdam) 124 (1961): 78–85.
General appreciation of the *OF*, noting that Ariosto, in his fantasy world, never completely loses touch with reality. Brief comments on Ariosto's frequent and unexpected transitions to humor and on his perfection of the *ottava rima*.

◄§ 875. VAN WOUDENBERG, GERDA. "Een sonnet van Joannes Six Van Chandelier geïnspireerd door een Motief uit Ariosto's *Orlando Furioso?*" *De Nieuwe Taalgids* 49 (1956): 81–83.
Suggests that Joannes Six Van Chandelier's (1620–1695) sonnet "Op twistige steeghjes gebuuren," on the quarreling of neighbors, was directly inspired by *OF* 5. 1–3. Briefly discusses the Dutch poet's stay in Rome and apparent familiarity with Italian culture.

◄§ 876. VARANINI, GIORGIO. "La Morte di Zerbino (*Orl. Fur.*, XXIV, ott. 76–86)." In *Annuario del Liceo R. Foresi*, pp. 121–33. Pisa: Giardini, 1967.
Observes that although psychologically simple, the characters of Zerbino and Isabella and the story of their tragic love leave an indelible impression upon the sensitive reader. Notes that contrary to a consuming passion that often leads to folly in the *OF*, the love binding this couple is a pure love perennially celebrated in poetry ("l'amore cantato da tutti i poeti," p. 125), a love that reveals its strength in the face of suffering and death. Argues that what the poet and his readers feel for the two unfortunate lovers is much more than a fleeting emotion, as De Sanctis and others after him have suggested. Sees in the noble theme and in the elegiac tone of the episode the poet's strong emotional participation, "il palpito del cuore del poeta" (pp. 130, 133).

◄§ 877. VARESE, MARINA FEDERICA. *Batjuškov. Un poeta tra Russia e Italia*. Padua: Liviana, 1970. 208p.

Passim comments on Batiushkov's interest in Ariosto, with an Italian translation of his essay on Ariosto and Tasso (pp. 179–84), first published in 1817
(in *Opyty v proze*, St. Petersburg, pp. 233–52).

✒ 878. VASOLI, CESARE. "L'astrologia a Ferrara tra la metà del Quattrocento e la metà del Cinquecento." In *Il Rinascimento nelle corti padane:
società e cultura*, ed. Paolo Rossi et al., pp. 469–94. Bari: De Donato,
1977.
Extensive discussion of the importance of magic and astrology in Renaissance Ferrara, noting its reflection throughout the OF and its documentation
in *Il Negromante* (pp. 469–71).

✒ 879. VAZZANA, STENO. "Romanticismo ariostesco." *Carovana* 10
(1960): 66–69.
Interprets the OF as an intimate spiritual diary of the poet, one whose
unity lies in an elegiac longing for personal ideals. Sees the projection of
Ariosto's own sentiments in the character of Medoro, whose role is central to
the poem in that he functions as the most profoundly human and truly heroic of all the protagonists.

✒ 880. VENTURI, GIANNI. "Il Giardino e la letteratura: saggi d'interpretazione e problemi metodologici." In his *Le Scene dell'Eden. Teatro, arte,
giardini nella letteratura italiana*, pp. 98–131. Ferrara: Italo Bovolenta,
1979.
Brief mention of the garden topos in the OF and the importance of garden
descriptions as "indicativi per l'encomiastica esaltazione della potenza estense e della sicurezza apportata a Ferrara dalla previdente politica dei duchi"
(p. 111). Also notes importance for the theory of *ut pictura poesis* and for the
Renaissance concept of the parallel between the arts of Vasari's discussion of
the Ariosto-Dossi relationship in the 1550 edition of his *Lives of the Artists*—
eliminated in the 1568 edition (pp. 112–13n35).

✒ 881. ———. "Le Scelte metriche e teatrali dell'Ariosto." In his *Le Scene
dell'Eden. Teatro, arte, giardini nella letteratura italiana*, pp. 3–34.
Ferrara: Italo Bovolenta, 1979.
Also in *Rivista italiana di drammaturgia* 1 (1976): 19–42.
Considers the reasons for Ariosto's choice of *endecasillabo sdrucciolo* in the
verse redactions of the comedies and concludes that although the dramatist
was seeking an appropriate equivalent to the classical meter of Plautine and
Terentian comedies, his major interest, as a writer involved in the production
of plays and recitation of the text, was in a theatrically effective language that
would satisfy the exigencies of both literary decorum and the evolving concept of theater as a composite metaphor of social realities. Focusing on the

use of the *endecasillabo sdrucciolo*, traces the critical fortunes of Ariosto's verse comedies from their reception by his contemporaries to the evaluation of nineteenth-century critics, especially Ginguené and Schlegel. Notes that the most lively interest in the function of verse in the comedies was in the eighteenth century, when in critical discussions of dramaturgy, Ariosto became a point of reference.

⚜ 882. ———. "Scena e giardini a Ferrara al tempo dell'Ariosto." In his *Le Scene dell'Eden. Teatro, arte, giardini nella letteratura italiana*, pp. 35–52. Ferrara: Italo Bovolenta, 1979.
Also in *Il Rinascimento nelle corti padane: società e cultura*, ed. Paolo Rossi et al. (Bari: De Donato, 1977), pp. 553–67, and in *Musei ferraresi*, nos. 5–6 (1975–1976): 152–59.
Discusses the aesthetics and symbolic function of the urban garden in Ferrara during the Renaissance, noting in particular the garden's association with the topoi of the Earthly Paradise and the Golden Age, assured and protected by Este rule. Considers several of the gardens in the *OF* as commemorations and exaltations of Este grandeur, the sole protector of the Edenic ideal.

⚜ 883. VENTURINI, GIUSEPPE. *Orazio Ariosti e la polemica intorno alla superiorità del Tasso sull'Ariosto*. Atti e memorie della Deputazione Provinciale Ferrarese di Storia Patria. Serie Terza, vol. 12. Ferrara: SATE, 1972. 93p.
Chapter 1 ("Il posto dell'Ariosto nella più grande polemica del Cinquecento") discusses the Camillo Pellegrino–Orazio Ariosti exchange and the latter's defense of Ludovico Ariosto. Chapter 2 ("Le *Difese* dell'*Orlando Furioso* e il pensiero critico dell'Ariosti") outlines the poetics of Ariosti and discusses how it was used to defend Ariosto. Notes that Ariosti argued for the use of discretion in applying Aristotelian rules and declared that the judgment of superiority relative to Ariosto and Tasso depends on the quality of their poetry, not their adherence to precepts. Ariosti explained away immoral passages in the *OF* as allegory. Second part of volume is entitled *Documenti* and includes a letter from Tasso to Ariosti (16 January 1577); "Le Risposte del sig. Orazio Ariosto ad alcuni luoghi del dialogo dell'Epica Poesia del Sig. Camillo Pellegrino; ne' quali si riprendeva l'*Orlando Furioso* dell'Ariosto"; and "'Delle differenze poetiche'—Discorso del signor Torquato Tasso per risposta al signor Orazio Ariosto."

⚜ 884. ———. "I Disticci di un gesuita sulla tomba dell'Ariosto." *Accademie e biblioteche d'Italia* 44, no. 6 (1976): 418–31.
On the basis of correspondence between Ariosto's *pronipote* Ludovico Ariosti and the poet G. B. Guarini, documents the authorship of three Latin

distichs engraved on Ariosto's tomb in the Biblioteca Ariostea in Ferrara. The distichs were composed by a renowned sixteenth-century Jesuit poet and dramatist, Bernardino Stefonio, whose career and works are briefly described.

≈§ 885. VERDIZZOTTI, GIOVAN MARIO. *Lettere a Orazio Ariosti.* Edited by Giuseppe Venturini. Bologna: Commissione per i Testi di Lingua, 1969 (printed in 1970). 92p.
Edition of eleven letters written by Verdizzotti to Orazio Ariosti from 1580 to 1585 in defense of Ludovico Ariosto. Introduction (pp. vii–xii) discusses Verdizzotti's role in the polemic between the *ariostisti* and the *tassisti*.

≈§ 886. VERKUYL, P. E. L. "Emulatio in een sonnet van De Harduyn naar Du Bellay" (*Emulatio* of Du Bellay in a sonnet of De Harduyn). *Spiegel der letteren* (Antwerp) 21 (1979): 49–62.
Extensive analysis of a sonnet by Justus De Harduyn (1582–1640) as an *emulatio* of Du Bellay's "Le grand flambeau" (*L'Olive*, sonnet 31), noting as sources for Du Bellay both Petrarch and Ariosto (*OF* 45.38–39) and suggesting that textual evidence is such to support the hypothesis that the Dutch poet was familiar with the text of the *OF*.

≈§ 887. VINAVER, EUGÈNE. *The Rise of Romance.* Oxford: Clarendon Press; New York: Oxford University Press, 1971. 158p.
Notes the significance of the medieval romance technique of interlace to Ariosto's narrative structure. See especially pp. 92–94.

≈§ 888. VINCENTI, LEONELLO. "Ariosto in Germania." In his *Alfieri e lo "Sturm und Drang" e altri saggi di letteratura italiana e tedesca*, pp. 57–87. Florence: Leo S. Olschki, 1966.
Also in *Nuove lettere emiliane*, nos. 9–11 (1965): 39–46; revision of "La Fortuna dell'Ariosto: In Germania," *L'Italia che scrive* 16, no. 9 (1933): 251–53; Fatini, 2993.
Reviews the critical reception of Ariosto in Germany during the eighteenth century, noting in particular the importance of Wieland's interest in the poet. Summary view of Ariosto's fortune among German romantics and nineteenth-century cultural historians (e.g., Jacob Burckhardt), concluding that modern critics and writers have shown a preference for Torquato Tasso.

≈§ 889. VISCARDI, ANTONIO. "Ludovico Ariosto: lingua, letteratura e poesia nel primo '500." In his *Storia della letteratura italiana dalle origini al Rinascimento*, pp. 555–86. Milan: Nuova Accademia Editrice, 1960.
General introduction to Ariosto following the critical perspectives of Atti-

lio Momigliano and Benedetto Croce. Discusses Ariosto's poetic language in the context of the linguistic canons of Pietro Bembo, noting that both writers belong to the same "sfera ideale: che è quella del classicismo del primo Cinquecento" (pp. 563–64). Brief "spiritual biography" of the poet, characterized as one anxious to escape into his own personal world of fantasy and study. Summary discussion of minor works, concluding that the satires, though a faithful autobiography (p. 572), have little literary value. Introduction to the *OF*, underscoring the poem's unity, as defined by Momigliano, and harmony.

◄§ 890. Visconti, Maria Luise. "Trionfo della favola bella della vita nel poema ariosteo." In her *Riflessioni letterarie*, pp. 5–11. Pompei: Tipografia S. Sicignano, [1969?].
Notes that the poet's genius is revealed in his capacity to control the variety of his material. Regards the *OF* as "[la] vita stessa rappresentata sotto la specie della fantasia" (p. 10).

◄§ 891. Visser, Fernando. "La Casa di Ludovico Ariosto in contrada del Mirasole." In *Musei ferraresi* (Bollettino annuale, 1971), pp. 81–91. Florence: Centro Di, 1972.
On the architectural problems and details of Girolamo da Carpi's plans for Ariosto's house.

◄§ 892. Vitale, Mario. "Ludovico Ariosto fra illusioni e conoscenza." Naples: Giannini, 1979. 12p. Address originally delivered at the *Convitto Nazionale*, Naples, n.d.
Brief observations on the *OF* in its portrayal of the complexity of human nature and as an example, in art, of the aesthetic resolution of the essentially irrational forces of the universe.

◄§ 893. Vitale, Maurizio, gen. ed. "Ludovico Ariosto." In *Antologia della letteratura italiana*, 2:1103–15. 5 vols. Vol. 2 (1966) edited by Alberto Asor Rosa; cited section edited by Carlo Salinari. Milan: Rizzoli, 1965–1968.
Summary introduction to Ariosto and to the *OF*, noting that the poem is essentially the product of an analysis of the complexity of human feelings and that its unity lies in the dialectic of multiplicity (p. 1109). Brief discussion of the poem's fundamental thematic elements and its structural components. Includes selected bibliography, pp. 1111–15. See also Salinari, Carlo, entry 730.

◄§ 894. Viti, Gorizio. *Guida all'"Orlando Furioso."* Florence: Le Monnier, 1964. 195p.

Introductory manual with a brief biography, as well as a description of the structure of the OF and its major motifs; summary of each canto, followed by a brief critical analysis. Appended anthology of selected commentaries by well-known critics. Index of characters included.

📎 895. VITTORINI, ELIO. "Ariosto e pittura. (Differenza tra il processo storico che sfocia nell'*Orlando* e quello che culmina nella pittura sua contemporanea)." In his *Diario in pubblico*, pp. 312–13. Milan: Bompiani, 1957.
Originally published as an introduction to three-volume edition of the OF (Turin: Einaudi, 1950); Fatini, 3462.

📎 896. WAKEFIELD, D. F. "Fragonard's Drawings for Ariosto's *Orlando Furioso*." *The Connoisseur* 200, no. 804 (February 1979): 131–34.
Observations on twenty-eight drawings "for an unpublished edition of Ariosto's epic" (p. 131), exhibited at Agnew Gallery, London. "It seems, in this case, that Fragonard almost certainly worked from the original text as no intermediary would have been available. . . . Fragonard stuck closely to the narrative. Detail is often sacrificed, but legibility always remains paramount" (p. 131). Notes that "action and movement were the prime concern" of the painter and that he had a remarkable ability to "portray a whole range of mood and emotion" (p. 131). Nine illustrations.

📎 897. WALDMAN, GUIDO. Introduction. In *Orlando Furioso, An English Prose Translation by Guido Waldman*, pp. vii–xvii. London, Oxford, New York: Oxford University Press, 1974.
Brief biographical sketch and discussion of the origins of the OF. Notes the poem's superiority to its predecessors in the Italian romance tradition, arguing, however, that as a laureate, Ariosto shows little interest in the encomiastic thread of his narrative. Reviews the history of English translations of the poem, the impossibility of rendering the *ottava rima* in English verse, and, consequently, the decision to translate it into prose, which captures the *narrative* art of the poet. Includes annotated index (pp. 574–630).

📎 898. WALEY, PAMELA. Introduction. In *Orlando Furioso: A Selection*, edited by Pamela Waley, pp. 1–25. Manchester: Manchester University Press, 1975.
General introduction to Ariosto and his writings, with observations on their social and historical context. Summary discussion of major thematic elements of the OF and on Ariosto's perspective on human nature and contemporary life. Traces important narrative lines in OI developed in the OF.

෫ 899. WARNKE, FRANK. "Baroque Transformations in the Romance Epic." In *Actes du VIᵉ Congrès de l'Association Internationale de Littérature Comparée* (1970), pp. 531–35. Stuttgart: Erich Bieber, 1975.

Considers transformations in the romance epic from Ariosto to the late Renaissance (Tasso, Marino, and Lope de Vega), using as a basis of analysis the archetypal figures of diverse aspects of woman in the *OF*: Angelica, Bradamante, and Alcina. Argues that the unity of identity of such figures undergoes a "phenomenon of contamination" (p. 532) by the late Renaissance and that such character types become mimetic: "Discrete symbolic or mythic identity is dissolved in the interpenetration of roles" (p. 533). Views such transformation as a movement toward the baroque and beyond to the modern (in character portrayal). Contrasts aesthetic distance in Ariosto and Tasso: "Whereas the older poet presents a scene pictorially, with a virtual absence of emotional involvement or emotional stimulus, Tasso consistently provides descriptive passages which, directly evoking the sensations and emotions of the participants, imply the emotional involvement of the poet and demand that involvement from the reader" (p. 533). Concludes with a comparative view of Renaissance and baroque styles, and, in particular, of Ariosto's perspective on the phenomenal world and that of fully baroque epic authors whose works evidence "severe doubts as to the validity of the phenomenal world" (p. 535).

෫ 900. WARREN, EMMA BRESCIA. "The Imagery of Ludovico Ariosto in *Orlando Furioso*." *DAI* 19, no. 1 (1958): 134. (Columbia University, 1957. 309p.)

Examines the variety of poetic figures in the *OF*, arguing that "comparison," in particular, is integral to Ariosto's poetic vision.

෫ 901. WEAVER, ELISSA B. "Lettura dell'intreccio dell'*Orlando furioso*: il caso delle tre pazzie d'amore." *Strumenti critici*, anno 11, 34, fasc. 3 (1977): 384–406.

Taking as a starting point the medieval romance tradition of literary *entrelacement*, or interlace, examines the structural, thematic, and linguistic affinities between three central episodes of the *OF*, all having to do with frustrated love (Orlando, Bradamante, and Rodomonte) and how their basic thematics—e.g., love-madness, the dangers inherent in knowing too much, and the relationship between reality and illusion—relate to the structural and thematic patterns of the work as a whole.

෫ 902. WEBBER, JOAN MALORY. *Milton and His Epic Tradition*. Seattle and London: University of Washington Press, 1979. 244p.

Considerable discussion (passim) of cultural perspectives, the ethics, and the structure of the *OF* in epic tradition; particular attention given to comparisons of the *DC* and the *OF* as important predecessors of *Paradise Lost*. Notes Ariosto's continuation of the diffuse structure of epic, observing that "it is just the 'diffuseness' of epic, in its capacity for encyclopedic choice, that enables it accurately to represent the human mind at any stage while still maintaining its own tradition" (pp. 7–8). States that in the *OF*, "The exaggeratedly episodic, fragmentary organization of *Orlando Furioso* is intended to demonstrate life's incoherence, the difficulty of achieving and maintaining any central purpose" (p. 57). Notes elsewhere, "In the *Orlando Furioso* good and evil exist side by side, in similar and indistinguishable forms, and it is impossible to tell which is which, or even to know that a particular thing, once identified, will maintain its identity. There is no question of searching below or beyond appearances to get to the truth. Ariosto certainly has no Christian solution to this problem, since for him Christianity is as pointless as everything else. To deal with the world is to learn that you cannot deal with it. His art gives him a kind of magicianship that enables him to see life as funny; symbols like Angelica's magic ring suggest the possibility of gaining enough transcendence over material things to become indifferent to them" (p. 180). Regarding Ariosto's reduction of the design of the *DC*, argues that Astolfo's trip from the underworld to the moon "is an obvious parody and rejection of Dante's experience. The only piece of wisdom given Astolfo here—and it is important—is that poetry creates value. He learns this in the moon, from St. John, and that is important too, for it denies the objective truth of the Bible, just as the whole sequence undercuts Dante's vision" (p. 23); and that with Ariosto, "Subjectivity . . . has been carried a step further than in Dante, whose universe had a generally accepted universal justification. And the relationship between language and sanity is total. In the *Inferno*, there is a margin of grace. The poet in a faint or in a dream may be carried from place to place, revived, set going again, because of Beatrice and all that she represents. The very title, *Orlando Furioso*, signifies the vast space between the two poems. Ariosto's fictional hero cannot depend upon his sanity, not because he ever tries to approach the limits of meaning, but because the world has none" (p. 25).

903. WEIDLICH, CARLO. "L'Ariosto a tavola." *La Lucerna* (Vittoria, Sicily) 19, no. 5 (1964): 14–18.

Uses biographical notes of Ariosto's son Virginio, among other documents, to prove the poet's temperate nature and cites passages from his writings in which his attitudes toward overindulgence are revealed. Notes that Ariosto was moderate in all his activities and abhorred excess in eating and drinking.

904. WEINBERG, BERNARD. "The Quarrel over Ariosto and Tasso." In his *A History of Literary Criticism in the Italian Renaissance*, 2:954–1073. 2 vols. Chicago: University of Chicago Press, 1961.

Extensive and authoritative account of the development of the polemic over Ariosto and Tasso during the sixteenth century, from the earliest commentary on the *OF* (Simone Fornari, 1549) to the comprehensive comparison of the two poets by Faustino Summo (1600). Divides history of the debate into two major periods, the first preceding the publication of the *GL* and concerning the development of polemical issues in connection with Ariosto's poem; the second, a period of seventeen years following the publication of Tasso's poem and of intense polemical activity. Passim discussion of the polemic throughout both volumes.

◄§ 905. WEINBROT, HOWARD D. *Augustus Caesar in "Augustan" England: The Decline of a Classical Norm.* Princeton: Princeton University Press, 1978. 270p.
On literary representation of the figure of Caesar Augustus, notes: "A sign of the consistent literary sniping at Augustus may be seen in the feline survival of the incipient anti-Augustanism in Canto 35, v. 26 of Ariosto's *Orlando Furioso*" (p. 66), in which the poet challenges Virgil's praise of the emperor. Cites the references to Ariosto's mention of Caesar Augustus in eighteenth-century England (p. 67).

◄§ 906. WELLES, ELIZABETH BASSETT. "Magic in the Renaissance Epic: Pulci, Boiardo, Ariosto, Tasso." *DAI* 32, no. 1 (1971): 461–62A. (Yale University, 1970. 264p.)
Surveys the use of magic in the Italian romance, noting that it is especially "complicated and ambiguous" in the *OF*, in which the enchanted castle of Atlante is used as the image of the poem. Discusses magic in relation to various aspects of the poem's themes and structure.

◄§ 907. WHITFIELD, J[OHN] H[UMPHRIES]. "Leon Battista Alberti, Ariosto, and Dosso Dossi." *Italian Studies* 21 (1966): 16–30.
Suggests that one of Alberti's recently discovered *intercenales* (L. B. Alberti, "Alcune intercenali inedite," ed. Eugenio Garin, *Rinascimento*, 2d ser., vol. 4 (1964): 125–258), the *Discordia*, was the source of inspiration for an episode in *OF* 14, the descent of the Archangel Michael to seek out Silence and Discord. Considers the possibility, too, of Alberti's dialogue, *Virtus*, as a source for Ariosto's contemporary, Dossi, in painting *Jupiter and Mercury* (Kunsthistoriches Museum, Vienna).

◄§ 908. WIGGINS, PETER DESA. "A Defense of the *Satires*." In *Ariosto 1974 in America*, edited by Aldo Scaglione (entry 760), pp. 55–68. Ravenna: Longo, 1976.
Defends the poetic quality and artistic originality of the satires against the reservations and evaluations of critics such as Ugo Focolo, Francesco De

Sanctis, and Benedetto Croce. Considers their autobiographical elements not as mere personal data, but as evoking "a poetic truth reaching far beyond the scope of [the poet's] private life" (p. 60). Suggests that the poetry of the satires is to be found in the fictional narrator who, created by Ariosto's skillful "selection and omission" of personal information, conducts himself like a "modern Horace" (p. 63). Concludes that they are intended as works of persuasion (p. 66) and that their originality lies in the self-awareness of the fictional narrator who, like the *cantastorie* of the OF, "suffers the torments of love along with his heroes, but is saved by his perception of the fact" (p. 68).

909. ———. Introduction. In *The Satires of Ludovico Ariosto: A Renaissance Autobiography*, translated by Peter DeSa Wiggins, pp. ix–xlv. Athens: Ohio University Press, 1976.

Revision of "The *Satires* of Ludovico Ariosto," DAI 34, no. 10 (1974): 6608–9A. (Columbia University, 1971. 238p.)

Reviews the critical reception of the satires, from the early recognition of their importance by Luigi Alamanni to Carlo Grabher's *La Poesia minore dell'Ariosto* (1947), "the most rewarding recent study of the *Satires* as poetry" (p. xv); concludes that much criticism has failed to recognize in the satires an ideal self-portrait, preferring instead to view them as pure autobiography (e.g., Croce). Considers Ariosto's use of classical sources, noting especially the nature of Horatian influences and Ariosto's use of Horace to underscore his own irony. Extensive discussion on the nature of irony in the satires and in the OF, noting that its source lies in the confrontation of illusion with reality, whether in the world of the poet's own experiences and disappointed expectations or in the fictive world of Orlando, for whom false illusions become an unbearable burden. Concluding discussion on the history of the text of the satires and their translators.

910. ———. "Galileo on Characterization in the *Orlando Furioso*." *Italica* 57, no. 4 (1980): 255–67.

Argues for the "modernity" of Galilei's reading of the OF and its potential for a more accurate assessment of the poem's position in the "spectrum of narrative art from Homer to the present" (p. 256). Discusses Galilei's observations on characterization in the OF, noting that his perspective is anti-allegorical and that he perceives Ariosto's protagonists as "complex representations of reality as opposed to signs pointing to easily recognizabale concepts or types in moral philosophy" (p. 257). Concludes that Galilei's concentration on the mimetic and coherent qualities of character makes him one of the earliest readers of narrative fiction foreshadowing the novel.

◆⅌ 911. WILKINS, ERNEST HATCH. "Ariosto." In A *History of Italian Literature*, revised by Thomas G. Bergin, pp. 185–95. Cambridge: Harvard University Press, 1974.
First edition 1954; Fatini, 3567.

◆⅌ 912. WISE, VALERIE MERRIAM. "Metaphors for the Imagination in Ovid, Ariosto, and Drayton." ADD (1978–1979): 295. (Harvard University, 1979.)
Ph.D. dissertation, not abstracted.

◆⅌ 913. W *Kręgu "Gofreda" I "Orlando."* Księga Pamiątkowa Sesji Naukowej Piotra Kochanowskiego (w Krakowie, dnia 4–6 kwietnia 1967 r). Wrokław-Warsaw-Cracow: Polska Akademia Nauk, 1970. 294p.
Proceedings of a congress devoted to Piotr Kochanowski (1566–1620) on the four-hundredth anniversary of his birth. Kochanowski completed a Polish version of the GL and translated portions of the OF. Includes an Italian summary of the articles (pp. 273–80).
Volume includes: Sante Graciotti, "Piotr Kochanowski W Polskim Oświeceniu Oraz Przekłady Ariosta I Tassa Pióra Krasickiego I Trembeckiego" (Piotr Kochanowski in the Polish Enlightenment and the translations of Ariosto and Tasso by Krasicki and Trembecki) (entry 383); Mieczysław Brahmer, "Kilka Uwag O Polskim *Orlandzie*" (Some considerations on the Polish *Orlando* (entry 127); Zofia Szmydtowa, "Lament Sakrypanta W Oryginale I Spolszczeniu Piotra Kochanowskiego Na Tle Renesansowych Przetworzeń Motywu" (The Lament of Sacripante in the original and in the version of Piotr Kochanowski against the background of the Renaissance versions of the theme) (entry 835).

◆⅌ 914. WLASSICS, TIBOR. "Il Tasso del Galilei." *Studi secenteschi* 12 (1972): 119–62. Biblioteca dell'*Archivum Romanicum*, 1st ser., vol. 118.
On the use of theatrical imagery in the GL and in the OF, notes, "La passione teatrale del Tasso, nettamente presecentesca, fa parte di quel suo amore per le apparenze, il quale, esteso ad una concezione della vita come effimera illusione e finale delusione, si indica come nucleo vitale della sua poesia nell'interpretazione di Giovanni Getto" (e.g., in his *Nel mondo della 'Gerusalemme,'* Florence, 1968, p. 138). Observes, in reference to Galilei's discussion in his *Considerazioni al Tasso* of OF 1.52 and GL 19.60–69: "L'accostamento galileiano dei due 'teatri' è eloquente in sé; a parte la goduta gradazione, da *voyeur*, del Tasso, e la diversità da fiaba dell'Ariosto, vi si nota il diverso significato della parola 'scena' nei due poeti. L'apparizione di Angelica assomiglia per un attimo ad una sorpresa o 'machina' da teatro che imita la natura; nel Tasso il teatro è la natura stessa, e si direbbe che, nella

sua concezione, la natura stia 'imitando' a sua volta, baroccamente, la propria imitazione ad arte" (p. 139).

915. WRIGHT, CAROL VON PRESSENTIN. "The Lunatic, the Lover, and
 the Poet: Themes of Love and Illusion in Three Renaissance Epics."
 DAI 30, no. 9 (1970): 3962A. (University of Michigan, 1969. 301p.)
 Considers illusion and reality in the *OF*, the *GL*, and the *FQ*, both as
themes and as elements informing the structure of the poems—each poet
having "considered the idea of a poem as itself a form of illusion and yet a
reflection of reality." Argues that the differing approaches to the themes in
the three poems determine their underlying differences as works of art.
Maintains that Ariosto, "focusing on psychological problems of perception,
develops in the *Orlando furioso* a metaphor of universal madness. If the
characters of his poem face a chaotic world, it is primarily their own, self-
caused blindness that causes them to fall. Through the device of a 'mad'
narrator, Ariosto extends the central paradox of knowledge beyond the limits
of the poem itself."

916. WYSS, IDA. *Virtù und Fortuna bei Boiardo und Ariost.* Beiträge
 zur Kulturgeschichte des Mittelalters und der Renaissance, band 48.
 Hildesheim, W. Ger.: H. A. Gerstenberg, 1973. 94p.
 Reprint of 1931 edition; Fatini, 2586.

917. YEOMAN, MARGARET ANNE. "Allegorical Rhetoric in *Orlando Furioso.*" *DAI* 39, no. 12 (1979): 7336A. (University of California, Irvine,
 1978. 231p.)
 "Irony, the feature of Ariosto's poem that has attracted modern critics the
most [has] a unique relation to allegory in the rhetorical tradition. This kind
of irony, which is based on the rhetorical concepts of *ethos* and *pathos*, is
recognized by the rhetoricians as closely akin to humor and therefore as
useful in both demonstrative and deliberative contexts. Developing a specific
ethos for his narrator, and playing on the potential for irony that *pathos* offers, Ariosto manages to comment seriously and consistently on his literary
tradition and especially on his moral and political milieu. Without being
offensive, he nevertheless develops and maintains a consistent moral position
that is revealed through his ironic manipulation of the plot and characters of
the *Orlando Furioso.* This technique and this point of view are illustrated in
the three main features of the narrative: Alcina's garden, the relationship of
Bradamante and Ruggiero, and Orlando's madness."

918. ZACHA, RICHARD BANE. "Ariosto and Spenser: A Further Study in
 the Relationship between the *Orlando Furioso* and the *Faerie Queene.*"

DAI 23, no. 5 (1962): 1690. (The Catholic University of America, 1962. 168p.)

Argues that Spenser, like the sixteenth-century allegorizers of the *OF*, considered Ariosto "a patriotic, ethical, and religious poet" and that Spenser is most successful as an allegorist in those matters in which he had Ariosto as a model, e.g., holiness and temperance.

৺ঠ 919. ———. "The Allegories of the 1542 *Orlando Furioso.*" *Allegorica* 1, no. 1 (1976): 166–85.

Notes that from 1542 on, almost all editions of the *OF* appeared with an allegorical explication preceding each canto and that the 1584 Venetian edition attempts to demonstrate a sustained, coherent allegory dominating the narrative. Provides a translation of the anonymously written allegories preceding each canto of the 1542 edition (Appresso Gabriel Iolito di Ferrarii, M.D. XLII).

৺ঠ 920. ZAMBONI, ARMANDO. "Il governatore Ludovico Ariosto e i briganti della Garfagnana." *Gazzetta di Reggio* 9, no. 244 (1959).

On the poet's hardships during his tenure as governor of the Garfagnana region (1522–1525) and his association with two particular bandits. Unavailable; cited in Medici, 49, without page reference.

৺ঠ 921. ZAMPOLLI, ANTONIO. "Le Concordanze diacroniche dell'*Orlando Furioso*: procedura per l'elaborazione automatica." In *Ludovico Ariosto: lingua, stile e tradizione*, edited by Cesare Segre (entry 789), pp. 237–64. Milan: Feltrinelli, 1976.

Details, with flowcharts, the operational procedures for a computerized diachronic concordance and indexes of the three editions of the *OF*. See also Segre, Cesare, entry 788.

৺ঠ 922. ZANETTE, EMILIO. *Conversazioni sull'"Orlando Furioso.*" Pisa: Nistri-Lischi, 1958. 395p.

Collection of essays, or "impressioni" (p. 55). "Dall'Ariosto al Boiardo," pp. 9–60: compares the styles of the two authors, their depictions of characters, and the structures of their epic poems, concluding that Boiardo's tone is "fresher" and less studied, his characters more "lifelike" and less stereotyped than Ariosto's, and his structure less programmed and more open ended (the two poems are "come due grandi sinfonie l'una compiuta e l'altra incompiuta," p. 52); "Frati ed eremiti," pp. 61–81: demonstrates the relationship between episodes in the *OF* and in Castellano Castellani's sacred drama, *Sant'Onofrio*, and that the poet reveals in his treatment of clerics and religious motifs a traditional Christian orthodoxy; "I due volti di Olimpia," pp. 82–111: considers the complexities and contradictions in Olimpia's character and discusses two particular classical sources suggested by earlier critics, Ariadne and Medea; "L'orca e l'orco," pp. 112–42: considers Ariosto's use of his primary sources (Ovid and Boiardo) for the two monsters; "Il palazzo di Atlante," pp. 143–64: concerns the indeterminate location of Atlante's palace and suggests that the reason might be due to the author's desire to heighten the sense of the fantastic or to accommodate inconsistencies in the narrative line, but without exploring either hypothesis discusses the palace as exemplary of picturesque variety in the poem and of the constant flux of its spatial dimension: "nella sua [Ariosto's] fantasia lo spazio non ha quell'aspetto di fisso e di stabile, con cui noi siamo abituati a pensarlo . . .; è uno spazio accomodante e arrendevole, che si allarga e si ristringe secondo le esigenze della poesia" (p. 164); "I gesti smisurati," pp. 165–83: examines the application of this Boiardesque motif to the *OF* and particularly to Rodomonte and to certain deeds of Orlando; "Due mori," pp. 184–209: considers the function of the Cloridano and Medoro episode in the structure of the poem and notes the supreme irony of the fact that their lowly origin and essential goodness, which endear Medoro to Angelica, are integral to the eventual madness of the poem's protagonist; "Prima della pazzia," pp. 210–31: analyzes the mental state of Orlando in the *OI* and up to the moment of his madness in *OF* 23; notes that he is perfectly sane until the moment he discovers Angelica's marriage to Medoro and that madness results from the shattering of his illusions regarding Angelica; "La pazzia," pp. 232–52: concludes that Orlando's madness, "medically" accurate in its details, provides a grotesque parallel to the hero's ideal self, in that the energy and heroic feats of the Christian paladin are translated into a mute display of destruction; "Astolfo," pp. 253–74: considers the changes in the character from the *OI* (handsome and fun loving) to the *OF* (the model English gentleman) and the resultant role of the character in the dimension of the poem's irony and ambiguity; "Anime dannate," pp. 275–88: relates Astolfo's journey to the underworld of Dantesque and Boccaccian models, noting that Ariosto's poem precludes a Christian visionary experience and that the damned are women who refused to reciprocate the affections of their lovers; "San Giovanni Evangelista," pp. 289–311: analyzes the paternal and loving nature of the saint as portrayed by Ariosto; "La fine della pazzia," pp. 312–31: interprets the final moments of Orlando's madness and his return to sanity in the context of Christian catharsis and regeneration, warning, however, against any attempt to impose upon the poem a consistently religious interpretation; "Cerco il vincitore," pp. 332–48: studies the final battle between Christians and pagans (canto 41) and the deterioration of the protagonist from hero to mere mortal; "Rodomonte," pp. 349–94: traces the development of the character, whose ugliness belies a heroic dimension fated to be sacrificed to the encomiastic ends of the poem.

923. ——. *Personaggi e momenti nella vita di Ludovico Ariosto.* Milan: Pan Editrice, 1970. 689p.

A number of chapters revised for this volume first appeared in journals. In such cases, the references are given after the chapter annotation. Chapter 1, "La sua mamma," pp. 7–31: speculations on the marriage of Ariosto's parents and the attitude of their children toward them based on extant documents, concluding that Ariosto found his father a more interesting personality than his mother. Chapter 2, "Infanzia fanciullezza adolescenza di un genio," pp. 32–38: concludes, upon the basis of Satire 6, 154–56, that Ariosto was not a child prodigy and that there exists no documented proof of his precociousness. Chapter 3, "Studente," pp. 39–54: discusses Ariosto's years as a student enrolled in the "Studio Ferrarese" (1489–1496), his early interest in law, the important influence of his teacher, Gregorio Ellio di Andrea d'Angelo, on his formation; concludes with earliest period as court poet. Chapter 4, "Hippolyti Cardinalis familiaris continuus commensalis," pp. 55–64: on initial period of Ariosto's employment in service of Ippolito d'Este; calls the three-distich epigram addressed to the cardinal, "Hippolytum Estensem Episcopum Ferrariae," the basis in spirit for the OF (pp. 59–61); considers Ariosto as initially a conformist and pleased with comforts of the cardinal's household (also in *L'Osservatore politico letterario* 15, no. 7 [1969]: 83–91). Chapter 5, "Il suo diffamatore," pp. 65–75: discusses the relationship between Ariosto and a contemporary poet, Ercole Strozzi, whose poem in Latin hexameters, "Venatio," ridicules Ariosto; concludes that Ariosto was fond of Strozzi, who did not reciprocate these feelings and did not appreciate his genius. Chapter 6, "Da Maria a Marta," pp. 76–106: Ariosto's claim in his satire to Bembo that personal tragedies resulted in a lack of poetic creativity prompts speculation on the poet's literary activities in the early years of the sixteenth century and particularly on the genesis of the OF. Chapter 7, "Il grande assente," pp. 107–33: considers political intrigue at the Este court as the basis for Ariosto's allegorical eclogue "Tirsi e Meliabeo," and conjectures on the absence of Cardinal Ippolito from the historical figures represented in the drama. Chapter 8, "'Cavallar mi feo,'" pp. 134–76: recreates Ariosto's several diplomatic missions on behalf of the Este to the court of Julius II during the period 1509–1510. Chapter 9, "Prima e dopo Ravenna," pp. 177–91: observations on the political events involving Ferrara and the Estensi from 1511 until early 1513, in particular, Julius II's seige of Ravenna; conjectures on Ariosto's reactions to the events and the degree of his involvement. Chapter 10, "Alessandra," pp. 192–222: narrates Ariosto's relationship with Orsolina Sassomarino, mother of his illegitimate son, Virginio, and with Alessandra Benucci, noting the purely conjectural aspect of any identification with Alessandra of the several unnamed women in Ariosto's writings. Chapter 11, "Durante la composizione," pp. 223–39: concludes that familiarity with the OF during the years of its compositions was limited to a very few of Ariosto's acquaintances; conjectures on Ariosto's psychological state during period of revisions (also in *L'Osservatore politico letterario* 14, no. 1 [1968]: 89–94). Chapter 12, "La musa contro la porpora," pp. 240–62: analyzes Ariosto's reasons for not accompanying Ippolito d'Este to Hungary in 1517; considers Ariosto's explanation of his decision in Satire 1. Chapter 13, "Il 'Sacro Cigno,'" pp. 263–94: considerations on the genesis of Ariosto's dedication of the OF to Ippolito d'Este and the cardinal's reactions to the dedication. Chapter 14, "L'altro padrone," pp. 295–320: narrates Ariosto's diplomatic and literary experiences while in the employ of Alfonso d'Este. Chapter 15, "Il suo cugino Rinaldo," pp. 321–47: biography of Ariosto's cousin, one of the most frequently mentioned relatives in Michele Catalano's life of the poet. Chapter 16, "Lucrezia Borgia," pp. 348–58: considers Ariosto's relationship with Lucrezia Borgia, concurring with her biographer, Maria Bellonci, that the OF was not appreciated by Lucrezia. Chapter 17, "Truffe di un poeta-editore," pp. 359–67: discusses Ariosto's preparation of the second edition of the OF (1521), commenting on the extent of the changes claimed to have been made from the original version (also in *L'Osservatore politico letterario* 14, no. 8 [1968]: 97–104). Chapter 18, "Il suo rivale," pp. 368–96: considers the relationship between Ariosto and a contemporary poet in the employ of the Este, Cassio da Narni, whose epic romance, *La Morte del Danese* (1521), reveals attempts at rivaling the OF; hypothesizes on Ariosto's failure to acknowledge Cassio da Narni in his own writings and discusses the significance of Cassio da Narni's references to Ariosto in his poem (with original title, "Il suo vicino di casa," in *Nuova Antologia* 484, fasc. 1934 [1962]: 191–220). Chapter 19, "Commissario in Garfagnana," pp. 397–413: notes that Ariosto's appointment as commissioner of the Garfagnana coincided with a period of great fiscal difficulties for the Este, who, unable to pay their functionaries, probably made potentially lucrative appointments as a means of compensation. Chapter 20, "Castagne e briganti," pp. 414–47: using Ariosto's correspondence, discusses his tenure as commissioner in the Garfagnana, with particular attention given to the poet's attitude toward the peasants, his problems with bandits, and his relationship with his patron, Alfonso I. Chapter 21, "A tu per tu con il sovrano," pp. 448–70: analyzes, through Ariosto's correspondence, his changing attitude toward Alfonso I during his assignment in the Garfagnana. Chapter 22, "La speranza folle," pp. 471–501: through an analysis of the texts of the satires, discusses Ariosto's constant but vain hopes for honors and benefices, proposing, in conclusion and in contradiction to traditional Horatian views of Ariosto's ethic, that Ariosto aspired to a cardinalate. Chapter 23, "Chierico anticlericale," pp. 502–13: speculates on the possibility of Ariosto's having seriously considered an ecclesiastical career. Chapter 24, "Il biscugino Alfonso," pp. 514–44: portrait of Ariosto's second cousin, Alfonso,

with particular regard to his relationship with Baldassare Castiglione; conjectures on Castiglione's views on the *OF*. Chapter 25, "Coniugi dell'ultima
ora," pp. 545–73: considers Ariosto's relationship with Alessandra Benucci
after his return from the Garfagnana and discusses their living arrangements
and the possibility of their marriage. Chapter 26, "'Ridiam di Marco
Guazzo,'" pp. 574–603: literary profile of Marco Guazzo, contemporary of
Ariosto and well-known author of romances, and his reception among his
contemporaries (also in *Nuova Antologia* 491, fasc. 1964 [1964]: 456–79).
Chapter 27, "Il suo mecenate," pp. 604–42: on the relationship between
Ariosto and the condottiero Alfonso del Vasto, who, in 1531, bestowed upon
the poet a pension for life and whose prowess as a soldier is celebrated in the
last edition of the *OF*; considers the historical validity of Ariosto's representation of Alfonso. Chapter 28, "Fra il 6 e il 7 luglio 1533," pp. 643–68:
conjectures on Ariosto's attitude toward death and discusses the reaction in
Ferrara to his death. Chapter 29, "Silenzi di Pietro Bembo," pp. 669–88: on
the extent of Ariosto's acquaintance with Bembo, the mysterious omission of
Ariosto's name from Bembo's extensive correspondence and his failure to
contribute to a collection of memorial lyrics planned to honor the poet after
his death (also in *Nuova Antologia* 480, fasc. 1919 [1960]: 305–22).

◆§ 924. ZERNER, HENRI. "Vitruve et le théâtre de la Renaissance italienne." See Klein, Robert, entry 440.

◆§ 925. ZINGARELLI, NICOLA. Introduzione. In *Orlando Furioso*, by Ludovico Ariosto, edited with notes by Nicola Zingarelli, pp. ix–lxxv. Edizione integra. 7th ed. Milan: Hoepli, 1973.
First edition 1934; Fatini, 3077.

◆§ 926. ZITAROSA, G. R. "Ludovico Ariosto." *Aspetti letterari*, n.s., fasc.
4 (1965): 35–52.
Summary discussion of Ariosto's life and character; observations of a general thematic nature on the *OF* and on the poet as reflecting the spirit and
aesthetics of his age.

◆§ 927. ZITNER, S. P. "Spenser's Diction and Classical Precedent." *Philological Quarterly* 45, no. 2 (1966): 360–71.
Notes, "Ideas on decorum in diction, and especially on the archaism and
license appropriate to epic, were in the Renaissance air. Epic, *romanzo* or
whatever, *Orlando Furioso* employed dialect, loan-words and archaism, this
despite Minturno's certainty in *L'Arte Poetica* of 1564 that Ariosto had not
written the sort of poetry that Aristotle taught. Yet Ariosto's verbal revisions
for the third printing of *Orlando* show his Bembian linguistic bias, though
he retains, significantly, non-Tuscan rhyme-words. And the welcomers after

his poetic voyage (*OF* 46.12) include Vida, who continually urged the wholesale plundering of the ancients for all purposes in *De Arte Poetica*, 1527 . . . and Trissino, who affirmed that foreign words were especially appropriate in heroic verse, where variety of languages was to be looked for" (pp. 366–67).

◆§ 928. ZORZI, LUDOVICO. "Ferrara: il sipario ducale." In his *Il Teatro e la città: saggi sulla scena italiana*, pp. 5–59. 2d ed. Turin: Einaudi, 1977.
   Theory and development of stage design in fifteenth-century Ferrara, particularly during the *signoria* of Ercole I (1471–1505). Cites the significance of Ariosto's theater in the evolution of the stage set as metaphor of a specific urban society. Discusses Pellegrino da Udine's set for the 1508 production of *La Cassaria* and interprets Bernardino Prosperi's reference to its perspective design.

Addenda

⋑ 929. CARTER, LIN. Introduction. In *Orlando Furioso, Volume I: The Ring of Angelica*, translated by Richard Hodgens, pp. xii–xvi. London: Pan Books Ltd., 1973.

Popularized introduction to Ariosto. Considers the *OF* as a continuation of the *OI*, noting, however, its superiority, with "a far larger cast of characters, a far richer and more varied landscape, and a plot infinitely more complex" (p. xiii). Suggests that "Ariosto's liveliness and sense of humor" (p. xiv) accounts for the modern reader's interest in the poem; states, however, that the *OF* lacks a "balanced plot structure . . . [and] organic unity" (p. xiv). Sees Ariosto as a major figure in the tradition of fantasy literature, a direct ancestor of writers such as Tolkien.

⋑ 930. SCHMIDGALL, GARY. "George Frideric Handel: Orlando, Ariodante, Alcina." Chap. 2 in *Literature as Opera*, pp. 29–65. New York: Oxford University Press, 1977. 431p.

Notes the importance of the *OF* as a source for the sixteenth- and seventeenth-century court masque, particularly because of its fantastic elements. Considers Ariosto's significance to eighteenth-century opera seria and the *OF* as an important source of operatic plots dealing with the illusionistic. Extensive discussion of Handel's use of the *OF* in three operas and the "affinities of personality and artistic sensibility shared by author and composer" (p. 49). Remarks especially on the human dimensions of Handel's operatic world and Ariosto's poem and their focus on emotions and passions; notes that pathos is fundamental to the *OF* as it is to Handel's *Furioso* operas. Considers the manner in which these operas foreshadow major operatic forms of the nineteenth century.

Subject Index

357, 359, 360, 400, 403, 416, 432, 445, 446, 505, 544, 548, 580, 614, 616, 621, 627, 693, 696, 727, 743, 746, 747, 758, 867, 876, 901, 915, 917, 922
Magic in the OF, 68, 103, 234, 304, 452, 489, 609, 634, 660, 870, 878, 906
Malaguzzi, Daria, 301
Malaguzzi, Sigismondo, 224
Mallarmé, Stéphane, 611
Malory, Sir Thomas, 242
Malraux, André, 157
Manara, Francesco, 474
Manfredi, Eraclito, 74
Manicardi, Cirillo, 313
Mannerism, 759
Manuel, Juan. *See* Juan Manuel
Manuzio, Aldo, 376
Manzoni, Alessandro, 509, 562, 668
Marfisa, 612, 844
Marganorre, 65, 237, 525
Marino, Giambattista, 55, 899
Marlowe, Christopher, 685
Marston, John, 482
Marti, Mario, 29, 308
Martin, Jean, 427
Martorell, Johanot, 138
Mazzolino, Ludovico, 486
Medici, Domenico, 74, 215, 232, 471, 473, 920
Medici, Giuliano de' (1453–1478), 736
Medici, Lorenzo de' (1492–1519), 687
Medoro. *See* Angelica; *see also* Cloridano and Medoro.
Melissa, 408, 416, 486, 532
Melo, Francisco Manuel de, 520
Merlin, 104
Metastasio, Pietro, 279
Michael, Archangel, 390, 907
Michelangelo, 59
Mickiewicz, Adam, 97, 477, 834
Milton, John, 144, 289, 419, 420, 570, 616, 808, 824, 902
Minturno, Antonio, 572, 927
Miollis, Sextius de, 31, 173
Miranda, Sá de, 520
Momigliano, Attilio, 220, 337, 441, 445, 506, 543, 696, 889
Monaci, Ernesto, 669
Mondolfo, Girolamo da, 737
Montaigne, Michel Eyquem de, 752

Mora, Vittorio, 711
Moreau, Gustave, 16
Morgante, Il. See Pulci, Luigi.
Muratori, Ludovico Antonio, 122

Neoplatonism, 39, 111, 112, 199, 432, 494, 612, 754
Nerval, Gerard de, 246
Niccolò degli Agostini, 151, 600, 607; borrowings in the OF, 7
Nicolay, Ludwig Heinrich von, 409
Niccolò dell'Abbate, 77, 374, 455
Novellino, Il (anonymous), 779
Núñez de Reinoso, Alfonso, 705

Olimpia, 23, 114, 118, 204, 237, 404, 550, 589, 616, 618, 709, 922
Oña, Pedro de, 76
Oprandi, Nicole, 63
Orlando, 56, 115, 140, 182, 184, 230, 236, 252, 279, 318, 334, 359, 360, 400, 403, 432, 494, 505, 571, 572, 601, 614, 621, 627, 681, 683, 693, 694, 696, 728, 744, 758, 859, 867, 901, 909, 917, 922
Orlando Innamorato, L'. See Boiardo, Matteo Maria
Orrilo, 728, 803
Ottava rima, 54, 61, 108, 127, 137, 160, 269, 344, 467, 470, 504, 541, 579, 642, 725, 743, 787, 798, 874, 897
Ovid, 23, 141, 404, 429, 456, 576, 616, 649, 719, 781, 912, 922

Palmarocchi, Roberto, 38
Panizzi, Antonio, 14
Papini, Pietro, 566
Paris, Gaston, 669
Parodi, Ernesto G., 90
Parrino, Leonardo, 862
Pastorini, Pastorino, 817
Pellegrino, Camillo, 147, 148, 883
Pellegrino da Udine, 653, 654, 928
Perillo, Marc'Antonio, 279
Pescatore, Giambattista, 564
Petrarch, Francesco, 94, 107, 108, 111, 312, 391, 395, 421, 459, 579, 655, 736, 776, 828, 841, 869, 886
Petrarchism (Petrarchan), 49, 93, 94, 312, 399, 691, 736
Philostratus, 435

Index of Ariosto's Works Cited

IN PRINT 32⁰⁰

LUDOVICO
ARIOSO